Mahara 1.4 Cookbook

Over 50 recipes for using Mahara for training, personal, or educational purposes

Ellen Marie Murphy

[PACKT] open source
PUBLISHING community experience distilled

BIRMINGHAM - MUMBAI

Mahara 1.4 Cookbook

First published: September 2011

Production Reference: 1080911

Published by Packt Publishing Ltd.
Livery Place
35 Livery Street
Birmingham B3 2PB, UK.

ISBN 978-1-849515-06-1

`www.packtpub.com`

Cover Image by Tom Glasspool (`t.glasspool@gmail.com`)

Credits

Author
Ellen Marie Murphy

Reviewers
Dominique-Alain JAN
Heinz Krettek
Samantha Moss

Acquisition Editor
Sarah Cullington

Development Editor
Pallavi Iyenger

Technical Editors
Joyslita D'Souza
Arun Nadar

Copy Editors
Brandt D'Mello
Leonard D'Silva
Laxmi Subramanian

Project Coordinator
Jovita Pinto

Proofreader
Aaron Nash

Indexer
Hemangini Bari

Production Coordinator
Shantanu Zagade

Cover Work
Shantanu Zagade

About the Author

Ellen Marie Murphy is a curriculum and learning technologies specialist with over 16 years of experience in education. She is an avid proponent of open source software. Her first Moodle and Mahara implementations were during her tenure at The Sage Colleges, where she was employed as Director of Instructional Technologies. More recently she served as the Director of Learning Technologies and Online Education at Plymouth State University, and Higher Education Liaison to the New Hampshire Society for Technology in Education, where she was actively engaged with all levels of education from K to 20. Currently, she serves as the Director of Online Curriculum at the State University of New York at Empire State College.

In 1998, while teaching at a middle school in Vermont, she was introduced to the concept of ePortfolios and has strongly supported the use of ePortfolios in teaching and learning since. She recently hosted a New Hampshire Statewide K-20 ePortfolio Day and hopes it will become an annual event. Additionally, she is a regular presenter at numerous educational conferences and Moodle Moots. Her current focus is on the development of Personal Learning Environments (PLEs) and furthering the cause of openness in education.

Acknowledgement

I've received a tremendous amount of encouragement and support during the writing of this book and would like to thank the following individuals in particular:

My family—my mother and father as well as Nick, Melanie, Keller, Maeven, Kateri, Maria, Anna, Charity, and Krystal, whose pictures and work appear throughout this book.

A friend and colleague John Harris, who installed and supported one of the Mahara instances in which I built portfolios for this book.

And the following wonderful educators in the State of New Hampshire, who provided me with questions to answer and an audience on which to test some of my recipes:

- Sonja Gonzalez, Director of IT at Oyster River Cooperative School District
- Danielle Bolduc, Director of Instruction, Oyster River Cooperative School District
- Kathy Weise, Windham High School, Windham School District
- Sharon Kondratenko, Mast Way Elementary School, Oyster River Cooperative School District
- Sarah Curtin, 4th Grade Teacher, Moharimet Elementary School, Oyster River
- Deb Boatwright, K-5 Tech Integrator, Newmarket School District
- Linda Heuer, Technology Coordinator, Timberlane School District
- Carol Liss, Tech. Educator Teacher, Middle School, Timberlane School District
- Lois Paul, Tech. Integrator Teacher, Timberlane HS, Timberlane School District
- Abby Fogerty, Tech. Teacher, Pollard (K-5) School, Timberlane School District

About the Reviewers

Dominique-Alain is a learning technologist, Mahara and Moodle consultant, and teacher in the Gymnase de Nyon, a secondary school near Lake Geneva in Switzerland. He is very active in developing new dimensions to teaching and learning. He defines himself as a 'techno sceptic', by which he means that technology without pedagogy and a real interest in human learning process is useless.

He is very involved as a Mahara and Moodle advocate and belongs to the French community of translators for both products, as well as leading the Mahara French community. He has been awarded "Mahara 1.4 Release crew" member by Catalyst, the Mahara core developers, for his help on this project.

For about four years, Dominique-Alain has been travelling worldwide—Australia (Estplan, The Australian National University), Tunisia, France, Germany, UK (Moodlemoot and Maharamoot) – to provide consulting and giving talks on eLearning, lifelong learning, and ePortfolio. For about five years he is a technology enhanced learning lecturer at the Teacher School of Canton Vaud, a one semester course on web 2.0, ePortfolio and reflexion on how/if technology should be use in schools.

He is now studying toward a PhD in eLearning. During his free time, Dominique-Alain likes water sports (sailing, swimming), golf, and walking through the Swiss vineyards, and when is he not talking about Mahara he loves to share his knowledge of Swiss wine with anyone. Come and drink a glass of Chasselat with him if you are passing by.

This is his third book he reviewed for Packt Pub, but not the last one.

Heinz Krettek is a German teacher at a school for vocational education. He studied business science and sports. His main job is to prepare socioeconomically deprived students for lifelong learning. In 2006, he discovered the Portfolio work and began to translate the German langpack for Mahara. The first translations for Mahara 0.6 were published on his own Moodle site. Soon after Nigel McNie installed a git repository, the actual files were published in the Mahara git. He has just finished the translation for the Mahara 1.4 release.

He has organized several education and training sessions for teachers and was a speaker at the German MoodleMoot. In 2010, Heinz started a part-time online study for eEducation at FernUni Hagen (Germany). He publishes postings about ePortfolio and related topics at `http://ewiesion.com`.

He lives with his wife and four kids in the Black Forest. In his spare time, Heinz enjoys the three M's—Mahara, Moodle, and marathons. He has run the New York Marathon. His motto is who finished a marathon will struggle all problems in school ;-)

Samantha Moss has a keen interest in how technology can enhance the teaching and learning experience for all in higher education. She works within the Learning Technology Unit at Southampton Solent University in the UK, a team that assists the staff and students in the development and use of eLearning tools and materials. She has been part of many internal projects that look into the potential uses of Mahara to promote personal development and career planning as well as the creation of online portfolios of work for 'self-promotion'. Samantha has presented Solent's work on Mahara at various conferences including the UK MoodleMoot 2010 and Mahara UK 2010.

I would like to thank both Roger Emery and Dr. Barbara Lee for originally asking me to get involved with the various Solent Mahara projects, as well as my manager Steve Hogg for allowing me the time to review this book.

www.PacktPub.com

Support files, eBooks, discount offers, and more

You might want to visit www.PacktPub.com for support files and downloads related to your book.

Did you know that Packt offers eBook versions of every book published, with PDF and ePub files available? You can upgrade to the eBook version at www.PacktPub.com and as a print book customer, you are entitled to a discount on the eBook copy. Get in touch with us at service@packtpub.com for more details.

At www.PacktPub.com, you can also read a collection of free technical articles, sign up for a range of free newsletters and receive exclusive discounts and offers on Packt books and eBooks.

PACKTLIB®

http://PacktLib.PacktPub.com

Do you need instant solutions to your IT questions? PacktLib is Packt's online digital book library. Here, you can access, read, and search across Packt's entire library of books.

Why Subscribe?

- Fully searchable across every book published by Packt
- Copy and paste, print and bookmark content
- On demand and accessible via web browser

Free Access for Packt account holders

If you have an account with Packt at www.PacktPub.com, you can use this to access PacktLib today and view nine entirely free books. Simply use your login credentials for immediate access.

Table of Contents

Preface

Mahara is an open source ePortfolio system that allows you to build dynamic and engaging portfolios in no time. Use Mahara when applying for jobs, creating portfolios for certification and accreditation, to support teaching and learning, for classroom projects, to create your own social network, and much more. This book will show you the many different ways in which you can use and exploit the various components of Mahara.

The *Mahara 1.4 Cookbook* will introduce you to features you may not have explored, and show you how to use them in ways you probably had not considered. The book also provides guidance in the use of GIMP, Picasa, Audacity, MS Word, and other programs that can be used to create artifacts. It will provide you with techniques for creating everything from dynamic and engaging web pages to complete projects, interactive groups, educational templates, showcase portfolios, and professional resume packages.

By exploring the recipes in this book, you will learn how to use each of the various blocks and content areas including the Resume sections, Journals, and Plans. You will learn how to archive a portfolio and set access levels. We will build an art gallery and a newspaper, use groups for collaboration and assessment, and use the Collections feature to build complex layered portfolios. You will also find recipes for building templates for standards-based report cards, college applications, and teacher certification. The book is packed with ideas from the simple to the extremely advanced, but each idea is supported with step-by-step instructions that will make all of them seem easy.

What this book covers

Chapter 1, Mahara for the Visual Arts, explores the use of Mahara for reflecting on process, and demonstrates various methods for showcasing work. Techniques for customizing image displays and protecting access to images are also covered.

Chapter 2, Literature and Writing, focuses on the uses of Mahara for language acquisition and for showcasing various forms of writing. Recipes include the use of various types of journals, the creation of a small poetry book, and the use of reflections in learning a second language. The chapter also includes a short tutorial on using GIMP for creating illustrations.

Chapter 3, The Professional Portfolio, provides ideas and templates for building resumes, resume packages, and portfolios for Promotion and Tenure. The recipes range from a very basic resume page, to a highly complex portfolio containing collections within collections.

Chapter 4, Working with Groups, takes an in-depth look at Groups, one of Mahara's most powerful features. Recipes include the building of a newspaper with student columnists, web pages that feature student work, and techniques for building templates.

Chapter 5, The Primary Education Portfolio, is comprehensive and packed full of ideas; all readers will benefit from the varied and creative uses of Mahara in this chapter. An example of these is the international project recipe that explains the technique for adding a banner to a Mahara page. Other examples are the use of plans for book reports, and the use of Secret URLs for setting access levels.

Chapter 6, The Social Portfolio, is simply a fun chapter that explores how to "pimp" your Profile page. Add a slideshow, write on a wall, add a counter so you can see how many visitors you get, or add a Twitter feed. Regardless of what else you choose to share, everyone in your Mahara instance can see your profile page. Learn how to make it much more reflective of who you are.

Chapter 7, The College Application Portfolio, talks about building a college entrance art portfolio, and the Common Application and its various supplements. Recipes follow the standard application procedures. The chapter also includes the use of code for creating tables in Mahara. This code is available for download from the Packt website. With modification, the code could be used for additional purposes in the ePortfolio process.

Chapter 8, Certification and Accreditation Portfolio for Higher Education, examines the various ways Mahara can be used by Colleges and Universities for the ePortfolios they use to meet certification and accreditation requirements. Since accreditation standards vary across disciplines and regions, the ECIS International Teacher portfolio is used to provide ideas for the development of other similar portfolios.

What you need for this book

This book uses Mahara out of the box—that is, without plugins. Some of the chapters, however, do use additional freeware as well as open source programs and applications. These include Audacity, GIMP, KompoZer, and Picasa.

Who this book is for

Anyone interested in using an ePortfolio or in helping others build one—teachers, professors, students, guidance counselors, advisors, mentors, career counselors, and individuals interested in building an online resume and/or portfolio.

Conventions

In this book, you will find a number of styles of text that distinguish between different kinds of information. Here are some examples of these styles, and an explanation of their meaning.

Code words in text are shown as follows: "The new file will appear in the same location as the original file, but will have a `.zip` extension".

New terms and **important words** are shown in bold. Words that you see on the screen, in menus or dialog boxes for example, appear in the text like this: "In the section labeled **Journal** click in the small bubble next to **My Research Paper**".

> Warnings or important notes appear in a box like this.

> Tips and tricks appear like this.

Reader feedback

Feedback from our readers is always welcome. Let us know what you think about this book—what you liked or may have disliked. Reader feedback is important for us to develop titles that you really get the most out of.

To send us general feedback, simply send an e-mail to `feedback@packtpub.com`, and mention the book title via the subject of your message.

If there is a book that you need and would like to see us publish, please send us a note in the **SUGGEST A TITLE** form on `www.packtpub.com` or e-mail `suggest@packtpub.com`.

If there is a topic that you have expertise in and you are interested in either writing or contributing to a book, see our author guide on `www.packtpub.com/authors`.

Customer support

Now that you are the proud owner of a Packt book, we have a number of things to help you to get the most from your purchase.

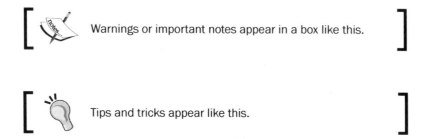

Downloading the example code

You can download the example code files for all Packt books you have purchased from your account at `http://www.PacktPub.com`. If you purchased this book elsewhere, you can visit `http://www.PacktPub.com/support` and register to have the files e-mailed directly to you.

Errata

Although we have taken every care to ensure the accuracy of our content, mistakes do happen. If you find a mistake in one of our books—maybe a mistake in the text or the code—we would be grateful if you would report this to us. By doing so, you can save other readers from frustration and help us improve subsequent versions of this book. If you find any errata, please report them by visiting `http://www.packtpub.com/support`, selecting your book, clicking on the **errata submission form** link, and entering the details of your errata. Once your errata are verified, your submission will be accepted and the errata will be uploaded on our website, or added to any list of existing errata, under the Errata section of that title. Any existing errata can be viewed by selecting your title from `http://www.packtpub.com/support`.

Piracy

Piracy of copyright material on the Internet is an ongoing problem across all media. At Packt, we take the protection of our copyright and licenses very seriously. If you come across any illegal copies of our works, in any form, on the Internet, please provide us with the location address or website name immediately so that we can pursue a remedy.

Please contact us at `copyright@packtpub.com` with a link to the suspected pirated material.

We appreciate your help in protecting our authors, and our ability to bring you valuable content.

Questions

You can contact us at `questions@packtpub.com` if you are having a problem with any aspect of the book, and we will do our best to address it.

1
Mahara for the Visual Arts

In this chapter, we will cover:

- Uploading and sharing a single image
- Protecting your opus
- Making a photo journal using Picasa
- Journaling a project from start to finish
- Building a simple gallery
- Using the Collections feature to build a gallery with an audio-guided tour

Introduction

*I*n this chapter, we serve up several recipes for the visual arts, particularly studio arts and digital arts. Learning how to market yourself and showcase your work is part of being an artist (and making a living out of it). The recipes in this chapter are designed to get your creative juices flowing regarding how you can use Mahara to showcase your work. The recipes will not only provide you with some creative ways in which to display your work, but will help you protect your ownership as well.

We will use a few additional programs, freely available on the Internet, in setting up our displays. The audio recording program, Audacity, can be found at `http://audacity.sourceforge.net/`. We will use it to create a guided tour of a gallery. Some of the recipes will require you to create and use an account on Picasa, a free image repository program hosted by Google at `https://picasaweb.google.com/`. Unlike text, images can take up a lot of space on a server and, consequently, storage space can be a problem. In addition to providing you with more space, Picasa gives you more control over how visitors access your images, in particular, blocking their ability to download images in their original size.

Finally, we will learn about the various ways in which you can establish usage rights. We will explore the Creative Commons License and how to apply it. We will also learn how to add a © to the work for which you wish to retain full rights. So, let's get creating.

Uploading and sharing a single image

This is one of the simplest recipes in this cookbook, but it can serve a variety of uses. We are simply going to do as the title says, namely, "upload and share a single image". This recipe can serve as a practice for other recipes, or it can be used to create a splash page in a collection (for example, it can be used with the recipe: *Using the Collections feature to build a gallery with an audio-guided tour*).

Getting ready

You should have the image you wish to use saved to your computer or some other accessible storage device.

How to do it...

1. Click on the **Content** tab in Mahara, and then on **Files**.
2. Put a check mark in the little box next to **Upload file**. Mahara will not allow you to upload a file unless this box is checked. Checking the box confirms that you either own the file you are uploading or you have been given the right to use it.
3. Select the **Browse** button and locate the image on your storage device. Double-click it, or select **Open**, to begin the upload process.
4. You will see a small green spinning circle, in the area just above **Upload file**. This tells you that Mahara is uploading the file. When your file is done uploading, you will see a small green check mark instead of the small spinning circle:

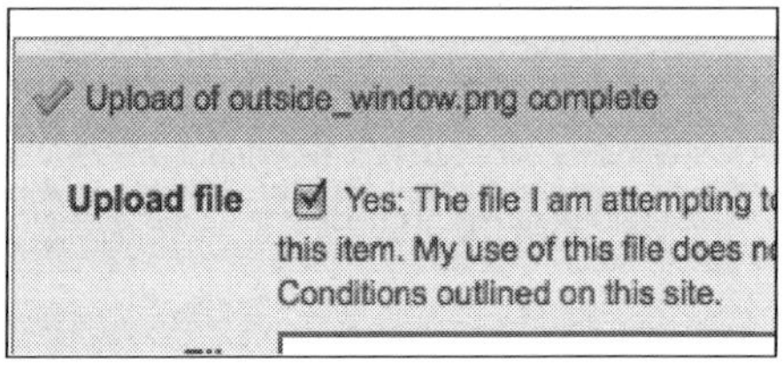

5. Your image is now stored in the **Files** section of your portfolio. Only you can see the file, and to do so you would have to click on the file in order to open it. Let's create a page and add the image to it.

How it works...

1. In the **Pages** section of the **Portfolio** tab, select **Create Page**.
2. By default, your new page has three columns of equal width—though you may not be able to tell that by simply looking at this new page. Let's change the format to one column. Select the **Edit Layout** tab at the top of your page.
3. Click in the bubble for **1 column, Equal widths**.
4. Click **Save**. You will be taken back to the editing window for your page.
5. If your admin has enabled themes, you will see a drop-down menu, near the middle of the page, labeled **Theme**. Select the theme you'd like to use. The example in this recipe uses **Fresh**.
6. Click on the tab labeled **Files, images and video**.
7. Click on the **An Image** block and drag it down into your page (below the line of text that says **This area shows a preview of what your Page will look like...**).
8. A window called **An Image: Configure** will open. In the **Block Title** area, delete the text **An Image** and leave it empty, or add the name of the image you will be displaying. I chose to delete the text and leave the **Block Title** field empty.
9. A little further down in this **Configure** window, you will see a list of all the files in your portfolio. Click the **Select** button next to the image you are adding to this page.
10. Click **Save**.

> If the **Block Title** is deleted for the **An Image** block, the words **[No title]** will appear above the image while you are editing the page, but only during editing. In the actual display view, there will be no title. To see how this appears, you can click the **Display my Page** link in the upper right-hand corner of the page. It will show you how your page will look when it is not in edit mode.

11. You will now see your image in the page. Select the tab labeled **Next: Edit Title and Description**.
12. Give this page a title. Because this is going to be a splash page for our gallery, we'll give it the title `A Gallery of Paintings`.
13. For this recipe, we are going to skip adding a **Description**. There are a number of very interesting things you can do with the description, which we will cover in other recipes.
14. Select the **Name display format** you'd like for this page. The name will appear at the top of your page. I chose to use my full name so the top of my page says **A Gallery of Paintings by Ellen Marie Murphy**.

15. Click **Save**.
16. Select the tab labeled **Share page.**
17. A list of all your **Collections** and **Pages** will appear; the page you are currently working on will be selected by default.
18. In the area labeled **Share with**, click the **Add** button next to **Public**. This will allow your page to be picked up by search engines, and for anyone to view it without logging in to Mahara.
19. You can set dates for when the page will be publicly accessible, but, for this recipe we will skip the additional settings.
20. Click **Save**.

There's more...

Mahara resizes large images to fit the page; however, the larger the image the more time it will take to load (the time it takes for the image to display when someone first comes to your page). This can be helped by setting the display width to no greater than `1000`.

When you click and drag the **An Image** block into your page and when the **An Image: Configuration** window opens, you will see an area at the very bottom labeled **Width**. This is where you type the display width. It's that simple! If you have already added the image you can go back and change this setting. Open the page and then click the **Edit** option in the upper right-hand corner. Click the small editing icon in the upper-right corner of the block that contains your image. This will open the settings and you will be able to set the width.

> If an image is only going to be displayed on the Internet, it does not need to have a resolution higher than 96ppi. When an image is going to be printed, it is often set to 300ppi or more. The higher the resolution, the longer the image will take to load. The file size also increases significantly as the pixel density increases. To check the ppi value of an image, open it in an image editing program like GIMP (see *Chapter 2, Literature and Writing*). You can also use the Preview program on a Mac, or the Paint program on a PC, to resize an image.

See also

- *Using the Collections feature to build a gallery with an audio-guided tour* recipe
- *The Art Portfolio and the Common Application*: Art Supplement recipe in *Chapter 7, The College Application Portfolio*
- *Creating a Poetry chapbook* recipe in *Chapter 2, Literature and Writing*.

Protecting your opus

The term "all rights reserved" means that no one, except the owner, has the right to publish, distribute, or modify a piece of work, without getting permission from the owner. An international agreement, known as the Bern Convention, ensures that published works automatically provide these rights to their owner whether there is an accompanying statement to that effect or not. Most artists add the statement, though, to remind people of those rights. It isn't always in your best interest, however, to retain "all rights reserved". For example, you may wish to allow others to distribute your work freely, as long as they give you credit for it, thereby increasing the number of people who become familiar with your work.

Since you will be publishing some of the work in your portfolio on the web, you will want to consider what kinds of rights you wish to establish and then put a statement to that effect on your work. Creative Commons licensing will allow you to do this more easily. In this recipe, we will learn how to add a Creative Commons license to your work, as well as a few other ways to protect your creations.

Here's a general description of a Creative Commons license (from the Creative Commons website `http://creativecommons.org/choose/`): "*With a Creative Commons license, you keep your copyright but allow people to copy and distribute your work provided they give you credit—and only on the conditions you specify...*"

Getting ready

In the **Pages** section of the **Portfolio** tab find the page you'd like to add the license to and open it by clicking on the name of the page. To begin editing, click the **Edit** option in the upper right-hand corner.

How to do it...

1. From the **General** tab, click and drag the **Creative Commons License** block into your page.
2. It is a good idea to leave the **Block Title** field as is.
3. You will need to select an option under **Allow commercial uses of your work?**, and an option under **Allow modifications of your work?**. The first set of options determines who has the rights to do the second. If a group is not granted rights, then they have no rights. Let's have a look at the first one. Commercial use refers to anything that generates income. So, for example, a company logo would be considered commercial use of an image. Do you wish to allow commercial use of your work?
4. Next, you'll need to answer how they can use your work. Regardless of which option you choose, they will be able to copy, distribute, and use your work (unaltered). **Yes** means that in addition to these rights, they can also change your work and use it (so they can add a hat to the picture of your dog). **No** means they can only use your work as is—they can't change your work (so the picture of your dog stays just as you took it). **Yes, as long as others share alike** means that they can do everything a **Yes** allows, but they must put a Creative Commons License on anything they create using your work and that license must be equivalent to the license you have on yours.
5. Once you've selected your options, click **Save**.

How it works...

Visitors who click on the Creative Commons License you applied to your work will be taken to a site on the Web that explains what your license means.

There's more...

Maybe, though, you want to keep "all rights reserved" and you wish to add an indication of that to your page:

If that is the case, follow these steps:

1. From the **General** tab, click and drag a **Text Box** block into your page.
2. Delete the text from the **Block Title** field, leaving it empty.
3. In the **Block Content** area, type the © symbol, followed by the year. To type the symbol: if you are on a Mac, hold the *option* key down and type the letter *G*; if you are on a PC, hold down the *Ctrl* key and the *Alt* key at the same time, then type the letter *C*.
4. If you are not able to get the symbol this way, you can always add the HTML code for it. Select **HTML** in the upper right-hand corner of the HTML toolbar. In the editing window that opens type `©`, that is, the & sign, the word 'copy' and a semi-colon. Select **Update**.
5. After the © symbol, add the words `All Rights Reserved`, and your name.
6. Click **Save**.

Adding copyright to the image description

Most of the artifacts you add to a page (for example, documents, images, and so on) have a **Details** page associated with them. Visitors to your portfolio will find the link to the Details page under the artifact. If they click the link to view the details, they will also have the option of downloading the artifact. While you may not want them to have this access, there is currently no way to prevent an individual with access from downloading the artifact. To add a © symbol to an artifact, so that it appears on the detail page, simply add the © symbol in the area for the description:

To add a **Description** to an artifact you've already uploaded to your files, click on the **Content** tab and then **Files**. Find the file you want to add the description to, and select the pencil tool next to it. The area will expand and you can add the description as shown in the image above. Click **Save changes**.

Making a photo journal using Picasa

Photo journalists can tell a story simply by using images. In this recipe, we are going to create a journal of images using Mahara's journal and the images we save to Picasa. While you can create an image journal using images that you store on Mahara, this recipe calls for using Picasa because most administrators will limit the storage space you are allotted and you may find it necessary to host your images elsewhere. Picasa gives you a gigabyte of space for free. Additionally, Picasa gives you greater control over viewers' access to your images. At the end of this recipe, you will be given a few options you can use to create slightly different versions of this recipe.

Getting ready

You will need to create an account on Picasa (`http://picasaweb.google.com/home`) and then create an album. Once you have logged into your new Picasa account, you will be taken to the **My Photos** section of your account. To create an album, select the button labeled **Upload**. Select the link to **Create a new album**. In the new window that comes up, you will give your album a name. You will also be asked about the **Visibility** of your album. If you do not want to make your images available to the general public, then select the option **Anyone with the link**. This will keep your images private but still accessible to individuals with whom you wish to provide access through Mahara. Visitors to the Mahara pages in which you've added your journal postings, will automatically see the images you've chosen to display there. They will not need to go to Picasa to see them. Upload the photos you wish to use. You can continue to add photos as you wish. Now we're ready to begin our journal.

How to do it...

You will want to have both your Mahara and your Picasa accounts open. In the window of your Picasa account, go to the album you will be using. Then go to the window with your Mahara account and we will begin by creating a new journal.

> By default, the option to have multiple journals is not enabled. To change your personal settings and allow for multiple journals, click the **Settings** link in the top right-hand corner on your Mahara window. In the section **General account options**, you will see the option **Enable multiple journals**. Click in the small box next to that option, and click **Save**.

1. Click on the **Content** tab, then click the tab labeled **Journals**.
2. Click the button **Create Journal**.
3. In the field for **Title**, type `Photo Journal`.
4. Leave the **Description** field empty.
5. If you wish to use **Tags**, add them.
6. Click **Create Journal**.
7. In the Picasa window, select the image you wish to add to your journal. It will open in a new window.
8. To the right of the photo, about halfway down the page, you will see a link labeled **Link to this Photo**. When you select the link, a set of options will open.
9. From the **Select size** menu, select **Large-800**.
10. Check the box labeled **Image only (no link)**. This will keep your images private, but still accessible to individuals to whom you wish to provide access through Mahara.
11. Copy the code from the box labeled **Embed image**. This code will contain the location of your image, information about the size, and a *Key* that allows individuals who access your image from within Mahara to see it (anyone with the link).

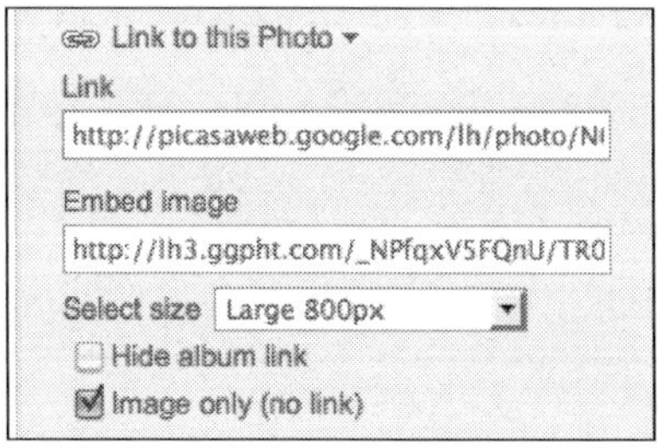

12. In your Mahara window, select the link labeled **New Entry** next to your newly created journal.
13. Give this post a **Title**.
14. Click inside the section for the **Body**.
15. Select the icon for **Insert/edit image** in your HTML editing tools (the one that looks like a picture of a tree):

16. In the small pop-up window that opens, locate the **Image URL** field and paste the code you copied in step 11.

17. In the box labeled **Description**, type a one- or two-word description of the image. This makes your page accessible to individuals who are using a screen reader and who may be unable to see the image or see it clearly.
18. Leave the **Alignment** field at the default setting. If we were going to be adding text that we wanted to wrap around our image, we would have set the alignment.
19. In the **Border** field, type `3`. This will put a 3-pixel sized black border around your image.
20. Leave the **Vertical space** field empty.
21. You do not need to put anything in the **Horizontal space** field either, as we will not be wrapping text around the image. Specifying the horizontal space puts white space on the left and right sides of the image.

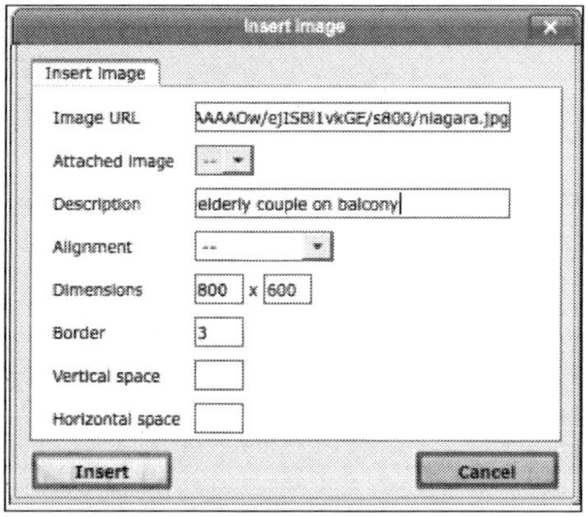

22. Select **Insert**.
23. Now let's add a little information about the image, or perhaps a reflection on the image. To begin: hit your *Enter* key to move the cursor down, so that the text will appear beneath your image. What text you enter is up to you; it can be a bit about the image, or the location, or a word the image represents, or a bit about the process you used in taking the image.

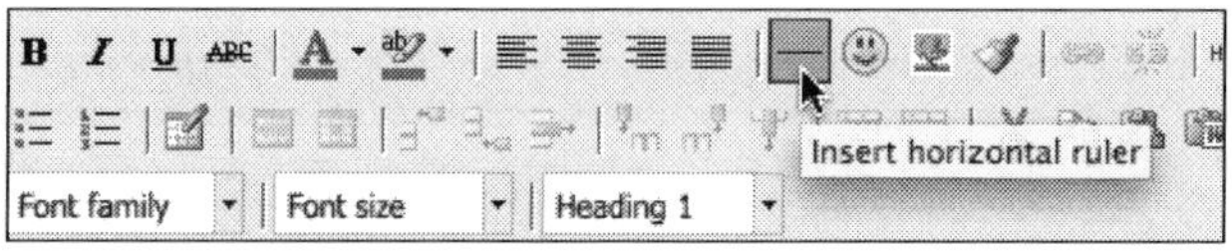

24. Next, we need to highlight all the text in the body of the post so that we can center it. Let's use our keyboard shortcuts to do that. If you are on a Mac, press the letter *A* key while holding the *command* key down; if you are on a PC, press the letter *A* key while holding the *Ctrl* key down. Now select the icon on the HTML toolbar that centers text.

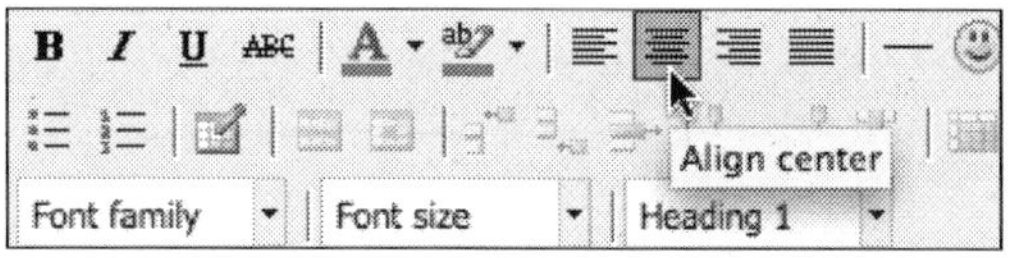

25. Now we can save the post. Select **Save entry**
26. Continue adding images to your journal. Keep in mind that, until you publish your journal, no one but you can see the images. When you are ready to share your journal, you will need to create a page for it. You don't need to wait until you've completed your journal as you can continue adding photos to it, even after publishing, and your page will automatically display your new photos. Publishing will allow others to comment on your photos as well.

    Let's publish the journal. It should appear similar to the following screenshot:

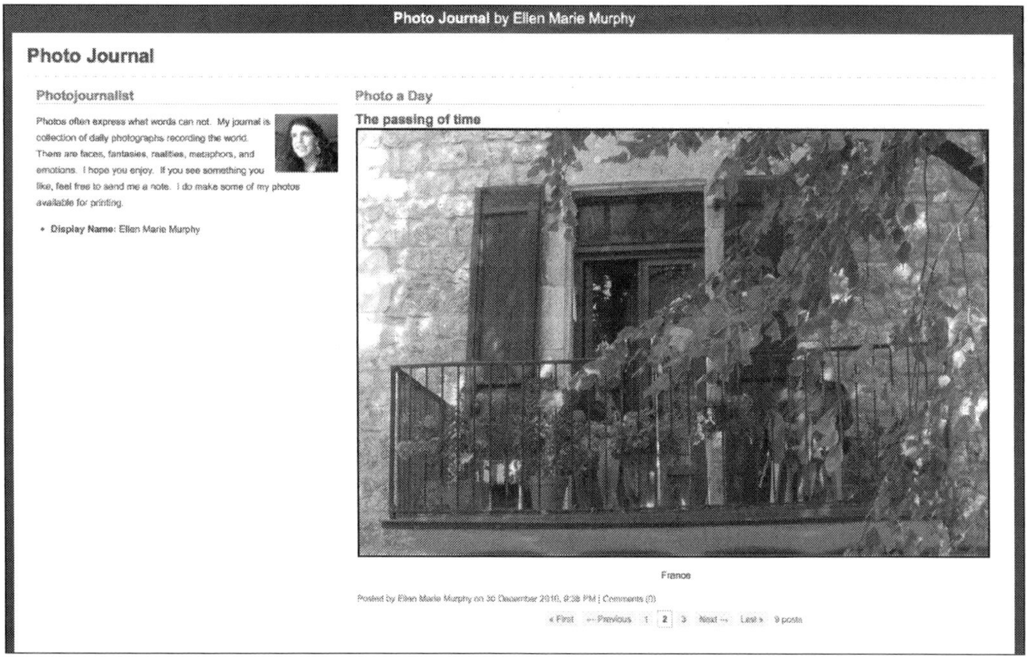

27. Click on the **Portfolio** tab and on **Pages**.
28. Click the button **Create Page**.
29. The page you created by clicking the button, will be in editing mode. You will see two rows of tabs. One row contains the blocks you will use to build your page; the other row contains options for Layout, Title, and Sharing.
30. Click the tab labeled **Edit Layout**.
31. Select the option **2 columns, Larger right column**.

32. Click **Save**.
33. From the **Profile** tab, drag a **Profile Information** block to the left-hand column. Delete anything in the **Block Title** field, leaving it empty.
34. Select **Display Name** and one of your **Profile icons**.
35. Enter information about yourself (the Photo Journalist) in the **Introduction Text Box**.
36. Click **Save**.
37. From the **Journals** tab, drag a **Journal** block to the left-hand column.
38. In the **Block Title** field, type a display name for your photo journal (I gave mine the name "Photo a Day"). If you leave this blank, Mahara will use the name you gave your journal in step 3 above.
39. Select your photo journal from your list of journals.
40. From the drop-down menu **Posts per page**, select **1**. This will post your most current photo to your page, and create automatic navigation at the bottom for viewers to browse your other photos.
41. You can skip the section labeled **Block copy permission** as you will not be granting permission to copy your page.
42. Click **Save**.
43. Select the tab labeled **Next: Edit Title and Description**.
44. You will need to give the page a **Title**. I called mine "Photo Journal".
45. You can skip the field for **Description**.
46. Add any tags you are using for these photos in the **Tags** field.
47. Click **Save**.
48. Click the tab labeled **Share page**.
49. In the **Edit Access** window, you will see this page listed in the area labeled **Pages**. It should have a check mark next to it. In the **Share with** area, click the **Add** button next to **Public**.
50. Click the **Advanced Options** link to expand the page. Leave **Allow comments** checked. If you wish to approve comments before they are posted then select **Moderate comments**. Make sure **Allow copying** is not checked.
51. Click **Save**.

How it works...

Your photo journal is now public! Because this slide show is actually a journal, and because it is public, viewers will be able to subscribe to your photo journal. When you add a new image, they will receive notification (see the information on RSS feeds in other chapters).

There's more...

You don't have to use Picasa to store your images. You can also store them in Mahara. In the section below we'll examine that option, as well as additional ways to use images in Picasa.

Giving visitors more access to the photo

If you follow the previous recipe, visitors will only be able to see your image as it appears in Mahara. They will not have access to the original. Using a slightly different method for embedding your images, you can provide visitors with access to your original photo on Picasa. You can also set certain privileges with regards to that image, such as the ability to order prints. Your Mahara visitors only need to click the image in order to be taken to the original. The following steps will outline how to give visitors more access.

In Picasa:

1. Select the photo you are adding to your journal.
2. In the right-hand panel, select **Link to this Photo**.
3. Select the size **Large-800**.
4. Select **Hide album link**.
5. Do *not* select **Image only**; if it is already selected, deselect it.
6. Click in the box labeled **Embed image** to highlight the code and copy it.

In Mahara:

1. Go to your journal and select **New Entry**.
2. Give the post a **Title**.
3. On the HTML toolbar at the top of the **Body**, select **HTML**. The **HTML Source Editor** will open.
4. Paste the code you copied from Picasa.
5. Click **Update**.
6. Click on the image that now displays in your post.
7. You will notice that the two link icons on the HTML toolbar are highlighted. Select the link icon in order to insert/edit a link:

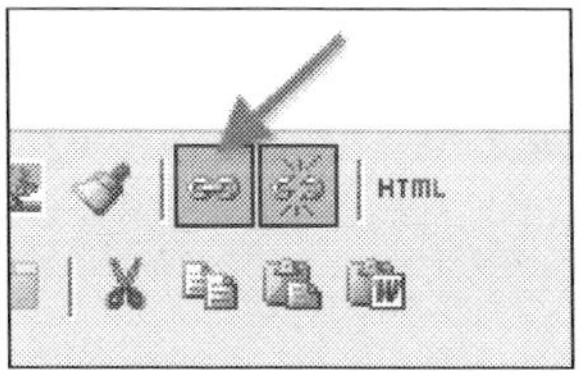

8. From the drop-down menu for **Target**, select **Open link in a new window** and then **Insert**.
9. Now click in the white-space area below your image (in the body of your post). This should deselect the image, and place your cursor in the post.
10. Hit the *Enter* key on your keyboard and add your text.
11. To center the image and all of the text, use your keyboard shortcut for "highlight all" (on a Mac: *command +A*; on a PC: *Ctrl+A*).
12. Select the icon on the HTML toolbar for center-alignment.
13. Click **Save entry**.

> By default, images can be downloaded and/or printed. You can edit your preferences to block downloading and the ordering of prints. At the very top of your Picasa page, in the right-hand corner, you will see the menu option **Settings**. Click on that and then on **Photo Settings** and **Privacy and Permissions**. Locate the area for **Allow any visitor to** and deselect the options **Order prints** and **Download my photos**. Click **Save changes**.

Adding a Picasa slideshow, or an entire album, to a journal entry

You can also add an entire Picasa album or slideshow to a journal post. Follow the ensuing steps in order to post an album:

1. Select the album (rather than an individual photo) you would like to post to your journal.
2. In the right-hand panel, select **Link to this album**.
3. Copy the code to the field named **Embed in website** and follow the same steps you used to embed a photo in More Info Section I.

To embed a slideshow of the album:

4. Select the album (rather than an individual photo) that you would like to post to your journal.
5. In the right-hand panel, select **Embed Slideshow**.
6. In the little pop-up window that opens, select a size for the slideshow, and choose whether you want autoplay.
7. Copy the code in the yellow box and then follow the same steps you used to embed a photo in More Info Section I.

Using images you have stored in Mahara (rather than Picasa)

You do not need to host your images on Picasa in order to have a photo journal. You can store your images on Mahara and embed them in your journal posts. This will require adding the photo as an attachment to your journal post, before embedding it in the post itself.

1. Click the option **New Entry**.
2. Give the entry a **Title**.
3. Under the **Body** is an area labeled **Attachments**. Select the button labeled **Add a file**. The page will expand.
4. Check the little box next to **Upload file**.
5. Select the **Browse** button, find the image, and click **Upload**.
6. Once it is uploaded, you will see it listed in the area labeled **Attachments**.
7. To add it to the body of your post, click the **Add/edit an image** icon in the HTML toolbar.
8. The **Insert Image** window will open. Skip the **Image URL** box and, from the menu for **Attached image**, select the image you just uploaded.
9. Continue with step 17 in the main recipe.

See also...

- *Using slideshow to create a book* recipe in *Chapter 5, The Primary Education Portfolio*
- *Creating a Poetry chapbook* recipe in *Chapter 2, Literature and Writing*
- *Creating a group newspaper using newsfeeds from student journals* recipe in *Chapter 4, Working with Groups*

Journaling a project from start to finish

There are a number of reasons why you might want to chart the progress of a particular art project from its inception to its completion. This recipe will use a journal in Mahara to post images as the project progresses and to provide reflections on why a particular technique was used, how it was used, or any other thoughts you may have as you work. Because we are using a journal, we can share our progress with others and allow them to comment on it and even provide ideas we might not have thought of. If you make the journal available to the public, they will be able to subscribe to an RSS feed of your journal. The recipe can also be used when creating a collaborative piece. Here is what a fragment of a project journal looks like:

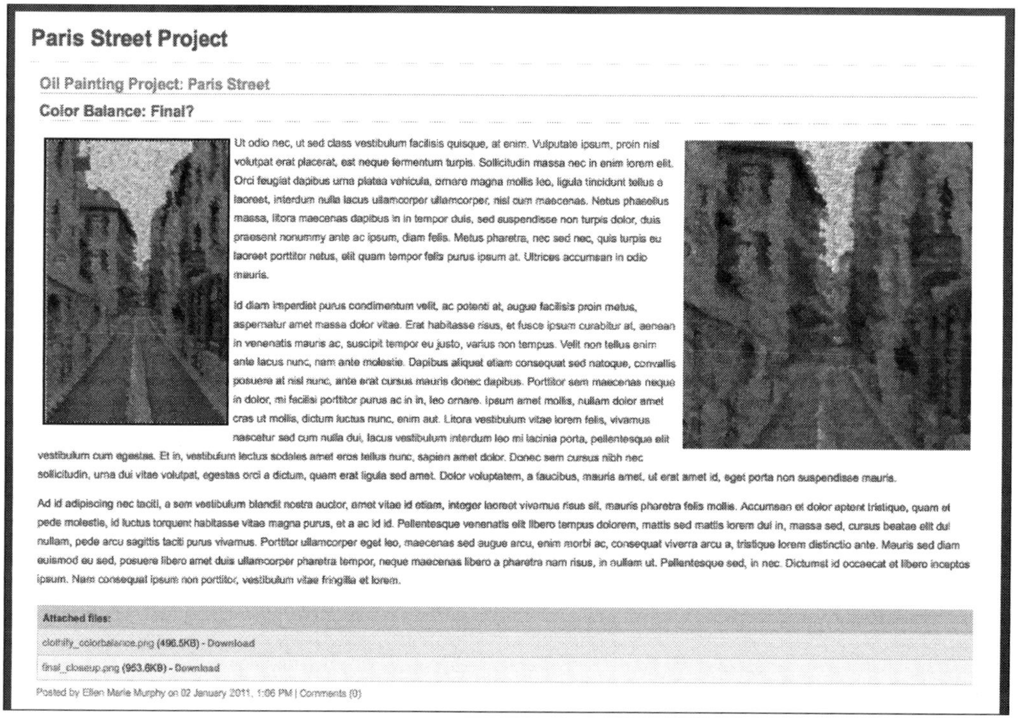

In the previous screenshot, the image on the right is a close-up of one section in the finished painting, which is on the left. Both of these images are smaller-sized versions of the original photos used for this post. Below the post, there are download links to the original photos, which can be accessed by anyone who has access to this journal. Below those is a link for comments.

Getting ready

You will need to have a way of capturing pictures of your project as you progress, for example, a digital camera for taking photos of the project. You will want to become somewhat familiar with how to capture and save pictures of your project to your computer. We will transfer them from your computer to a file folder in your Mahara portfolio.

To begin the journal, create a folder in the **Files** section of the **Content** tab. We will be storing our project images in this folder. To create the folder, type a name for the folder in the textbox next to the **Create Folder** button. Then click the **Create Folder** button.

Create a new journal in the **Journals** section of the **Content** tab.

How to do it...

1. Select **New Entry**.
2. Give your post a title.
3. Skip the **Body** for now and go down to the area labeled **Attachments**.
4. Click the button labeled **Add a file**. The area will expand, and you should see a list of your folders.
5. Click on the folder you created for this project. The list of folders will disappear, and the breadcrumb trail should indicate that you are in the folder for this project:

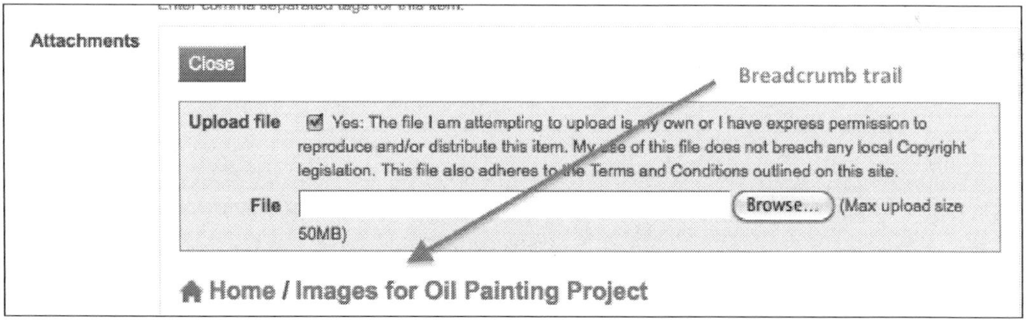

6. Put a check mark in the small box next to **Upload file**.
7. Select the **Browse** button, find the picture you previously saved to your computer, and upload it. A green circular icon will appear above **Upload file** showing you that the file is being uploaded. When it has finished, a green check mark will appear next to the file name.
8. If you have more than one picture to upload for your post, you can begin uploading the next image immediately. You don't need to wait for the previous image to finish being uploaded.

9. When you have finished uploading all of the images for this post, select **Close**. You will see a list of the pictures in the area labeled **Attachments**.
10. Place your cursor in the **Body** of your post and select the **Add/edit Image** icon in the HTML toolbar (it is a picture of a tree).
11. An **Insert image** dialogue box (pop-up window) will open. Skip the box labeled **Image URL**. From the drop-down menu for **Attached image**, select the first image you'd like to add to your post. We will need to add images one at a time. Each time you add a new image, it will appear below, or next to, the previously added image. Much depends on the type of alignment you assign to each image. Before you do that, however, type in a brief **Description** of the image you are adding. (This is for screen readers).

> It is important to be aware of issues of accessibility when designing for the Web. Using the **Description** field creates what is known as an **alt tag**. It allows individuals who are using a screenreader to know that there is an image in the text. For further reading regarding web accessibility, see `http://www.w3.org/WAI/`.

- **Alignment**: You will want to choose an alignment that allows the text to float around the image. The best options to choose are either **Left alignment** or **Right alignment**. You can place images right next to each other by paying attention to where your cursor is when you add an image.
- **Dimensions**: Because visitors will be able to access the full-sized image by clicking on the attachment link, you can resize the image in the post to be smaller than the original. You can either type in the measurements or you can adjust the size after you've added the image to the post by clicking on a corner and dragging it in or out. The preferable method is to type the size in, while making sure the proportions are kept the same. You will see the dimensions of the original image in the fields **Height** and **Width**. Divide both dimensions by the same number. For example, if the image measures 1200 X 1600, divide both 1200 and 1600 by 4. The result is 300 X 400. Type those numbers into the fields that specify the **Dimensions**.
- **Border**: This places a black border around the image. In the example project journal, a border of 3 pixels was used for images of the full painting, while no border was used around magnified selections of the image.
- **Vertical space and Horizontal space**: These settings provide the ability to set a white space around the image. This allows for a bit of space between the text and the image. Without the space, the text will be right up against the image. It can make reading the text a little uncomfortable. Set both options to `5`.

12. Click **Insert**.
13. Your image now appears in your post. You can begin adding text, or you can add another image by clicking the **Add/Edit Image** icon, and repeating steps 11 and 12.
14. When you have finished with your post, make sure **Allow comments** is checked, and then click **Save entry**.

As you progress through your work, you'll add new posts using the steps outlined previously. Let's make this journal available to someone, though—a professor, a friend, or the public, so they can follow your progress and provide feedback. Follow the ensuing steps:

15. On the **Pages** section of the **Portfolio** tab click **Create Page**.
16. Click on the **Edit Layout** tab.
17. Select the option **1 column, Equal widths**.
18. Click **Save**.
19. Select your theme from the drop-down menu for **Themes**. We've used the example **Aqua**.
20. From the **Journals** tab, click and drag the **Journal** block into your page.
21. By default, the title of the block will become the title of your journal. If you wish the block to display some other title, type it in the field named **Block Title**.
22. Select your project journal from the list named **Journals**.
23. By default, your five most recent posts will be shown on your page. There will be a small navigation option added at the bottom, which visitors can use to see prior posts (five to a page). You can change what is shown by changing the number in **Posts per page**.
24. We are not using this page to create a template, so you can skip the **More options** section.
25. Click **Save**.
26. Select the tab **Next: Edit title and description**.
27. Give this page a **Title**. Our example is called "Paris Street Project".
28. Leave the **Description** field blank.
29. By default, your **Display name** will appear at the top of your page. If you wish to use one of the other options available to you (first name, last name, full name) select it from the drop-down menu for **Name display format**.
30. Click **Save**.
31. Select the tab named **Share page**.
32. You have many options available. You can choose to share this with specific individuals (by selecting their names), or with a group, or the public. To select your option, click the **Add** button next to your choice.

33. Click the **Advanced options** link near the bottom to expand additional options. Since we have already allowed comments on individual posts, we do not need to select **Allow comments**, which would add an unnecessary feedback link at the bottom of each page in the journal. Deselect **Allow comments**. Also make sure that the option **Allow copying** is turned off.
34. Click **Save**.

How it works...

To add entries to your journal, you will need to actually go to the journal itself, rather than the page that contains the journal. That is, to add new entries, you will need to go to **Journals** on the **Content** tab and add your posts there. Your page will automatically be updated and will reflect any new posts you've added. Mahara was designed in this way, so you can add the journal to any number of pages, or so you can add individual posts to a page. This is different from the way other online journals and blogs work, but it gives you the ability to repurpose everything you write.

Subscriptions to your journal

If you make your journal public, viewers will be able to choose to subscribe to your journal. This means that when you add a new post to your journal they will automatically receive a notification via their RSS feed reader. You do not need to do anything in order for this to happen. To subscribe to your journal, they will need to click the RSS icon (a little orange icon) shown in the next screenshot:

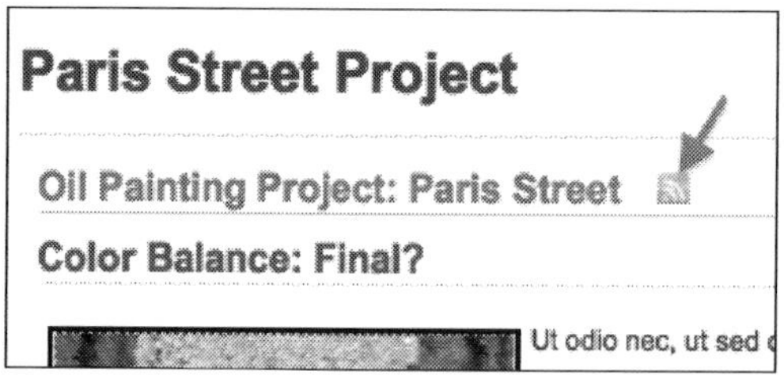

See also

- *Language acquisition journal* and *A Daily Gazette* recipes in *Chapter 2, Literature and Writing*

Building a simple gallery

You can build a simple, and somewhat elegant, gallery to display images you've saved to your files in Mahara. See the example in the following screenshot:

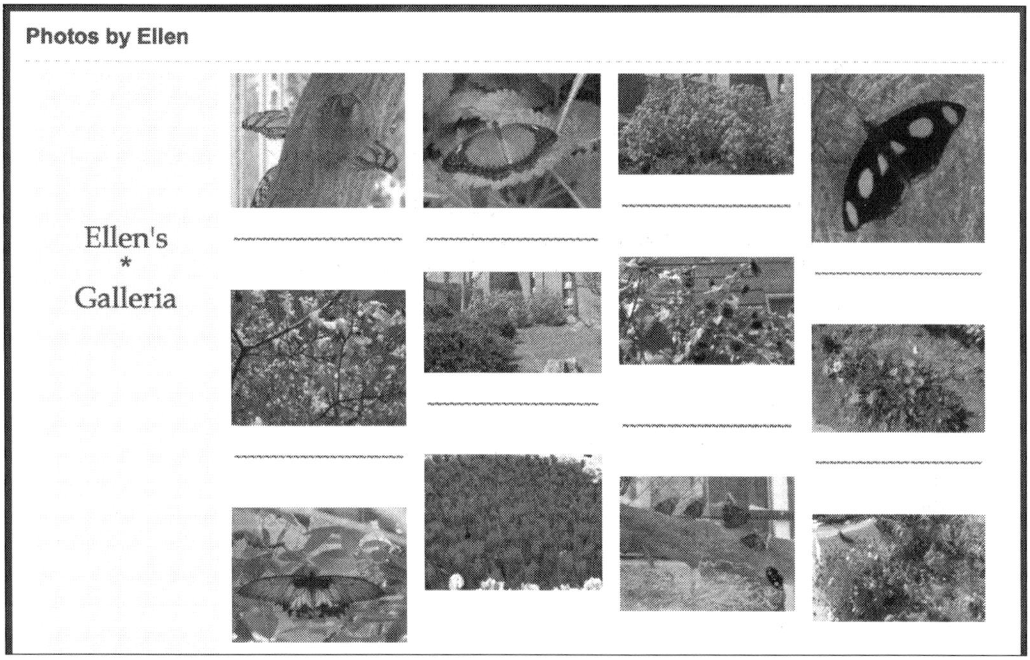

Getting ready

Locate all of the photos you wish to use in your gallery. If they are not already in your Mahara folder, upload them first.

How to do it...

1. Create a new page in the **Pages** section of the **Portfolio** tab.
2. Click the **Edit Layout** tab.
3. Select **5 columns, Equal width**.
4. Click **Save**.
5. Select a theme from the drop-down menu for **Themes**. I chose **Aqua**.
6. From **Files, Images, and video** click-and-drag the **An Image** block into one of the columns. Do not drag it to the first column as we're going to use that column to create a decorative sidebar.

7. Delete the text in the **Block Title** field, leaving it empty.
8. Click the word **Select** next to the image you wish you add.
9. Do not select **Show Description**.
10. In the box named **Width,** type `250`. If you were to set it higher, Mahara would still fit it into the column, but it would take longer to load the page.
11. Click **Save**.
12. Now, we will add the little lines you see between the pictures, to give us some extra white space. From the **General** tab, click-and-drag the **Text Box** block to the same column as the picture you just added and put it underneath the image.
13. Delete the text from the **Block Title** field, leaving it empty.
14. Place your cursor in the **Block Content** field and click the center alignment icon on the HTML toolbar.

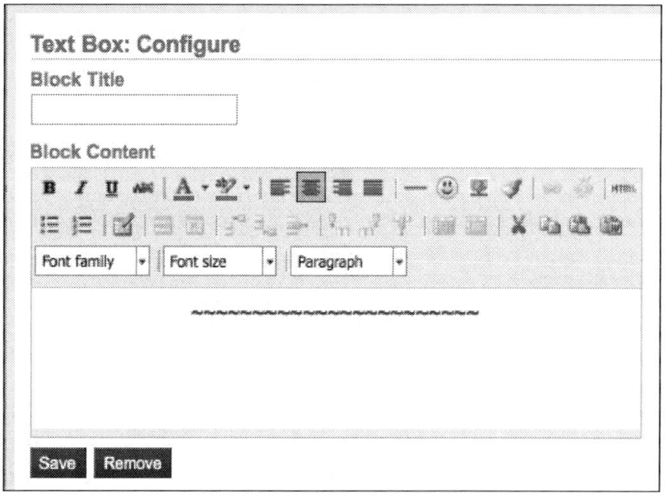

15. Make a line using the tilde key (~). Highlight the line, choose the color you would like it to be, and make it bold.
16. Click **Save**.
17. Continue adding images and spacers (textboxes) until you have a nice-sized gallery.
18. Now, let's make that sidebar. From the **General** section, click on the **Text Box** block and drag it to the left-hand column.
19. Delete the text in the **Block Title** field, leaving it empty.

20. Click the icon in the HTML toolbar to add a table:

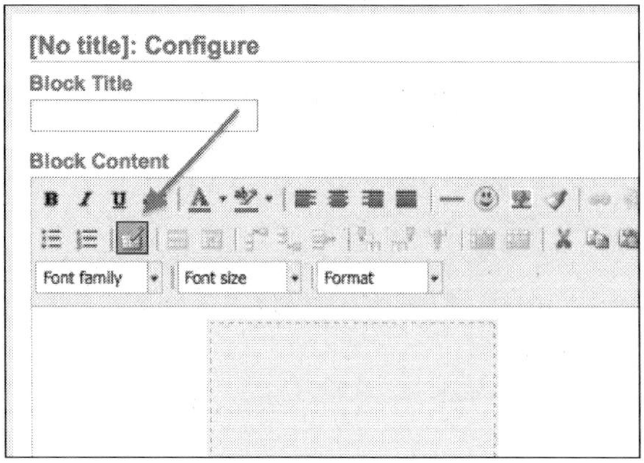

21. The **Insert/Modify table** dialogue box will open.
22. On the **General** tab set the table to **1 row** and **1 column**. Set the **Alignment** to **Center** and the **Width** to `200`.
23. Next, click on the **Advanced** tab, and set the background color of the table by clicking the small box furthest to the right of **Background color**. Then, to make the selection of a color easy, select the **Palette** tab. Click on the color you'd like your background color to be.

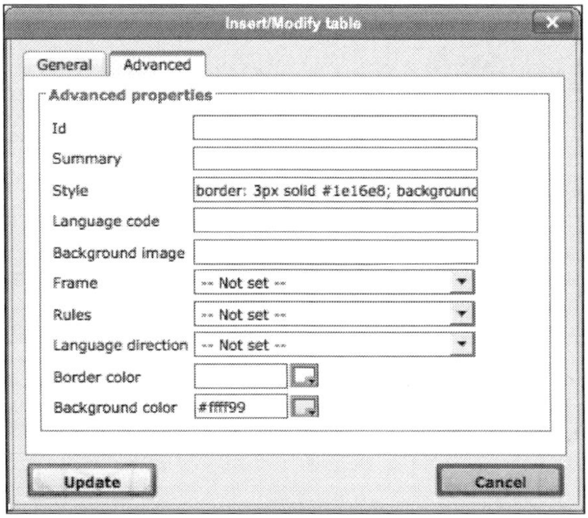

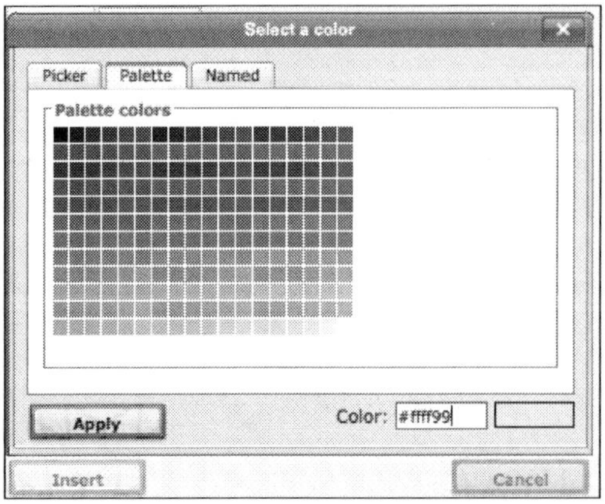

24. Select **Apply** and then **Insert**.
25. You will now see a narrow table in the **Body** of the **Text Box**. Place your cursor inside your new table and insert a few spaces. Using the various options in the HTML toolbar, set your **Font type**, **Color**, and **Size** (I chose **Book Antiqua** size **36**). Then, type the name of your gallery as you wish it to appear in your sidebar.
26. Insert a few more spaces. Click **Save**.
27. Finally, add a Creative Commons License to your gallery. From the **General** tab, select the **Creative Commons** block and drag it underneath your sidebar (to the bottom of the column on the far left). Set your preferences. Click **Save**.

How it works...

The images in your gallery are referred to as **thumbnails**; this means they are smaller pictures of larger images. They are also links to the original images. When visitors click one of your thumbnail images, they will be taken to a larger view of the image. Below the image will be a small link labeled **Details**, which takes visitors to a page with details about the image. For an example, see the following screenshot:

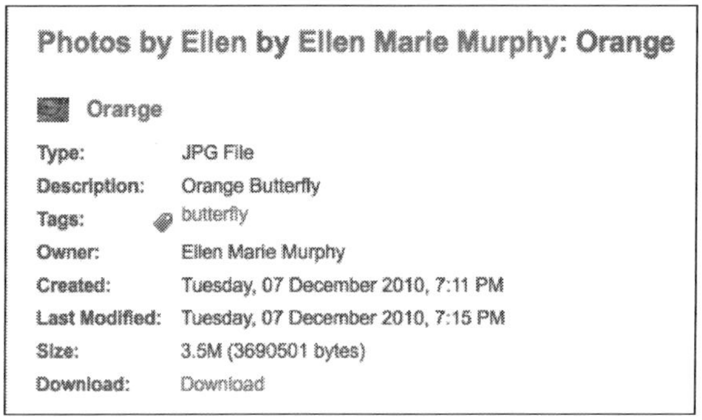

Adding titles and captions

You can choose to provide titles, as well as descriptions, for each of your images. To add a title, simply enter it in the **Block Title** field when you add the image to your page. If you choose the option **Show descriptions**, descriptions will appear centered underneath your photos (like captions). If your photos do not already have descriptions, you will need to add them first by going to the Mahara file section where they have been stored (**Files** on the **Portfolio tab**). Click the **Edit** link next to the photo you wish to add a description for. The image information section will expand and there will be a place where you can add a description of the photo.

Lining up the images more precisely

If you prefer to have all of your images in a neater line than in the example, you can use the **Text Box** blocks to add additional spacing between your images. When you add these blocks in steps 12 and 13, use the *Enter* key to add white space above the line you add. You can add space underneath the line as well. Sometimes it takes a little tweaking to get it exactly as you want. You can edit the text in the **Text Box** until you are happy with the way it looks.

> Changing the font size for an empty line, that is the line you simply used to create white space, changes the size of that space.

Using the image gallery block

Mahara 1.4 has an **Image Gallery** block that will create a gallery for you. While it is a much easier way to create a gallery than the method we used previously, it gives you fewer options for design. The number of images per row changes, depending on the size of the window. Resizing a window (making it wider or narrower) will change the display of the gallery.

To use the **Image Gallery** block, apply the following instructions:

1. Set the **Layout** to **2 columns, Larger right column** or **3 columns, Much larger center column**.
2. From the **Files, Images and video** tab, click-and-drag the **Image Gallery** block into the larger column.
3. You can leave `Image Gallery` in the **Block Title** field.
4. Under **Image Selection**, choose the option **I will choose individual images to display**.
5. Click the **Select** button next to each of the images you wish to include in this gallery.
6. Under the option for **Style**, select **Thumbnails**.
7. In the box for **Width**, type `250`.
8. Click **Save**.

See also...

- *The Art portfolio and the Common Application: Art Supplement* recipe in *Chapter 7, The College Application Portfolio*

Using the Collections feature to create a gallery with an audio-guided tour

In this recipe, we will create a gallery with several pages (or rooms) of your work. We will also add a self-guided tour using audio. Unlike the gallery in the previous recipe, we will be using photos we've saved on Picasa to create our tour. This is for two reasons: one, we don't want to go over our allotted storage space and two, doing so will enable us to have more control over the access we give visitors to our pictures. We will create multiple pages, each one representing a room in our gallery, and then join them together in a Collection.

> A Collection joins pages together into a type of website. A set of tabs can be automatically created as well, to provide navigation.

Getting ready

In addition to Mahara, we are going to be using two other programs: Picasa, which is an image-hosting site, and Audacity, which is an open source audio recording program.

Picasa: You will need to create a free account on Picasa (`http://picasaweb.google.com/home`), and an album. Once you have logged into your new Picasa account, you will be taken to the **My Photos** section of your account. To create an album, click the button labeled **Upload**. Click the link **create a new album**. In this new window, you will give your album a name. You will also be asked about the **Visibility** of your album. Select the option **Anyone with the link**. This will keep your images private yet accessible to individuals to whom you wish to provide access through Mahara. They will not need to go to Picasa to see them, and this will give you greater control over the information individuals can access regarding your photos. Upload the photos you wish to use.

Audacity: Download and install Audacity (`http://audacity.sourceforge.net`). You will also need to download and install the LAME MP3 Encoder (there is a link for this on the download page for Audacity). Make sure you remember where you save the LAME file as you will need to find it the first time you make a recording. You will also need a microphone, if you do not have one built into your computer.

Create a folder in the **Files** section of the **Content** tab to hold your audio files. You do not need to upload your audio files ahead of time.

How to do it...

You will need to have two windows or two tabs open; your Mahara account should be open in one of them and your Picasa account in the other. We will be shifting back and forth between the two. Do not close either of the tabs/windows in between the steps listed next:

1. Go to the Mahara window. In the **Pages** section of the **Portfolio** tab, create a new page.

2. Deciding on how many columns to have in your page will be the tricky part as each individual image may be a different size. If you have a particularly wide image, you may want to use one or two columns; if you have tall and narrow images, you may want to use three. Each room in your gallery can have a different number of columns, based on how you would like to showcase your work. Here, in the following screenshot, is an example of a finished room that uses three columns of equal width:

In the next screenshot is an example of a two-column room:

3. After you have selected the number of columns you wish to start with (you can always delete or add a column later), select the theme you wish to use. For this project, I used **Ultima**.
4. Before adding any blocks to your page, go to your album in Picasa and locate the first image you wish to place in your gallery. Click on the image so that it opens in its own window. You will see a panel to the right of the image. Click the link labeled **Link to this Photo** and the area will expand, providing you with several options.
5. The first thing you will need to do is to select a size. It is best to begin with either **Medium 400** or **Medium 640**. When you select a particular size in Picasa (such as **Medium 640**) the image's largest dimension will be set to the number specified in the size. So, if you choose **Medium 640** and the image is taller than it is wide, Picasa will make the height of the image **640px**; the width will be proportionately set. After adding a few pictures, you will get the feel for what approximate sizes to choose. Even so, once you add the image to Mahara, you can resize it, if need be.
6. After selecting the size, put a check mark in the box labeled **Image only (no link)**. This will allow visitors to see your image in Mahara, and will not provide a link back to Picasa.
7. Click inside the box labeled **Embed image** and copy the code. Now you are ready to add your first image to your gallery.
8. Go back to Mahara. In your page, drag the **Text Box** block from the **General** tab to the column you wish to place this image into.

9. Delete everything in the **Block Title** field so that it is empty.
10. With your cursor inside the **Body** field of the textbox, click the "**Insert/edit image**" icon on the HTML toolbar.
11. Paste the code you copied from Picasa into the area for **Image URL**.
12. Type a one- or two-word **Description** of the image.
13. Set the **Alignment** option to **middle**.
14. In the **Border** field, type `10`. This will give you a black frame around your image. The frame thickness will be `10` pixels. At the end of this recipe, I will show you how to make frames with other colors, and frames that appear 3D).
15. Click **Save**.
16. Repeat the previous steps until you've added all the images you wish to add to your first room.
17. Next, we will add little placards underneath each picture. To begin, click-and-drag a **Text Box** block to the area underneath one of your images.
18. Delete the text in the **Block Title** field, leaving it empty.
19. Click in the **Body** field of the **Text Box** and then click the **Insert a new table** icon from the HTML toolbar.
20. On the **General** tab, in the **Insert/Modify table** window, set the following parameters: **Cols**=`1`, **Rows**=`1`, **Cellpadding**=`3`, **Alignment**=`center`, **Border**=`2`, and **Width**=`150`.
21. Now, select the **Advanced** tab. From the drop-down menu labeled **Frame**, select **vsides**. This will place the border on the right and left sides (vertical sides).

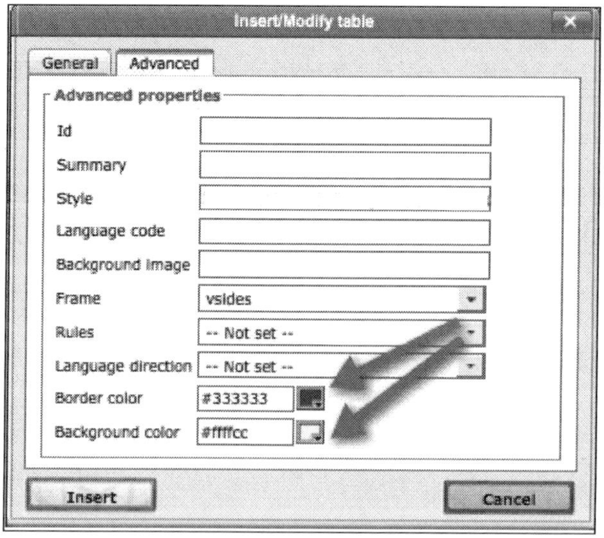

22. Select a border color by clicking on the small box at the far right of the **Border color** option. It will open a palette of colors from which you can select the color you want.
23. Select a **Background color** by clicking the small box to the far right of that option.
24. Click **Insert**.
25. You will be taken back to the editing window for the **Text Box**. We will now add some text to our newly-created placard. Make sure your cursor is in the table you just created. Select the **Book Antiqua** font, and click the center alignment icon. Type the title of your piece and then make it bold. Space down and provide a little information about the piece, for example, `Oil on canvas`.
26. Click **Save**.
27. Continue adding placards for the images in this first room.

    Now we can add a guided tour.

    We're going to add an audio recording to our room. This will provide more details about the images to our visitors. We will also add a transcription of the recording for our visitors who are not able to listen to the audio tour.

28. Leave your Mahara window open to the page you are editing and open Audacity.
29. Click on the button with the red dot to begin recording your voice. You should see a blue wavy line in the grey area with the timeline. You should also see a red line in the upper right-hand area of the recording window. These will tell you that your microphone is picking up your voice and Audacity is recording it. Tell your visitors about the images they are seeing in the room that you will be adding this recording to:

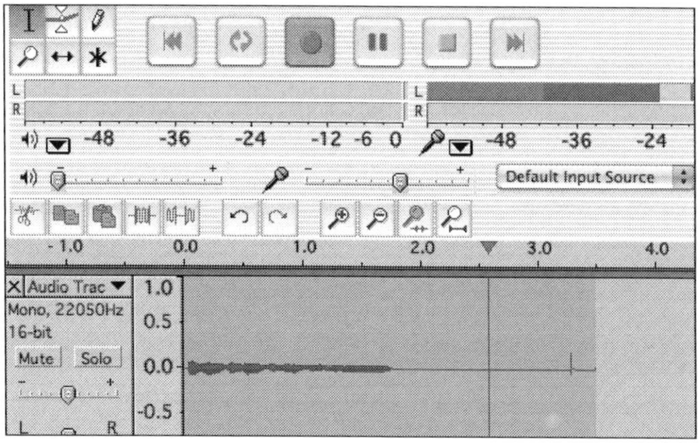

30. When you have finished your recording, click the button with the yellow square. This will stop your recording.

31. From the **File** menu, select **Export as MP3**. The first time you save an MP3 file, you will be asked to locate the LAME encoder file. Just browse to the location you saved it to and select it. You won't need to do this again. You will also be asked to give the file some additional information, but it is not necessary to do that for this project. Simply save the file to a location you will remember. We will be uploading it to Mahara shortly.
32. Back in Mahara, from the **File, Images and video** section, click-and-drag the **Embedded Media** block to a location under one of your images.
33. Delete the text in the **Block Title** field and add `Guided Tour` instead.
34. You will see a list of files and folders in this window. Click the folder you created at the beginning of this recipe to open it.
35. Put a check mark in the box next to **Upload file** and select the **Browse** button.
36. Find the audio file you saved in step 31 and begin uploading it.
37. In the box labeled **Width**, type `300`. This will set the width of your playback controls to 300 pixels. You can set it to a different size, if you prefer.
38. Click **Save**.
39. To add a text-based tour for visitors who cannot hear the audio tour, create and save a transcript of your audio file to your computer. It is a good idea to give the file a name like `Text for Guided Tour of Room #1`, because visitors will see the name of the file.
40. From the **Files, Images and video** section, click-and-drag a **Files to download** block to the area underneath your audio recording.
41. You can delete the text in the **Block Title** field, leaving it empty.
42. Put a check mark next to **Upload file** and click the **Browse** button to find and upload your transcript.
43. Click **Save**.
44. Click on the tab **Next: Edit Title and Description**.
45. In the field for **Page Title**, give your page a title.
46. You can skip the **Description** field, add **Tags** if you like, and click **Save**.
47. Do not assign access at this time. We will do that when we build the gallery (this is just one room in that gallery). Click **Done**.
48. Continue building the rest of your rooms (pages), following the steps outlined above. When you have finished building your rooms, it will be time to put them all together into one marvelous gallery!
49. This is the easiest and quickest part, combining all of your rooms into your gallery. To begin, select **Collections** on the **Portfolio** tab.
50. Click the button **New Collection**.

51. In the **Collection name** field, give this collection the name of your gallery. It will contain all of the rooms you've previously created. Add a description if you'd like to.
52. The option for **Page navigation bar** should have a check mark next to it.
53. Select **Next: Edit Collection Pages**.
54. A list of all your pages will appear in a box labeled **Add pages to collection**. Click the little bubble next to each of the pages (rooms) that you want as part of this gallery.
55. Click the button **Add Pages**.
56. These pages will now appear in the area labeled **Edit Collection Pages**.

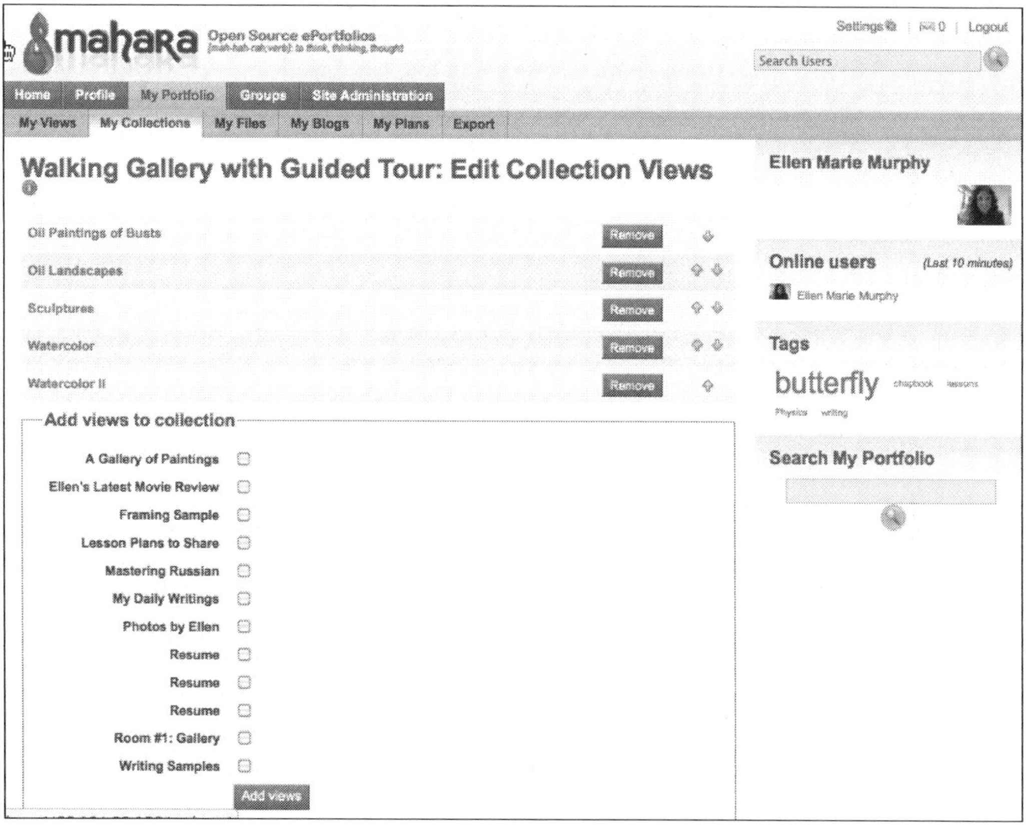

57. If the rooms are not in the proper order (room 1 at the top, room 2 next, and so on), use the little gray arrows on the right to move them up and down into their proper order.
58. Click **Done**.
59. To set the access, click the tab labeled **Share**.
60. You will see a list of all your Pages and Collections. Find the Collection you just created and click the small icon opposite it in the column labeled **Edit access**.

61. In the **Edit Access** window, make sure that this Collection has a check mark next to it, then click the button labeled **Add**, next to the access level you would like to set.
62. The rest of the options can remain at their default settings, so simply skip them.
63. Click **Save**.

That's it! Your gallery is now open!

How it works...

Your pages will now have tabs at the top, which visitors can use to navigate through your gallery. There will be an audio player on each page that they can use to listen to the recordings that you made. They can also download the transcript.

There's more...

Next, you will find a few additional ideas for creating frames and a welcome page.

Creating frames

In this recipe, we set the frame to 10 pixels, but you can set the size of the frame to any thickness you prefer by simply typing in a different number; the larger the number, the thicker the frame. By default, the frame is solid black, but, with a little tweaking of the code, you can have just about any color you want, and you can make a frame that appears 3D.

The following instructions outline how it's done:

1. After adding your image to your **Text Box** block (step 14) but before saving it (step 15), click **HTML** in the upper right-hand corner of your HTML toolbar.
2. A window will open with a few lines of code that look similar to the snippet in this screenshot:

```
<p><img style="border: 25px solid black;" src="http:/
/AAAAAAAAAPk/EzmsWvhT5Uk/s640/beachcomber.png" alt=""
```

3. Locate `<img style="border:`, following which is the size you set for your border (I set mine to `25px`), then the type of border (`solid`), and then the color (**black**).
4. To change the solid border to one that appears 3D, carefully change the word `solid` to either *one* of the following options: `groove`, `ridge`, or `outset`.
5. To change the color of the border, carefully change the word `black` to another color. You can find a list of web-friendly color names here: `http://www.w3schools.com/HTML/HTML_colornames.asp`. I've found that some of the names do not work in all browsers, but using the **Hex codes** does. You can try using a color name (type it exactly as the color name indicates), but if your color isn't working, try typing in the Hex code for the color instead.

> Hex codes contain a combination of six letters and/or numbers and begin with a # sign. The code for red is #FF0000. Rather than explaining how to figure out the codes (which can be done because they are actually mathematical expressions), I'm going to suggest simply finding the hex codes on the Web (by the way, `Hex` is short for Hexadecimal). Hex codes can contain letters: A-F and/or numbers 0-9. So, you will never see a hex code that contains the letter O. Characters that look like that are *always* zeroes.
>
> I have created a tutorial that will help you to understand hex codes so that you don't have to rely on a table. It also contains a page in which you can enter hex codes and see them displayed. You can find it at the following website: `http://visibledreams.net/Web/color/color_1.html`.

6. Click **Update** and then click **Save**.

To make the frame for the previous image, the color was changed to DeepSkyBlue, but, instead of using the words, the Hex code #00BFFF was used. The solid border was changed to groove. Here is what the new code looks like:

```
><img style="border: 25px groove #008B8B;"
AAAAAAAAPk/EzmsWvhT5Uk/s640/beachcomber.pn
```

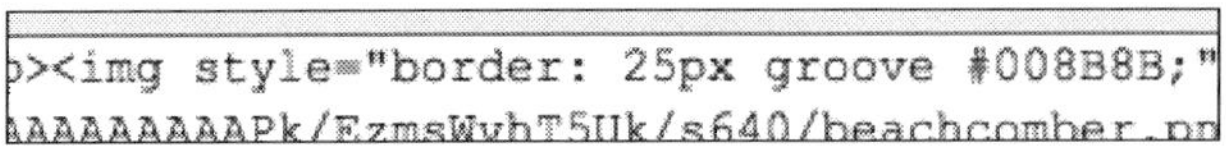

Adding a splash page

Currently our gallery is set up to open to our first room, but you may want to create a splash page or a welcome page. You can create one using the first recipe in this chapter and add it to the collection you created when you made your gallery. Once you've created the page for your gallery entrance, and saved it, go to the **Collections** section on the **Portfolio** tab. You will see three icons to the right of your gallery collection. Click the one closest to the title of the collection. Once you select that link, you will see a list of all of the pages in your portfolio that are not part of another collection. Your splash page will be there. Select it and then select **Add page**. Once it is added to the list of pages that are part of your gallery collection, you will need to use the small arrows to make sure this welcoming page is the first one in the collection. Then click **Done**.

See also

- *Language acquisition journal* recipe in *Chapter 2, Literature and Writing*
- *Making a photo journal using Picasa* recipe

2
Literature and Writing

In this chapter, we will cover:

- Uploading a group of documents and sharing them using the Secret URL
- A "Thought a Day" journal
- A Page of writing samples
- A poetry page with a faux woodblock print created using GIMP
- Creating a poetry chapbook
- Thesis/Research planning
- Language acquisition journal
- A daily gazette

Introduction

The saying goes "You can't tell a book by its cover" but there's a lot to be said about the way "packaging" affects perception. In this chapter, we will explore several creative ways for packaging your writing. Many of the recipes use journals in ways you might not expect.

Mahara allows the creation of an unlimited number of journals, and journals can be used for a variety of purposes. The advantage of using a journal for reflections on artifacts, and for simply creating artifacts of writing, is the ability to use and reuse a single post, a group of posts, or an entire journal, for many different types of Pages. And, if you delete the Pages, your writing will still be saved in your journal. This is not the case with adding writing to a Page using a textbox; if you delete the Page, the textbox and all it contains is deleted as well. Additionally, the text in a textbox cannot be repurposed.

Nevertheless, there are times when textboxes in Pages are the perfect venue for your writing, and you'll see a few examples in this chapter. You'll also learn that textboxes can be extremely *versatile.*

In addition to learning some creative ways to use Mahara, the chapter acquaints you with a digital image editing program called GIMP. GIMP is another Open Source product that is freely downloadable from the website: `http://www.gimp.org/`.

I hope the chapter stimulates your own creative ideas for using Mahara to "put a cover on your book". Have fun!

Uploading a group of documents, and sharing them using the Secret URL

We're going to imagine we've developed a series of lesson plans that a colleague in another school would like to use. With this recipe, we will upload the series of lesson plans (documents) and then share them using the Secret URL. The following screenshot is what your colleague will see:

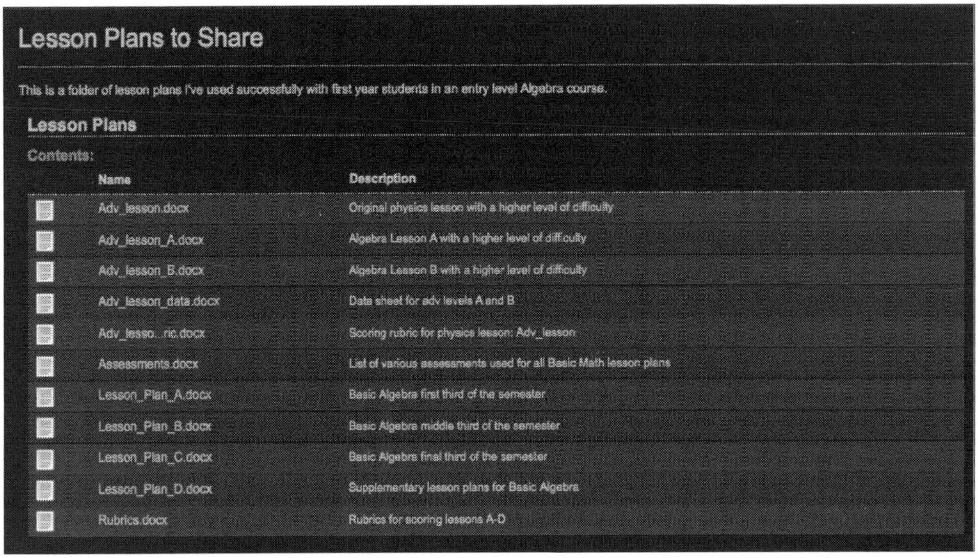

Getting ready

It is best to begin by putting all of the documents you will be uploading into one folder.

How to do it...

1. Select the **Content** tab, and then **Files**.
2. In the box labeled **Create folder** type the name of the folder you wish to create for this recipe. Our example is called: Lesson Plans.
3. Select the button labeled **Create folder**.
4. Your new folder will appear in the list of folders under **Home**.
5. To add our files, we will first need to open this new folder. To do so, click on the name of the folder.
6. Now that we are in the folder, let's put a checkmark in the little box next to **Upload file**—this certifies that you have the right to use this file.
7. Select the **Browse** button. Find the document you wish to upload and select **Open**.
8. A little green spinning wheel and the name of the document you are uploading will appear above **Upload file**. You do not need to wait for the wheel to stop spinning before you begin uploading your next document. The **Upload file** box will still be checked; simply select the **Browse** button again and upload your next document. If all of your documents have been stored in the same file, this can be a relatively quick process, as the browse window will open to the same location you attained the previous document.
9. Documents that have finished uploading will have a green checkmark next to them, and will appear in the bottom half of the **Files** window.
10. Next to each file, there will be two small icons: the first icon is for editing and the second one is for deleting the file. Select the icon for editing next to the first document.
11. The file information will expand and you will see areas where you can add additional information about the document. This information will be displayed in the Page you will create to give your colleague access to the documents. In the area labeled **Description**, add a brief description of the document:

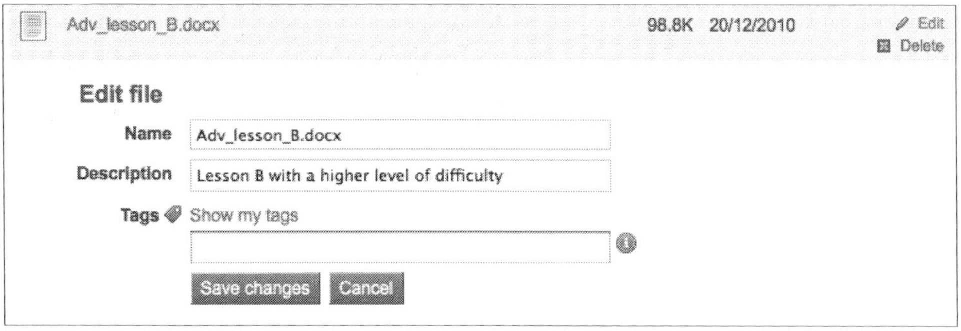

12. Select **Save changes**.
13. Repeat steps 10-12 for each document. This will create a better looking table when we go to share it, and it will provide you with additional information for future reference.

Okay, now let's share these lesson plans:

1. In the **Pages** section of the **Portfolio** tab select **Create Page**.
2. On this next page, you will see two rows of tabs. Click the tab labeled **Edit Layout**.
3. Select the option for **1 column, Equal widths**.
4. Click on **Save**.
5. Select a theme from the **Theme** drop-down menu.
6. On the **Files, Images and video** tab, select the block: **A Folder**, and drag it down to the bottom of the page (into your Page).
7. A window **A Folder: Configure** will open. There will be a space for you to add a **Block Title**. You do not need to add one as Mahara will use the title of your folder; just leave it empty.
8. Under **Block Title** you will see three tabs: **My Files**, **Group Files**, and **Site Files**. The tab "My Files" will be the one that is selected, and that is the one we want to be selected. You should see a list of your folders and two buttons next to each: **Edit** and **Select**. Click on the button **Select** next to the folder you created for this recipe.
9. Select **Save**.
10. Select the tab: **Next: Edit Title and Description**.
11. Provide a **Title** and a **Description** of the Page. Descriptions can be seen by anyone who has access to the Page. They will be displayed at the top of the Page.
12. Use the **Tags** field to add keywords that you can use to locate this Page more easily in the future (when you have lots of Pages).
13. Click on **Save**.
14. You will be back at the Page you are creating. Click on **Done**.
15. You will now be on the **Pages** section of the **Portfolio** tab. Click the tab labeled **Share**.
16. In the next page, you will see a list of all your **Pages** and **Collections** (if you have any). Next to each Page, you will see a small icon under a column labeled **Secret URLs**. Click that icon for the Page you just created.

17. In the next page, simply click the **Add** button.
18. A URL will appear above the **Add** button. Copy that URL.

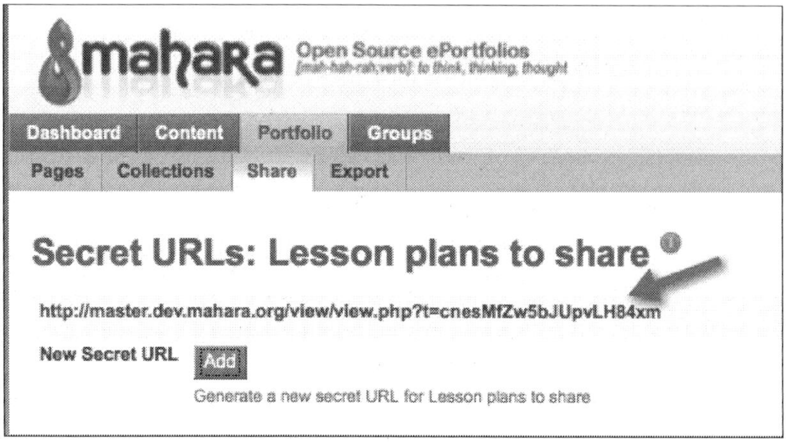

19. Paste this URL into an e-mail, and send it to the person with whom you wish to share this Page.

How it works...

The Secret URL is a web address (URL) that allows a Page to be accessible to individuals who do not have an account on your system, without making the Page accessible to the general public. Only individuals who have the Secret URL will be able to access your page. It is not because the program knows who you sent it to, but because they will be accessing your Page directly. Search engines will not pick this page up.

There's more...

Below are a few additional steps that might enhance the presentation of your materials, and a method for uploading all of your files with one upload, instead of many.

Adding a Creative Commons License

Whenever you make your work accessible to someone else, it is a good idea to include a notification regarding how you would like to share your work. The default is "All rights reserved", whether you put the statement on your work or not. However, you may want others to be able to use your work without your permission.

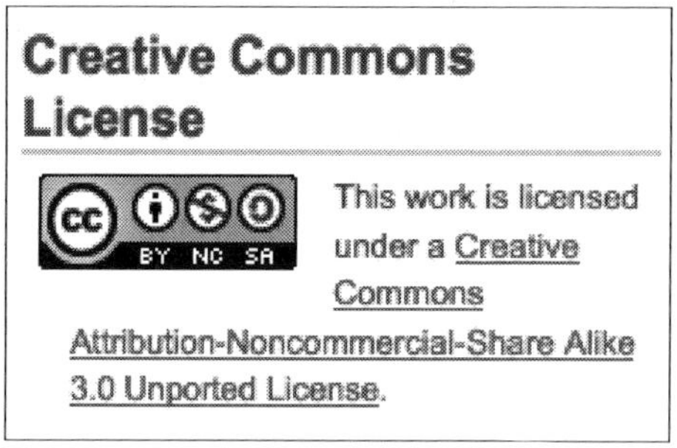

Putting a Creative Commons License notification on your work, will remind the viewer that you own the rights to the work, and it lets them know how they can use the work.

Adding a Creative Commons License is very easy. Simply add it when you are creating your Page by dragging the **Creative Commons** block from the **General** tab into your Page. Select the options you wish to allow. If you are unsure of what the various options mean, select the little **i** next to the **No** options:

How to edit a filename after upload

You can change the way the filenames display on your Page. For example, I uploaded a file called `Adv_LessonA.docx`. Currently, that's the name of the file that appears on my page. However, I might want a "nicer" name, maybe something like "Advanced Lesson A". I can change the display name in Mahara, without affecting its ability to locate the file. To do so:

1. Go to **Files** on the **Content** tab and locate the file you'd like to edit. Don't click on it; instead select the **Edit** icon next to it. The file information will expand.
2. Replace the text in the box labeled **Name** with the title you would like the file to have instead.
3. Click on **Save changes**.

See also

- *Protecting your opus recipe in Chapter 1, Mahara for the Visual Arts*
- *A page of writing samples* recipe

A "Thought a Day" journal

With this recipe, we will use a journal to create a Daily Reflection book-like journal. Wow, that's a mouthful, but this is an easy recipe, and the following screenshot shows how it might look when we're all done:

How to do it...

Establish a journal for daily journaling:

1. On the **Content** tab, select **Journals**.
2. Select the button labeled **Create Journal**.
3. Give the journal a title. The example uses "A Thought a Day". Give the journal a short description and **Tags**, if you want.
4. Select **Create Journal**. You will be taken back to the **Journals** section of **Content**. Your new journal will be listed there.
5. Select the button labeled **New Entry**, and begin your first entry in your new journal by giving this entry a **Title**.
6. Type your entry in the Body, using the options in the HTML toolbar to select the fonts you wish to use.
7. Click on **Save Entry**.

The journal now exists, but no one can read it except you. Let's add it to a Page, so that it can be shared with others.

To create the Page:

1. Go to the **Pages** subtab on the **Portfolio** tab and select **Create Page**.
2. Change the Page format to *one column*.
3. From the **Journals** tab, select the **Journal** block and drag it into your Page.
4. In the window that opens, you will see a list of your journals. The **Block Title** will be empty. You can choose to add a title; if you leave it empty, Mahara will use the title of your journal for the title of the block.
5. From the list of journals, select your daily journal.
6. In the **Post per page option**, type the number "`1`". (Mahara will automatically create navigation, to each journal entry, at the bottom of the Page).
7. Click on **Save**.
8. Select the tab labeled **Next: Edit Title and Description**.
9. Give this Page a title. The title you choose will appear in the very upper left-hand corner of the finished Page.
10. You can add a description in the area labeled **Page Description**, but it is not required. If you would like to add a banner (like the one in the example) this is where you would put the image. For now, just leave the description empty: I'll explain how to add the banner in the *There's more...* section.
11. Click on **Save**.

12. Select the tab labeled **Share page**.
13. In the page that opens, select the type of access you want by clicking the **Add** button next to that option. You could even choose to make it publically accessible—meaning anyone can see it.
14. Click on **Save**.

How it works...

New entries in your Journal must be added directly to the Journal (in the Journals section of the Content tab). The Page will automatically add the new posting. The Page will also automatically create a navigation menu beneath your posts, so that viewers can see previous entries. The most current entry will always be the one initially displayed.

There's more...

The previous example has a banner (an image of a book). Banners are relatively simple to make and we'll look at that in the following steps:

Adding an image banner to your page

The banner in the example is a single image 800 X 100. Images for the Web need to be in one of the following formats: `.png`, `.jpg`, or `.gif`. The sample banner was created using a digital image editing application called GIMP. GIMP can be downloaded from the site: `http://www.gimp.org`.

To add a banner:

1. Upload your saved image to the **Files** area of the **Content** tab.
2. After it is uploaded, you will see that the name of the image is a link—select the link by clicking on it.
3. The image will open in a new window. Copy the URL at the top of the window (in the address bar):

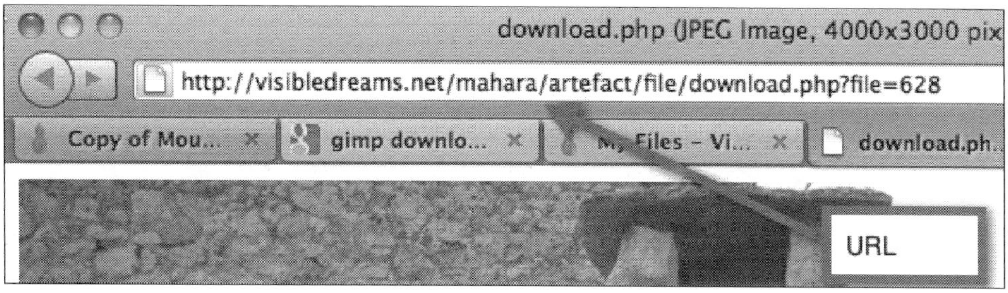

4. Close that window and click the **Portfolio** tab.
5. You should, then, be at the **Pages** section.
6. Find the Page for your journal and click on it to open it.
7. Once the Page opens, click the **Edit** option in the upper right-hand corner.
8. Click the tab labeled: **Edit: Title and Description**.
9. Place your cursor in the box labeled **Page Description** by clicking in it.
10. Select the **Insert/edit image** icon in the HTML tools (it looks like a little picture of a tree):

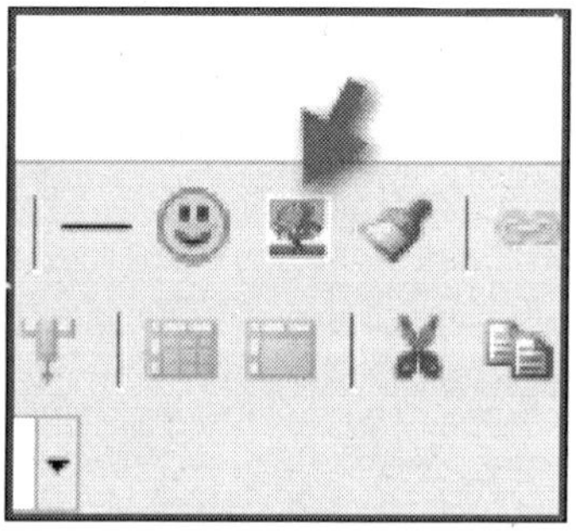

11. A small window will open.
12. Paste the URL you copied in step 3, into the area labeled **Image URL**.
13. In the **Description** field type: "`banner`".
14. Set the **Alignment** to **left**.
15. Select **Insert** and then **Save**.

There are a number of sites on the Internet that will allow you to create a banner in your web browser (for example, `http://www.createbanner.com/`). The images are usually stored on their servers, however, and you might lose your banner if the website goes away. If you choose to use this option, copy the URL of your completed banner. Then follow steps 5-11, adding the URL of your web created banner in step 9.

See also

- *Chapter 5, International project* recipe

A page of writing samples

With this recipe, we will create a delicious looking Page of writing samples, sure to make a viewer explore further. The following screenshot is an example of the same:

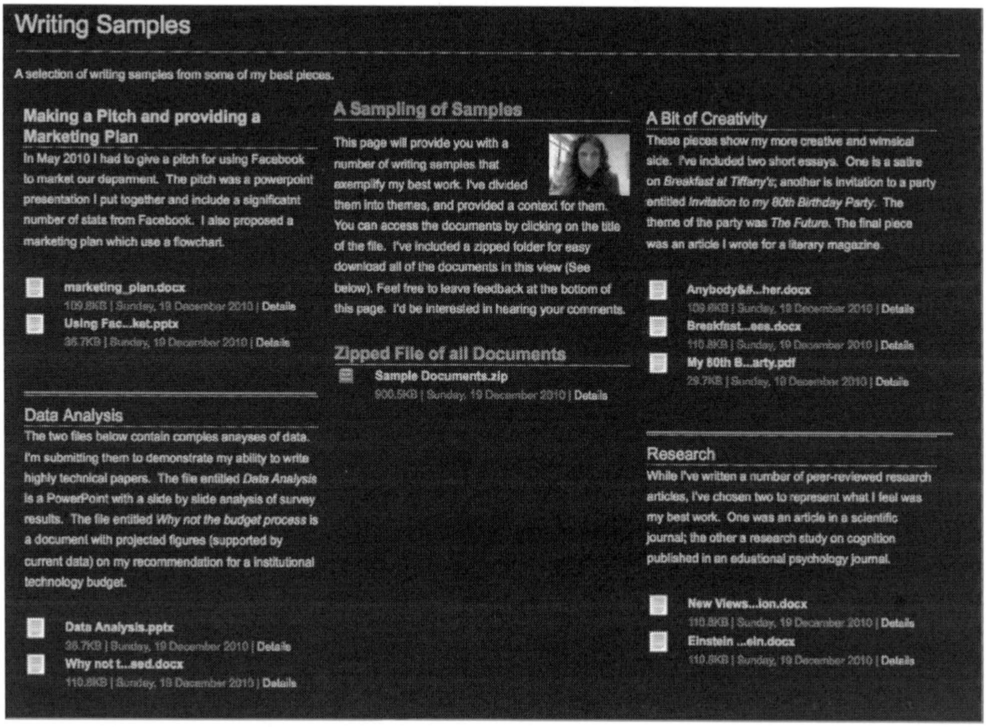

Getting ready

If your writing samples are not already in your portfolio, create a folder in the **Files** section of the **Content** tab and upload the documents you wish to use.

Optional: If you are able, make a zipped folder containing all of the documents as well, and upload the zipped folder to your **Files** section. You will have to create the zipped folder on your computer as Mahara does not currently provide a way to do that.

How to compress (.zip) a folder

To make a zipped folder of all your documents, you will need to have a folder somewhere in your computer that contains all of the documents. If you have not kept a copy of the documents on your computer (in other words: the only copies are on Mahara) then you will need to create a folder on your computer, download the documents from Mahara, and save them to the folder you created on your computer. After you've put all of the documents into the folder, you're ready to "zip" it.

To make a zipped folder on a Mac, hold down the *control* key and click on the folder. From the menu that opens, select **compress folder**. This will automatically create a zipped folder, with the same name as the original folder. It will appear in the same location as the original folder, but will have a `.zip` extension.

To make a zipped folder on a PC: right-click the folder. From the menu that opens, select **Send To** and **Compressed Folder**. The new file will appear in the same location as the original file, but will have a `.zip` extension.

How to do it...

1. Click the **Portfolio** tab to get to the **Pages** section. Select **Create Page**.
2. Set the theme you wish to use from the drop-down menu for themes. For my example, I used **Ultima**.
3. Leave the default format (three columns of equal width).
4. Select the **Profile Information** block from the **Profile** tab and drag it to the center column.
5. Change the **Block Title** to suit your Page: In the example, I used "A Sampling of Samples", but you can use whatever works for you. You will want text in the **Block Title** because it will keep this block slightly higher on the page.
6. Deselect items in **Fields to Show** so that none of the items is checked.
7. Select a **Profile Icon**. If you do not have one, you can upload one using the link provided.
8. In the **Introduction Text** box, provide a general overview of what your visitors will find. I've included a sentence telling them that, for ease of downloading, I've included a zipped folder of all the documents in the Page.
9. Click on **Save**.
10. Next, we are going to add Text Boxes and Files to download in both the right-hand and left-hand columns. Let's start with the left-hand column first. Drag a **Text Box** block from the **General** tab to the column.

11. Delete the **Block Title** so that it is empty and, instead, add the title in the Body of the textbox itself.
12. Highlight the title and apply **Heading 2** from the drop-down menu for **Paragraphs**.
13. Using your *Enter* key, insert a space and begin typing your reflection or description of the writing samples you will be adding below this box.
14. Click on **Save**.
15. Beneath the textbox, drag a **Files to Download** block from the **Files, Images and video** tab.
16. Delete the **Box Title** so that it is empty.
17. Select the files for this section using the **Select** button next to those specific files. Then **Save**.
18. Now, we'll create the next set of samples for this column. Drag a **Text Box** block to the bottom of the column.
19. Type an underscore (line) in the **Block Title**, and then add the title as you did in steps 11 and 12.
20. Repeat steps 13-17.
21. To build the right-hand column, repeat steps 10-19, dragging the blocks to that column.
22. Finally, we will give the visitor the opportunity to download all of the samples in a zipped file. From the **Files, Images and video** tab, select a **Files to download** block and drag it to the area underneath your profile block (in the center of the Page).
23. Change the **Block Title** to: `Zipped Folder of all Documents`.
24. Use the **Select** button next to the zipped file and **Save**.
25. When you've finished adding all of the writing samples you wish to showcase, select the **Next: Edit title and description** tab.
26. Provide a **Title** and a brief **Description** (it makes the Page look more professional).
27. Add Tags that will help you easily locate this Page in the future.
28. Click on **Save**.
29. Select the tab: **Share page**.
30. Set your access levels and **Save**.

A poetry page with a faux woodblock print is created using GIMP.

So you've written a poem you'd like to share? Have you considered adding an illustration to accompany it? In this recipe, we'll create a Page of your poem, and a woodblock print to accompany it—a poetry page that can later be added to a small book.

To create images that look like woodblock prints, we will use a software program called GIMP (an open source image-editing program), and pictures taken with a digital camera. GIMP is available at: `http://www.gimp.org/`.

A screenshot of one poetry page is as follows:

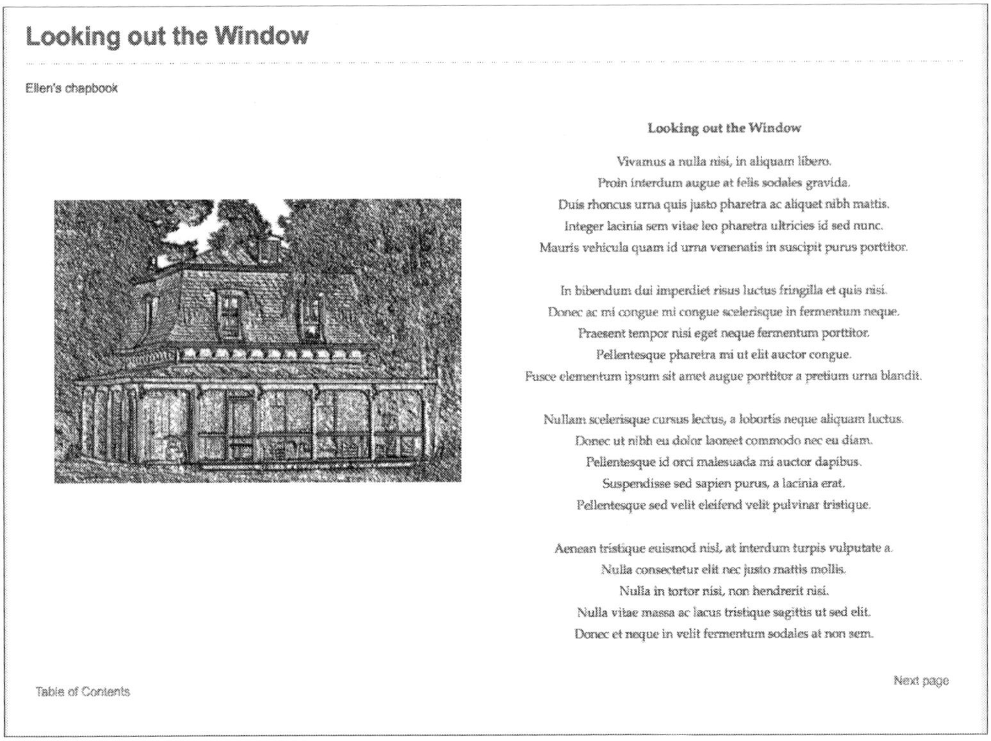

Getting ready

To make the poetry page, you will use **Text Blocks** and **Image Blocks**. Because this recipe is so addictive, and you'll want to create several poetry pages, you should create a folder in Mahara to hold the images you will be using. Finally, you will need to download and install GIMP: `http://www.gimp.org/`. For this example, we are going to use poetry, but this could also be a page of another genre (short essay for example).

How to do it...

To create your images:

1. Using GIMP, open the digital images you wish to edit (**File | Open**).
2. To crop the image: In the GIMP toolbox, select the **Rectangle Select Tool** (it's in the upper left-hand corner).
3. Draw a rectangle around the area you wish to use for your woodblock print.
4. In the menu at the top of the image, select **Image** and then **Crop to selection**.
5. Now, from that same top menu select **Filters**, then **Distorts**, then **Emboss**. The default settings are generally sufficient.
6. Before we finish, let's check the size of the image. Click the **Image** menu and then **Scale Image**:

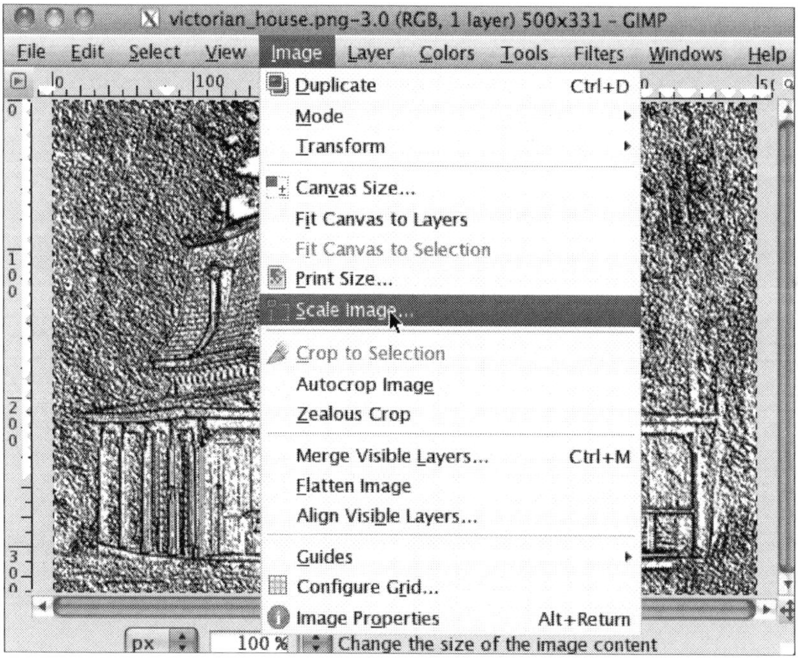

7. You will see a number of settings. The first one you will want to change is the setting for the **X** and **Y resolution**. Set them both to: `96.000` pixels/in; this setting will significantly decrease the file size and not affect the clarity of the image.
8. Next, set either the **Width** or the **Height** to no more than `500` pixels, and then type your *Enter* key. It will resize the image proportionately.
9. **Save** the image, and then upload it to the folder you created in Mahara for this project.

Building your poetry pages:

1. Log into Mahara.
2. On the **My Portfolio** tab, select **Pages** and then **Create Page**.
3. Click the tab labeled: **Edit Layout**.
4. Select **2 columns, Equal widths**.
5. Click on **Save**.

We are going to begin with building the right-hand side of the page:

1. From the **General** tab select the **Text Box** block and drag it to the right-hand column.
2. Delete the words **Text Box** in the **Block Title**, leaving it empty.
3. Either copy and paste your poem into the textbox, or type it directly into the textbox.
4. Highlight the text and center it using the center-alignment icon in the HTML toolbars.
5. With the text still highlighted, select the font **Book Antiqua** from the **Font Styles** drop-down menu.
6. Make the title **Bold**.
7. Click on **Save**.

To build the left-hand side:

1. From the **Files, Images and video** tab, drag the **An Image** block to the left-hand column.
2. Delete the words **An Image** from the **Block Title**, leaving it empty.
3. Find the image you wish to add and choose the **Select** button next to it. If you have not already uploaded the image, you can do so now and then select it.
4. Set the **Width** to **400**.
5. Click on **Save**.

To add the proper amount of whitespace around the image, and/or the text:

1. From the **General** tab drag a **Text Box** block into the area you wish to add whitespace.
2. Delete the words **Text Box** from the Block Title, leaving it empty.
3. Use your *Enter* key to space the cursor down the approximate amount of whitespace you need in the area. This does not need to be exact, as you can always go back and adjust it.
4. Click on **Save**.
5. Repeat steps 1-4 in this section to add additional areas of whitespace.
6. To adjust the whitespace, select the **Configure this block** icon on the text block you wish to edit.

7. Add or delete whitespace using the *Enter* or *Delete* key on your keyboard.
8. Click on **Save**.

The following screenshot shows how the page looks in editing mode:

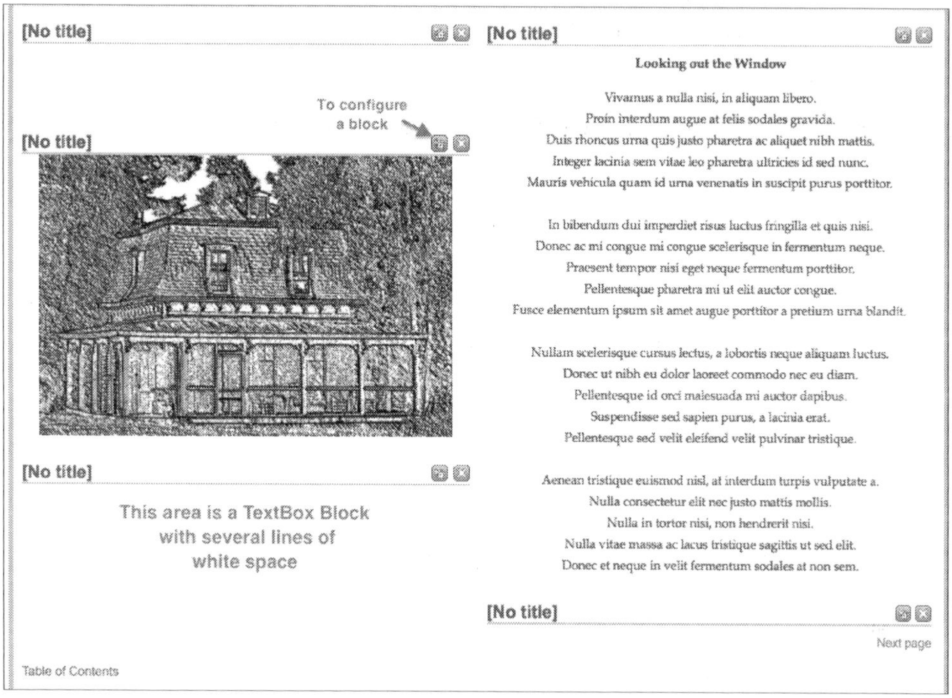

The next step is to name the page:

1. Select the tab labeled **Next**: **Edit Title and Description**.
2. In the **Title** area type the name of the poem; in the **Description**, type the name of the book (if it will be part of a book—see the next recipe).
3. Select **Save**.
4. To set your access, click the tab labeled: **Share page**.
5. Choose the access level you would like to set by selecting the **Add** button next to that option.
6. Click **Advance Options** to expand that portion of the page.
7. Turn off the option **Allow Comments**.
8. Click on **Save**.

After you've created several poetry pages, you may want to bind them into a little book. The next recipe can help you with that.

There's more...

When you use a textbox to create your poem, or to add any text to a Page, you are not creating nor using an artifact. The text in the textbox cannot be repurposed in another Page without copy/paste. And if you delete the Page, the text will be deleted as well. You can create the poem in a word processing program (like Word), or a web page composer (such as KompoZer), and save the document as an HTML file. Then upload the documents to Mahara and using the **Some HTML** block, add it to your Page. This will create a permanent artifact in your portfolio, and the text will display almost exactly, if not exactly, as the Page created using a Text Box block. Let's see how to do this using a word processing document.

Using the Some HTML block to create your Page (creating an artifact of your poem)

1. Open Word and then **File** and a **New Blank Document**.
2. Type your poem and then format it as you would like it to appear in your Page (set the Font, the Alignment, and so on).
3. From the **File** menu, select the **Save as Web Page**.
4. Give the file a name and save it to your computer (Note the file extension will be `.htm` instead of `.docx`).

The steps we are going to follow now, should replace steps 14-20 in the main recipe:

1. From the **Files, images and video** tab, click-and-drag a Some HTML block to the right-hand column.
2. Delete the text from the **Block Title**.
3. To upload the `.html` file you created in Word, click in the small box next to **Upload file** (to put a checkmark in the box).
4. Click the **Browse** button to locate and upload the `.htm` document you saved on your computer.
5. When it has finished uploading, you will see it listed above the tabs labeled: **My Files, Group Files, Site Files**.

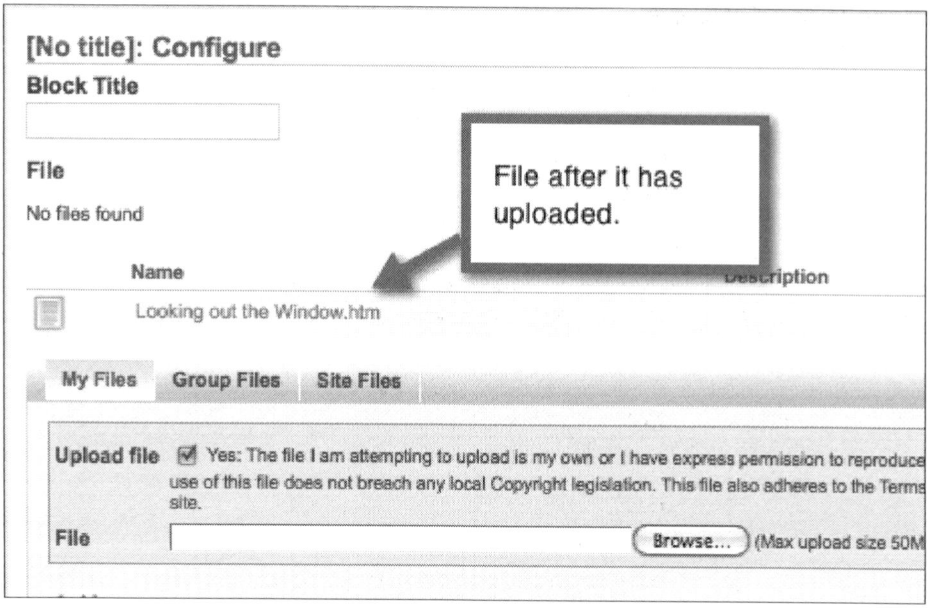

6. Save and you will see your text displayed in your Page.

See also

- *A poetry chapbook* recipe
- *Using HTML to create your official transcript recipe in Chapter 7, The College Application Portfolio*
- *Templates for meeting teacher certification standards recipe in Chapter 8, Certification and Accreditation Portfolio for Higher Education*

A poetry chapbook

As you've already seen, there are a number of ways that artifacts can be stored and shared in Mahara. In this recipe, we will create a poetry chapbook (which is simply a small book) using the poetry pages you may have created using the previous recipe.

> Though the term chapbook usually refers to a pocket-sized book, we're kind of going to stretch the meaning a bit here when we refer to this digital book with a style similar to a paperback poetry book you might find in a local bookstore.

Getting ready

Using the recipe for poetry pages (earlier in this chapter), create all the Pages (pages) of your chapbook; you'll need to group them into a collection (a little like bookbinding). Then, we will create a cover page and table of contents. We'll use the built-in navigation for Collections, but the *There's more...* section will provide you with the option of creating links at the bottom of each page to take readers through the book page-by-page.

Let's begin and create our collection.

How to do it...

1. Select the subtab labeled **Collections** on the **Portfolio** tab.
2. Select the button labeled **New Collection**.
3. Give the collection a name (the name of your book would be a good choice).
4. You can provide a Description, if you want, but it is not necessary.
5. The option for a **Page navigation bar** should be checked.
6. Select **Next: Edit Collection Pages**.
7. Click to put a checkmark next to each Page that will be a page in your chapbook.
8. Select the button labeled **Add Pages**.
9. You will see the list of Pages you've added. Next to each will be a button labeled **Remove** and arrows. To change the order of the Pages, use the arrows. First page should be at the top, and the last page at the bottom.
10. Click **Done**.
11. You will find yourself back at the **Collections** page. To set the access level for your collection, click the **Share** tab.
12. Locate this Collection in the list of **Pages** and **Collections** on the **Share page**. Click the small icon next to it in the Edit Access column.
13. In the next page, you will see the list of Collections and Pages again, only this time they will run horizontally. Ensure there is a checkmark next to this Collection.
14. Click the **Add** button next to the access level you would like to set.
15. If you want to turn off the ability to let viewers comment on your book, click that **Advanced Options** link, and uncheck the option to **Allow comments**.
16. Click on **Save**.

> The access level you set for a collection overrides all previous access settings that may have been applied to individual Pages in the Collection.

We're going to create a cover page with a Table of Contents. The Table of Contents will provide links to each of the pages in our book.

The cover page is another Page. The Table of Contents is actually a **Navigation Block**. The following is an example of a cover page:

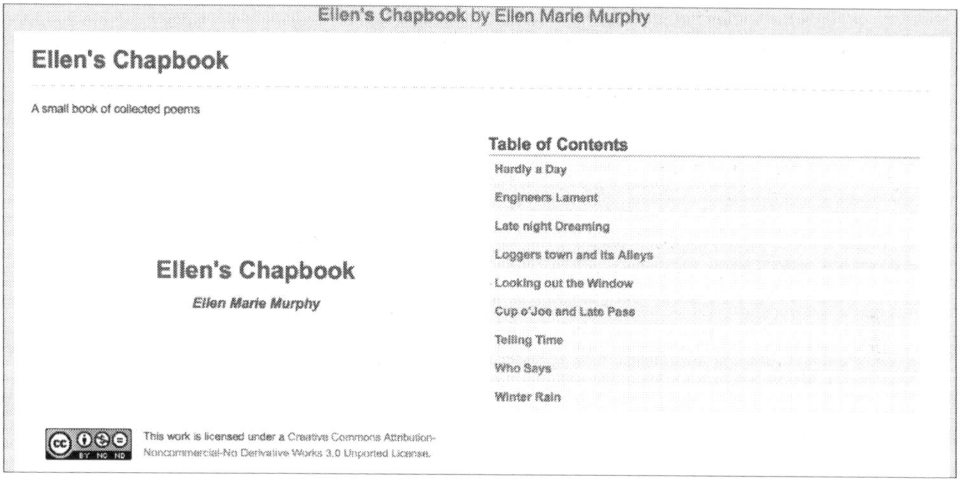

Implement the following steps to create a cover page:

1. On the **Portfolio** tab, select **Pages**, and then **Create Page**.
2. In this next window, you will see two rows of tabs. Click the **Edit Layout** tab in the top row.
3. Select the option: **2 columns**, **Equal widths**.
4. Click on **Save**.
5. From the **General** tab select the **Text Box** block and drag it to the left-hand column.
6. Delete the words **Text Box** in the **Block Title**, leaving it empty.
7. Using the *Enter* key on your keyboard, insert several spaces.
8. From the drop-down menu labeled **Paragraphs**, select **Heading 1**.
9. Select the center-alignment icon on the HTML toolbar.
10. Type the title of your book.
11. Insert one space using your *Enter* key.
12. Change the **Paragraph** menu to **Heading 4**.
13. Select the option to center the text.
14. Type your name (the author).
15. Insert a few more spaces and then **Save**.
16. From the same **General** tab, click on the **Creative Commons** block and drag it to the bottom of the left-hand column.

17. You can either delete the **Block Title** or leave it; it's up to you. Select the licensing options you would like.
18. Click on **Save**.
19. From the **General** tab, select the **Navigation** block and drag it to the right-hand column.
20. In the **Block Title** type `Table of Contents`.
21. From the drop-down menu under **Collections**, select your chapbook collection. If you have not created any other Collections, then you will already see the Collection in the drop-down menu.
22. Click on **Save**.
21. If you need to adjust the whitespace in the left-hand column (the Text Box that contains the Title and Author's name), select the icon **Configure this Block** in the upper right-hand corner of the textbox.
22. The block will reopen in edit mode. Click in the space where you wish to add or delete space, and use the *Enter* and/or *Delete* keys on your keyboard to do so.
23. Click on **Save**.
24. Select **Next: Edit Title and Description** tab and add your **Title** and a brief **Description** of your book—just one line.
25. Click on **Save**.
26. Select **Done** and set your access to the same access you set for your collection.

How it works...

We now have a collection of Pages. They are currently connected, though it would not be easy to tell that because there is currently no navigation between the pages. (We did not add a Navigation Bar when we created the Collection). In fact, if you opened any one of the Pages, you would not know it was part of a collection, and you would not have a way to get to any of the other pages in the collection. Mahara has another method for navigation which we will explore next, and provide a way for our readers to get to the various pages in our book.

There's more...

Below we offer an alternate method for creating navigation, as well as a way to add the Title Page to your collection:

Using page corner links for navigation instead of the tabs

You may not like the look of the tabs at the top of your book, and prefer to have little links at the bottom of each page (to take readers through the book in a more linear fashion).

This is a bit tricky—mostly because it requires a little extra concentration and organization—but it can be more aesthetically pleasing. The first thing you'll need to do is open Notepad (PC) or TextEdit (Mac).

1. Go to **Pages** on the **Portfolio** tab.
2. Click each Page in the chapbook, one at a time, so that they open. Copy the URL (address of the Page):

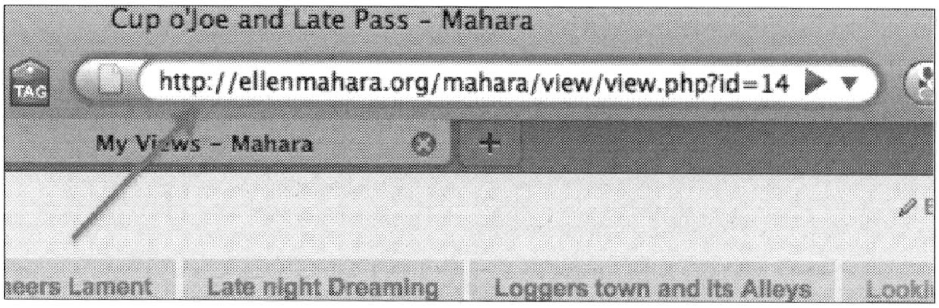

3. Paste each URL into your text window (Notepad or TextEdit).
4. When you've finished this, you should have a list of the URLs for each page. Make sure you know which page each of those URLs are for.
5. Back in the **Pages** section of **Portfolio**, click on the first page in the Chapbook to open it (not the title page). Then click the **Edit** option in the upper right-hand corner to go to the editing mode.
6. From the **General** tab, select a **Text Box** block and drag it to the bottom of the left-hand column.
7. Type the word `Home` and highlight the word you just typed. Select the link icon in the HTML editing tools. A window will open:

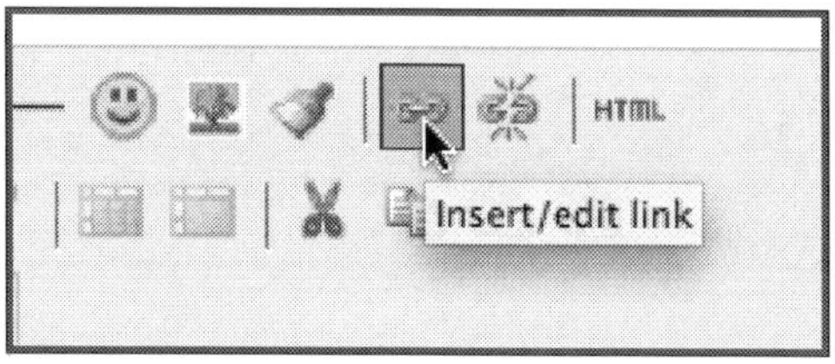

8. Without closing the window with Mahara, go to the text window (in TextEdit or Notepad) with your list of URLs. Copy the URL for the Title Page.
9. Go back to the window with Mahara, and in the small window that opened in step 7, paste that Title Page URL into the **Link URL** area.
10. Select **Open link** in the same window from the drop-down menu for **Target**.
11. In the **Title** area, type the title of the page you are linking to (`Title Page` in this case).

12. Select **Insert**:

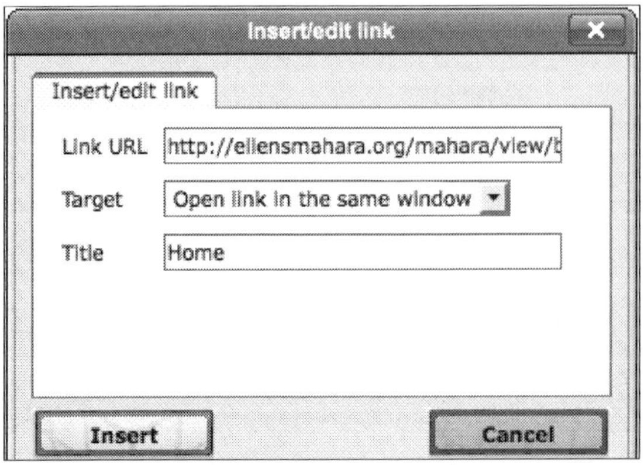

13. From the **General** tab, select a **Text Box** block and drag it to the bottom of the right-hand column.
14. Select the icon in the HTML toolbar for right-aligning the text. Type the words `Next Page`.
15. Highlight the word you just typed. Select the link icon in the HTML editing tools. A window will open.
16. Go back to the list of URLs in your text window. Copy the URL for the next page (Page 2) in the chapbook.
17. Go back to Mahara and paste that URL into the **Link URL** area.
18. Select **Open link** in the same window from the drop-down menu for Target.
19. In the **Title** area, type the title of the page you are linking to.
20. Select **Insert**.
21. Select **Save**.
22. Repeat steps 5-21 for each page in the Collection.

Another option: Adding the Title Page to the Collection

Another option is to add the Title Page to the Chapbook collection. After creating the title page, select **Collections** from the **Portfolio** tab. You will see three icons to the right of each collection. Select the icon for **Manage pages** for the chapbook collection:

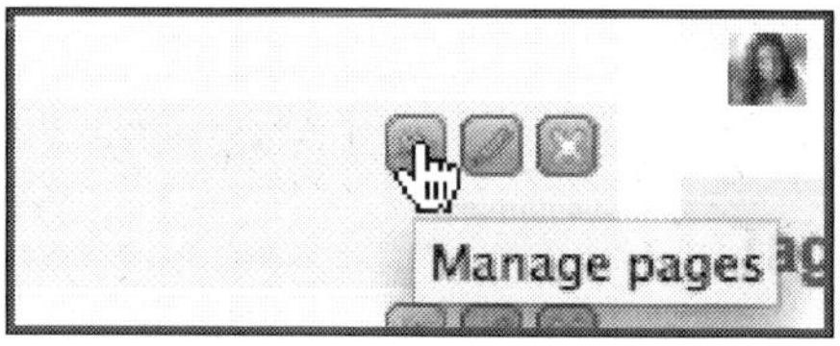

Put a checkmark next to the Title Page and select **Add Pages**. Use the arrows to move it to the top of the list. Select **Done**.

See also

- *Complex resume recipe in Chapter 3, The Professional Portfolio*

Thesis/research planning

Using the planning tool in Mahara, we will build a project plan and then send it to an advisor for feedback.

Getting ready

For Advisors/Instructors: To facilitate submissions, you will want to create a **Course Group**. This will provide a quick and easy way for you to view and comment on your advisees' plans. It also provides an easy way for students to submit the plans to you and allow you to follow their progress.

How to do it...

1. Select **Plans** on the **Content** tab.
2. Select the button labeled **New Plan**.
3. Give the plan a **Title** and a **Description**. These should reflect what the plan is for.
4. Click on **Save plan**.
5. Select **New Task**.
6. Give this task a title, for example: `Determine topic of research`.

7. Select a **Completion date** for this task by clicking on the small calendar icon next to the area for the date. You can use the small arrows to scroll through the various months and years, or you can click and hold your mouse down on the small arrows to pull up drop-down menus of the months and years. Note that the date will appear with the year first, then the month, then the day.

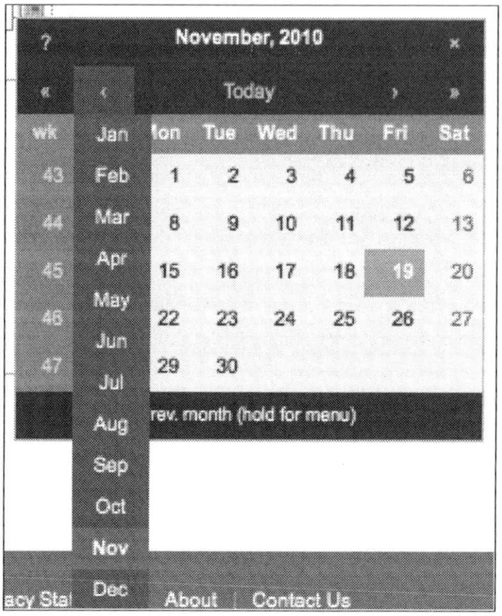

8. Add a description of the task you will be undertaking.
9. Click on **Save**.
10. Repeat steps 5-10 to complete your entire plan.

How it works...

When a task is past due, it will be highlighted in red on your plan. Any plans you've completed will have small green checkmarks. To show that you've completed a task:

1. Select the plan from the list of **My Plans** in the **My Portfolio** tab.
2. Select the word **Edit** next to the task you wish to show you've completed.
3. Put a checkmark in the box labeled **Completed** by clicking in the box. If you wish to add comments regarding the completed task, add them in the box labeled **Description**.
4. Click on **Save task**.

There's more...

The plan can be added to various Pages for various purposes. In your dashboard, it will be a reminder of tasks to do each time you log into Mahara or you can add it to a Page you create so you can share the plan with others.

Adding the plan to your dashboard

It is a good idea to add your plan to your dashboard, so that you will see it every time you log into Mahara. Your dashboard is simply another Page; however, it's a Page that only you can see. To add your plan to your dashboard:

1. Go to **Pages** on the "**Portfolio**" tab.
2. Click the small pencil icon to the right of the **Dashboard Page**.
3. Your dashboard will open in Edit mode. On the **General** tab, select the block labeled **Your Plans** and drag it into your Dashboard in the location you'd prefer.
4. Select the plan you wish to add.
5. Select **Done**.

The following screenshot shows how a plan would look on a dashboard:

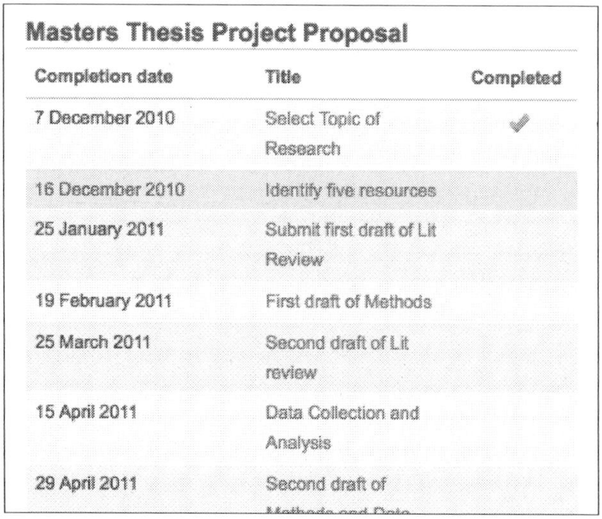

Masters Thesis Project Proposal
Completion date
Title
Completed
7 December 2010
Select Topic of Research
16 December 2010
Identify five resources
25 January 2011
Submit first draft of Lit Review
19 February 2011
First draft of Methods
25 March 2011
Second draft of Lit review
15 April 2011
Data Collection and Analysis
29 April 2011
Second draft of

Note the green checkmark for a completed task, and the bright red task indicating that the task is overdue. If you've added a description to your tasks, the titles of the tasks become links. When they are clicked the task expands, revealing the description.

> When you pull a **Your Plans** block into a Page you can always name it anything you want by simply typing a name in the area for **Block Title**. If you do not supply a name, Mahara will use the name of your plan.

Sharing the plan with an advisor:

1. **Create Page** using the button with that label in the **Pages** section of **Portfolio**.
2. Click the tab labeled: **Edit Layout**.
3. Select the option for **1 column**, **Equal widths**.
4. From the **General** tab, click-and-drag and the **Your Plans** block into the Page.
5. Select the plan you wish to show on this Page.
6. Click on **Save**.
7. Select the tab: **Next: Edit Title and Description**.
8. Provide a **Title** and **Description**.
9. Click on **Save**.
10. Select the tab labeled: **Share Page**.
11. In the next page, you should see a checkmark next to your Page; if not, click the small box next to the name of your Page.
12. Click the **Share with other users and groups** to expand your options.
13. If your Advisor has asked you to submit the Page to a group, or through a group, then skip down to step 17, otherwise go to the next step.
14. In the Search area, leave the drop-down menu set to **Users**. In the search box next to that drop-down menu, type your Advisor's name and click the magnifying glass.
15. Click the **Add** button next to your Advisor's name.
16. Click on **Save**.

Submitting a Page to a group or to a specific individual in a group:

1. In the Search area, change the drop-down menu to **Groups**.
2. In the Search box, type in the name of the group (or part of the name).
3. Find the group, and from the drop-down menu underneath it, select whether you are submitting this to **Everyone in the Group**, or **Member**, or **Admin**. If your Advisor is the administrator for your group, simply select **Admin**:

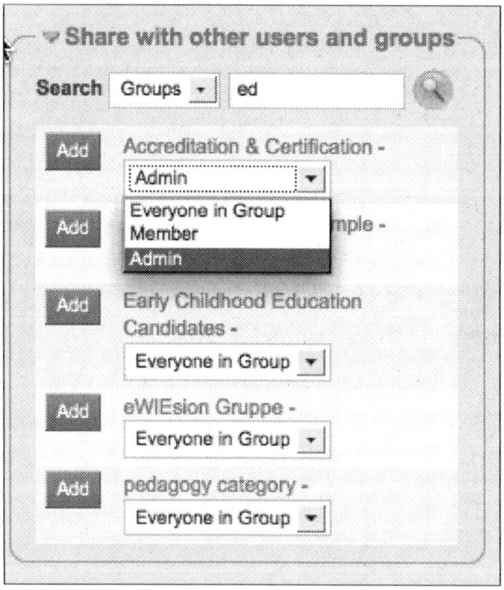

4. Click the **Add** button next to the group.
5. Click on **Save**.

See also

- *A reading list (book reports) recipe in Chapter 5, The Primary Education Portfolio*

Language acquisition journal

Journals are wonderful tools for developing metacognition, that is, knowing about our own learning and thinking. Using a journal in the process of learning a new language, can provide you with the means to reflect on your own progress, and provide evidence of growth over time. The journals can also provide artifacts of learning that can be repurposed. For example, you may wish to apply for a job that requires the ability to learn other languages and respect cultural differences; selections from your journal could provide your potential employer with examples of how you work through a new language and your understanding of the cultures in which the language is spoken.

Getting ready

Download and install Audacity from the website `http://audacity.sourceforge.net`. You will also need to download and install the LAME MP3 Encoder (there is a link for this on the download page for Audacity). Make sure you remember where you save the LAME file, as you will need to find it the first time you make a recording. You will also need a microphone, if you do not have one built into your computer.

How to do it...

Let's make an audio recording first:

1. Open Audacity.
2. From the **File** menu, choose **New**.
3. An audio recording/editing window will open. When you are ready to begin recording, select the button with the **red dot**; when you are done, select the button with the **yellow square**. To listen to your recording, use the **green arrow**. If you don't like what you hear, simply undo the recording (*Ctrl+Z* on a Windows; *command+Z* on a Mac) and start over. When you are satisfied with the recording, go to the next step.

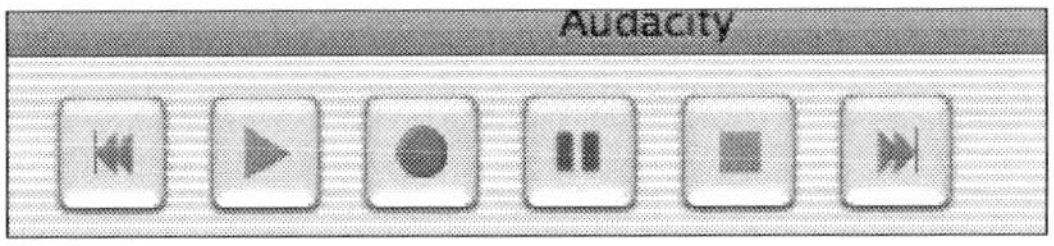

4. From the **File** menu, select **Export as MP3**. A window will open with fields that allow you to add information about the recording—these are helpful if the recording is going to be accessed via a program like iTunes; for our purposes, these are optional.

> The first time you export an Audacity file as an MP3, a window will open asking you to locate the LAME file. Simply browse for it and select **Open**. You will not have to do this again.

Now, let's journal about our recording:

1. Click on the **Content** tab, then **Journals**.
2. Select the button labeled **Create Journal**.

> If you do not have that option, you may need to enable multiple journals. Click **Settings** at the very top of the window in the right-hand corner. Scroll down to about the middle of the page and put a checkmark next to the option **Enable multiple journals** and save

3. Give the journal a title and a description.
4. Select **Create Journal**.
5. You will see your new journal in the list of journals. Click the option **New Entry**.
6. Give this new post a name: maybe something like `First Recording`.
7. In the section labeled **Body**, type your reflections on the recording. For example, you might explain what the recording is about, and how well you think you articulated what you were trying to say. You might even talk about the process—how many times you re-recorded your monologue before you were satisfied enough to upload it.
8. Under the **Body**, in the area labeled **Attachments**, select the button labeled **Add a file**.
9. Put a checkmark in the box next to **Upload file**; this certifies that the file you are uploading does not violate copyright laws, nor your host's Terms and Conditions.
10. Select the **Browse** button, locate your recording, and select **Open**.
11. When your file has finished uploading, select the button labeled **Close**, and then **Save Post**.

How it works...

Remember, no one can see your journal until you provide access to it. To share your progress with others you will need to put the journal, or select postings from the journal, into a Page. Your postings and the associated audio files will be accessible in the Page. If you have chosen to share the entire journal, or recent journal posts, your Page will automatically update when you add new postings to your journal; you do not need to go and edit your Page as well.

The following is an example of a post, with its associated audio file in a Page:

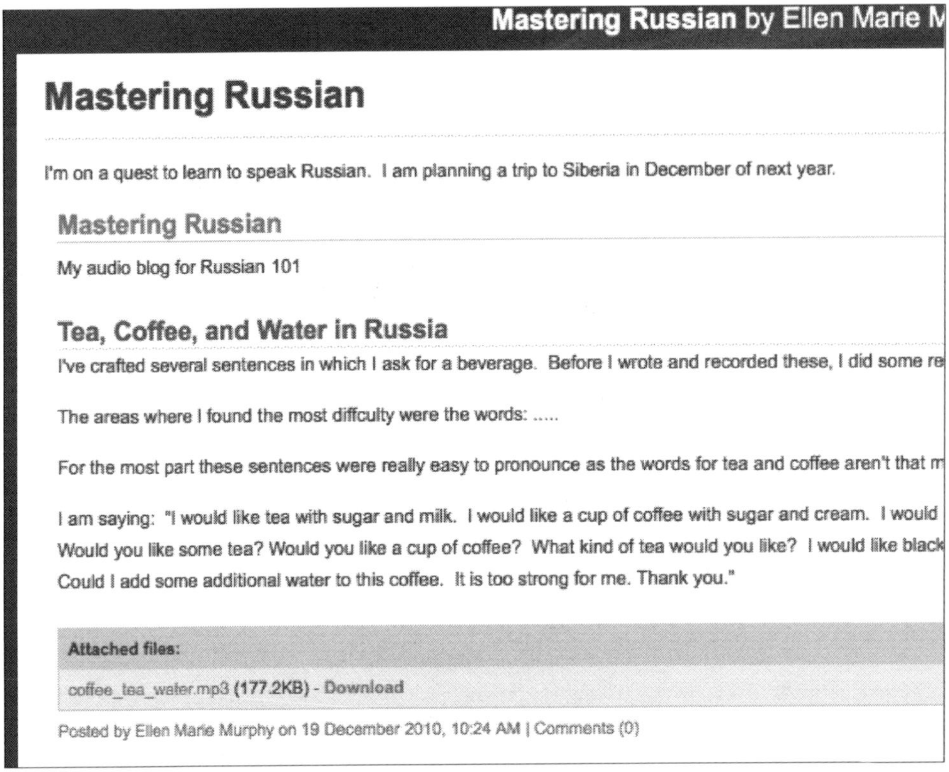

Mastering Russian by Ellen Marie M
Mastering Russian
I'm on a quest to learn to speak Russian. I am planning a trip to Siberia in December of next year.
Mastering Russian
My audio blog for Russian 101
Tea, Coffee, and Water in Russia
I've crafted several sentences in which I ask for a beverage. Before I wrote and recorded these, I did some re
The areas where I found the most diffculty were the words: .....
For the most part these sentences were really easy to pronounce as the words for tea and coffee aren't that m
I am saying: "I would like tea with sugar and milk. I would like a cup of coffee with sugar and cream. I would
Would you like some tea? Would you like a cup of coffee? What kind of tea would you like? I would like black
Could I add some additional water to this coffee. It is too strong for me. Thank you."
Attached files:
coffee_tea_water.mp3 (177.2KB) - Download
Posted by Ellen Marie Murphy on 19 December 2010, 10:24 AM | Comments (0)

Settings in Audacity that can affect file size

Audio files can be quite large, and the storage your Mahara administrator has allotted to you might get used up pretty quickly. There are some settings you can change in Audacity, which will create smaller sized files and not significantly affect the quality of your recording. The default settings in Audacity are for very high quality recording (for lots of different sounds and a wide range of frequencies). However, speech recording does not need, and usually doesn't significantly benefit from settings that high. To change the settings:

1. Open Audacity and go to **Preferences** (on a PC you will find this under the **File** menu; on a Mac it is under the **Audacity** menu).
2. Select **Quality**.
3. Set the **Default sample rate** to **22000Hz**. You can lower this even more, if your file size is still too large; just make sure to do a sample recording and see what you think about the quality. I have often recorded at 8000Hz with little loss of quality.

4. Set the **Default sample format** to **16-bit**. I usually leave all of the other default settings alone.
5. Select **Okay**.

See also

Using the Collections feature to build a gallery with an audio-guided tour recipe in *Chapter 1, Mahara for the Visual Arts*

A Daily Gazette (Journalism page)

In this recipe, we are going to create a little newspaper. With a couple of RSS Feeds from outside sources, and regular postings in a couple of your own journals, you will have a "newspaper" with frequently updated content. The following screenshot shows how this would look:

Getting ready

You will need to have two journals in which you will regularly post the news you wish to be a part of your Gazette. The text in these journals should be **fully justified**—that is the text is aligned on the left and the right. It would be a good idea for the journals to have specific themes, but they don't have to.

> By using journals for your stories, the stories will become part of your permanent portfolio, and an archive of news articles will be created automatically in your Gazette as well. If you were to simply use Text Box blocks for your stories, then every time you changed the story in the Text Box, you'd lose the story you had before.

How to do it...

1. In the **Pages** section on the **Portfolio** tab create a **New Page**.
2. Leave the default format to three columns of equal width.
3. For my Gazette, I chose the theme called **Sunset**, but you can select the theme that you prefer from the drop-down menu for **Themes**.
4. In the upper left-hand column we will add a weather feed from the National Oceanic and Atmospheric Administration's website `http://www.weather.gov/alerts-beta/`.
5. Open a new tab or window in your browser, and go to the previous URL.

Find the state you would like to get the weather for; you will see an RSS icon and the word **ATOM** next to it. Click on **ATOM**. A new window will open with the feed; copy the URL from the **address bar** at the top of the window:

1. Go back to the window with Mahara, and the page you were building. From the **External feeds** tab, select the **External Feed** block and drag it to the top of the left-hand column.
2. In the **Block Title** put the name of your feed.
3. In the **Feed location**, paste the URL of the RSS feed.
4. Select the number of items you wish to show, and select **Show feed items in full**, which means that the feed will include descriptions of the items in the feed.

5. In the upper right-hand corner, let's put another RSS feed. The feed in the example is from Google Video, and the code for this little trick can be found on this website: `http://googlesystem.journalspot.com/2006/09/secret-feeds-in-google-video.HTML`. This feed displays the latest videos for a predetermined topic of your choice. The URL you'll need to use for this feed is `http://video.google.com/videosearch?q=XXXXXXXX&output=rss`. Where there is a string of Xs, you will want to add your search term. For example, if you would like videos on "owls", your URL will look like this: `http://video.google.com/videosearch?q=owls&output=rsshttp://video.google.com/videosearch?q=owls&output=rss`.
6. From the **External feeds** tab, select the **External Feed** block and drag it to the top of the left-hand column.
7. In the **Block Title** put the name of your feed.
8. In the **Feed location**, type the URL of the Google Video feed you would like (as explained previously).
9. Select the number of items you wish to show (I chose 3), and select **Show feed items in full**.
10. The other two news items in the Daily Gazette are postings from two separate journals. One is in the center column, and one in the left-hand column under the weather feed. Both use the **Journal** block from the **Journals** menu.
11. When you have dragged the **Journal** block to the area where you would like your news story to show, select the journal that will feed stories to this area.
12. You can put a title in the **Block Title** if you'd like; the default title will be the title of your journal.
13. Type the number `1` in the area labeled **Posts per page**.
14. Click on **Save**.
15. Repeat items 16-20 for the other news story, selecting a different journal to feed from.
16. Select the tab labeled **Next: Edit title and description**.
17. Give your journal a title. This title will not appear in the center of your journal.
18. Instead, the **Description** area will be used to create the Journal title text that will display across the top center of your journal. Type the journal title in a large font and center align it.

> To add a large display title like the one I have, you will need to add an image to the description. Yes, that's right, the description can be an image. Instructions for this are in the *There's more* section below.

19. Click on **Save**.
20. Select the tab labeled: **Share Page**.
21. In this next window, you will see a list of your Pages and Collections. Make sure this Page has a checkmark next to this Page.
22. Click the **Add** button next to **Public**.
23. Click on **Save**.

Now you have a Daily Gazette that others can follow.

How it works...

When you post New Entries in the journals associated with your Gazette, your Gazette will automatically display the new posts. Beneath the latest posting (story) a small navigation menu will allow readers to read previously posted stories. To add new posts to your journals, go to **Journals** on the **Content** tab. Look for the journal you wish to add a post to, and select the **New Entry** link to the right of it. Adding regular posts to your Gazette will keep it fresh and interesting.

Readers can also subscribe to a newsfeed from your Gazette. They will actually be subscribing to your journals (each one separately). Every time you update a post, your subscribers will receive notification in their feed readers.

There's more...

The Header on our Gazette was an image created using GIMP. It was added to the Description of our page. The stories in our Gazette also contain images. We'll explore both of these in the next couple of sections.

Adding an image banner to your page

The "Daily Gazette" banner, at the top of Page is an image created using a program called GIMP `http://www.gimp.org/`. GIMP is freely available for download. To create a banner using GIMP:

1. From the **File** menu select **New**.
2. In the window that opens, set the **Width** to 840 and the **Height** 100.
3. Select **Okay**.
4. In the **Toolbox**, select the large black letter **A**. This is the Text tool.
5. Select your font (I used **Bernard MT Condensed**); set the size to 80, and the color to black.

6. Click in the image window and draw a box (you can adjust it later if need be).
7. A small window will open in which you will type the text of your title.
8. Select **Close**.
9. You will see the text in your image. To move it, select the move tool in the Toolbox (it's a blue crosshatch), click on the text and adjust its location.
10. To add the two decorations on either side of the title, select the Text tool again, and change the font to **Wingdings 2**. I also changed the size to 60.
11. Repeating steps 6-9, type a lowercase "h" on the left of your title; type a lowercase "g" on the right.
12. From the **File** menu select **Save As**.
13. Give the image a name and select the location where you wish to save the image; then, on the lower-left corner select PNG from the **Select file type** menu.
14. Click on **Save**.
15. In Mahara, upload the image to the **My Files** section of **My Portfolio**.
16. Once the file has uploaded, you will see it in your list of files. Click the file and it will open in your browser window.
17. Copy the URL in the address window at the top of your browser.
18. Every file has an address. That is its location on the server where all of your artifacts, Pages, and so on are stored. The address we just copied is the location of this image on the server.

Now we will add the image to the description of your Page:

1. When your Page is in edit mode, choose the tab **Edit Title and Description**.
2. Click inside the textbox for the **Description** and delete any text that might be there.
3. Select the Add/edit image icon (it looks like a tree) on the HTML toolbar.
4. In the small window that opens, you will see a field for Image URL. Paste the URL that you copied in step 17 into that field.
5. In the **Image Description** area, type the text that appears in your image. (The example used is Daily Gazette).
6. Leave everything else blank, and select **Insert**.
7. Select **Save** and then **Done**.

Adding an image to your stories (journal posts)

You'll notice that my journal posts had images in them. It's fairly easy to add an image to a journal post. While you could use an image that is hosted on another site, I'm going to give you directions for using your own images (uploaded to Mahara):

1. Attach the image to your journal posting, using the **Add a file** button.
2. Click in body of your journal and then select the **Insert/edit image** button on the HTML toolbar.
3. Select your image from the **Attached image** menu; set the alignment (left is what's usually chosen).
4. Add the number 5 to the **Vertical Space** and 5 to the **Horizontal space** (this will give you some whitespace around your image, so that the text won't be right up against it).
5. Select **Insert**.
6. Resize the image by clicking on it and then dragging a corner in the direction you wish to resize the picture.
7. Click on **Save**.

See also

- *Journaling a project from start to finish* recipe in *Chapter 1, Mahara for the Visual Arts*
- *A poetry page with a faux woodblock print created using GIMP* recipe
- *Creating a group newspaper using newsfeeds from student journals* recipe in *Chapter 4, Working with Groups*

3
The Professional Portfolio

In this chapter, we will cover:

- Adding content to the resume
- A simple Curriculum Vitae
- The cover letter
- References and recommendations
- The complete package: Cover letter, resume, and letters of reference
- Complex resume
- The promotion and tenure portfolio

Introduction

The recipes in this chapter cover various aspects of professional portfolio design. A single chapter on this topic can really only scratch the surface of what you can do when building a website that reflects your skills, talents, and accomplishments. Becoming familiar with the other recipes in this book, in order to incorporate into the design of your professional website the ideas they present, will give you many more options for presenting your accomplishments and skills.

This chapter contains recipes for a simple resume, an entire application package, and even a portfolio for promotion and tenure.

It is a good idea to think of your professional portfolio as a website. People often claim that employers aren't interested in looking at a portfolio. That might be the case if you refer to your professional portfolio as a portfolio, but if you provide them with a link to your website, many, if not most, will look at it. Employers, for the most part, want to know what you are truly capable of. What better way to showcase that than a compilation of artifacts of things you've already done, nicely packaged and easy to navigate?

Adding content to Résumé

In this recipe, we will add material to the **Profile** section of your portfolio, in particular those fields that may later become part of a constructed resume or curriculum vitae. We will primarily be working in fields on the **Résumé** tab in the **Content** section of your portfolio. Nothing of what we create with this recipe is available for others to see, until you put it into a page.

> **Education History**, **Employment History**, **Certifications**, **Accreditations and Awards**, **Books and Publications**, and **Professional Memberships** do not have HTML editing toolbars. When added to a page, these sections will appear in a table with formatting determined by the theme chosen for that particular page. They will be in a collapsed format, but can be easily expanded by the viewer. This allows you to add a great deal of text to these fields, without worrying about how they will fit into a page.

Getting ready

Gather any documents you may need to compose your resume.

How to do it...

1. Select the **Content** tab and then **Résumé**.
2. On the Résumé page, you will see several tabs; select the one labeled **Education & Employment**.
3. Click the **Add** button to begin adding information. Note which fields are red as these are required fields.
4. Click on **Save**.
5. Click the **Edit** icon next to any item that you wish to edit.
6. If you add more than one entry for either **Education** or **Employment**, you will see small arrows to the left of the item. Use the arrows keys to place them in chronological order.
7. Click on **Save**.

8. Next, select the **Achievements** tab. You will see three areas to which you can add information: **Certifications, Accreditations and Awards**, **Books and Publications**, and **Professional Memberships**.

> The headings for the sections on the **Achievements** tab may not be appropriate for you. Keep in mind that you can rename these (and any of the section headings) when you pull them into a page. For example, because I do a large number of conference presentations, I list them in the **Books and Publications** section. When I pull this section into a page, I rename it to **Publications and Presentations**. Students may wish to use the section titled **Professional Memberships** to list participation in various co-curricular activities (clubs, sports, and so on).

9. Select the tab for **Certifications, Accreditations and Awards**.
10. Repeat steps 3-7.
11. Continue with the **Books and Publications** area and the **Professional Memberships,** repeating steps 3-7 for each of these.
12. Click on **Save**.

How it works...

Each of the sections in the **Résumé** part of your **Content** tab can be added individually to a page. This is the best method for creating a resume you wish to share. It is the only method used in this book. There is another option however, which I *strongly* caution against: you can choose to add the entire **Résumé** to a page by simply dragging the **Your Entire Résumé** block into a page. Again, I do not recommend using this method, because the order of the items is predetermined and cannot be changed. Also, all items are displayed and cannot be removed, including **Personal Information**.

Let's talk a little about some of the sections in **Résumé** and how they work:

Education:

- A little bit about some of the fields in this section that might not be clear: **Qualification Type** is the type of degree, for example, Masters of Science; the **Qualification Name** (for example, Curriculum Development) and the **Qualification Description** can be used if the **Qualification Type** or **Qualification Name** needs further clarification.

▶ In the table this qualification information is displayed as follows: under the **Qualification** heading the **Qualification Type** will be listed first, followed by the **Qualification Name** (which will be in parenthesis). Then the word **at** and then the name of the **Institution**. Any information you put in the **Description** will be hidden, but the **Qualification** information will become a link. When it is clicked, the table will expand revealing the text you entered in the **Description**. If you did not enter any information in the **Description**, then the **Qualification** will not display as a link.

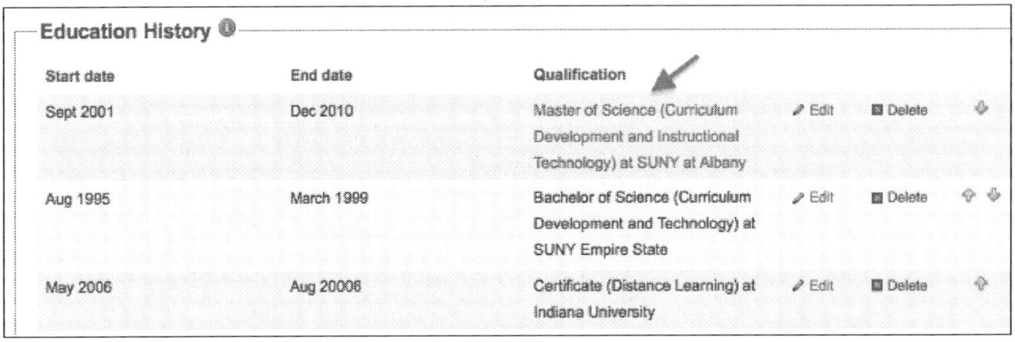

Education History ⓘ					
Start date	**End date**	**Qualification**			
Sept 2001	Dec 2010	Master of Science (Curriculum Development and Instructional Technology) at SUNY at Albany	✎ Edit	☒ Delete	⬇
Aug 1995	March 1999	Bachelor of Science (Curriculum Development and Technology) at SUNY Empire State	✎ Edit	☒ Delete	⬆ ⬇
May 2006	Aug 20006	Certificate (Distance Learning) at Indiana University	✎ Edit	☒ Delete	⬆

Employment:

▶ The collapsed format of this section will show the **Start date**, the **End date**, and the **Job Title**. The **Job Title** will appear under the heading **Position**. The **Position** description will be hidden, but when the **Job Title** is selected the field will expand showing the description. This means you can write a thorough job description, and it will not overwhelm a page.

▶ You can copy and paste from a Word document, but your formatting will be lost. The formatting is controlled by the theme(s) you choose for the page(s) you place this into.

Books and Publications:

▶ In the **Books and Publications** section, the **Date**, the **Title**, and the **Contribution** are required fields. The **Title** would be the actual title of the book, journal article, presentation, and so on; the **Contribution** would be the type of publication (for example, video, journal article, book, conference presentation, and so on).

▶ Use the **Details of your contribution** section to provide the citation or other pertinent information.

There's more...

There are four additional tabs in the **Résumé** section: **Introduction**, **Goals**, **Skills**, and **Interests**. We will look at the **Introduction** tab later in this chapter while Goals, Skills, and Interests we'll take a brief look at now. There are other recipes in this book that use those areas as well.

Goals, Skills, and Interests

- Each of these sections provides HTML editing toolbars. This means that you can embed images and use various forms of formatting. This allows you to use these fields in very creative ways.
- As your skills and goals change over time, and you update these fields, prior entries will be lost. If there are any pages that contain these sections, they will be automatically updated to reflect the new information. This is important if you are using these fields for pages that record educational progression.

See also

- *The Athletic Supplement* recipe in *Chapter 7, The College Application Portfolio*
- *The complete package*: *Cover letter, resume and letters of reference* recipe

A simple curriculum vitae

This **Curriculum Vitae** can be described as "classic", yet it produces a document that can contain a lot of information without appearing as overwhelming as the same amount of information might, if presented on paper. Individuals, to whom you provide access, have a number of ways they can choose to view and print a copy of your curriculum vitae.

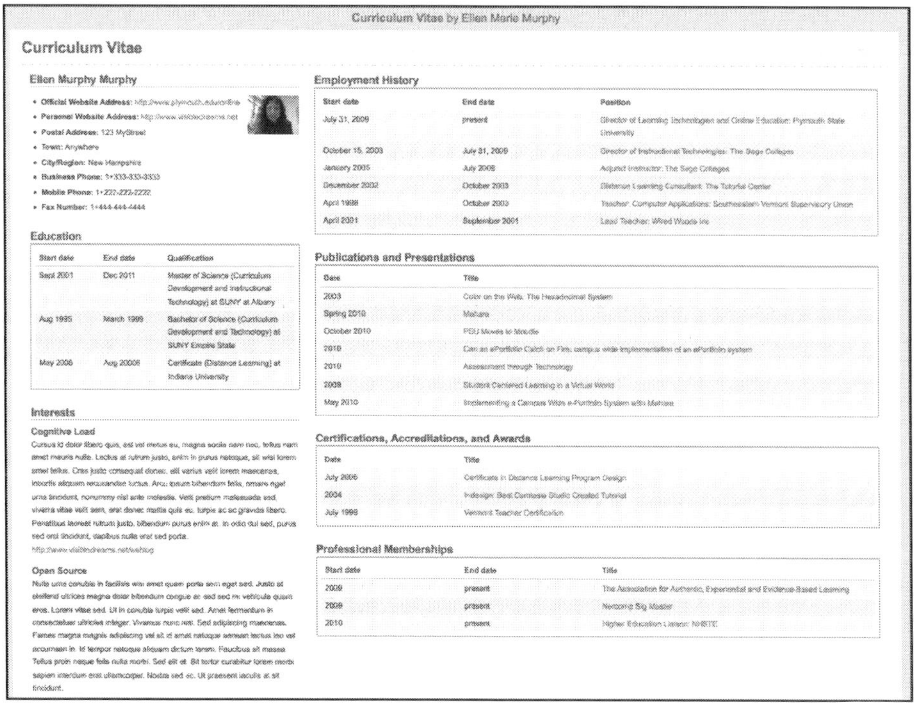

Getting ready

For this recipe, you will need to prepare the following areas in your **Content/Résumé** section beforehand: **Employment History**, **Education History**, and **Achievements**. You will also need to have **Contact Information** in the **Content/Profile** section, and a **Profile Icon** in the **Contnet/Profile Icons** section. In **About Me**, make sure that your full legal name is available as either your **Display name** or a combination of your **First Name** and **Last Name** (this will be important when we get near the end of the recipe). You will add additional information as we proceed with the recipe.

How to do it...

We're going to begin this by adding some additional information to our profile first. On the **Content** tab, click on **Résumé** and then **Interests**. Choose two of your interests that will provide a potential employer with a clearer picture of who you are, and what motivates and/or inspires you:

1. With your cursor in the **Interests** text block, type the title of your first interest.
2. Highlight the title and from the formatting drop-down menu (**Paragraph**), select **Heading 3**.

> When you apply a heading format to text, it ensures the colors and formatting of the text will always match the style and color of other headings and block titles in whatever page this text appears. The formatting will be determined by the theme you choose.

3. Using the *Enter* key on your keyboard, space down to the next line.
4. Type a short paragraph about this interest and what it means in your life.
5. Using the *Enter* key on your keyboard, space down to the next line.
6. Type the title of your next interest and apply **Heading 3** formatting to this title.
7. Space down to the next line and type a small paragraph about this interest.
8. Click on **Save**.

Now let's actually build the curriculum vitae that you see above:

1. Go to **Pages** on the **Portfolio** tab and select **Create Page**.
2. Change the column layout to **Larger right column** in the **2 columns** section.
3. You can pick a theme from the **Theme** menu, but I simply used the **Site Default (Default)** theme for my page.

4. From the **Profile** tab, click on the **Profile Information** block and drag it to the top of the left-hand column.
5. In the **Block Title**, type your full name.
6. Select the information you would like to display, such as addresses, phone numbers, and websites.
7. Select the **Profile Icon** you would like to display.
8. Select the e-mail address you'd like visitors to use to contact you.
9. Make sure the **Introductory Text** is empty.
10. Click on **Save**.
11. From the **Résumé** tab select the **One Résumé Field** block and drag it to the left-hand column underneath the profile information.
12. In the **Block Title**, type `Education`; in the **Field to Show**, select **Education History**.
13. Click on **Save**.
14. Drag another **One Résumé Field** block to the left-hand column, underneath **Education**.
15. Leave the **Block Title** empty (it will take on the name of the field you choose) and select **Interests** from **Field to Show**.
16. Click on **Save**.

Let's build the right-hand column now. We will be using the **One Résumé Field** block multiple times. We're going to build from the bottom up.

17. Drag a **One Résumé Field** block to the right-hand column and select **Professional Memberships**.
18. Click **Save**.
19. Drag another **One Résumé Field** block to the right-hand column, above the one you just added, and select **Certifications, Accreditations and Awards.**
20. Click **Save**.
21. This time, when we drag the block to that right-hand column, we're going to enter the text `Publications and Presentations` into the **Block Title**. We're going to select **Books and Publications** from the **Field to Show** options.

> Of course, you do not need to change the title of the block if **Books and Publications** suits your information better. The point is that you can adjust any of these fields to meet your needs. You can enter content that is more applicable to you and your field, and you can change the name of the field when you add it to a page.

22. Click **Save**.
23. Finally let's add **Employment History** by dragging the **One Résumé Field** block into the **Page** and selecting **Employment History** from the field options.
24. Click **Save**.
25. Select **Edit Title and Description**.
26. For the **Title**, add the text `Curriculum Vitae`.
27. Leave the **Description** empty.
28. In the drop-down menu for **Name display format**, select the option that will provide your full name (legal name), as this will display at the top of your page.
29. Select **Next: Edit Access**.
30. Whether or not you would like viewers to add comments is up to you. Personally, I would uncheck that option.
31. Choose the level of access you would like by selecting the **Add** button next to your choice(s), for example, **Secret URL** or **Public**.
32. Click on **Save**.

How it works...

When you drag the various résumé fields into your page, you see them in their expanded format, which can give the impression of clutter. However, when the page is displayed in the non-editing format, information is collapsed and can be expanded by clicking on the links. Below is an example of how the information will look when you display the page. The items in the column labeled **Title** are links. When they are clicked, the area below the link will expand to reveal the additional information you've added.

Professional Memberships

Start date	End date	Title
2009	present	The Association for Authentic, Experiential and Evidence-Based Learning
2009	present	Nercomp Sig Master
2010	present	Higher Education Liaison: NHSTE

This allows the document to contain a lot of information without appearing overwhelming, and without requiring a great deal of scrolling. Individuals with whom you share your page can see the expanded formats by clicking on the various links created for each title or position. They can open each of them by expanding the entire page, or just open selected items. They can also print them in either format.

Here is a partially expanded page of the previous item:

Professional Memberships

Start date	End date	Title
2009	present	The Association for Authentic, Experiential and Evidence-Based Learning
2009	present	Nercomp Sig Master * Organize one full-day workshop on a specific and timely topic. * Work with NERCOMP's Board and Events Coordinator to decide on a location and a date for the workshop. * Work with the NERCOMP Event Coordinator, create and work within a budget, the goal of which is to break even (see budget section below) * Procure agreements from speakers, presenters, and vendors to participate in the workshop. SIG Masters may also come up with someone else who wishes to organize the day, set up speakers, etc. * Provide a preliminary outline of the day's events, and a solid paragraph of description for NERCOMP to use in announcements and on the web. This is due by September 1st , for posting on the web site. * Provide speaker contact information for *NERCOMP's coordinators so that they can communicate directly with speakers. This is due four months prior to the SIG Day. * Work with the NERCOMP coordinators to set up chat rooms and list-servs on the NERCOMP list server. The SIG Master is required to moderate and stay involved in these chat rooms and list-servs. * Work with other SIG Masters and the NERCOMP annual conference program chair as appropriate.
2010	present	Higher Education Liaison: NHSTE

As you add information to your **My Résumé** sections in your profile, your pages will automatically update as well.

There's more...

You may wish to add some additional text to provide a clearer picture of who you are. Let's look at one method we can use to do that now.

Elaborating on your interests

The **Interests** section of the **Résumé** tab has an HTML toolbar, whereas the textboxes for **Employment History**, **Books and Publications**, and so on, do not. This provides you with the opportunity for adding information that the other sections didn't. For example, in my curriculum vitae I included a paragraph describing my interests in open source. I included links to the various websites I've created using different open source products. Doing so not only indicates my interest in the open source movement, but also illustrates my knowledge and application—all in one small paragraph.

The cover letter

Potential employers almost always request a cover letter, resume, and list of references. In this recipe, we will create a basic cover letter—one that can be reused multiple times, yet one that can be easily customized for each new instance, so you can use the same letter for a variety of potential employers (without typing it multiple times). Here's an example of what this might look like:

Cover Letter

Ellen Marie Murphy
1 My Home Road
My City, St 12345
Phone: 555-555-5555
Email: admin@visibledreams.net

January 1, 2011

Dr. Anybody Somebody
Stargate University
23 This Lane Street
Suffolk, ZZ, 55555

Re: Director of Emerging Technologies

Et augue libero habitasse magna justo volutpat, eu amet tristique velit odio egestas, nulla lacus ornare maecenas risus ut. Vel erat ac in, morbi pede class, varius amet, enim ipsum suscipit cras, in vulputate vel non etiam. Ultricies sem, sem a, aliquet nullam semper, ipsum vivamus adipiscing convallis tempor ligula. Eget magna mi, sit arcu, ullamcorper viverra sollicitudin metus in, lorem at eu. Mauris purus mauris sed sagittis, laoreet eros a ac ipsum metus. Lectus amet magna eu, nullam donec, sit in dis in, sem consectetuer, enim amet vestibulum lobortis ante donec adipiscing. Ullamcorper sapien penatibus mauris consectetuer in, accumsan sed morbi nisl pretium ante, pede in egestas in, amet lacinia sapien et. Phasellus enim, nunc euismod, dolor convallis arcu pede libero volutpat a. Ut placerat penatibus bibendum.

Ipsum eu nulla sed id, congue diam, risus eu, nam hac porttitor. Quis at lorem nibh. Turpis massa in eu phasellus mattis diam. Suspendisse rhoncus cras sit luctus pharetra, aliquam sint vitae pulvinar, eu ligula massa nunc justo metus pellentesque. Aliquet rhoncus rhoncus vehicula dictum ante donec, ac duis a urna eget, quis turpis vulputate.

Quis consectetuer, et pharetra amet sit consectetuer sit nec, venenatis ut et bibendum ligula. Sit ut sapien mi tristique feugiat imperdiet, ligula rhoncus fringilla facilisis sed vestibulum. Amet sed tincidunt ac fusce luctus nisl. Sollicitudin nunc nullam lectus, mauris ultrices ut eget donec vestibulum. Sodales magna mauris varius, rutrum a vel maecenas vitae. Vestibulum nunc sodales commodo orci, ipsum pede per imperdiet luctus, nulla in hendrerit ut magna commodo et, velit at amet. Nulla faucibus neque vitae, sit ullamcorper felis sociis eleifend, sed praesent, integer semper eros ornare nunc. Eget tempus, fringilla ridiculus vel leo maecenas, velit adipiscing nunc, in eu, sed fusce vitae tortor elit eu non. Est odio fermentum eu eu tristique, erat ultricies, in non consectetuer tincidunt purus proin, ante lobortis vestibulum tempor dictum vel. Ipsum integer, wisi ac ac leo elit tellus felis. Velit malesuada, blandit at nulla lectus amet.

Varius placerat integer nunc, consectetur lorem dignissim viverra varius. Blandit sem sapien in vitae. Massa potenti aliquam, ut magna. Facilisis aliquet potenti non sem luctus, lectus faucibus adipiscing magna viverra dui molestie, a dolor volutpat tortor aenean ut, orci turpis at consequat odio. Rutrum ac nunc cumque, odio morbi est porta quam. Suspendisse eu, etiam iaculis facilisis eu vitae justo, vulputate magna gravida, dictumst et felis a, ac convallis et in quam. Urna consectetuer metus et justo. Id mattis pede hendrerit, viverra laoreet facilisis leo lorem, dis sit sociis justo elit. Montes vitae pharetra quam ac neque, sed ipsum massa porta amet.

Very truly yours,

Ellen Marie Murphy

Getting ready

If you already have a cover letter written in a word processing program, you can open that; otherwise, there are no required preparations.

How to do it...

1. On the **Content** tab, select **Résumé**; you should find yourself at the **Introduction** section.
2. On the **Introduction** tab, you will see a textbox labeled **Cover Letter**.
3. This is the area where you will type the body of your cover letter. *Do not type any addresses or greetings in here*. If you composed your letter in MS Word, and you want to paste it into Mahara, *do not paste directly into the textbox*. Instead, click the **Paste from Word** icon on the HTML toolbar, paste it into the window that opens, and click **Insert**.

4. Space down three lines. Type your closing and your name.
5. Click on **Save**.

Now, to share your work, follow the ensuing steps:

6. In the **Pages** section of the **Portfolio** tab, select **Create Page**.
7. Click the tab labeled **Edit Layout**.
8. Select **1 column, Equal widths**.
9. Click on **Save**.
10. Choose your **Theme.**
11. From the **Résumé** tab, click and drag the **One Résumé Field** block into your page.
12. In the **Block Title** type `Re:` and the name of the position you are applying for (for example, Re: Director of ePortfolios).
13. Select **Cover Letter** in **Fields to Show**.
14. Click on **Save**.
15. From the **General** tab, click and drag a **Text Box** block into your page above the body of your cover letter.

16. Delete the **Block Title**, leaving it empty.

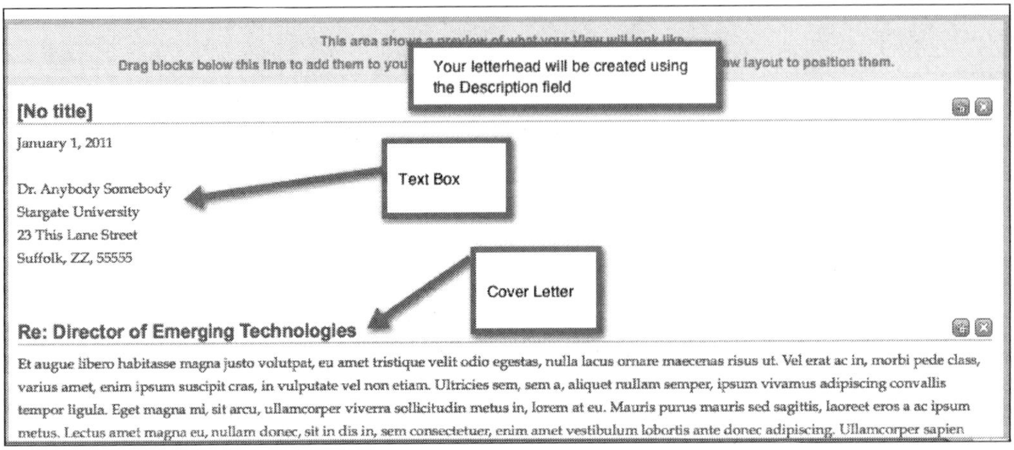

17. In the body of the **Text Box**, type the date and the address of the individual(s) for whom the cover letter has been written.

> To avoid the double-spacing that occurs when you hit the *Enter* or *return* key, hold down the *Shift* key while you space down.

18. Click on **Save**.
19. Select the tab labeled **Edit Title and Description**.
20. In the **Title**, type `Cover Letter`.
21. We will use the **Description** to create the letterhead; type your name, address, phone, and e-mail. The text you put here will appear at the top of your page and look like a header.
22. Highlight your text and use the center-alignment icon to center it.
23. Make your name **Bold**, and set the **Font size** to **24**.
24. Click on **Save**.
25. Click **Done**.
26. You should now find yourself on the **Pages** tab in the **Portfolio** area. Select the tab labeled **Share**.

27. On the **Share** page, you will see four columns. The first column contains a list of all pages and collections in your portfolio. On the right there are three additional columns: **Access list**, **Edit Access**, and **Secret URLs**. Find your **Cover Letter** page in the list of pages and click the icon for this page in the column labeled **Secret URLs**.
28. Click the **Add** button next to **New Secret URL**. Copy the URL that you are given. You will need to provide this to the individual(s) for whom the letter is written.
29. You do not need to click **Save**.

How it works...

The body of the cover letter can be used multiple times because you can rename the block when you pull it into a page. So, if you wished to create another cover letter for a different job, you would simply follow steps 6-24. The Secret URL generated for the new pages will be different than that for the other pages, ensuring that prospective employers only see the cover letter you designed for them.

The cover letter can be added to a collection that contains a resume and references, providing a complete package. There is a recipe in this chapter that explains how to do that.

There's more...

You cover letter can include hyperlinks to other websites containing your work (for example, `http://www.slideshare.net`) or documents you've stored in your portfolio. Your letter can also contain images. Adding any of these to your cover letter can provide a way for you to go beyond simply telling to showing. Here's how you would do that.

Adding a link to an external website

1. Open two tabs or windows in your browser. In one window, navigate to the **Résumé** section of the **Content** tab, where the **Cover Letter** field is located; in the other window, navigate to the website you wish to provide a link to in your cover letter.
2. Copy the URL (address) of the website.

3. Go back to the window that contains your **Cover Letter**, and highlight the text you will be using to represent the link. For example, in a sentence that includes **well received presentation on Mahara**, I might highlight this entire phrase:

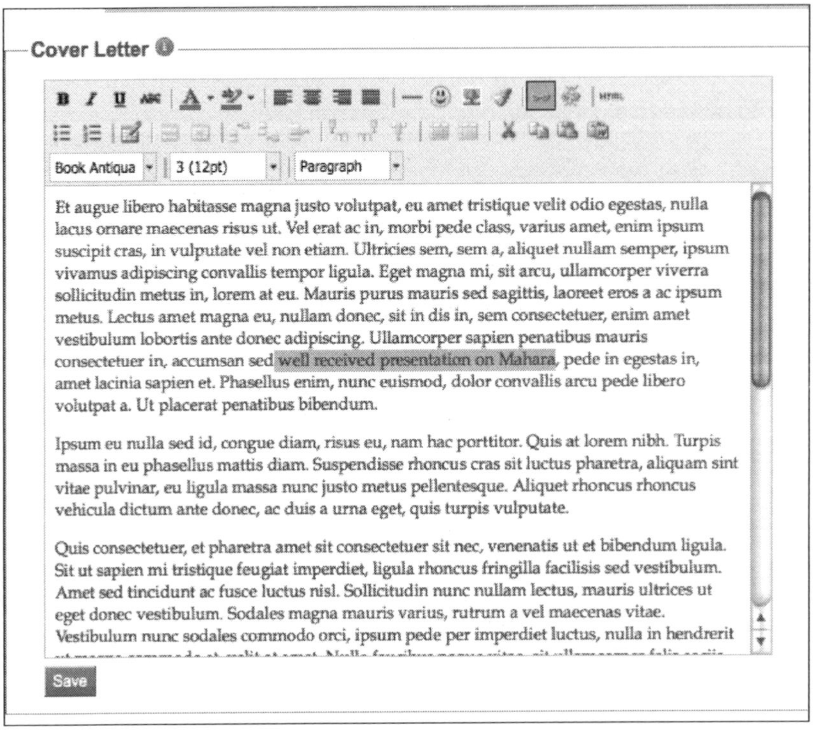

4. Click the icon that looks like a link in the HTML toolbar.
5. In the window that opens, paste the **URL** you previously copied.
6. In the drop-down menu for **Target**, select **Open link in new window**.
7. Provide a **Title** for the link (this is optional).

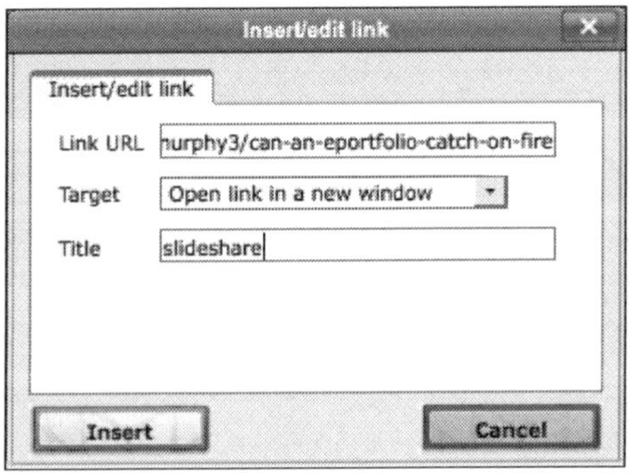

> The information you add in the **Title** field is displayed whenever a cursor hovers over the link. Title codes provide the reader with information regarding where the link will take them. It is a good idea to keep this in mind when adding text to the **Title** field.

8. Click **Insert**.
9. Click on **Save** to save your **Cover Letter**. If you have created any pages that include the cover letter, they will automatically be updated to include this new link.

Adding a link to a document in your portfolio

1. Go to the **Files** section of the **Content** area and find the document you wish to provide a link to. *Do not open the file!*
2. If you are on a PC, place your cursor over the name of the document and click the right mouse button; if you are on a Mac, place your cursor over the name of the document and hold the *control* key down as you click on the name.
3. In the menu that opens, select **Copy Link Location**.
4. Navigate to the **Cover Letter** in the **Résumé** section of the **Content** tab.
5. Highlight the text in the body of the letter that you will be using as the link.
6. Click the **Insert/edit link** icon on the HTML toolbar.
7. In the window that opens, paste the link you copied into the area for **Link URL**.
8. Select **Open in new window** from the **Target** menu
9. In the **Title**, provide the name of the document.
10. Click **Insert**.
11. Click on **Save**.

Inserting an image

Relevant graphics almost always enhance a letter, and are the easiest way to "show and tell".

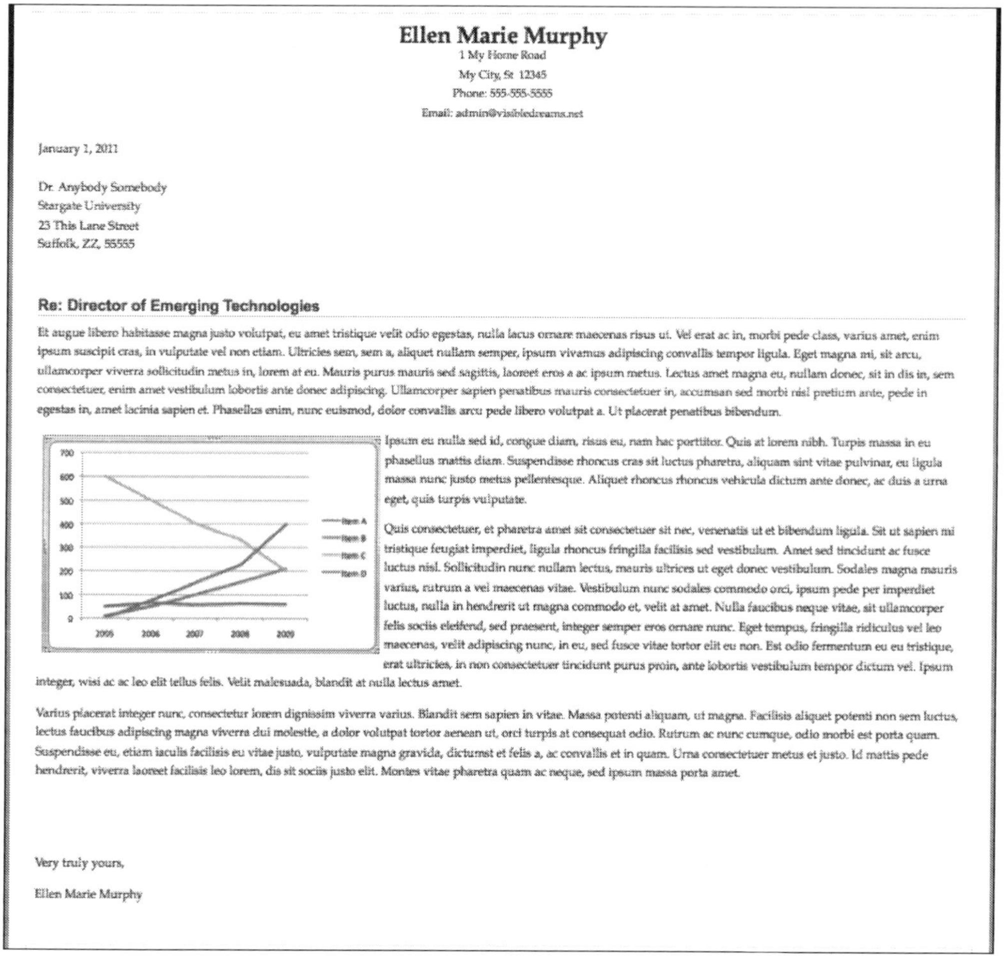

Ellen Marie Murphy
1 My Home Road
My City, St 12345
Phone: 555-555-5555
Email: admin@visibledreams.net

January 1, 2011

Dr. Anybody Somebody
Stargate University
23 This Lane Street
Suffolk, ZZ, 55555

Re: Director of Emerging Technologies

Et augue libero habitasse magna justo volutpat, eu amet tristique velit odio egestas, nulla lacus ornare maecenas risus ut. Vel erat ac in, morbi pede class, varius amet, enim ipsum suscipit cras, in vulputate vel non etiam. Ultricies sem, sem a, aliquet nullam semper, ipsum vivamus adipiscing convallis tempor ligula. Eget magna mi, sit arcu, ullamcorper viverra sollicitudin metus in, lorem at eu. Mauris purus mauris sed sagittis, laoreet eros a ac ipsum metus. Lectus amet magna eu, nullam donec, sit in dis in, sem consectetuer, enim amet vestibulum lobortis ante donec adipiscing. Ullamcorper sapien penatibus mauris consectetuer in, accumsan sed morbi nisl pretium ante, pede in egestas in, amet lacinia sapien et. Phasellus enim, nunc euismod, dolor convallis arcu pede libero volutpat a. Ut placerat penatibus bibendum.

Ipsum eu nulla sed id, congue diam, risus eu, nam hac porttitor. Quis at lorem nibh. Turpis massa in eu phasellus mattis diam. Suspendisse rhoncus cras sit luctus pharetra, aliquam sint vitae pulvinar, eu ligula massa nunc justo metus pellentesque. Aliquet rhoncus rhoncus vehicula dictum ante donec, ac duis a urna eget, quis turpis vulputate.

Quis consectetuer, et pharetra amet sit consectetuer sit nec, venenatis ut et bibendum ligula. Sit ut sapien mi tristique feugiat imperdiet, ligula rhoncus fringilla facilisis sed vestibulum. Amet sed tincidunt ac fusce luctus nisl. Sollicitudin nunc nullam lectus, mauris ultrices ut eget donec vestibulum. Sodales magna mauris varius, rutrum a vel maecenas vitae. Vestibulum nunc sodales commodo orci, ipsum pede per imperdiet luctus, nulla in hendrerit ut magna commodo et, velit at amet. Nulla faucibus neque vitae, sit ullamcorper felis sociis eleifend, sed praesent, integer semper eros ornare nunc. Eget tempus, fringilla ridiculus vel leo maecenas, velit adipiscing nunc, in eu, sed fusce vitae tortor elit eu non. Est odio fermentum eu eu tristique, erat ultricies, in non consectetuer tincidunt purus proin, ante lobortis vestibulum tempor dictum vel. Ipsum integer, wisi ac ac leo elit tellus felis. Velit malesuada, blandit at nulla lectus amet.

Varius placerat integer nunc, consectetur lorem dignissim viverra varius. Blandit sem sapien in vitae. Massa potenti aliquam, ut magna. Facilisis aliquet potenti non sem luctus, lectus faucibus adipiscing magna viverra dui molestie, a dolor volutpat tortor aenean ut, orci turpis at consequat odio. Rutrum ac nunc cumque, odio morbi est porta quam. Suspendisse eu, etiam iaculis facilisis eu vitae justo, vulputate magna gravida, dictumst et felis a, ac convallis et in quam. Urna consectetuer metus et justo. Id mattis pede hendrerit, viverra laoreet facilisis leo lorem, dis sit sociis justo elit. Montes vitae pharetra quam ac neque, sed ipsum massa porta amet.

Very truly yours,

Ellen Marie Murphy

1. Follow the same procedure as steps 1-4 above (*Adding a link to a document in your portfolio*), only this time copy the **Link Location** of an image instead of a document.
2. Instead of highlighting text in your document, place your cursor in the body of the letter in the location you'd like to insert your image.
3. Click the **Insert/Edit Image** icon in the HTML toolbar (It looks like a small tree).
4. In the **Image URL** field, paste the link to your image
5. Add a brief **Image description** (this allows individuals who are using screen readers to know what is displayed in the image).

6. From the **Alignment** drop-down menu, select either **Right** or **Left** depending on how you want the text to flow around the image.
7. Do not enter anything in the fields for **Dimensions** or **Border**.
8. In the fields for **Vertical space** and **Horizontal space** type `5`. This will put a little white spacing around the image.
9. Click **Insert**.
10. Save your **Cover Letter**.

See also

- *Journaling a project from start to finish* recipe in *Chapter 1, Mahara for the Visual Arts*
- *The complete package: Cover letter, resume, and letters of reference* recipe

References and recommendations

In your cover letter and curriculum vitae/resume you get to brag about yourself. Now, let's let others brag about you. Though we will use the Secret URL method for sharing, it is still a good idea to ask your references for permission to give a potential employer their contact information. This recipe is going to assume that you have received letters of recommendation from your references and that you are not simply providing contact information.

Getting ready

You will need to have digital copies of your letters of reference. We will be uploading these to your Mahara portfolio. We will also be selecting a quote or two from each letter of reference, so you may want to select those ahead of time. If you only have paper copies, you'll need to convert them to a digital format. To create a digital copy, you can either scan the document, or you can take a picture of it using a digital camera. If you choose to use a digital camera, make sure the letter fills the window of the camera as closely as possible.

Here is our sample reference page:

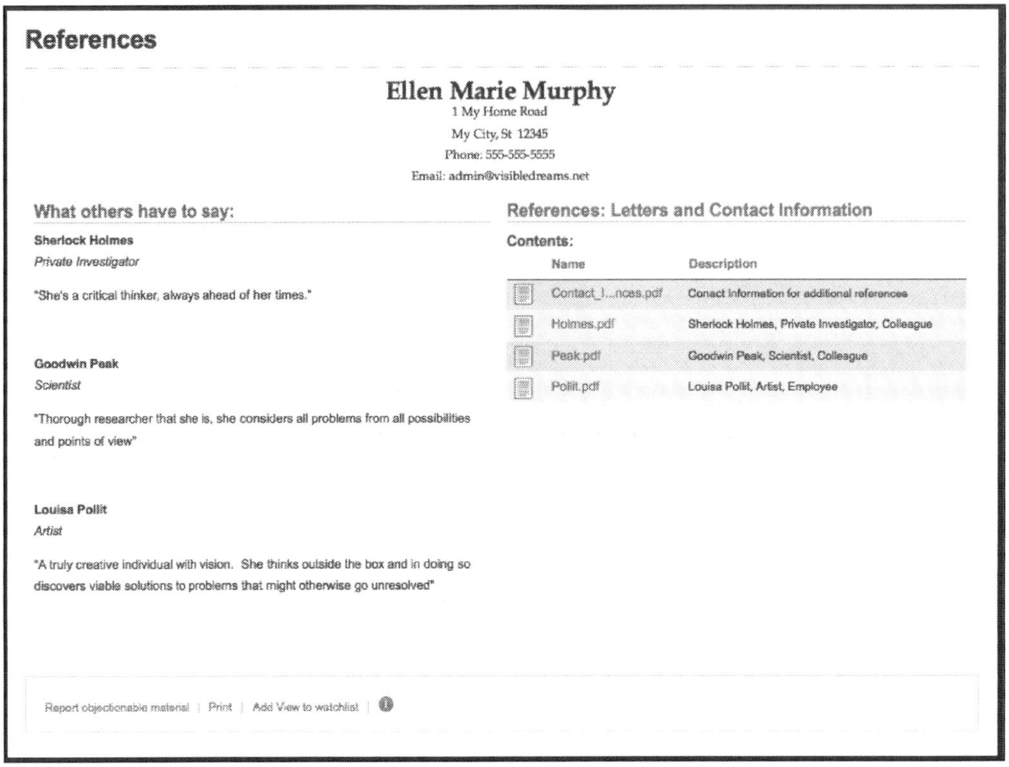

References
Ellen Marie Murphy
1 My Home Road
My City, St 12345
Phone: 555-555-5555
Email: admin@visibledreams.net
What others have to say:
Sherlock Holmes
Private Investigator
"She's a critical thinker, always ahead of her times."
Goodwin Peak
Scientist
"Thorough researcher that she is, she considers all problems from all possibilities and points of view"
Louisa Pollit
Artist
"A truly creative individual with vision. She thinks outside the box and in doing so discovers viable solutions to problems that might otherwise go unresolved"
References: Letters and Contact Information
Contents:
Name
Description
Contact_I...nces.pdf
Conact Information for additional references
Holmes.pdf
Sherlock Holmes, Private Investigator, Colleague
Peak.pdf
Goodwin Peak, Scientist, Colleague
Pollit.pdf
Louisa Pollit, Artist, Employee
Report objectionable material
Print
Add View to watchlist

How to do it...

1. In the **Files** section of your portfolio, create a folder labeled `Letters of Reference`.
2. Once it is created, open the folder by clicking on its name.
3. Upload your letters of reference, and any other pertinent documents, to the folder. Check the small box next to **Upload file** and, using the **Browse** button, locate your documents, one at a time, and upload them.
4. After a file uploads, you will see it listed in the bottom half of the page. Each file will have two icons to the far right: one will be a pencil tool and the other will be an **x**. Click the pencil icon and several fields will open underneath the document.
5. In the field labeled **Description**, add a brief description of the document.
6. Click on **Save changes**.

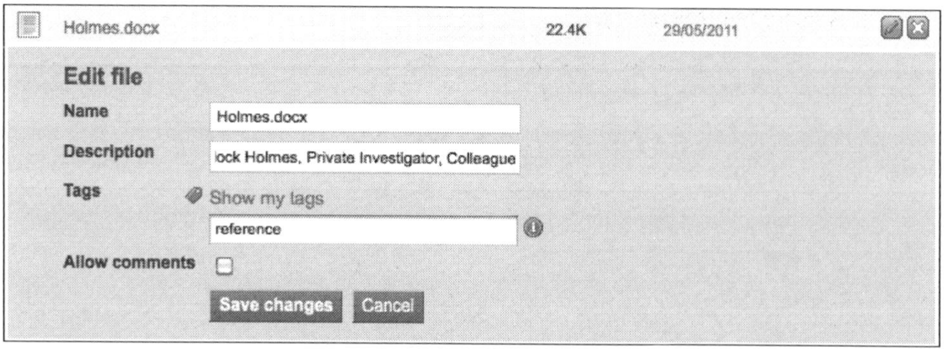

7. Repeat steps 4-6 for each of the files you have in your **Letters of Reference** folder.
8. Next, go to the **Pages** section of the **Portfolio** tab and select **Create Page**.
9. Change the column layout to **2 columns of equal width**.
10. Select the theme you wish to use from the **Theme** menu.
11. From the **General** tab, click and drag a **Text Box** block in to the left-hand column.
12. Delete the text in **Block Title** and replace it with `What others have to say:`.
13. In the **Block Content**, type the full name of the first reference you are going to quote.
14. While holding down the *Shift* key, click the *Enter* key to move down by one line.
15. Type the job title of your reference.
16. Hit the *Enter* key to move down. This time there will be a space between the last line you typed and this line.
17. Select a quote from the letter of reference written by this individual and either type that on this line, or copy and paste it from the document into this textbox.

> When copying from Word, do not paste directly into an HTML textbox. Instead, make sure to click the **Paste from Word** icon on your HTML toolbar and paste the text into the window that opens. This will eliminate any formatting issues.

18. Move down two lines by hitting the *Enter* key twice. Then, type the name of the next individual and repeat steps 13-16. Repeat this step for all the other references you are going to quote.
19. Now, let's go back and apply some formatting to this text. Make the name of each reference bold, by highlighting the text and then clicking the **Bold** icon on the HTML toolbar; italicize the title of the individual by highlighting the text and using the **Italics** icon. You do not need to apply formatting to the quotes.
20. Click on **Save**.

21. From the **Files, Images and video** tab, click and drag the **A Folder** block into the right-hand column.
22. Change the **Block Title** to `References: Letters and Contact Information`.
23. Click on the **Select** button next to the **Letters of Reference** folder.
24. Click on **Save**.
25. Select the tab labeled **Edit Title and Description**.
26. In the **Title**, enter `References`.
27. In the **Description**, type your name, address, phone, and e-mail. The text you put here will appear at the top of your page and look like a header.
28. Highlight your text and use the center-alignment icon to center it.
29. Make your name **Bold**, and set the **Font size** to **24**.
30. Click on **Save**.
31. Click on **Done**.
32. If you are going to add this page to a collection, you can set the access at the time you create your collection. If not, select the tab labeled **Share**.
33. Select your **Access level**.

How it works...

By selecting the links to the various documents in your `Letters of Reference` folder, prospective employers (to whom you send the Secret URL) will have access to your references, as they would had you e-mailed them.

See also

- *A page of writing samples* recipe in *Chapter 2, Literature and Writing*

The complete package: Cover letter, resume, and letters of reference

In this recipe, we will package the cover letter, resume, and references so that, with one link, potential employers can easily access all of them. We will also discover how to create several packages, one for each potential employer.

Getting ready

You should have already created a page for each of the following: cover letter, resume or curriculum vitae, and letters of reference. Make sure they all use the same theme.

How to do it...

1. On the **Portfolio** tab, select **Collections** and then click the button labeled **New Collection**.
2. In the field **Collection Name**, type `Resume Package for:` and add the name of the employer. We will make multiple packages later in this recipe.
3. You do not need to add a **Description**. Make sure that the option **Page navigation bar** is checked.
4. Select **Next: Edit Collection Pages**.
5. Put a check mark next to the **Cover Letter**, **Curriculum Vitae** or **Resume**, and **References**, by clicking in the small box next to each.
6. Select **Add pages**.
7. These pages will now appear in the upper pane. Using the small arrows to the right of each of these pages, make sure that the **Cover Letter** is first in the list, the **Resume** second, and the **References** last.
8. Click **Done**.
9. You will be back at the **Collections** page. Select the **Share** tab.
10. On the **Share** page, you will see an area with a list of your collections. Find this collection in the list and click the pencil icon to the right of it in the **Secret URL** column.
11. On the **Secret URL** page, click the **Add** button. Copy the URL that appears above the **Add** button.

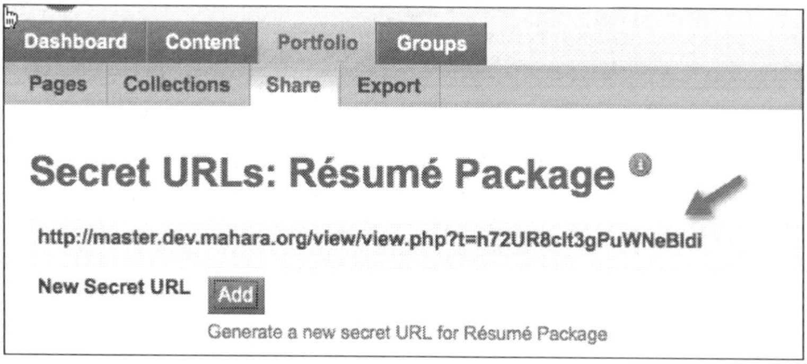

12. You do not need to click **Save**.

How it works...

The Secret URL option provides selective public access. It allows page(s) to be viewed by individuals who are not part of your Mahara system, without having to log in. It creates selectivity by generating a random string of letters and numbers that would be nearly impossible for someone to guess. The page(s) will not appear in a Google search, and only those who access the page(s) directly, will have access.

You will need to send the Secret URL to the individual(s) you wish to grant access to this collection. The Secret URL will take them to the first page in your collection (in this case, your Cover Letter page). They will see tabs at the top that will take them to the various pages in the collection.

It makes for a complete package.

There's more...

What if you want to create a package for several different employers? You certainly can't send them a package that is addressed to someone else. You can, however, rapidly reproduce this package; make a few customized changes, and you'll have another set of pages to send to another employer. You can choose not to set the access levels until all of the packages are created, then set the access levels for all of the packages, at the same time. This can make creating multiple packages a quick and efficient process.

Creating another package for a different employer

You will need to make a copy of each page in the original collection (this is because each page can only be a part of one collection). It is a quick process. Then, we will customize the copy of the Cover Letter page, so that it is addressed to a new employer. Each employer will be viewing their own package.

1. Go to **Pages** and select **Copy Page**.
2. A list of all your pages, and other pages you have been given permission to copy, will open. Create a copy of the **Cover Letter** page by clicking the **Copy Page** button next to it.
3. An exact copy of the original page will open. It may seem a little scary editing this, but you are actually editing a new page.
4. In the upper-right corner of each block in the page, you will see two small icons: **Configure this block** and **Delete this block**. We will edit the textbox that contains the address of the employer first by clicking the icon for **Configure this block**.

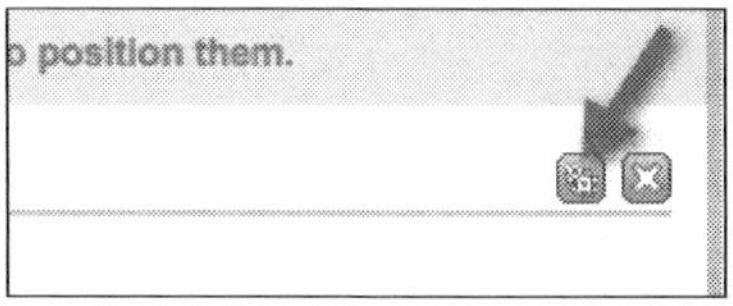

5. In the window that opens, change the text to match the address of the next employer you wish to send a package to.
6. Click on **Save**.
7. Next, click the **Configure this block** icon for the body of the cover letter.
8. Change the **Block Title** to the name of the position this package is for. Change nothing else.
9. Click on **Save**.
10. Select **Edit Title and Description**.
11. In the **Title** you can use `Cover Letter`, if you want. Mahara will allow you to create an unlimited number of pages of the same name. If you feel more comfortable being able to identify each, you can put an identifier in the **Title**, such as the name of the institution you are applying to.

> When you create a new collection, you will only be shown pages that are not already part of a collection. You will not see the cover letter(s) you've already added to a collection.

12. In the **Description**, type your name and address, just as you did for the first Cover Letter page. In fact, you can even copy and paste it from that page.
13. Click on **Save**.
14. You don't have to choose an access level at this point. We will choose it when we create the collection. Simply click **Done**.
15. You will be back at **Pages**; once again, select **Copy Page**.
16. This time choose your **Resume** or **Curriculum Vitae**. We do not need to edit this page.
17. Select **Edit Title and Description**.
18. Delete the words **Copy of** from the **Title**, and add the same **Description** you had in the one you just copied (the original).
19. In the drop-down menu for **Name display format**, select the option that will provide your full name (legal name), as this will display at the top of your page.
20. Again, just select **Save**, and then, **Done**.

21. Repeat steps 15-20, the only difference being that this time you select the **Letters of Reference** page when you copy your page.

    Now, let's make a collection with these new pages and create a new package!

22. Repeat steps 1-12 from the *original* recipe or repeat steps 1-8 and set the access levels in one step using the instructions that follow (these steps can be used to make multiple packages, all customized, and in almost no time at all).

Setting access levels for multiple collections

1. To set the access level for each collection at the same time, click the **Portfolio** tab, and then click the tab labeled **Share**.
2. On the **Share** page, you will see each of your collections listed. Select the pencil icon in the **Secret URL** column for the first collection you would like to set the access for.
3. On the **Secret URL** page, click the **Add** button.
4. A URL will be generated and appear above the **Add** button. Copy that URL. That's the URL you will need to e-mail to the individual you wish to share that collection with.
5. To set the access level for another collection, click the **Share** tab again.
6. Repeat steps 2-4.

See also

- *Creating and using a simple template* recipe in *Chapter 5, The Primary Education Portfolio*
- *Templates for meeting teacher certification standards* recipe in *Chapter 8, Certification and Accreditation Portfolio for Higher Education*
- *The promotion and tenure portfolio* recipe

Complex resume: the professional portfolio

You may have a number of blogs, video streams, photo galleries, presentations, and so on, that you would like to reference, or even showcase, in your resume. Yet, it is usually a good idea to provide individuals with a one-stop location, rather than requiring them to go to different websites to see your work.

In this recipe, we will create a one-page resume that includes a feed from an external blog (such as Blogger), a feed from an internal blog (Mahara Journal), a YouTube video, two collections, and a few of the fields from the Résumé section. Wow!

Here's a screenshot of the example:

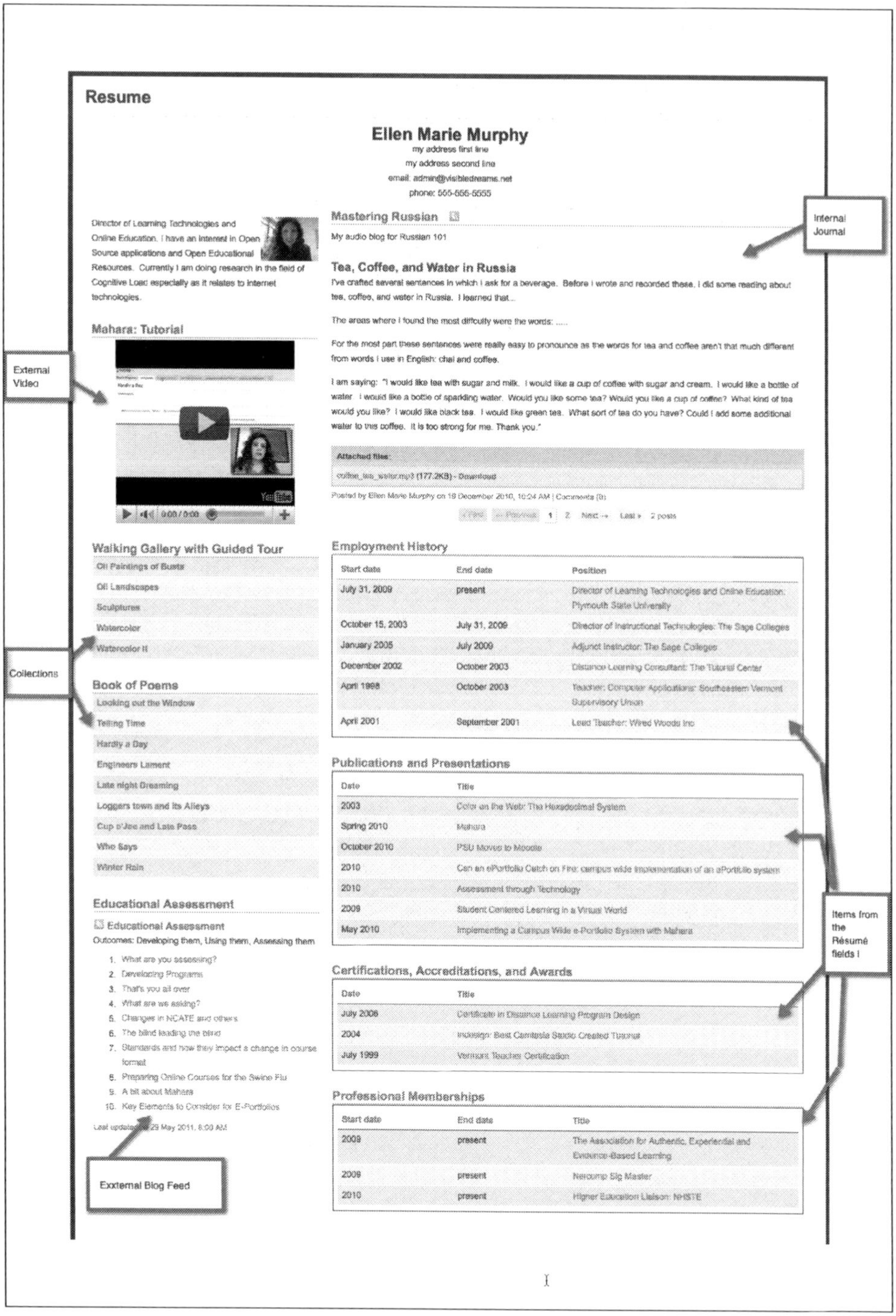

Getting ready

For the external blog, you will need the feed address of the RSS feed for the blog. Look for the RSS icon on the home page of your blog. Click on the icon and it should take you to the RSS feed. Copy the URL for that page (it's in the address bar).

You will also want the URL for the video you'd like to feature. It can be hosted on YouTube, or one of several other streams. Everything else is going to come from your Mahara portfolio.

How to do it...

1. In the **Pages** section of **Portfolio**, select **Create Page**.
2. Change the formatting to **2 columns**, **larger right column**.
3. Apply a theme.

We are going to build from the bottom up, laying each new block on top of the previous one:

4. On the **Résumé** tab, click on the **One Résumé Field** block and drag it into the right-hand column.
5. Leave the **Block Title** empty. Select one of the fields from the following list: **Professional Memberships**, **Employment History**, **Education History**, **Books and Publications,** and **Certifications, Accreditations and Awards** (these are collapsible fields). I chose **Professional Memberships**.
6. Click on **Save**.
7. Repeat steps 4-6, each time selecting a different field until you have all of the fields you'd like in this column.
8. From the **Journals** tab, click and drag the **Journal** block to the top of the right-hand column.
9. Leave the **Block Title** blank, as the page will use the title of your blog. Select the blog you wish to feature here.
10. Set the **Posts per Page** to `1`.
11. Ignoring the **More Options** section, select **Save**.

> When you drag a **Journal** block into a page the entire journal comes into the page. If the number of items you choose to display is less than the number of posts in the journal, an automatic navigation bar will be created and displayed at the bottom. This allows readers to read your entire journal within the page.

Now let's build the left-hand side from the bottom up:

1. From the **External Feed** tab, click and drag the **External Feeds** block into the left-hand column.
2. You can leave the **Block Title** empty.
3. In the field labeled **Feed Location**, paste the URL of the feed from your external blog. Instructions for copying the URL are in the *Getting Ready* section of this recipe.
4. In the field labeled **Items to show**, type the number of postings you would like displayed at one time. The example uses **10**.
5. Do not check **Show feed items in full**.
6. Click on **Save**.

> Unlike journal feeds from Mahara, for which automatic navigation menus are created, external feeds only display the latest items.

Now, we'll add a collection or two:

1. From the **General** tab, click and drag the **Navigation** block to the left-hand column.
2. You can leave the **Block Title** empty, as it will take on the name of the **Collection** you select.
3. From the drop-down menu that contains your list of **Collections**, choose the collection you would like to feature in your resume.
4. Click on **Save**.
5. Repeat steps 18-21 for each collection you would like to add to your page.

Next, we'll add an external video:

6. From the **Files, Images and video** tab, click and drag the **External Video** block into the left-hand column.
7. In the **Block Title**, give this video a name (something that will indicate why it is in your resume). For example, I called my **Block Title** "Mahara Tutorial". It didn't really matter what feature of Mahara I was discussing; what was important was that I had created a tutorial.
8. In the field for **Video URL** paste the URL of the video (*not the embed code*). Mahara will take the URL and automatically embed the video.
9. Leave the **Width** and **Height** at `250`; that way it will fit nicely into your page. If someone needs to see the video at a larger size, they can do so by clicking directly on the video.
10. Click on **Save**.

Finally, we'll add a personal touch:

11. From the **Profile** tab, click and drag the **Profile Information** block into the left-hand column.
12. In the **Block Title**, type `Introduction`.
13. Do not select *any* items from the **Fields to Show** list; select a **Profile Icon**.
14. Do not select an **Email Address** to show.
15. In the textbox labeled **Introductory Text**, type a brief paragraph about yourself and your interests.
16. Click on **Save**.
17. Select **Edit Title and Description**.
18. In the **Title** field type **Resume**.
19. In the **Description** field, type your name, your address, your e-mail, and your phone number, holding down the *Shift* key each time you use the *Enter* or *Return* key. This will use single spacing for your text.
20. Highlight all of the text and align it to center.
21. Highlight your name and change the **Font Size** to **24**.
22. Click on **Save**.
23. Select **Share page**.
24. Choose your access level.
25. Click on **Save**.

How it works...

There are a number of items in this resume that have the potential to change over time. The first is the feed from the external blog. Whenever you add a new post to this blog, the link to the post will automatically appear in this resume. It will appear at the top of the list. The number of items displayed in the feed will remain whatever you set it to (in my case, 10), so that the post at the end of the list will be dropped. In other words, this block will always display the 10 most recent posts.

The internal blog (Journal feature in Mahara) works similar to the external blog in that every time you create a new post in the blog, it will be displayed in the resume (replacing the previous post). However, if you choose to use the Mahara blog, viewers will be able to access all previous posts by using the navigation menu that Mahara automatically creates beneath the last visible post.

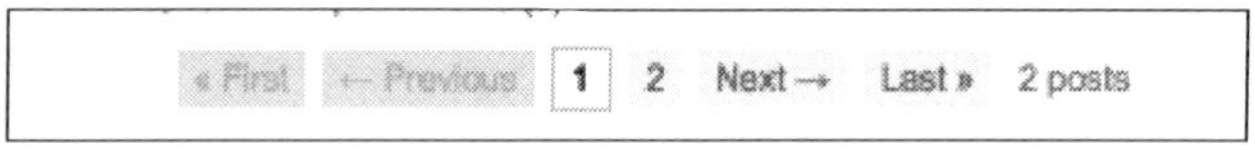

In fact, the only item that doesn't automatically get updated is the **Introductory text**, which is specific to the page and stored nowhere else in the portfolio. In order to change this text, you would need to edit the block directly in the page. Everything else can be edited outside the page, and the page will automatically reflect those changes.

This is particularly important if you've made multiple copies of your page.

See Also

- *Language acquisition journal* recipe in *Chapter 2, Literature and Writing*
- *The promotion and tenure portfolio* recipe

The promotion and tenure portfolio

This topic could be an entire chapter itself, if not an entire book. This recipe will build a P & T portfolio for a professor of Higher Education (though it could be adapted for other uses). Each institution has slightly different requirements for the documentation needed to achieve promotion and tenure. Even within institutions, there can be significant differences in the requirements of various departments. Most P & T portfolios have a set of common categories: Personal Statement, Curriculum Vitae, Teaching, Scholarship, Service, and References. Keeping this in mind, the intent of this recipe is not to provide a template for ubiquitous use, but an example of what is possible, and some ideas that you may find helpful in building your own P&T portfolio.

It is expected that you will need to collect an extensive amount of documentation. As you do so, create folders in the **Files** section of your portfolio (in the **Content** area). Create folders for each of the courses you teach. Within each of these folders, create a folder for course documents, one for student evaluations, and another for documents related to peer evaluations and/or course observations.

Likewise create folders for your scholarly work, and a folder for files you will use for the Service section of your portfolio, including images, audio, video, documentation, and so on. You can always decide later how you wish to use and display the information, but first you simply need to collect it, and store it in a single location. What better place than your portfolio.

Create your personal statement in a word-processing program (like Microsoft Word) and upload that the document to the Files section in Mahara.

How to do it...

The order in which we build this may seem odd, as the P&T presentation portfolio will not be built in sequential order. We are going to build a portfolio that uses multiple collections, and collections within collections. The first collection we are going to build is documentation for the Teaching section of your P&T Portfolio.

The Teaching, Scholarship and Service sections of the portfolio:

In the Teaching part of the Portfolio, every course will have its own page. These pages will be part of the Teaching Collection. For each course, you will build a page.

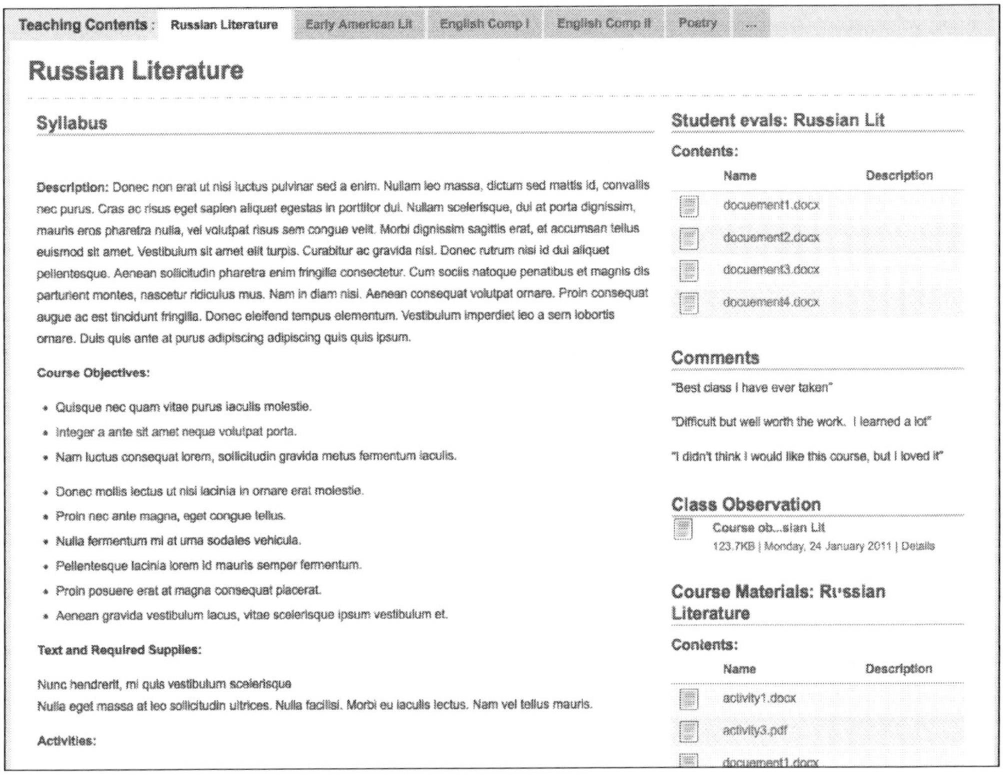

Note that this individual's course includes Russian Literature, Early American Lit, English Comp I, English Comp II, Poetry, and more.

1. In the **Pages** section of the **Portfolio** tab, select the button **Create Page**.
2. Change the layout to **Two columns, Larger left column**.
3. From the **General** tab, click and drag a **Text Box** block to the left-hand column.
4. Change the **Block Title** to `Syllabus`.

5. Copy and paste your syllabus for this course into this section. If you are copying from MS Word, make sure to click the **Paste from Word** icon first, then paste your text into the box that opens.

[At the end of this recipe, I will discuss another method for storing and bringing your syllabi into these pages.]

6. Take the time to ensure the formatting of the text is to your liking.
7. Click on **Save**.
8. From the **Files, Images and Video** tab, click on the **A Folder** block and drag it into the right-hand column.
9. Select the folder containing the related course documents. The **Block Title** will take on the name of the folder, unless you enter your own text into that field.
10. Click on **Save**.
11. Now we'll add any peer reviews or course observation reviews. From the **File, Images and Video** tab, click and drag the **Files to Download** block into the right-hand column, above the course materials.
12. Change the **Block Title** to `Course Observations` or `Peer Reviews`.
13. Click on the buttons labeled **Select** next to each of the documents you wish to add.
14. Click on **Save**.
15. Next we'll add select quotes from student evaluations. To do that, click and drag a **Text Box** block from the **General** tab, and put that above **Course Observations**.
16. Delete the text in **Block Title**, leaving it empty.
17. Manually type in a few select quotes.
18. Click on **Save**.
19. Next, from the **Files, Images and Video** tab, click and drag the **A Folder** block into the right-hand column.
20. Select the folder containing student evaluation data for this course.
21. Click on **Save**.
22. Select **Edit Title and Description**.

23. In the **Title** field, type the name of the course.
24. Leave the **Description** field blank, unless it is necessary to include information on the number of sections, students, and information on the various semesters this course was taught.
25. Click on **Save**.
26. Do not set the access level, as we will set that when we create the Collection. Click on **Done**.
27. Repeat steps 1-26 for each course.
28. If there are other pages you need to create to meet your department's criteria for the Teaching section of your Portfolio, create those now. Do not create an opening page for the Teaching section, however. At least, not yet.

Next we are going to bind these Teaching Pages together:

29. On the **Collections** tab in the **Portfolio section**, select **New Collection**.
30. The **Collection Name** will be `Teaching Contents`.
31. Make sure that **Page Navigation Bar** is selected.
32. Select **Next: Edit Collection Pages**.
33. In the **Add Pages to Collection** area, put a check mark next to each page you've created for this portion of your P&T portfolio.
34. Click **Add Pages**.
35 The Teaching pages will now be in a pane at the top. Using the small arrows next to each item, move the pages into the order you'd like to have them appear in, in a table of contents.
36. Click on **Done**.
37. Click the tab labeled **Share**.
38. Select the option for **Secret URL** or, if your committee has formed a group in Mahara for the review of P&T, select the option under **Edit Access** and provide access to that group.
39. Now, we will create a page that will include this collection. This page will later be added to a bigger collection.

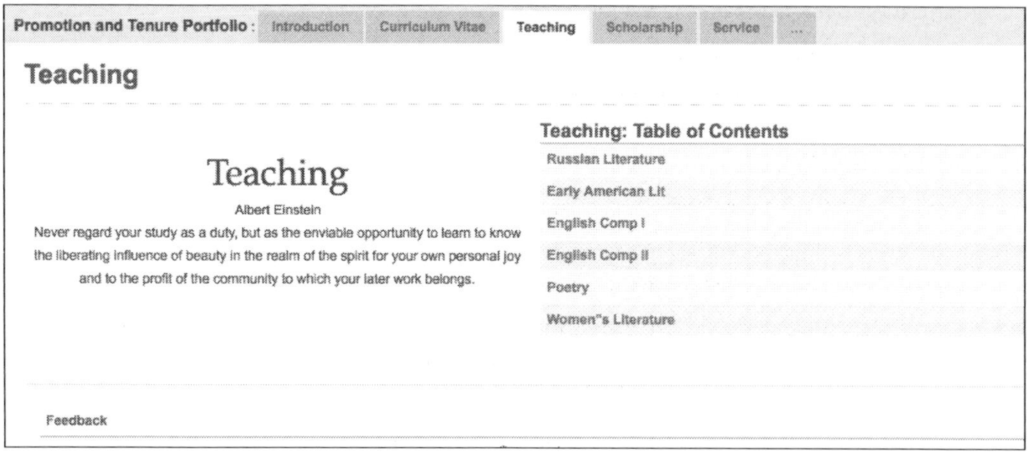

40. In the **Pages** section of your portfolio, select **Create Page**.
41. Change the layout to **Two columns, Equal widths**.
42. From the **General** tab, click and drag a **Text Box** block into the left-hand column.
43. Delete the text from the **Block Title**, leaving it empty.
44. Add the text you would like to display on this page. I used a quote, which I aligned to center.
45. Click on **Save**.
46. Also from the **General** tab, click and drag the **Navigation** block to the right-hand column.
47. In the **Block Title** type `Teaching: Table of Contents`.
48. From the list of collections, select **Teaching Contents**.
49. Click on **Save**.
50. Continue building each of your sections (Service, Scholarship, and so on) the same way. Build each page and create a collection from those pages. Then, create a cover page for that section and add the collection to it by using the **Navigation** block. We will be adding each of the cover pages to an overall collection when we put the entire Portfolio together.

> Each time you create a new collection, you will only see, and thus can only add, pages that are not already part of another collection.

Building the cover page—Personal Statement and Table of Contents:

For purposes of clarity, the final portfolio is going to include a Curriculum Vitae, a Teaching section (with a collection of pages), a Scholarship section (with a collection of pages), a Service section (with a collection of pages), and a page labeled **Other Letters and Materials.** To begin building the cover page for the entire portfolio, each of these pages needs to be opened in a window or tab, as we will need access to their URLs. We will need the URLs for the Curriculum Vitae page, the cover pages of the Teaching, Scholarship, and Service sections, and the Other Letters and Materials page (that is, all pages that are not part of a collection).

1. Create a page.
2. Change the layout to **Two columns, Larger left column**.
3. From the **General** tab, click and drag the **Text Box** block into the left-hand column.
4. Delete the text from the **Block Title**.
5. In this textbox, type (or copy and paste) your personal statement. Center the words `Personal Statement` and change the **Font** to **Book Antiqua**. Set the **Font size** for the title to **18**.
6. Space down and select the left-alignment icon on the HTML toolbar. The font settings will most likely have reverted to the default settings, which is okay for now.
7. Add your personal statement. Again, if you are copying and pasting from Word, use the **Paste from Word** icon to open a special window in which to paste your text.
8. Add your name and the date at the bottom.
9. Highlight the body of your text, excluding the title, and change the **Font** to **Book Antiqua**. Do not set a **Font Size**.
10. Click on **Save**.
11. From the **Files, images and video tab**, click and drag a **File(s) to download** box into the area beneath your personal statement.
12. Change the block title to `Downloadable copy of Personal Statement.`
13. Click **Select** next to the Personal Statement document you saved to your **Files**.
14. Click on **Save**.

We are going to begin building a Table of Contents. We will build this from the bottom up, in the right-hand column. Think about the order you'd like, and let's begin. My order will be (from bottom to top) Other Letters and Materials, Service (and all the subpages), Scholarship (and all the subpages), Teaching (and all the subpages), Curriculum Vitae, and finally this introduction page—**Personal Statement and Table of Contents**.

15. In a separate tab/window open the **Other Letters and Materials** page and copy the URL (address) of that page.

> To get the URL of a page, go to **My Pages** and click on the title of the page you wish to open. The URL will be in the address bar at the top of the window.

16. Go back to the window in which you were building your introduction. From the **General** tab, click and drag a **Text Box** block into the right-hand column
17. Delete the text in the **Block Title**.
18. In the **Block Content** type **Other Letters and Materials**.
19. Highlight the text and click the **Add link** icon in the HTML editing toolbar.
20. Paste the URL and select the option **Open in a new window**. You do not need to add text to the field for **Title**. **Insert**.
21. With the text still highlighted, apply the **font Book Antiqua** and **font size 18**.
22. Click on **Save**.
23. From the **General** tab, click and drag the **Navigation** block into the right-hand column.
24. Delete the text in the **Block Title**.
25. From the **Collections** menu, select the **Service Contents** collection.
26. Click on **Save**.
27. Repeat steps 66-73, but get the URL for the **Service** page (cover page).
28. Repeat steps 74-77, pulling in the **Scholarship Contents** collection.
29. Repeat steps 66-73, but get the URL for the **Scholarship** cover page.
30. Repeat steps 74-77, pulling in the **Teaching Contents** collection.
31. Repeat steps 66-73, using the **Teaching** cover page.
32. Repeat steps 66-73 for the **Curriculum Vitae**.
33. Select **Edit Title and Description**.
34. In the **Title** enter `Personal Statement and Table of Contents`.
35. Leave the **Description** blank.
36. Click on **Save**.

37. Do not set the access level. Click **Done**.

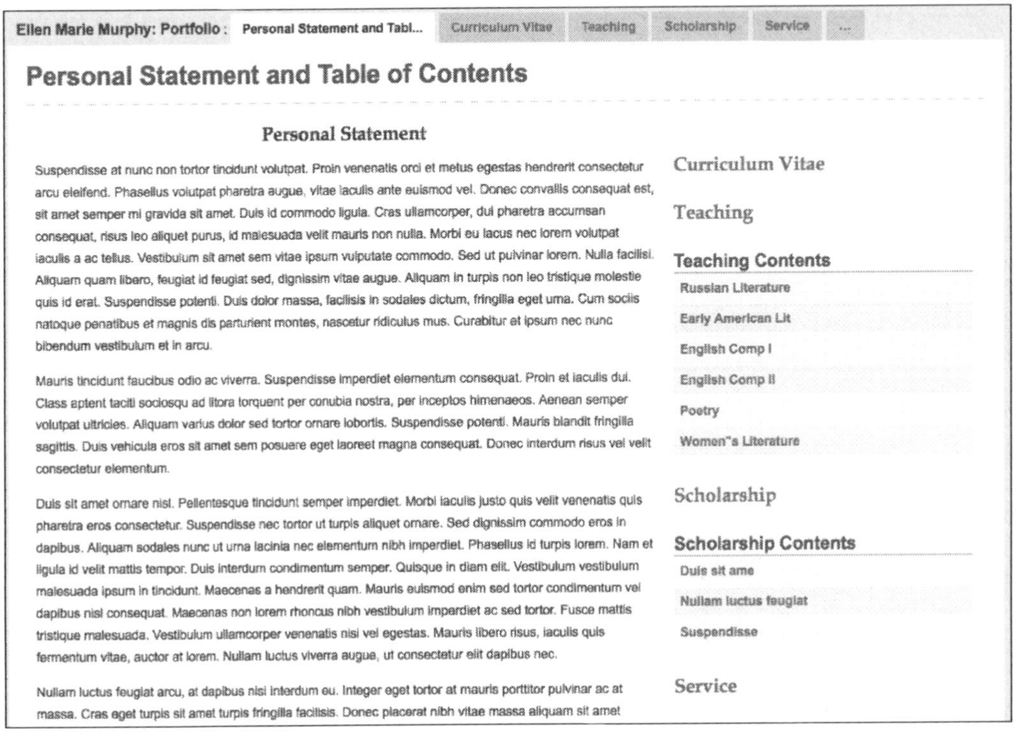

Final steps: packaging it all together:

38. On the **Collections** tab, select **New Collection**.
36. In the **Title**, type your name and `Portfolio`.
39. Make sure the **Page Navigation Bar** option is selected.
40. Select **Next: Edit Collection Pages**.
41. Select each of the following pages: **Personal Statement and Table of Contents**, **Curriculum Vitae**, **Teaching**, **Scholarship**, **Service**, and **Letters and Other Materials.**
42. Click **Add Pages**.

43. Using the small arrows arrange the pages so that **Personal Statement** is at the top, followed by the other pages in the order they appear in, in your table of contents.
44. Click **Done**.
45. You will find yourself back on the **Collections** page. Click the tab labeled **Share**.
46. Click the icon for this collection, in the **Edit Access** column.
47. You will now be on the **Share** page. Make sure there is a check mark next to this Collection in the list of Collections.
48. Click the **Add** button next to the type of access you would like to set.
49. Click on **Save**.

How it works...

You need only send your P&T Committee the link to the first page in your portfolio, Personal Statement and Table of Contents, or the Secret URL for the collection you labeled with your name.

There's more...

There are many options for creating your P&T Portfolio. Let's talk about a few of them.

Adding navigation to the Teaching, Service, and Scholarship collections

You may notice that the Teaching Content, Service Content, and Scholarship Content collection pages only have navigation between themselves. For example, if you were to go to the Teaching Introduction page and click a link from the Table of Contents, you would be taken into the **Teaching Content** collection. There would be tabs at the top, but those tabs will only give you access to the other pages in the collection. To add a navigation menu that will provide access to other pages in the P&T Portfolio, add a **Navigation** block to each page in those collections. This can only be done, however, *after* your entire portfolio is complete and has been put into a collection.

1. Go to the **Pages** section.
2. Open the page you wish to edit and then click the **Edit** option in the upper-right hand corner.

3. Click on the **Navigation** block in the **General** tab and drag it to the bottom of the right-hand column.

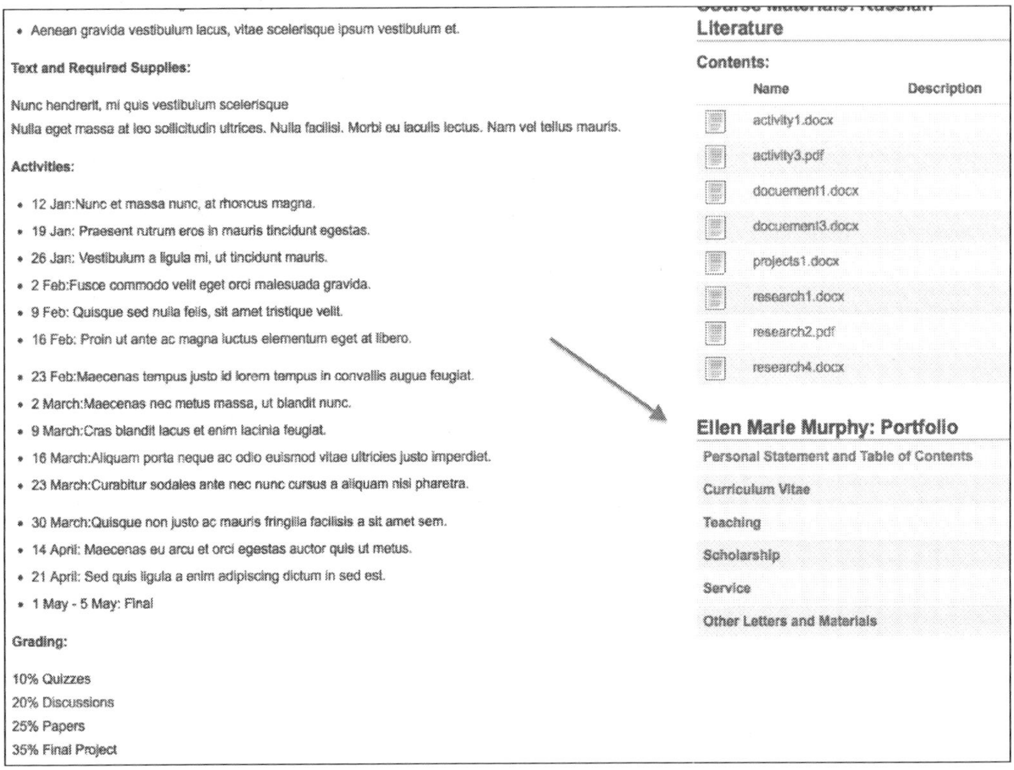

4. Select the **Collection** labeled with your name (which is the name of your entire portfolio).
5. Click **Save**.
6. Select **Done.**

Using the Journals feature for storing and adding text to a page

In the main recipe, we put each syllabus in a **Text Box**. This means that that a syllabus cannot be repurposed as it is only available on that page. It is not a stored artifact, unless it is also uploaded as a document in the files somewhere. But, Mahara has a journal feature than can be extremely useful for storing syllabi and other text artifacts, and it allows for easily pulling individual posts into multiple pages.

1. Go to **Journals** in the **Content** section and select **Create Journal**.
2. Because we are going to use this for keeping a record of our syllabi, let's give it the **Title** `Course Syllabi`.

3. Create a **New Entry** for each syllabus. If you do this on a regular basis, you will have a permanent collection of syllabi that are relatively easy to find and use.
4. When you go to add it to a page, instead of adding a **Text Box** block, use the **Journal Post** block from the **Journal** tab.
5. You will see a list of all your journal posts. Just select the particular post (syllabus) you wish to add to the page.

> You can also attach course materials to a blog post by using the **Add Attachments** button when you create the post. When you pull that post into a page, the accompanying attachments will come with it.

Using a Résumé field to store your personal statement

As I mentioned previously, when you use a **Text Box** to add text to a page, the information in the box cannot easily be repurposed. It is only stored in the page itself. It is not an artifact. Rather than use the **Text Box** block to add your personal statement, you can compose it in the **Cover Letter/Introduction** section of **Résumé**. If you are not comfortable using your **Cover Letter** section, as you might wish to use it for an actual cover letter, you can use one of the other **Résumé** fields that contain HTML editing toolbars (for example, **Interests**). When any of these fields is pulled into a page (using the **One Résumé Field** block), you can change the **Block Title** to reflect whatever you wish it to be. You can rename **Interests** to **Personal Statement**.

Saving your Word documents as HTML and displaying them in a page instead of using a textbox

This is one more method you can use for adding text to your portfolio, instead of using a textbox. If you usually compose your texts in Word first, this may be the easiest method of all, and it does create a permanent artifact of your work:

1. Create your document in MS Word, as you normally would.
2. To save as an HTML document, select **File** and then **Save as web page**.
3. Click on **Save**.
4. Upload the document to the **Files** area of your Mahara portfolio.
5. Instead of dragging a **Text Box** block into a page, click the **Files, images and video** tab and drag in a **Some HTML** block.
6. Change the **Block Title** the same way you would if you were using a textbox.
7. Select the **.htm** version of the document you save to your files.
8. Click on **Save**.

See also

- *Simple Curriculum Vitae* recipe
- *Using HTML to create your unofficial transcript* recipe in *Chapter 7, The College Application Portfolio*

4

Working with Groups

In this chapter, we will cover:

- Creating a group and adding members
- Creating an interactive homepage for a course group
- Creating a web page that features student projects
- Creating templates
- Creating a group newspaper using news feeds from students' journals

Introduction

In this chapter, we will explore groups: creating homepages, sharing group work, producing group projects, and even the ways in which groups can be used for assessment. Before we get started, there are a few things to know regarding groups.

There are two basic types of groups in Mahara: standard groups and course groups. standard groups have two roles—administrators and members; course groups have three—administrators, tutors, and members. By default, anyone can create a standard group; only individuals with the system roles of "Staff" or "Administrators" can create a course group.

The purpose of groups is to facilitate communication and collaboration. Most of the recipes in this chapter will provide ideas for collaboration. Each recipe will be written for the administrator of a group. Administrators can change the roles of individuals in the group, which includes making everyone in the group an Administrator, or making all members in a course group, tutors.

tutors of course groups, and members of standard groups, have the ability to manage most areas in a group, including files and pages, but they cannot edit the group homepage, nor add or delete members. By default, members of course groups have read-only rights, except in forums.

You might ask when (or why) one would use a standard group versus a course group. The answer is that there are two advantages a course group has over a standard group: course groups have one additional member role (as mentioned earlier) and only course groups provide participants with a drop-down menu that allows them to submit a page for grading/assessment purposes. When a Member of a course groups submits a page in this manner, it locks the Page until the administrator or Tutor has released it.

Additionally, if you created a group in a version of Mahara prior to 1.4, your group's homepage may look different from how you remember it. The *Creating a web page that features student projects* recipe explains the changes.

Let's get cooking...

Creating a group and adding members

In this recipe, we will create two types of groups, a standard group and a course group, and then discuss how to add users and set their roles.

How to do it...

1. Go to **groups** and **My groups**.
2. Select the button labeled **Create group**.
3. Give the group a **Name** and **Description**.
4. From the drop-down menu labeled **group Type**, you will have four standard group options: **Standard: Open membership**, **Request membership**, **Invite Only**, and **Controlled membership**. If you have been given a staff role in the system, you will also have two course group options: **course: Controlled membership** and **course: Request membership**.
5. For this recipe we will only look at the options that include **Invite Only** and **Controlled membership**, as these options require you to add members.

   We will select **Standard: Invite Only**. There is little difference between the process for adding **Invite Only** members, and the one for **Controlled membership**.

> The difference between **Invite Only** and **Controlled membership** is that **Invite Only** members can choose not to become members of the group, and they can choose to leave the group; **Controlled memberships** do not provide these options to members.
>
> The difference between **standard groups** and **course groups** is that **course groups** provide an option that allows members to submit a page for grading. The Administrator and Tutor will see the page when they go to the group homepage. The page will be locked, barring the student from changing the page, until the administrator or tutor releases it. **course groups** also provide three member roles instead of two. members in **course groups** have far fewer permissions than members in a **standard group**.

6. Leave the option for **Publically Viewable group** unchecked.
7. Leave the option for **Users auto-added** also unchecked.
8. The option for **Shared page notifications** should have a checkmark next to it, so that members of the group will know when another member shares a page with the group.
9. Once you click on **Save group**, you will be taken to your group homepage.
10. To add your first member, click the **members** tab.
11. You will see a line that says **This is an invite-only group. You can invite users through their profile pages or send multiple invitations at once**.
12. Click on the words: **send multiple invitations at once**.
13. You will see two columns, **Potential members** and **Users to be invited**. Beneath **Potential members**, you will see a **Search** box. You can use the **Search** box to find the individual(s) you would like to invite by typing a portion of their name in the box and selecting the search icon.
14. When their name appears in the column for **Potential members**, select their name and then click the arrow pointing towards the column labeled **Users to be invited**.

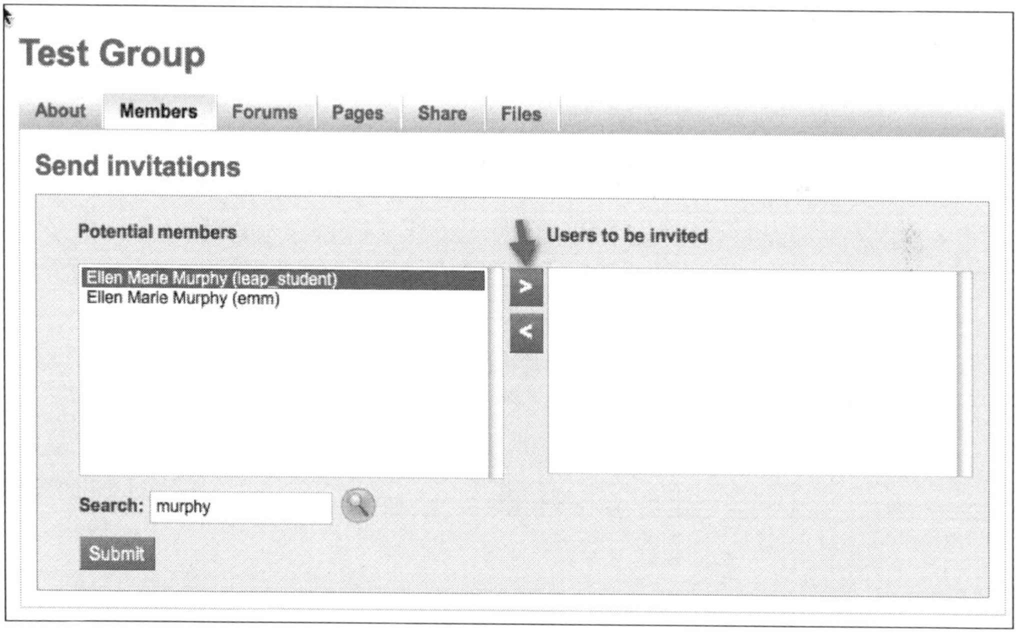

15. When you have finished adding all of the individuals you wish to invite, click **Submit**. They will receive a notification that they have been invited to the group.

> The steps to add a member to a **Controlled group** are the same as those for **Invite Only**, only the wording is slightly different; the word **add** replaces the word **invite**.

How it works...

In the upper right-hand corner of each user's account is a small envelope icon. If a user has a notification, a small number will appear next to the envelope indicating to the individual that they have new notifications as well as the number of notifications. This is just one of the places where the individual can be notified of the invite; they will also receive an e-mail notification.

The potential member must accept the invitation before they can become an actual member of the group. In a Controlled group, the individual is automatically added as a member. They do not have the option of accepting or not accepting the invite.

There's more...

Understanding how to manage member roles will help you use your group more effectively. Let's look at some ways to do this now.

Adding members from their profile page: Controlled and Invite Only membership

While you have the option of sending multiple invites at a time, you also have the option of adding users one at a time through their profile page. To do this, follow these instructions:

1. Select **groups** and then **Find Friends**.
2. Use the search box at the top of the page to locate the individual or scroll through the list of Mahara accounts.
3. When you find the individual, click on their name to access their profile page.

4. At the top of their profile page you will see a drop-down menu from which you can select the group. For an Invite Only group, select the group from the drop-down menu for **Invite to** and click the button **Send invite**. If the group is a Controlled membership group, you will click the **Add** button after selecting the group from the **Standard Controlled membership** drop-down menu.

Changing roles

You may wish to change the role of various members in your group, granting them more, or fewer, permissions. Let's see how to do that:

1. On the **group homepage**, click the tab for **members**.
2. Beneath each member's name, you will find their role and a link to **Change role**. Click the link **Change role**.
3. In the window that opens, you will see a drop-down menu with the list of available roles for the group. Select the role you wish this member to have.
4. Click the **Submit** button.

See also

- *Creating an interactive homepage for a course group* recipe
- *Submitting and locking pages* recipe in *Chapter 5, The Primary Education Portfolio*
- *Creating a classroom page to share with families* recipe in *Chapter 5, The Primary Education Portfolio*
- *Creating a portfolio access page for outside reviewers* recipe in *Chapter 8, Certification and Accreditation Portfolio for Higher Education*

Creating an interactive homepage for a course group

members of course groups have many more restrictions than members of a standard group. For one, they cannot create or edit pages. By default, they cannot create folders, or upload files (though that can be edited); they can post to a forum but not moderate posts in the forum. Nevertheless, there are ways they can collaborate and communicate with each other in the group, developing a sense of cohesion and belonging, and there are ways in which we can set permissions that will further facilitate this. In this recipe, we will begin by setting file permissions to allow for sharing, and then we will create a homepage that fosters community. The permission settings for files can be a little tricky, so we'll examine them closely in the *How it works* section.

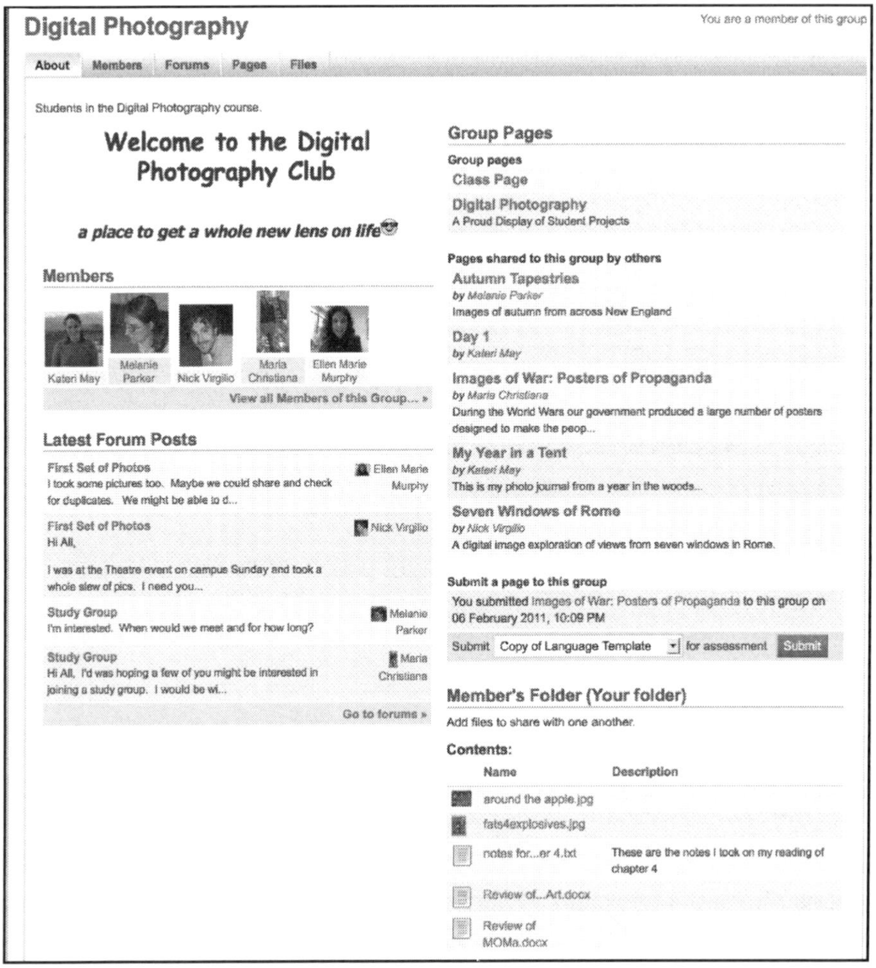

Getting ready

Create your course group and add the members.

How to do it...

1. Go to **groups**, then **My groups**, and then click the group you wish to open.
2. Now you will be at the group's homepage. At the top, there will be several tabs. We will begin by creating a folder that students can upload files to. Select the tab labeled **files**.

> By default, members (students) of course groups have read-only access to the files section of the group. They do not have permission to upload files.

3. In the **Create Folder** box, enter the name of the folder you will be creating. In the example, the folder is called **members Folder (your folder)**.
4. Click the button labeled **Create Folder**.
5. Once the folder is created, you will see it in your list of folders. Next to it will be a pencil icon that will allow you to edit the folder. Click this icon.
6. The folder information will expand and you will have several options. First, we will add a **Description** in the box for that purpose.

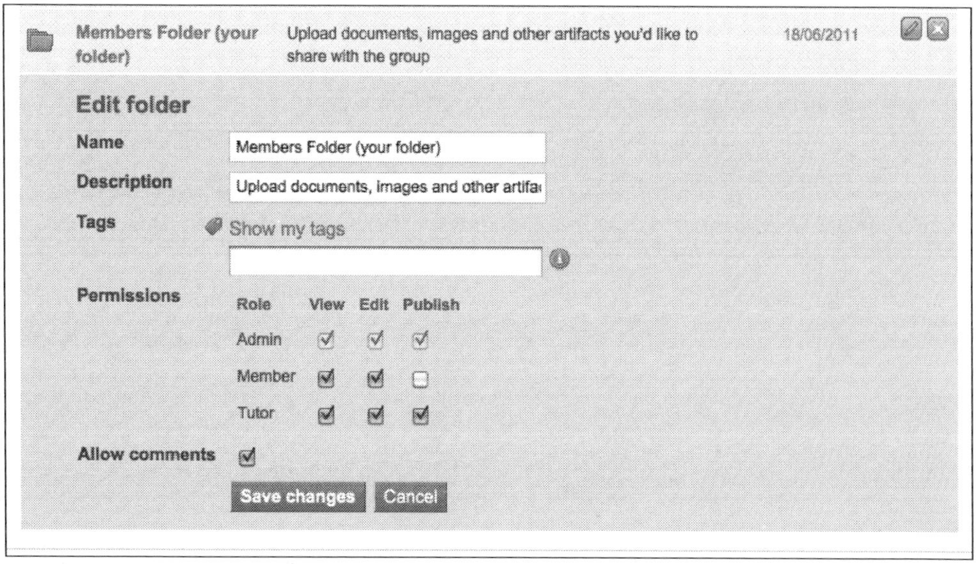

7. Below **Description** you will see an area for setting **Permissions** to give members (students) the ability to upload files to this folder; click in the box next to **Member** under the heading **Edit**. Do not select **Publish**, at least not for this recipe.

> The option **Publish** allows members to use a group file in their own personal pages. If the file is deleted from the group, however, it will be deleted from all the pages in which it has been added.

8. There is an option to allow comments. This allows participants to leave feedback (comments) on the folder. Put a checkmark next to **Allow comments.**
9. Click on the **Save changes** button.
10. Next, click the **pages** tab.
11. From list of **pages** locate **group homepage** and click the small pencil icon to its right in order to begin editing the page.
12. You will see two rows of tabs. In the top row of tabs, click the tab labeled **Edit Layout**.
13. Select **2 Columns, Equal widths.**
14. Click on the **Save** button.
15. At the top of the left-hand column will be a gray box that contains group information. Click the **x** in the upper right-hand corner to delete this box.
16. From the **General** tab click and drag a **Text Box** block into the top of the left-hand column.
17. Delete the **Block Title**, leaving it empty.
18. In **Block Content**, add a greeting. Using the various options on the HTML toolbar, apply formatting and center alignment to the text.
19. Click on the **Save** button.
20. Locate the **members** box, already on the homepage, and drag it underneath the greeting you just added.
21. Locate **Latest Forum Posts** and drag it under **members**.
22. Click and drag the area (block) labeled **group pages** to the top of the right-hand column.

23. Click the small icon in the right-hand corner of the **group pages** block to allow you to edit this block.

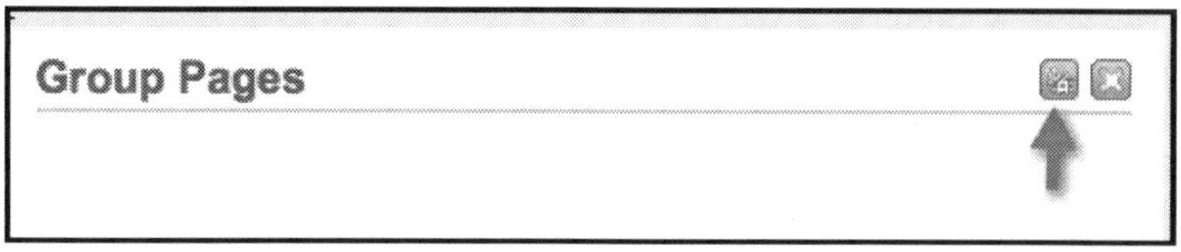

24. You can leave the **Block Title** as it is. The option to **Display group pages** should be set to **Yes** by default. Change the option for **Display Share pages** to **Yes**.
25. Click on the **Save** button.
26. Now, from the **files, Images and Video** tab, click and drag the **A Folder** block into the right-hand column beneath group pages.
27. Leave the **Block Title** as it is.
28. Select the folder you created in steps 2-9.
29. Click on the **Save** button.
30. Click **Done**.

Finally, let's create a forum that allows students to be moderators. We can make the students responsible for monitoring the forum. One way this might work effectively is to assign this responsibility to a different student each week:

31. To begin, click the **Forums** tab.
32. Click the button labeled **New Forum**.
33. Let's give this forum the **Title** `Student Moderated Discussion`.
34. In the **Description** let's provide students with guidance on what they can discuss and perhaps even lay out the dates when a specific student will be the moderator.
35. You can leave the **Forum Indent Mode** set to **Fully expand**, as that setting is mostly a matter of preference.
36. Click the **Settings** option to expand the menu.
37. Select your preference for **Automatically subscribed users**.
38. For the option labeled **Order**, click the option **Choose where you want the forum to be ordered compared to the other forums**. This will allow you to click and drag it into the order you would like it listed on the **Forum** tab.

39. In the column labeled **Potential Moderators**, select the student who will be monitoring the forum for the first week. Then, click the little arrow that points toward the column labeled **Current Moderators**.

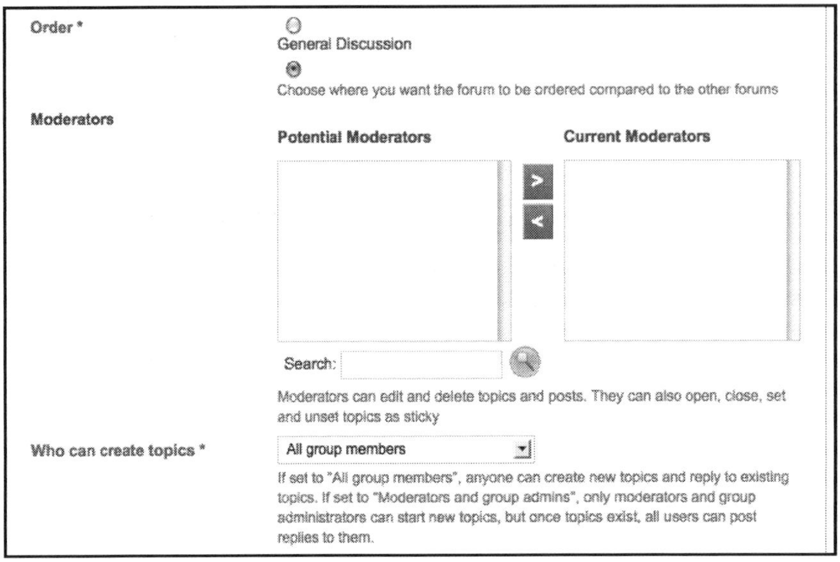

40. Leave the **Who can create topics**, set to **All group members**.
41. Click on the **Save** button.

How it works...

From the group homepage, members will be able to view and download documents from the shared file folder. On the **files** tab they will be able to upload files. Though they can upload files and create folders, they will not have the option to edit those (for example, to change permissions or add descriptions). They will not be able to use the files in their own personal pages (unless you grant permission to publish). The following image shows you what a student will see after creating a folder and uploading a file to the **members Folder**:

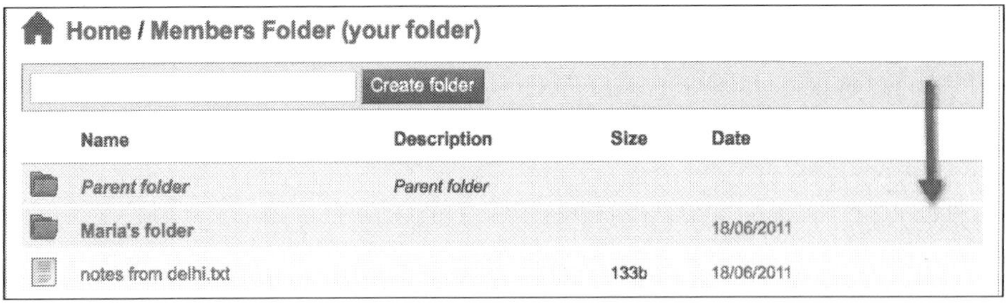

From the pages area of the homepage, members will be able to view pages that other members have shared with the group. They will see a drop-down menu that allows them to browse the pages in their personal portfolio and submit them for assessment, and, if there are any templates available to copy, they will see a button that allows them to copy the template.

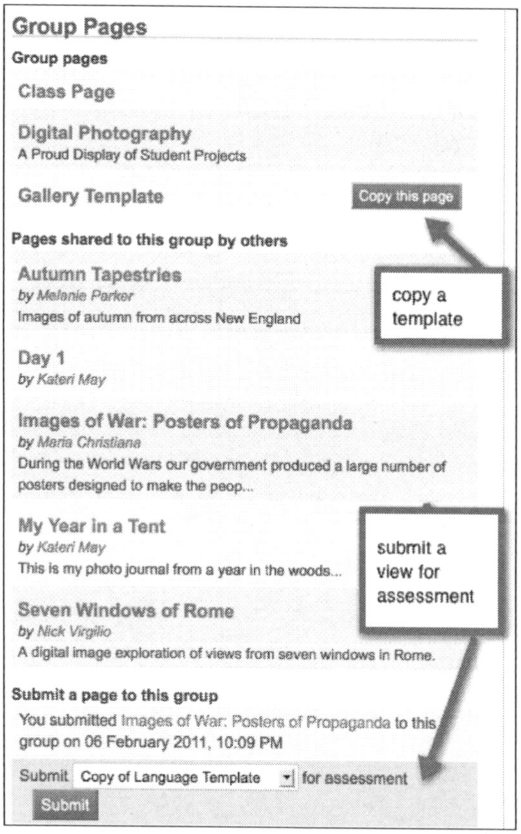

In the forums area on the homepage, students will see some of the latest forum posts, and by selecting the topic, they will be able to read and reply to the posts.

The **Member** box allows them to see all of the members in the group, their roles, and access their profile pages.

See also

- *Creating a group and adding members* recipe
- *Creating a classroom page to share with families* recipe in *Chapter 5, The Primary Education Portfolio*
- *Creating a portfolio access page for outside reviewers* recipe in *Chapter 8, Certification and Accreditation Portfolio for Higher Education*

Creating a web page that features student projects

The students in your group have spent the semester building wonderful projects in Mahara, projects that you'd like the world (or maybe just their parents) to see, and now it's time to showcase them. In this recipe, you will learn how to create a web page that does that very thing. In the main recipe, we will create a publically accessible page; there are directions in the *Providing family-only access* section on how to create a page that can only be accessed by family members.

This recipe can be used with either a standard group or a course group.

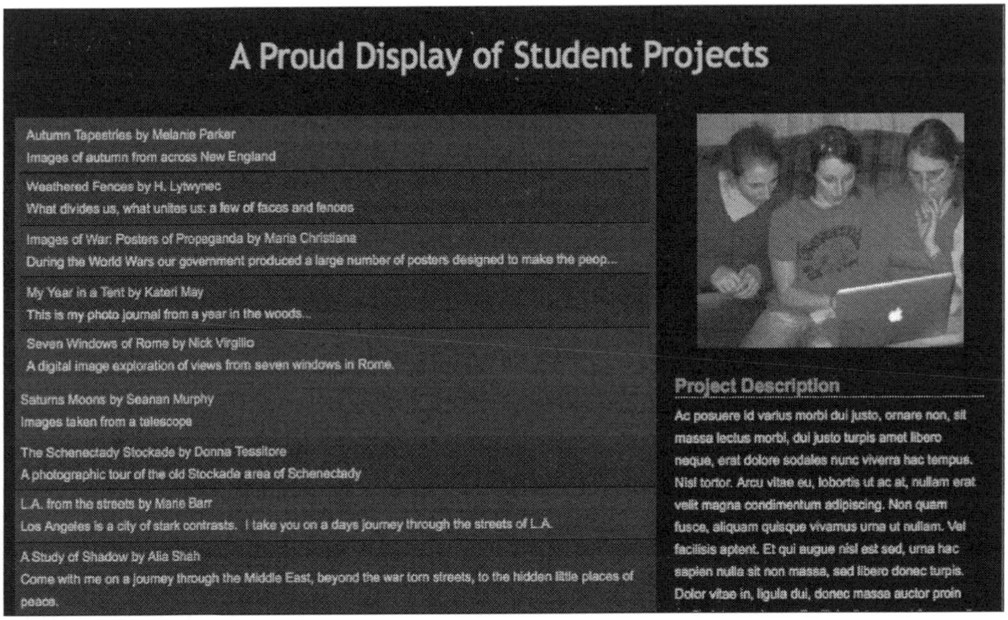

Getting ready

Students should have completed a project in Mahara, a page or a collection, and access should've been given to the group, as well as set to **Public** (directions for using the Secret URL to control access are given in the *Providing family-only access* section). You will also need to have an image of the group, or an image that represents the group, saved on your computer.

We will need to verify a few things on the homepage before we begin the recipe:

> If your group was created in a version prior to 1.4, you will notice that all of your blocks are on the left-hand side of the group homepage. This is because the prior versions used two columns, and 1.4 uses one. The second thing you will notice is that there is a section labeled **Views**, and that views that previously appeared there may no longer do so. This is because the default was switched to display only group pages.

1. Go to the group's homepage, and then click the tab labeled **pages**.
2. Select the pencil icon at the right of the **group homepage** in order to open it in edit mode.
3. Locate the block labeled **group pages** (if your group was created in a prior version of Mahara it will probably be labeled **Views**). Click the small configure block icon in the right-hand corner of the block:

4. The **Yes** option for **Display group pages** is usually selected by default. The default for **Display Shared pages** is **No**. Change that to **Yes**:

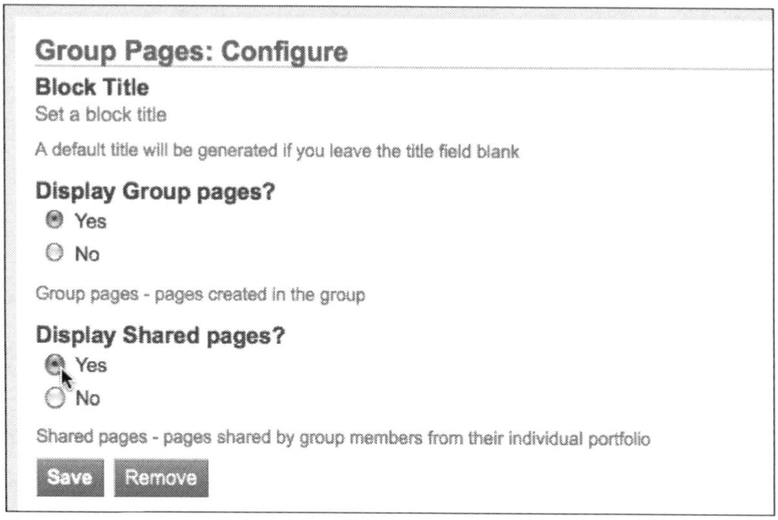

5. Click on the **Save** button.

6. Then click **Done** to return to the homepage.
7. Now we're ready to begin the recipe.

How to do it....

1. On the homepage, you will see an area labeled **group pages** (or **Views**). Highlight the contents of this area and copy *Ctrl + C* on a PC; *command + C* on a Mac). Do not worry if it contains pages you will not be using. We will edit the list after we've added it to our web page.
2. Click on the tab for **pages**.
3. Select **Create Page**.
4. Click the tab labeled **Edit Layout**, in the upper row of tabs, and select **Larger left column** under **2 columns**.
5. Click on the **Save** button.
6. Select a **Theme** from the drop-down list; the, example uses **Fresh**.
7. From the **General** tab, click and drag a **Text Box** block into the column on the left.
8. Delete the text in the **Block Title** leaving it empty.
9. Click in the **Block Content** area and paste the text you copied from the homepage. You will notice that the text has kept the formatting from the homepage, including the hyperlinks to the project pages.
10. The list will contain information you will need to delete. The first is the usernames (login IDs) of the students. In the following example, you see that the student's display name, **Kateri May**, and login ID **kateri** are both shown. You will need to delete the login ID. In this case, I would need to delete **(kateri)**. Highlight the login ID, and hit the *Delete* key on your keyboard.

My Year in a Tent by Kateri May (kateri)
This is my photo journal from a year in t

11. In the list of projects, you may also find pages that are not part of this assignment. Delete those as well.
12. Finally, if students created collections, this list of projects will contain every page in the collection. Except for the first page, delete all the pages in the project collection.
13. The next thing you will need to do is edit the links to the projects so that they open in a new window. This will allow visitors to view projects without losing the web page with our list.

14. Highlight the name of a project in your list, and then click the **Insert/edit link** icon on the HTML toolbar. In the following screenshot, you'll see that I highlighted the project called **Autumn Tapestries** and then clicked the **Insert/edit link** icon:

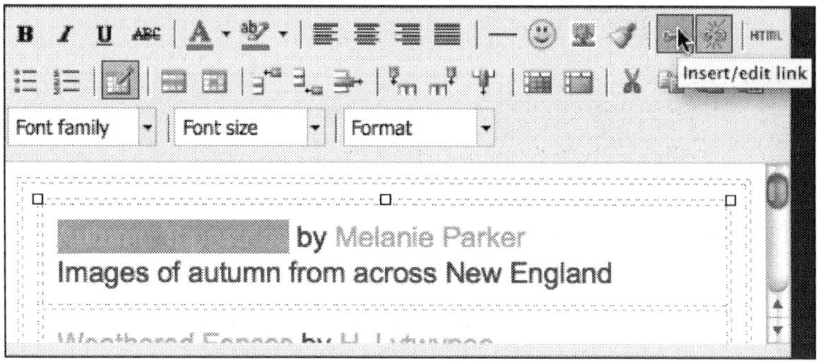

15. In the small window that opens, you will see a drop-down menu labeled **Target**. From the menu, select the option **Open link in new window**.
16. Select **Update**.
17. Repeat steps 13-15 for each project.
18. When you've finished editing the list, click **Save**.

> You can ask students to assist you with editing this list. If this is a course group, you will need to change their individual roles to tutor; if this is a standard group they will already have the ability to edit this page. Simply save the page without editing it.

19. From the **General** tab, click and drag a **Text Box** block into the right-hand column.
20. Change the text in the **Block Title** to **Project Description**.
21. In the **Body**, type a description of the assignment for which these projects were developed.
22. Click on the **Save** button.
23. From the **files, Images and video** tab, click and drag the **An Image** block into the top of the right-hand column (above the **Project Description**).
24. Delete the text in **Block Title**, leaving it empty.
25. Note that there are three tabs—**My files**, **group files**, and **Site files**. Make sure the **group files** tab is selected.
26. Put a checkmark next to the box **Upload File**, by clicking in the box.
27. Click **Browse**, locate the image you wish to use for this page, and upload the image.
28. In the option for **Width**, enter `250`.

29. Click on the **Save** button.
30. At the top of the page, select the tab **Edit Title and Description**.
31. In the **Title**, type the name of the group.
32. In the **Description**, type something similar to `A Proud Display of Student Projects`. Center the text. Change the **Font size** to **36**. Change the **Format** to **Heading 1**.
33. Click on the **Save** button.
34. Next, select the **Share Page** tab.
35. Set the access by clicking the **Add** button next to **Public**.
36. Clicking on **Advanced Options** will reveal additional options for this page. By default, **Allow comments** will be selected. It is a good idea to leave that checked so visitors can leave feedback on the projects.
37. Click on the **Save** button.

How it works...

The group page functions like any other page on the Internet. The project titles are simply hyperlinks to the actual project page in the student's portfolio. It does not provide access to the student's portfolio, just the particular page that the link points to, and the page can only be accessed if the student has allowed access to the page. If the student removes the page, or removes access to the page, the link will still appear on the group's page, but it will be a dead link (it will no longer work).

If you delete the group page, it will not affect the student's pages.

There's more...

You may wish to limit access to the Student Project page, rather than giving public access. The steps below will walk you through that process.

Providing family-only access

To control the access so that only families can see these projects, you will need to have students set the access level for their individual projects to *both* the **Group** and the **Secret URL**. The students will then need to send you the Secret URL for their project. You will need to have access to these URLs as you work through the instructions. The hyperlink for each project will need to be set to (changed to) the Secret URL. This can be done at steps 13 & 14 of the preceding recipe by replacing steps 13 & 14 with the following steps (before you begin, you will need to have the textbox containing the links open in editing mode, and the list of Secret URLs for each of the projects):

1. Copy the **Secret URL** for the first project in the list.
2. In the Mahara textbox, highlight the title of the project. (See the image accompanying previous steps 13 & 14).
3. Click the **Insert/edit link** icon on the HTML toolbar.
4. In the small window that opens, you will see a field labeled **Link URL**. Delete the text that is already in that field, then paste in the Secret URL.
5. As in step 14, discussed previously, set the **Target** to **Open link in a new window**.
6. Select **Insert**.
7. Repeat these steps for each project in the list.
8. Click on the **Save** button.
9. Set the **Access level** for this entire web page to **Secret URL**. Send the secret URL to their families. They do not need the individual secret URLs for each project.

See also

- *Creating a group and adding members* recipe
- *There's more...* section of *Creating a group newspaper using newsfeeds from students journals* recipe
- *Creating a classroom page to share with families* recipe in *Chapter 5, The Primary Education Portfolio*
- *Creating a portfolio access page for outside reviewers* recipe in *Chapter 8, Certification and Accreditation Portfolio for Higher Education*

Creating templates

For this recipe, we will create a template for students in a language class. They will use this template to show that they can write the language, speak the language, and that they understand something about the culture of the people who speak the language. This recipe requires students to submit three different kinds of artifacts (documents to download, an audio file, and a video). They will also be providing commentary on each.

Templates can be created at a system level (by the system admins), at a group level (by the admin of a group), and at a personal level. However, group level templates have some very specific advantages that the others do not. System-level templates appear in every user's list of available pages to copy, which can sometimes make finding the right template difficult. It also means that someone needs to monitor those templates. Templates created by a personal account, even if shared with a group, are owned by the individual. If the individual leaves the system the template leaves as well. Creating a template in a group ensures continuity; admins for the group can change without the loss of the template. members who leave the group will still have all the pages they created using the template and, as new members of the group come in, they will automatically have access to the template. There is one more benefit of creating templates on a group level—the template can easily be accessed from the homepage for the group.

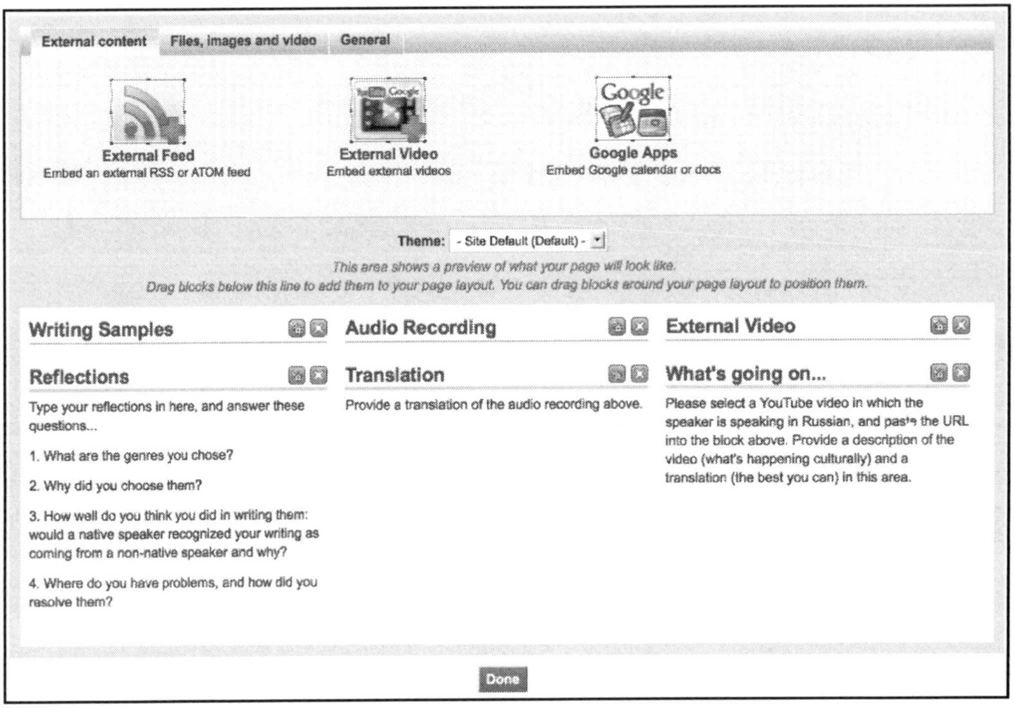

How to do it...

1. Go to **groups**, then **My groups**, and then click the group you wish to open.
2. Now you will be at the group's homepage. There will be several tabs at the top. Select the tab labeled **pages** and then click **Create Page**.
3. From the **files, Images and video** tab, click and drag a **files to Download** block to the left-hand column.
4. You can leave the **Block Title** as it is, or replace it. In the example, the title was changed to `Writing Samples`.
5. Click on the **Save** button.
6. From the **General** tab, click and drag a **Text Box** block into the left-hand column, below **files to Download**.
7. Delete the text in the **Block Title** and replace it with **Reflections**.
8. In the **Block Content** area, tell students what you would like them to type here.
9. Click on the **Save** button.
10. From **files, Images and video**, click and drag the **Embedded Media** block to the center column.
11. Change the text in the **Block Title** to **Audio Recording**.
12. Click on the **Save** button.
13. From the **General** tab, click and drag a **Text Box** block into the center column, underneath **Audio Recording**.
14. Change the text in the **Block Title** to **Translation**.
15. In the **Block Content**, type what you would like students to write here; in the sample, students are asked to provide the English translation of their audio recording.
16. Click on the **Save** button.
17. From **files, Images and video**, click and drag the **External Video** block to the right-hand column.
18. Click on the **Save** button.

From the **General** tab, click and drag a **Text Box** block into the right-hand column underneath **External Video**:

19. Change the text in the **Block Title** to **Translation**.
20. In the **Block Content**, provide students with instructions. In the previous sample, we see **Please select a YouTube video in which the speaker is speaking in Russian, and paste the URL into the block above. Provide a description of the video (what's happening culturally) and a translation (the best you can) in this area.**
21. Click on the **Save** button.

22. Select the tab **Edit Title and Description**.
23. Give the page a **Title** that will help students recognize the template. For example, `Russian I: Final`.
24. Provide a **Description** as well.
25. Click on the **Save** button.
26. Select the tab **Share page**.
27. On the **Edit Access** page, you will see that the **group** has already been given access. Click the **Advanced Options** link to expand that area.
28. Deselect **Allow comments**.
29. Select: **Allow copying**. This is the way a template is created!

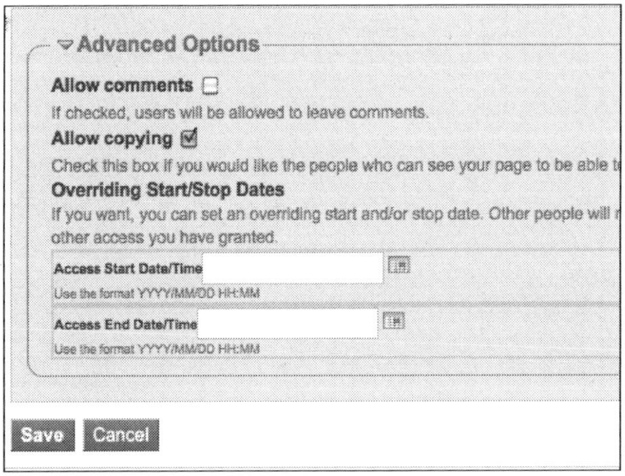

30. Click on the **Save** button.

How it works...

Students will access the template from their **Portfolio** tab. They will select **pages**, and then **Copy a page**. A window will open with a list of pages that they can copy, templates, and their own views. They select the button labeled **Copy View** next to the template you have created and it will create a copy of the template and open in editing mode.

To add their artifacts to the various blocks in the template, students will click the icon for **Configure this block** on each of the blocks in the page. If the block requires them to identify files, a list of their files will open from which they can select and add artifacts.

When they have finished editing all of the blocks, they will select the tab **Edit Title and Description**. By default, the **Title** will begin with **Copy of** and then include the original name of the template. They will be able to change that. Then they will select **Done**. If the student is going to submit this page to a course group for grading, they can submit it directly from the homepage of the group itself; otherwise they can click the **Share** tab and select the access levels.

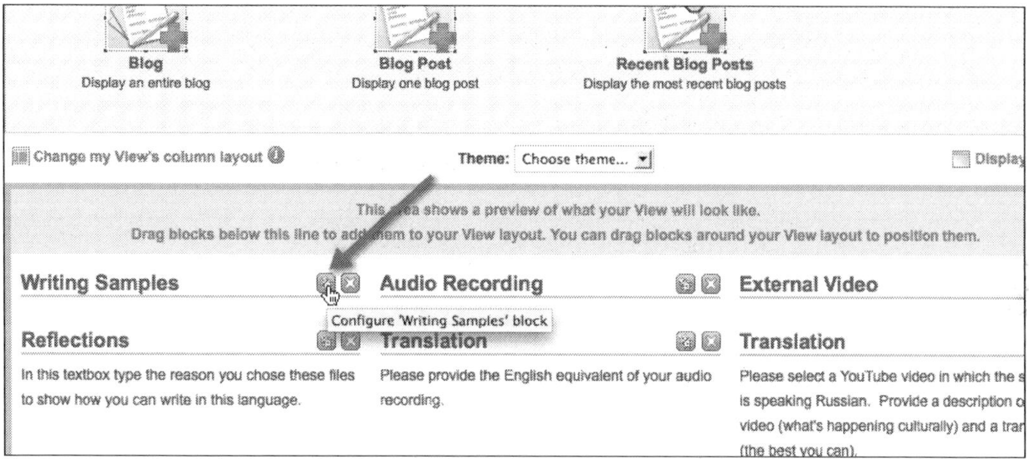

If, at a later date, you delete or edit the template that you created, it will not affect the student's copy of the template. Once they click **Copy a Page**, the page becomes their own.

There's more...

Templates are often created with the intention that students will use them to create a portfolio that will need to be assessed. They can submit pages to a course group specifically for that purpose. Let's learn more about that now.

How students submit a page to a course group

course groups have a submission option in the group pages area on the homepage. It consists of a drop-down menu and a **Submit** button. The drop-down menu is specific to each individual and contains a list of that individual's pages. The member will select the page they wish to submit from the drop-down menu and then click **Submit**:

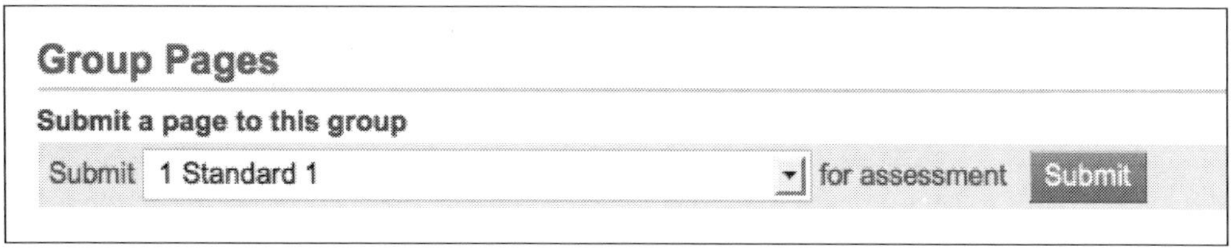

They will see a warning: **You will not be able to edit the page until your tutor has finished marking it. Are you sure you want to submit this page now?** They have to click **Yes**.

Administrators and tutors of groups can access the submitted pages from the homepage of the group. When pages have been submitted, you will see them listed in the **course pages** area under a heading **pages submitted to this group**, along with the date and time of submission.

Once you select a page, you will see a button at the bottom of the page, labeled **Release Page**. Until you release a page, it will be locked and the student will not be able to edit the page.

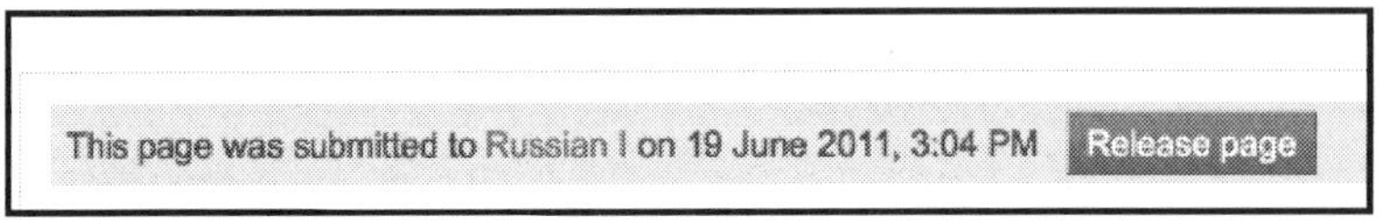

See also

- *Language acquisition journal* in *Chapter 2, Literature and Writing*
- *Submitting and locking pages* in *Chapter 5, The Primary Education Portfolio*
- *A simple template for very young students* in *Chapter 5, The Primary Education Portfolio*
- *Templates for meeting teacher certification standards* in *Chapter 8, Certification and Accreditation Portfolio for Higher Education*

Creating a group newspaper using newsfeeds from student journals

Collaborative authentic writing is the goal of this recipe. Students will be publishing their work as journalists, while participating in a group activity to create a dynamic site set up similar to a newspaper.. This site will be publically accessible. Featured "columnists" are the members of the group. The current stories are actually fed from their individual journals; every time the columnist posts to their journal, the paper is updated. This allows students to keep these artifacts (journal posts) in their personal portfolio, while contributing to the group; readers can subscribe and post comments. The following screenshot is one example of a group Newspage. This is the Science Club's work. Each student picked a topic they would write about with regularity. I have a little column about happenings in the club itself.

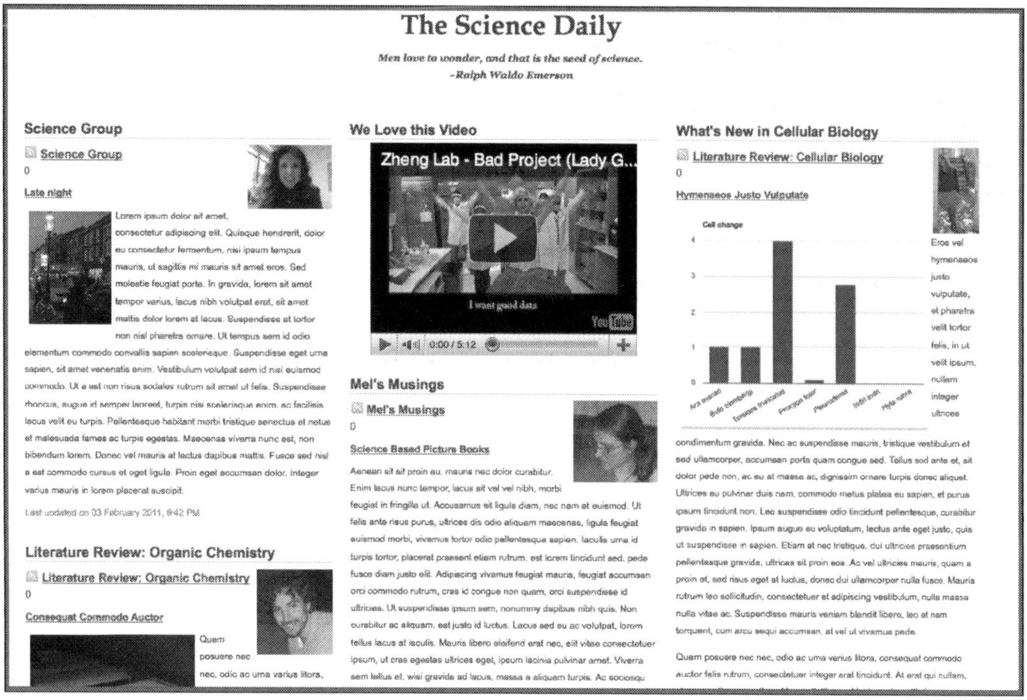

Getting ready

Create your group and add the members. If this is going to be a course group, change the role of members to tutors, otherwise they will not be able to create or edit pages.

How to do it...

One member (or admin) of the group will need to create the page.

1. Go to **groups** and then **My groups** in your portfolio.
2. You will see a list of the groups you belong to. Click on the group you want to work with.
3. You will be taken to the **group homepage**. At the top you will see several tabs. Select the **pages** tab.
3. Click on **Create Page**.
4. At this point, you do not need to add content to this page. Select **Next: Edit Title and Description.**
5. Give this page a title. **News** would be sufficient. It is actually the **Description** that will be used to create a header for your page.

6. To make a large and centered title for your journal, type the name of the journal in the **Page Description** field. For example, mine is called **The Science Daily**.
7. Highlight the title and set the **Font size** to **36**, set the **Format** to **Heading 1**.
8. Use the center-align icon in the HTML editing toolbar to center the text.
9. Using your *Enter* key, move down one line.
10. Type a subheading.
11. Highlight the subheading and set the **Format** to **Heading 5**. You can also italicize the text by using the **Italics** icon in the HTML editing toolbar.
12. Click on the **Save** button.
13. Select the tab **Share page**.
14. Set the **Access** to **Public**, by clicking the **Add** button next to **Public**.
15. Click on the **Save** button.

The next steps will need to be repeated by each individual member that will be contributing journal postings to this group page. This is written so that you can give these directions to the members of your group:

16. Go to the **Journals** section on the **Content** tab and select **Create Journal**.

> If you do not have this button, you will see a sentence similar to: **You have one journal. If you would like to start a second one, enable the multiple journals option on the account settings page**. Click on **Settings** in the upper-right corner of the page, and you will be taken to your personal settings. Under **General Settings**, you will see the option **Enable Multiple Journals**. Click the small box next to the option to enable multiple journals. Click **Save** and return to **Journals.** Now click **Create Journal**.

17. Give the journal a **Title** and a **Description** (the description is optional).
18. Click **Create Journal**. You will now see this new journal in your list of journals.
19. To add your first post, click the link **New Entry**.
20. Give this post a **Title** and, in the **Body**, write your first posting.
21. Select the option **Allow comments**, if it is not already selected.
22. Save the post.
23. To enable your posts to become part of the group's newspaper, you will need to put it into your own page first, and allow public access to your posts. To do this, go to the **pages** section of the **Portfolio** tab and select **Create Page**.
24. In the top row of tabs, select the tab labeled **Edit Layout**.
25. Select the option **1 column**, **Equal widths**.

26. Click on the **Save** button.
27. Next, on the second row of tabs, find and select the **Journal** tab. Click and drag the **Journal block** into your page.
28. Select the journal you've created to share on the group's News page (the journal you created in steps 1 – 3).
29. Click on the **Save** button.
30. Select the tab labeled **Edit Title and Description**.
31. Give this page a **Title** and a **Description**. It might seem redundant, but you can give this page the same title and description as the journal. We are going to create an RSS feed of this page. The **Title** and **Description** you provide will appear in the feed (in this case, the News page for your group). Note that this will also be a publically accessible journal.
32. Click on the **Save** button.

> In very simple terms, the RSS feed provides a way for fans of your journal to receive a notification when you add a new post. It also provides the title of the post and either a synopsis of the post or the entire text (this is determined by the settings in the reader's Feed aggregator). Only **pages** that have **Public Access** enabled will have RSS feed capability.

33. Select the tab labeled **Share page**.
34. Click the **Add** button next to **Public**.
35. Click on the **Save** button.
36. In the **pages** section, open the page you just created by clicking on the name of the page.
37. You will see a small orange icon next to the title of your journal. This icon is used to represent RSS feeds. You will see this icon on many web pages on the Internet. Clicking this icon will take you to the page that generates the feed for your journal. We will need the address of that feed in order to add your journal to the group's newspaper. Click on the little orange icon:

38. You will now be on the feed page for your journal. You will notice that readers have the option of getting this feed through a number of different aggregator including Google. If you don't understand feeds or what this means, you don't really need to worry about that at this point. For this recipe, you will need to copy the URL for this page (in the address bar) and then proceed to the next steps:

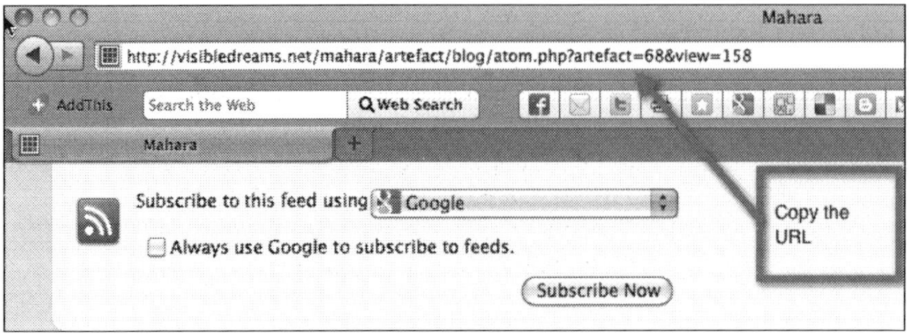

39. Now, we will add this journal to the news page for your group.
40. Select **groups** and then **My groups**.
41. Find your group and click on its name.
42. On the **group homepage**, click the tab for **pages**.
43. Find the Page for your group's Newspaper and select the small pencil icon to its right. The page will open in edit mode.
44. From the **External feeds** tab, click and drag the **External Feed** block into the page.
45. Paste the URL you copied in step 23 into the box labeled **Feed location**.
46. Set the **Items to show** to **1**.
47. Select **Show feed items in full**.
48. Click on the **Save** button. Your journal post will now appear in the page, as will your default profile icon.
49. Additional items can be added to this page to make it more interesting. In the example, members have added a YouTube video they all liked. When you're done, select the **Done** button.

How it works...

Whenever a member adds a new post to their journal, the new story will appear in the group's newspaper, replacing the previous post from that member. members do not need to go into the group page in order to update the content. The feeds ensure new content will appear on the news page. Readers will be able to subscribe to individual columnists, if they wish. Since comments are allowed, the contributors are able to receive feedback posted by readers.

There's more...

You may wish to create a multi-page newspaper, or add a YouTube video like the sample page. We'll now explore both of these options.

Creating a multiple-paged paper

If you have a large number of contributors, one page might not be enough. You can create multiple pages and a table of contents, so that you can accommodate a large number of contributors. To begin, decide how many columnists you'd like to feature on each page. This will largely depend on how long you'd like your page to be and how long each post will be (most likely you will not want more than 4-6 feeds on a page). Then, create a page for each group of columnists using the previous recipe. For example, if there are 24 members, you might create four pages with six journal feeds per page. Be sure to give each page a different title.

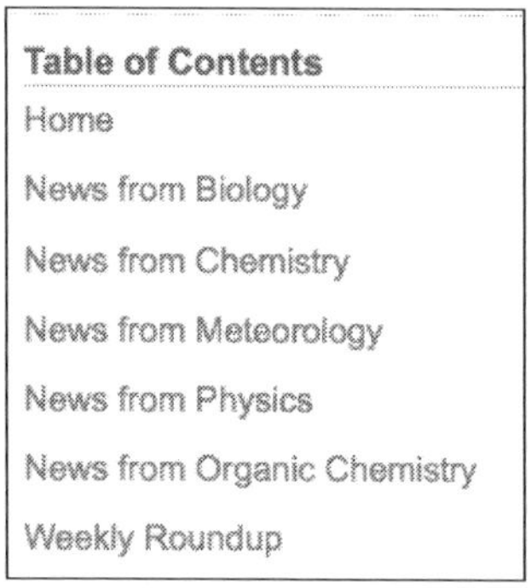

Here's how you build a Table of Contents and add it to your pages:

1. Open two windows or tabs in your browser—we will refer to these as "Window 1" and "Window 2" (we will be going back and forth between these windows/tabs). In both windows, go to your group's homepage, and then **pages**, to see a list of your group's pages.
2. We'll start in Window 2. In the list of pages, find the first page of your newspaper and click its title so that it opens in display mode (not edit mode).
3. Copy the URL for this page (it is in the address bar at the top of the window).
4. Now, go to Window 1.
5. In Window 1, find the first page for your newspaper and select the pencil icon to the right of it so you can open the page in edit mode.
6. From the **General** tab, click and drag a Text Box block into the page where you would like the Table of Contents to be located.
7. Change the **Block Title** to **Table of Contents**.

8. In the **Block Content** type `Home`
9. Highlight the text you just typed (`Home`) and click on the **Insert/edit link** icon on the HTML toolbar:

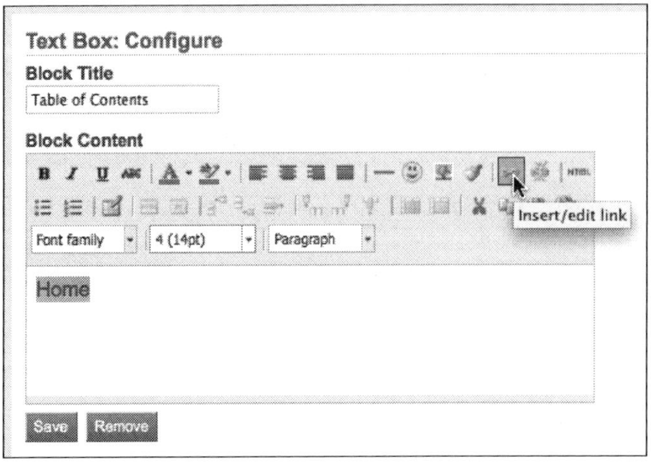

10. In the **Link URL** field, paste the URL you copied in step 3.
11. Set the **Target** to **Open link in the same window**
12. In the **Title**, type the title of the page (`Home`).
13. Click **Insert**. Do not save the textbox at this point, just leave it open in editing mode.
14. Go back to Window 2.
15. Click the **Back** button in your browser to go back to your list of pages.
16. Click and open the next page in your newspaper (as you did for the home page in step 2).
17. Copy the URL.
18. Go back to Window 1.
19. In the textbox block you currently have open, space down one line and type the next entry in your **Table of Contents**.
20. Repeat steps 9 – 13.
21. Repeat steps 14 – 20 until you have added all of the pages for your newspaper to the **Table of Contents**.
22. With the textbox block still open in edit mode, highlight the **Block contents** and copy (*Ctrl* + *C* on a PC; *Command* + *C* on a Mac).
23. Click **Save**.
24. Click **Done**.

25. You can remain in the current window for the rest of the steps. In your list of group pages, find the next page in your newspaper and select the pencil icon to the right to open the page in edit mode.
26. From the **General** tab, click and drag a **Text Box** block into the page where you would like to add the Table of Contents.
27. Change the **Block Title** to **Table of Contents**.
28. Click in the box for **Block Content** and paste (*Ctrl* + *V* on a PC; *command* + *V* on Mac). The text you copied in step 22 should now appear in this box.
29. Select **Save**.
30. Select **Done**.
31. Repeat steps 25 -30 until you have added the Table of Contents to all of the pages in the newspaper.

Adding a YouTube video

The top center of our paper had a YouTube video that course members particularly liked. Adding a YouTube video is extremely easy, and does not require you to copy any code from the YouTube site.

1. Go to YouTube (`http://www.youtube.com`) and select the video you would like to use.
2. Copy the URL (the address in the address bar).
3. Go to your group's homepage, then **pages**, and then select the pencil tool to the right of the page you wish to edit.
4. From the tab labeled **files, Images and video**, click and drag the **External Video block** into your page.
5. Delete the text in the **Block Title**, leaving it blank.
6. In the **Video URL** box, paste the URL you copied in step 2.
7. Leave the **Width** and **Height** at the default settings (you can always edit them later).
8. Click **Save**.

See also

- *A Daily Gazette* in *Chapter 2, Literature and Writing*
- *Adding an external blog to your profile page* in *Chapter 6, The Social Portfolio*

5

The Primary Education Portfolio

In this chapter, we will cover:

- Submitting and locking pages
- Using a student journal to help students learn how to write a research paper
- Progress reports and the transference of artifacts
- A simple template for very young students
- Creating and using a simple template
- A student portfolio of the primary education years
- A reading list (book reports)
- Using slideshow to create a book
- International project
- Creating a classroom page to share with families

Introduction

Every classroom is unique, as is every school. This chapter will offer some ideas that may not fit with what's available at your school, or maybe the way you teach a particular subject. The hope is, though, that the recipes can be adapted so that they do fit in your classroom. Where a journal is used for weekly spelling lists, you might see an idea for journaling a weekly math problem. Where a project on France is used, you may see a Science Fair project. Some of the recipes in this chapter require the teacher to create the page first as a template; some are designed to be created exclusively by the student. Some could be done either way. The goal of this chapter is to inspire you, to give you some possibilities you may not have thought of, and to make building ePortfolios fun for you and your students.

Submitting and locking pages

This is a basic recipe that can be used with nearly all of the other recipes in this chapter, if you choose. The primary focus of this chapter is the assessment of portfolios, that is, setting up a method for the submission of locked portfolios that you can easily access and assess.

The submission of pages can only be done through a course group, which is a certain type of group. (This is not the same as providing page access to a group). This method allows a teacher easy access to a page, while ensuring that the portfolio page will only be seen by teachers and tutors. And, it locks the page (we'll discuss this later). Because these features require the creation of a course group, this particular recipe could have been included in the chapter on groups. You may wish to review that chapter.

This recipe contains two parts: one that has been written for the instructor, and one for the students. Each has its own set of instructions.

How to do it...

For the instructor/teacher:

1. Go to the **My Groups** section on the **Group** tab.
2. Click the button to **Create Group**.
3. Provide a group **Name** and **Description**.
4. From the drop-down menu for **Group Type**, select **course group Controlled Membership**.

> Only administrators and staff can see the option to select a **course group**. If you do not have this capability, you will need to ask the administrator to add you to the list of s\taff in Mahara. Using a **Controlled Membership** as opposed to **Invite Only** means that you do not need to wait for students to accept your invitation. They are automatically added to the group when you add them. It also means that they cannot choose to leave the group.

5. If your school has created various **Group Categories**, select the one that is most appropriate for this group from the drop-down list for **Group Category**.
6. Make sure that **Publically viewable group** and **Shared page notifications** are *not* checked.
7. Click on **Save**.
8. You will be taken to the home page for the group. Click the tab labeled **Members**.

9. You will see a sentence that says something similar to **This is a controlled membership group. You can add users through their profile pages or add many users at once.** It is up to you how you would like to add the members of this group.
10. All members of this group will now have a drop-down menu at the bottom of their pages that will allow them to submit the page to this group.

For the student – submitting a page:

1. Go to the **pages** section on the **Portfolio** tab.
2. Click on the page you wish to submit.

> Students do not need to provide access to the teacher in order for the teacher to see the page. Submitting the page will automatically provide access.

3. At the bottom of the page, locate the drop-down menu that begins with **Submit this page to**. From the drop-down menu select the group you wish to submit this page to.
4. Click on the **Submit** button.
5. When you see the message asking if you are sure you want to submit this, click **Yes**.

For the instructor/teacher – accessing the page and releasing it:

1. Go to **My Groups** on the **Groups** tab and click on the **course group** to open it.
2. In the **pages** area on the group homepage, you will see a section labeled **pages submitted to this group**. pages that have been submitted will be listed there along with the name of the owner and the date and time of submission.
3. To view a page, click the title of the page.
4. At the bottom of the page you will find a statement that tells you to which groups the page was submitted, along with the date and time of the submission. Directly to the right of that is the **Release page** button. To release a view, click the button.

> Once the page is released, you will no longer be able to access it from the group homepage, unless the student provides access to the group. You will not be able to access it outside of the group, if the student has not provided you access.

How it works...

When a page is submitted to a course group it gets locked. This means that the student cannot add or delete blocks on the page, unless and until the teacher releases it. However, the student can edit the content of the blocks. For example, if the page contains a journal, a File folder, or a plan the student can continue adding items to them and the submitted page will include them—that is, it will automatically update to include those changes. You will want to keep this in mind when assessing portfolio using this method—in some ways it is a work in progress. There are methods for acquiring portfolios in a finished format—that students cannot edit at all. This would require exporting the portfolio. This is covered in other recipes listed further in this chapter.

There's more...

A little more about locked pages:

Managing classroom journaling

Locked pages can be particularly helpful when you would easily like to manage a classroom full of journaling students. Have each student create a journal and then put the journal in a page. Have the students submit their pages to your course group. At this point, the pages will be locked and accessible to you via the group page. As the students add entries to their Journals, the pages will automatically update. You can read and respond to entries on the locked pages.

Using a locked page to follow progress on a research project

Ask the students to create a plan for their research projects and drag their plan into a page. Once they submit the pages, you will be able to access the plans, provide feedback, and watch as your students progress through their projects, all from the home page of the course group.

See also

- *Chapter 4, Working with Groups*
- *Archiving portfolios* recipe in *Chapter 8, Certification and Accreditation Portfolio for Higher Education*

Using a student journal to help students learn how to write a research paper

The journal tool can be used for a large number of different purposes. In this recipe, we will see how the journal can be used to document the progress of a research paper, and teach students how to use resources without plagiarizing—something that students often have a difficult time with. As the students progress through the process, they will cite their sources and provide links to web resources from which they are gathering information. They will journal about the information they received from each source, in their own words.

As this is a journal, they will be able to receive feedback from the teacher on each post. This will help guide the process even further, and provide an excellent teaching tool. The completed project will be a collection of very good notes from which they can write the first draft of their research paper.

This recipe will familiarize the reader with the journal tool.

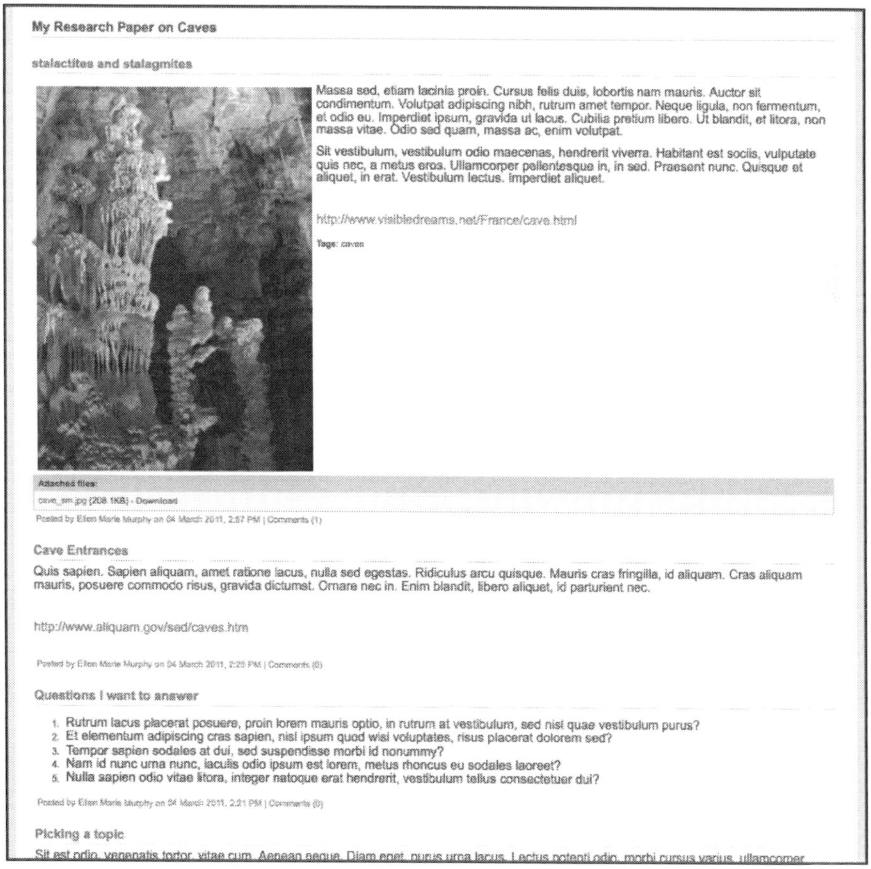

Getting ready

Students will need an outline of the required steps and the due dates for each. It is assumed that at the time of beginning this paper, they would not have chosen a topic. You will also need to create a course group and add your students. (See the recipe *Submitting and locking pages* in this chapter). The following instructions are written for the students.

How to do it...

We will first create the journal and add it to a page:

1. Click the **Content** tab and then **Journals**.
2. Click the button **Create Journal**.

> If you do not have the button allowing you to create a journal, you will need to change the settings in your account to allow multiple Journals. Click the **Settings** link in the upper-right corner of the page. In the **General Account Options** section, you will see an item labeled **Enable Multiple Journals**. Put a checkmark next to that item by clicking in the little box next to it. Save.

3. In the **Title** field type `My Research Paper` (this title can be changed once the topic has been chosen).
4. A **Description** is optional; put the grade level in the field for **Tags** (additional tags can be added later).

> **Tags** are key words that facilitate sorting and searching the portfolio. Each new tag is added to the **Tags** area that appears on the right-hand side of the **Content** and **Portfolio** sections in the student's portfolio. The more frequently a particular tag is associated with artifacts, the larger the tag becomes in the tag cloud.

5. Click **Create Journal**. This will take you back to the **Journals** area where you will see your list of Journals. This new journal should appear there.
6. Now, click the **Portfolio** tab and **pages**.
7. Click **Create page**.
8. Click the **Edit Layout** tab.
9. Select **1 column, Equal widths** by clicking the small bubble above that option.
10. Click on **Save**.

11. From the **Journals** tab click and drag a **journal** block into an area beneath **Themes**.
12. Leave the **Block Title** empty. This block will take the name of the journal.
13. In the section labeled **journal**, click in the small bubble next to **My Research Paper**.
14. In the field for **Entries per page** type `10`.
15. Skip over the section **More options**.
16. Click on **Save**.
17. Click the tab labeled **Edit Title and Description**.
18. In the **page Title** field type your name and `Research Paper` (for example, Keller's Research Paper).
19. You can leave the **Description** blank. You can add to that later, after you've chosen your topic.
20. In the **Tags** field type your grade level. Again, we can add to this field later.
21. Check the **Name display format** to ensure your full name is the name that appears in that field. If not, choose your proper name from the drop-down menu.
22. Click on **Save**.
23. Click the tab **Display page**.
24. At the bottom of the page, you will see a small drop-down menu and a button labeled **Submit**. From the drop-down menu find the group that you need to submit this page to. Click on **Submit**. Click on **Yes**.
25. Click **Done**.

Now you are ready to add your first post. Your posts will automatically update the page you submitted in steps 24 and 25. Your teacher will be able to follow your progress, and provide feedback as you go along:

26. Go to the **Content** area of your portfolio and click the tab for **Journals**.
27. Click the **New Entry** button next to your **Research Paper** journal.
28. Each post will need a title. In the **Title** field type `Choosing my topic`.
29. Click inside the box labeled **body** and begin typing your first post. You can use the HTML toolbar at the top of the box to help you make this post look the way you want it to. The first entry will be the topics you are considering for your research paper and your thoughts about each. If you have decided on your topic, write why you chose that topic.
30. When you have finished typing your first post, type the name of your topic in the field labeled **Tags**. If you are not sure about your topic, leave it blank.
31. Make sure **Allow comments** is checked.
32. Click **Save entry**.

In the second post, you will list the questions your research paper will answer:

33. Repeat steps 26-28, but this time the Title field should say **Questions I want to answer**.
34. Click the icon in the HTML toolbar that allows numbered bullets. This will put **1.** and your cursor inside the **body**:

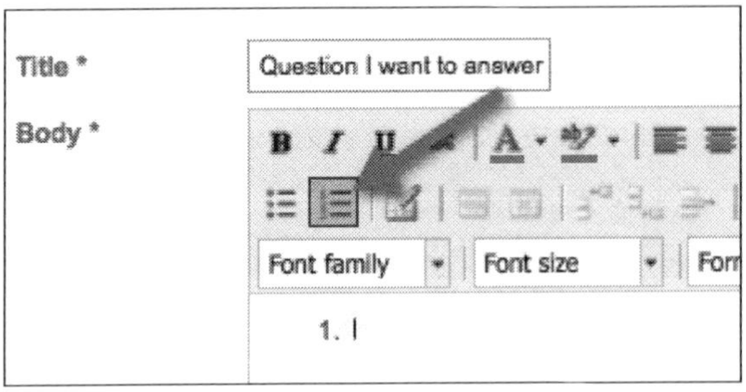

35. Type your first question and then click the *Enter* key on your keyboard. You are ready for your next question.
36. Repeat step 35 until you've added all of the questions you wish to list.
37. Click on **Save entry**.
38. Each of the remaining entries will be summaries of what was learned from a particular source. The **Title** of each post should be the main topic of the post. The body will contain the summary, and the citation. If the source was taken from the Web, the URL should be included. Mahara will automatically make the link live, if it is typed in the proper format (for example, http://www.somewhere.com). `http://www.somewhere.com`. All sources should use the format required by the teacher. The posts can include images and diagrams that will be included in the final paper.

How it works...

The pages submitted by the students, will be accessible by the teacher on the homepage of the group. Only the teacher will be able to see these pages. As the students add entries to their Journals, the pages will automatically display them. The teacher can follow the progress of the students, and provide feedback. Students will receive notification when a teacher leaves feedback on the page.

Feedback can be quite detailed and include file attachments, hyperlinks, embedded images, and more.

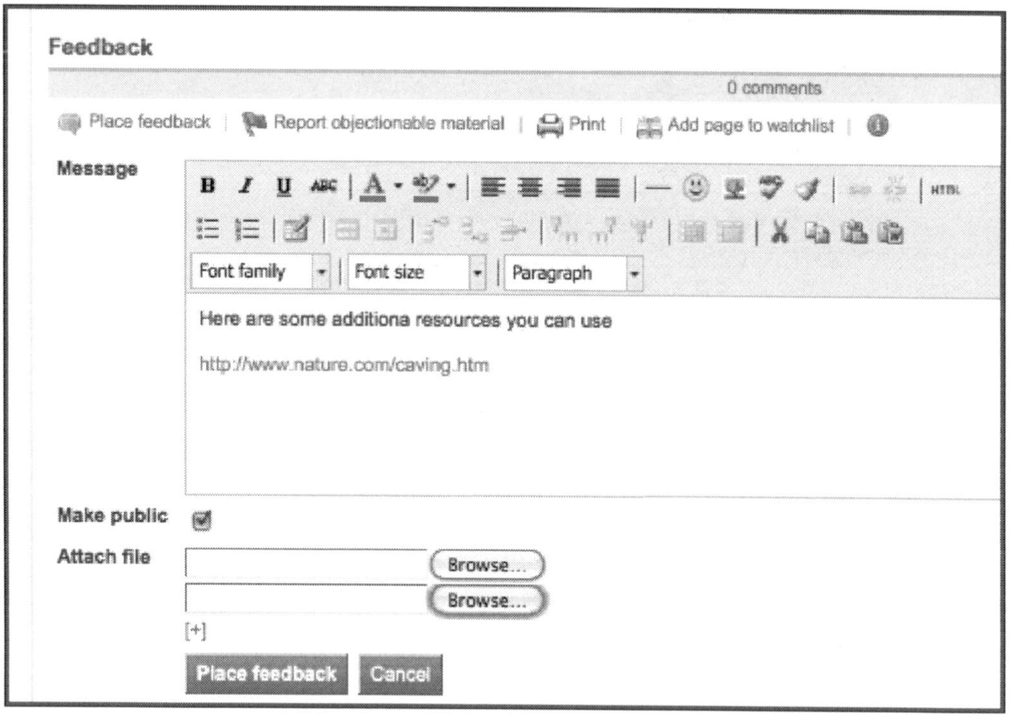

Students can be asked to provide copies of the resources, if the teacher feels it would be beneficial. To do so, a student would attach the file to the journal post by clicking the **Attach file** button underneath it.

When the Journals are complete, the students will have a fairly good beginning to their first drafts, if not the first drafts themselves.

There's more...

The following points provide some ideas for much more completed drafts.

Getting and embedding images from the Web

Since this is a research paper, you will most likely need to use images from sources on the Web. Keep in mind that you must cite the source of your image the same way you would if you were using someone else's words:

1. Put the cursor on the image you wish to use and click the right mouse button (PC), or (on a Mac) hold the *control* key down and click.

2. From the menu that opens, select **Copy Image Location**:

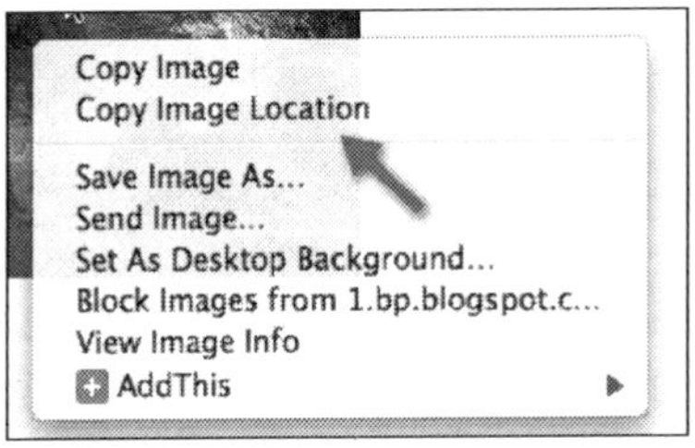

3. If the post you wish to add this to is not already open, let's open it by going to Journals in the **Content** section and clicking on the title of the journal.
4. Find the post you wish to add this to, and click the **small pencil tool** in the upper right-hand corner.
5. Put your cursor into the **body,** at the very start of your post.
6. Click the small tree icon in the HTML toolbar. This will open a window labeled **Insert image**.
7. Click in the field labeled **Image URL** and paste the **Image location** you copied in step 2.
8. In the field labeled **Description**, type a one or two word description of the image (this is so that individuals who cannot display the image, will know that there is one there and what it is an image of).
9. From the **Alignment** drop-down menu, select either **Right** or **Left**. This will put the image to either the left-hand side of your post or the right-hand side, and it will allow the text to flow around it.
10. You can skip the **Dimensions**, as the program will use the original dimensions of the image.
11. You can skip the **Border**.
12. In the fields for **Vertical** and **Horizontal space**, type `5`. This will put five pixels of whitespace around the image, so that the text is not right up against it.
13. Click on **Insert**.

Writing the first draft from the notes by using a page to rearrange paragraphs

Using feedback from your teacher, and your own reading of your journal, edit your journal entries, so that each post is written with complete sentences.

1. Go to the **Content** area of your portfolio and click the tab for **Journals**.
2. Click the title of your **journal** in order to open it.
3. To edit a particular post, click the small pencil in the upper right-hand corner of the post.

4. Change the **Title** of each post to the first sentence in the post. To do that highlight the first sentence; using *Ctrl* + *X* on a PC or *command* + *X* on a Mac, cut the first sentence from the body of the post.
5. Click in the field for the **Title**, highlight the text already in the field, then hold down *Ctrl* + *V* (on a Mac the keys are *command* + *V).*
6. Make the changes you wish, and then click on **Save entry**.
7. Continue editing posts, by repeating steps 3 and 4, until you have complete sentences, have added any additional information you needed to, and have deleted any irrelevant information. Now it's time to rearrange the information into paragraphs and a rough draft.
8. Click the **Portfolio** tab and then **pages**.
9. Click the button **Create page**.
10. Click the **Edit Layout** tab.
11. Select **1 column, Equal widths** by clicking the small bubble above that option.
12. Click on **Save**.
13. From the **Journals** tab click and drag a **journal Entry** block into the area beneath **Themes**.
14. Leave the **Block Title** empty.
15. Click the bubble next to the post you think should be the first in your paper.
16. Click **Save**.
17. Repeat steps 13-15, dragging and dropping posts into your page.
18. Once you have all the posts—you think you will be using—in your page, you can begin rearranging them. Simply move your mouse up to the top of the post you wish to move, until you see a small hand appear. Click and hold down your mouse button while you drag the post to where you wish to move it. Release the mouse button and the post will drop into the new location.

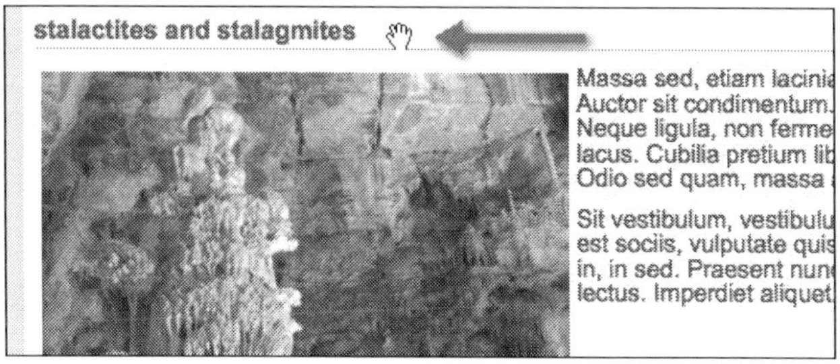

19. When you have dragged the posts into the order that you wish, click the **Display page** tab.
20. Find your group in the drop-down menu at the bottom of the page and click the **Submit** button.
21. Click on **Yes**.

Your teacher can now leave you feedback regarding this first draft. If you need to move posts after you've submitted your page, your teacher will need to release the page. When the final draft is ready to become your final paper, you can copy and paste from the page into the document for your final draft, or you can print the page as a PDF.

See also

- *Chapter 4, Working with Groups*
- *Journaling a project from start to finish* recipe in *Chapter 1, Mahara for the Visual Arts*

Progress reports and the transference of artifacts

Students do not need to save all of their artifacts themselves in order to have them in their portfolio. Teachers can create a page for each student that can contain a number of artifacts including a journal, which can later be copied into the student's own portfolio for permanent keeping. All of the files associated with that page will come over to the student's portfolio. This allows the teacher to do some of the building for the student. In this recipe, we will look at how that works in the context of creating progress reports that demonstrate how a particular student meets the grade level standards.

In this recipe, we will create a page that contains a folder of a particular student's work, a journal for reporting on the student's progress which will include related documentation, media including a picture of the student, and finally a link to the student's own portfolio. The entire page, and all of the items associated with it, will transfer to the student's own portfolio when the page is copied at the end of the year. This will allow the teacher to delete the artifacts and the page from his/her own personal portfolio, while allowing the student to keep them as part of his/her permanent portfolio. The page and artifacts can be archived, if a permanent record needs to be maintained, by exporting the page (all associated files will come with it) as an HTML site.

The page can also be printed and mailed home if need be, or parents can print it at home themselves.

The following screenshot is an example of what this will look like:

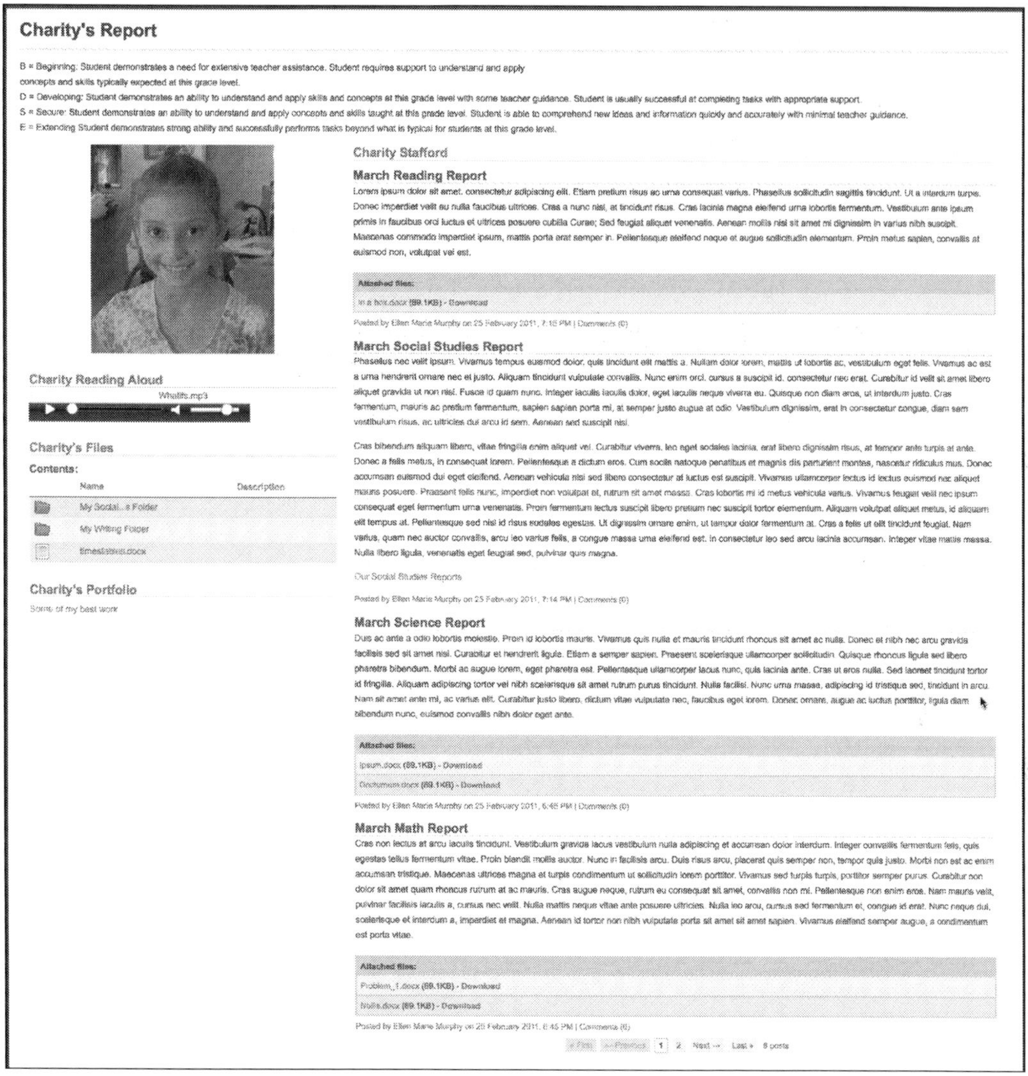

Getting ready

You will need to create a journal for each student, and a file folder for each student as well, in which to store artifacts of work. The Journals and file folders will need to be created in your personal portfolio (they will not remain there permanently). The title of each should contain the student's name.

It is assumed that students will also have their own grade-level presentation portfolio page that they will be working on from time to time. Access to this page should be set to Secret URL. You will need that URL in this recipe to provide a direct link to the student's portfolio page, so that parents can access it from the report.

The report created by the teacher includes an assessment of the student's reading level and the ability to read aloud. You will want to make a recording of each student reading aloud and upload it to the file folders you created for the students.

Finally, since we will be adding a photo of each student to his/her report, you will need to take a picture of each student and upload it to the folders you created for the students, or have access to photos of the students from some other source. You may need to obtain permission from parents to use the student's photos, but the reports will only be accessible to individuals who have been given the Secret URL.

How to do it...

We will begin with the journaling aspect. The journal will contain a post for each subject in each term. So if, for example, the school has only two terms: Midterm, and Final, and it has five subjects you will be writing narratives for: Reading, Writing, Mathematics, Science, and Social Studies, then you will be writing five posts for each term. The title of the posts should reflect the term and the subject, for example: Midterm Reading Report, Midterm Writing Report, and so on. Any documents you attach to these narratives will become part of the student's portfolio when the student copies the page at the end of the school year.

To begin building the page:

1. Select the **Portfolio** tab, and then the tab labeled **pages**.
2. Click on **Create page**.
3. On the top level of tabs, click the tab labeled **Edit Layout**.
4. Select the option for **2 columns, larger right column**.
5. Click on **Save**.
6. From the **journal** tab, click and drag the journal block into the right column of your page.
7. Leave the **Block Title** empty.
8. Select the journal you've created for this student.
9. In the small box for **Entries per page**, type the number of *subjects* you will be journaling on for each semester. So, if there are five subjects (Reading, Writing, Math, Social Studies, and Science), type `5`.

> When an entire journal is displayed in a page, and the number of entries is more than the number of entries per page, the page will automatically display the most recent postings and create navigation that will allow readers to view older journal entries. In the case of this report, then, the final report will display the final journal narratives, but the navigation area will allow parents to see all of the reports for the year. One page can contain an entire year's worth of reports.

10. Click the link labeled **More options** to expand that area.
11. From the drop-down menu for **Block copy permission**, select **Others will get their own copy of your journal**.

> The option **Others will get their own copy of your journal** means that when someone copies the page, they will get a copy of your entire journal, as it is at the time they copy it. The copied journal will become part of their portfolio. If you delete or update the journal, it will not affect the copy in their portfolio.

12. Click on **Save**.

We'll build the left column from the bottom up. We will begin with providing a link to the preselected page in the student's own portfolio:

13. From the **General** tab, click and drag a **Text Box** block into the left-hand column of your page.
14. In the field for **Block Title** add a title that indicates this area provides a link, or links, to the student's own portfolio pages.
15. In the **Block Content** area type `Some of my best work`.
16. Highlight the text you just typed and select the **Insert/edit link** icon in the HTML toolbar:

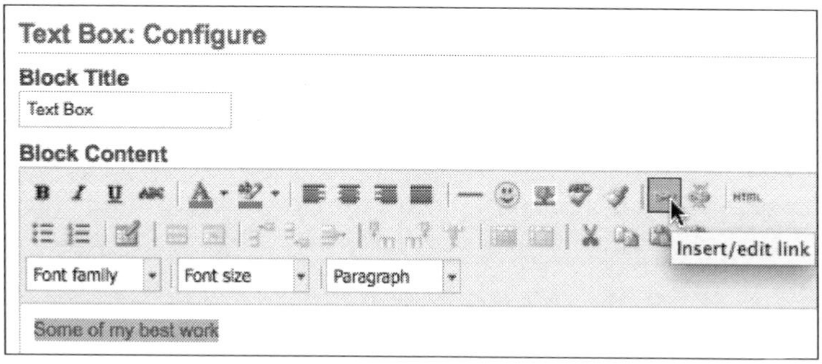

17. In the field for **Link URL**, paste the Secret URL to the student's page.
18. From the **Target** drop-down menu, select **Open link in a new window**.
19. In the **Title** field, type the student's name and then `portfolio`.

> The text in the title field appears when an individual holds his/her cursor over the link.

20. Click on **Insert**.
21. Click on **Save**.
22. From the **Files, images and video** tab, click and drag the **A Folder** block into the left-hand column.
23. Leave the **Block Title** empty.
24. Click the **Select** button next to the folder you created for this student's documents.
25. Click on **Save**.
26. From the **Files, images and video** tab, click and drag the **Embedded Media** block into the left-hand column.
27. Change the **Block Title** to **Reading Aloud** and add the student's name.
28. In the list of folders, find this student's folder and click on the folder to open it.
29. Click the **Select** button next to the audio recording.
30. You can leave the options for **Width** and **Height** blank, as the default settings for the audio player are generally sufficient.
31. Click on **Save**.
32. From the **Files, images and video** tab, click and drag the **An Image** block into the left-hand column.
33. Select the appropriate tab from **My Files**, **Group Files**, and **Site Files**, in order to go to the area where the student pictures were stored, and click the **Select** button next to the image of this student.
34. Delete the text in the **Block Title**, leaving it empty.
35. Click the option to **Show description** (if no description was added to the image, none will be displayed).
36. In the box for **Width**, type `250` (this will automatically and proportionately resize the image to fit a width of 250 pixels).
37. Click on **Save**.
38. On the menu of tabs at the top of the page, select **Edit Title and Description**.
39. In the field for the **page Title**, type the student's name and `Report`.
40. In the field for **Description**, type any pertinent information regarding grading. For example, B=beginning, D=developing, S=secure, E=extending.

41. **Name display format**, should show your professional name.
42. Click on **Save**.
43. From the top-level tabs, select **Share page**.
44. A list of all your **Collections** and **pages** will appear; the page you are currently working on will be selected by default.
45. In the area labeled **Share with**, click the **Add** button next to **Secret URL**.
46. In the **Access Date/Time** area add the beginning and ending dates for the viewing of this report, by adding them in the areas labeled **From:** and **To:**. It is a good idea not to leave the page open indefinitely.
47. Open the **Advance Options** by clicking the link to do so, and make sure that there is a checkmark next to **Allow Comments**. Do *not* select the option to allow copying. You will do this at the end of the year, when students will be allowed to copy the final reports to their permanent portfolios.
48. Click on **Save**.

To export the page and all associated content:

49. Click on the **Portfolio** tab and then the **Export** tab.
50. In the options under **Choose an export format**, select **Standalone HTML website**.
51. In the options under **What do you want to export?**, select **Just some of my pages**.
52. Select the page for a particular student (it is a good idea to export each student's report separately, so that it can be stored as part of their permanent record).
53. Click to **Generate export**.
54. When the export has finished generating, a window will open asking you whether you wish to **Open** or **Save** the file. Select the option to **Save**. You may want to change the name of the file so that it can easily be found later. Select a location. **Save**. The entire page and all associated files will be saved in a compressed/packaged format that contains the report as its own website.

How it works...

As you add the entries for this student in your journal, the Report page will automatically display the latest posts. A navigation bar will be added to the page, which will provide access to the previous entries. Setting the display number to the number of subjects you will be commenting on, will display an entire semester's worth of posts with one click.

Parents will be able to comment on each post as well as the overall report. They can also print the entire report and/or save the report as a PDF.

> Apple computers come with the ability to print a webpage or document to `.pdf` format. For those who use PCs, there are a number of free programs that can be downloaded and used for printing (or saving) in the `.pdf` format; for example, PDF printer for Windows 7 `http://download.cnet.com/PDF-Printer-for-Windows-7/3000-18497_4-10964932.html`.

After the *final report* has been written, go back to the access settings for the page and choose to **Allow copying**. Also give the student access to the page. The student can go to **pages** in the **Portfolio** section of their own Mahara account and click the button to **Copy a page**. They will see this page in the list of pages they can copy. When they select to copy this page, not only will the page be added to their pages, but they will also get a copy of the journal and all artifacts associated with the page. The artifacts will be found in the **Files** section of the student's portfolio, in a folder labeled **viewfiles**.

Once the page has been copied, and you have exported the page, you can delete the page and all associated documents, including the journal, from your portfolio. This will not delete them from the student's portfolio.

See also

- *Language acquisition journal* recipe in *Chapter 2, Literature and Writing*
- *Templates for meeting teacher certification standards* recipe in *Chapter 8, Certification and Accreditation Portfolio for Higher Education*
- *Archiving portfolios* recipe in *Chapter 8, Certification and Accreditation Portfolio for Higher Education*

A simple template for very young students

Kindergarten is not too early to introduce students to ePortfolios. At this stage though, they do need to be kept simple. This Kindergarten page has two artifacts: a journal and a video recording of the student answering the question **What do I want to be when I grow up?** (thank you Danielle Bolduc of Oyster River Middle School in New Hampshire for this idea). Keep in mind that the teacher will initially build this with the expectation that the student will copy the page. This will bring both the video and a journal for Kindergarten journaling into the student's own portfolio.

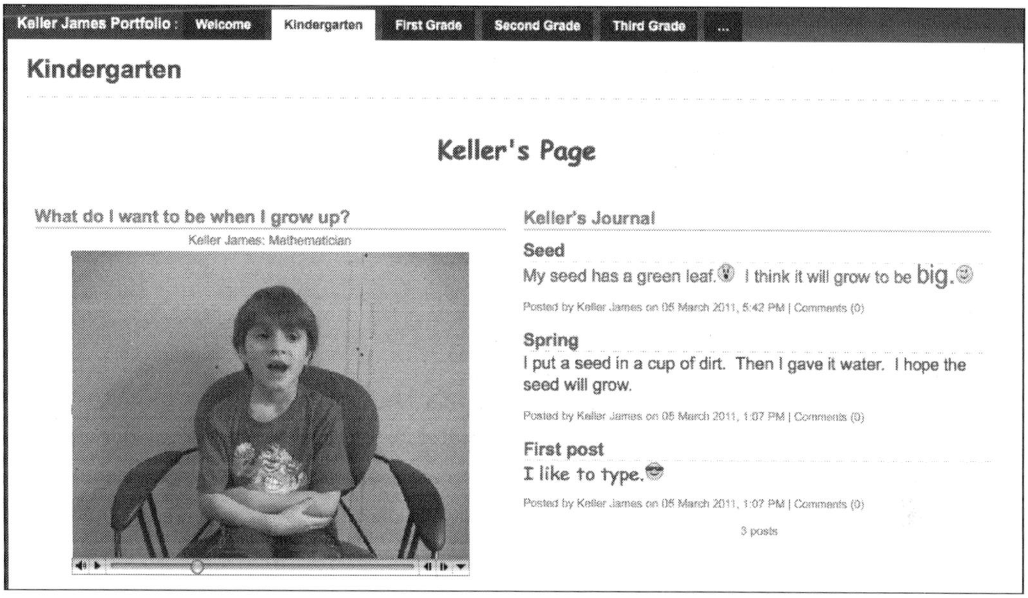

Getting ready

This recipe requires a video recording of the student answering the question **What do I want to be when I grow up?** Since the video will be transferred to the student's own portfolio after copying, it does not need to take up permanent space in your portfolio. If space is an issue, it can be saved to site files and deleted once the student copies the page.

> Mahara will display nearly all video formats with no difficulty. If you have trouble displaying a video, check to make sure the System Administrator has enabled the plugin for the file format you are using. It is best to avoid formats like Windows Media, which require special players.

Students will need to have **Multiple Journals** enabled in their settings.

How to do it...

1. Click the **Content** tab, the **Journals** subtab, and then the button labeled **Create Journal**.
2. In the **Title** field type `Kindergarten journal`.
3. The **Description** is optional.
4. In the field for **Tags**, type `Kindergarten`.
5. Click **Create Journal**. You do not need to post anything in the journal.

6. Go to the **pages** section in the **Portfolio** tab.
7. Click **Create page**.
8. Click the tab **Edit Layout**.
9. Select **2 columns, Equal widths.**
10. Click on **Save**.
11. From the **Files, images and video** tab, click and drag the **Embedded Media** block down into the left-hand side of the page (below the drop-down: **Theme**).
12. Change the **Block Title** to `What do I want to be when I grow up?`.
13. In the **Media** section, you will see three tabs: **My Files**, **Group Files**, and **Site Files**. Click on the tab for the appropriate file area (where you uploaded the video files). Browse for this student's video and click the **Select** button next to it.
14. In the field for **Width**, type `400`. You do not need to add the **Height** as Mahara will automatically size the video.
15. Click on **Save**.
16. From the **Journals** tab, click and drag a **journal** block into the right-hand side of the page.
17. In the **Block Title** field put the student's name and the word journal (for example, Keller's journal).
18. In the list of **Journals**, click the bubble next to **Kindergarten journal**.
19. Leave the **Posts per page** at **5**.
20. In the **More options** area, select **Others will get their own copy of your journal** from the drop-down menu for **Block copy permission**.
21. Click on **Save**.
22. Click the tab labeled **Edit Title and Description**.
23. In the **page Title** field, type `Kindergarten`.
24. In the **Description** type the student's name and the word `page`. Highlight the text and center it using the center-align icon on the HTML toolbar. Using the drop-down for Font family, change the font to Comic Sans. Using the drop-down for Style (it has the word Paragraph in the drop-down), choose Heading 1.
25. Click on **Save**.
26. Click the tab labeled **Share page**.
27. You will see that this page is selected by default—there will be a checkmark next to it.
28. Click on **Share with other users and groups** to expand the menu.
29. Find the student in the list of users. To facilitate this, type either the student's first or last name in the **Search** box and click the icon that looks like a small magnifying glass. Click the **Add** button next to the student's name:

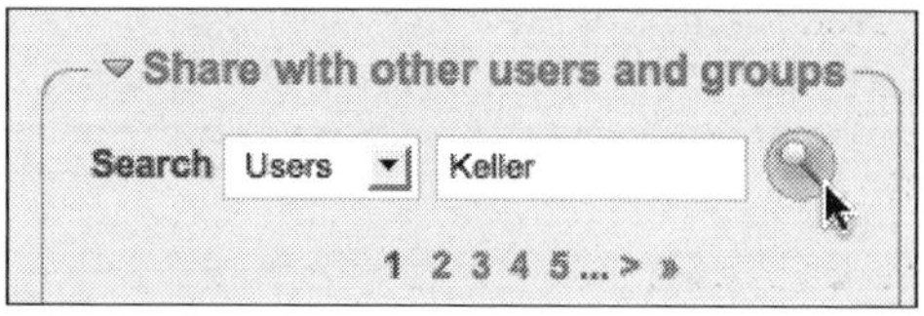

30. Click the **Advanced Options** link to expand the menu.
31. The option **Allow comments** should be checked by default; put an additional checkmark next to the option **Allow copying**:

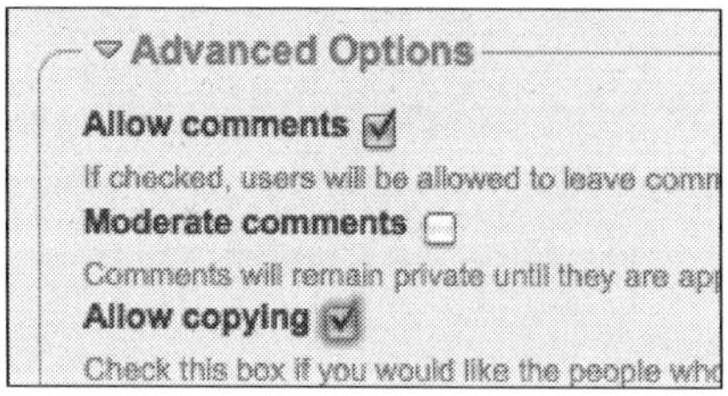

32. Click on **Save**.
33. Repeat steps 6-32 for each student.

How it works...

Each student will need to copy this page. After they have copied the page, they will have a new journal called Kindergarten journal in their list of journals (each student will have their own). Each student will have a copy of their video in the files area of their portfolio, and they will have a page called **Copy of Kindergarten**. They do not need to do anything with the page at this point. As they post to their journal, the posts will automatically show on their page.

See also

- *Progress reports and transference of artifacts* recipe
- *Creating and using a simple grade level template* recipe
- *Templates for meeting teacher certification standards* recipe in *Chapter 8, Certification and Accreditation Portfolio for Higher Education*

Creating and using a simple template

In this recipe, we will create a very simple template that can be used in the primary grades for showcasing student work. It is not meant to be a complex standards-based template. Rather, it is a template that students should be able to manage pretty much on their own. The recipe includes a journal for reflections and one for "My Weekly Spelling Lists". These journals will automatically be created in the student's portfolio when the template is copied. The assumption is that students will have at least some time each week in a computer lab when they can type their spelling words and create sentences for them. Perhaps this is something students could even work on at home.

The following screenshot is an example of the template:

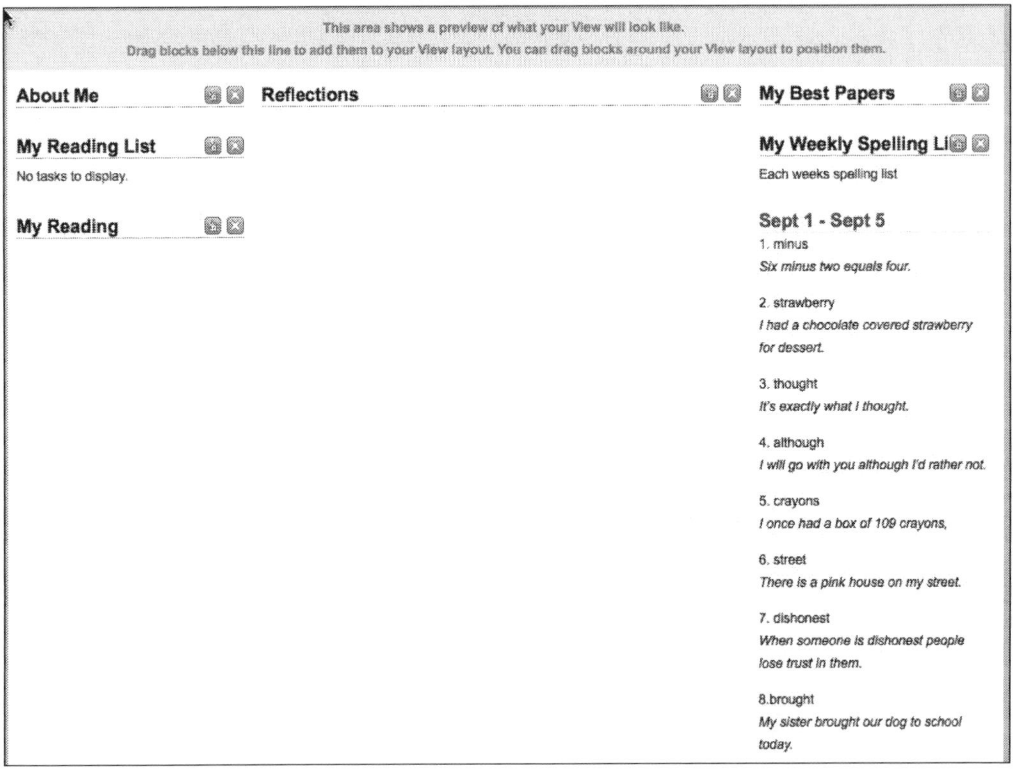

Getting ready

Students will need to go to the plans section in the Content area of their portfolio and create a plan titled "My Reading List". Students will use the list to keep book reports. They will also need to create a folder in the Files section of their Content area. It is a good idea to have them label this folder with the grade level, as they will be collecting a good number of file folders in the years ahead.

You will need to create a journal titled `My Reflections`. Do not add postings to this journal.

You will also need to create a journal titled `My Weekly Spelling Lists`. Add the first entry simply as an example for students—to show them what's expected of them each week. The first entry should have a title that indicates the week either by date or by sequence; and the body should contain a list of words with sentences that show how the word is used.

Students will need to have **Multiple Journals** enabled in their settings.

How to do it...

1. On the **Portfolio** tab, select the subtab **pages** and click the button labeled **Create page**.
2. Select the **Edit Layout** tab from the menu of tabs at the top of the page.
3. Select **3 columns, Larger center column**.
4. Click on **Save**.
5. From the **Files, images and video** tab, click and drag an **Embedded Media** block to the left-hand column (this will be used for an audio or video recording).
6. Change the **Block Title** to **My Reading**.
7. Set the **Width** to `200`.
8. Click on **Save**.
9. From the **General** tab, click and drag a **Your plans** block to the top of the left-hand column, above the block you added in step 6.
10. Change the **Block Title** to `My Reading List`.
11. Click on **Save**.
12. From the **Profile** tab, click and drag a **Profile Information** block to the top left-hand column.
13. Change the **Block Title** to `About Me`.
14. Click on **Save**.
15. From the **Journals** tab, click and drag a **journal** block to the right-hand column.
16. You do not need to put anything in the **Block Title** as it will take the name of the journal.

17. Click in the bubble next to the journal you created for **My Weekly Spelling Lists**.
18. Change the **Posts per page** to `1`.
19. In the **More options** area, select **Others will get their own copy of your blog** from the drop-down menu for **Block copy permission**.
20. Click on **Save**.
21. From the **Files, images and video** tab, click and drag the **A Folder** block to the top of the right-hand column.
22. Change the **Block Title** to **My Best Papers**.
23. Click on **Save**.
24. From the **Journals** tab, click and drag a journal block to the center column.
25. You do not need to put anything in the **Block Title** as it will use the title of the journal.
26. Select the **My Reflections** blog you created by clicking in the bubble next to it.
27. Change the number of **Posts per page** to **3**. (The number can be set to anything you feel is appropriate).
28. In the **More options** area, select **Others will get their own copy of your blog** from the drop-down menu for **Block copy permission**.
29. Click on **Save**.
30. Click the tab for **Edit Title and Description**.
31. In the **page Title** field, provide a title that indicates the grade level (for example, My Third Grade Portfolio page). You can enter a description and/or tags, but it is not required.
32. Make sure the display name is what you'd like to appear in the student's list of copiable views.
33. Click on **Save**.
34. Click on the tab **Share page**.
35. You will see a list of all your **Collections** and **pages**. By default, there should be a checkmark next to this page. You will need to provide access to each student. If you have a class group of which they are members, you can simply provide access by clicking the **Add** button next to the group.
36. If you do not have a class group, you will need to provide individual access. To do this, click the option **Share with other users and groups** to expand your options. You can use the search box to search for students. Click the **Add** button next to each of your students as you find them.

37. When you have finished providing **Access**, you will need to set a few more options. Click the link for **Advanced Options**. You should see a checkmark next to **Allow comments**. You can leave that checked. Put a checkmark next to **Allow copying**.
38. Click on **Save**.
39. Have students copy the view by going to the **pages** tab in the **Portfolio** section, and click the button to **Copy a page**.
40. A list of pages they can copy will appear. Have students locate the page and click the **Copy page** button next to it.
41. Have students click the tab to edit the **Title and Description**.
42. Have students delete the words **Copy of** from the title.
43. Click on **Save**.
44. Click on **Done**.

Students now have a copy of the view and the two Journals.

How it works...

Students will find their new Journals in the **Journals** section of the **Content** area. They can add postings by clicking the **New Entry** button next to the journal. Every time they add a new post, the new post will automatically be displayed in their page. When they have more posts than the display number set for that particular journal block, Mahara will create a navigation menu at the bottom of the block so that previous posts can be accessed. The most recent posts will always be displayed in the page. Students do not need to go to the page to add the journal content.

Students are often asked to upload an artifact to their portfolio and then add a reflection about the piece. Journals are a good way to do this, because the journal entries become a permanent part of the student's portfolio. While adding content to Text Boxes may serve a similar purpose—that is, reflection—they are not artifacts and consequently cannot be repurposed. They are not stored in the Content area of the portfolio. When the page that contains them is deleted, the content in the textbox is also deleted. This is not true of artifacts. When a page that contains a specific artifact is deleted, the artifact is unaffected.

To configure the other blocks, the students will need to go the **pages** section of their **Portfolio** and select the **Edit Content and Layout** icon next to the page for this recipe:

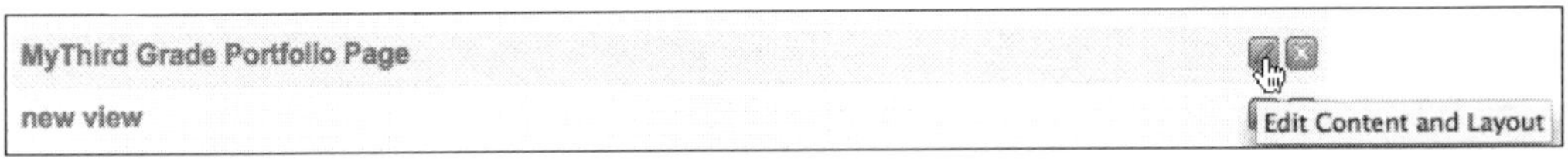

The page will open in the editing view. The title of each block will contain two icons: one deletes the block; the other configures the block. Let's configure the **My Best Papers** block first. Students should click the icon for **Configure "My Best Papers" block**. This will open a window containing a list of their folders. They should click the **Select** button next to the folder for their work and then click **Save**. This block will now automatically display any content added to this folder:

To add information about themselves, students should select the configure icon for the block we titled **About Me**. Their profile content options will open from which they can select to display their first name, last name, a profile icon if they have one, and any information they would like to add in the **Introduction Text** box. Unlike the folder and journals, this is static content.

To point the **Reading List** block to the correct plan, students will select the icon to configure this block. A list of their plans will open. They should click the bubble next to the plan titled **My Reading List**. This block will automatically update as they add new books to the plan.

Finally we will add a media file—either a prerecorded audio recording, or a prerecorded video. Again, students will click the configure icon. They will see a list of files and folders that are contained in the **Content** area of their portfolio. They will either need to click the **Select** button next to the media they will embed here or, if they have not already done so, they will need to upload the media file. The **Width** should be set to 250. The **Height** should automatically adjust itself. **Save**. This is static content.

When the blocks have all been configured, students should select **Done**.

The following screenshot is an example of a complete page created using the template:

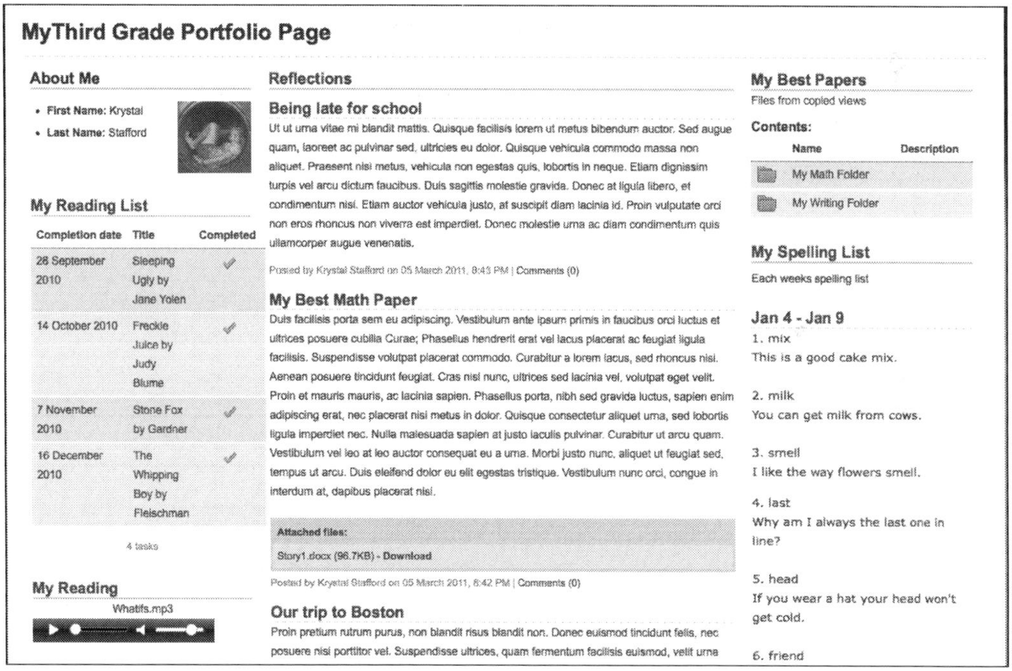

There's more...

During the course of the school year, students may use Mahara for any number of projects. Links to these pages and collections can be added to this page using the Navigation block, which we will discuss next:

Adding a Navigation block for links to other pages in the student's portfolio

If the student has created or will be creating other pages as they go through the school year, they will want to provide access to those pages from this Grade Level page. Students will need to first create a collection and add each of those additional pages to it. A single page can be its own collection.

1. To create a Collection, students will need to click the **Collections** tab in the **Portfolio** section, and then the button labeled **New Collection**.
2. They will need to provide a **Collection name**. The **Description** is optional. For now, let's leave it blank.
3. The small box under **page navigation bar** should be checked.
4. Click the button **Next: Edit Collection pages**.
5. The list of available pages will appear in an area labeled **Add pages to collection**.

> pages that are already part of a collection will not show up in the list. If the page we are currently working on (the page created by the Grade Level Template) is later going to be part of its own collection of pages (such as in the *A student portfolio of the primary education years* recipe, do not add it to the collection we are currently creating).

6. The student should click in the small boxes next to each of the pages that need to be added to this collection, and click the button **Add pages**.
7. The pages can be reordered using the small arrows that appear next to them.
8. When finished click **Done**.
9. Now, we'll add these to our Grade Level page. Click **pages** in the Portfolio tab.
10. Click the **small pencil tool** next to the page you will be editing.
11. From the **General** tab, click and drag a **Navigation** block into the left-hand column.
12. You can leave the **Block Title** empty. It will take on the name of your collection.
13. From the **Collection** drop-down menu, select the collection you wish to add.
14. Click **Save**.

15. If you have more than one collection to add, repeat steps 12-15 for each one.
16. When you are finished, click **Done**.

The following screenshot shows a page that was created using the template, and to which a Navigation block was added:

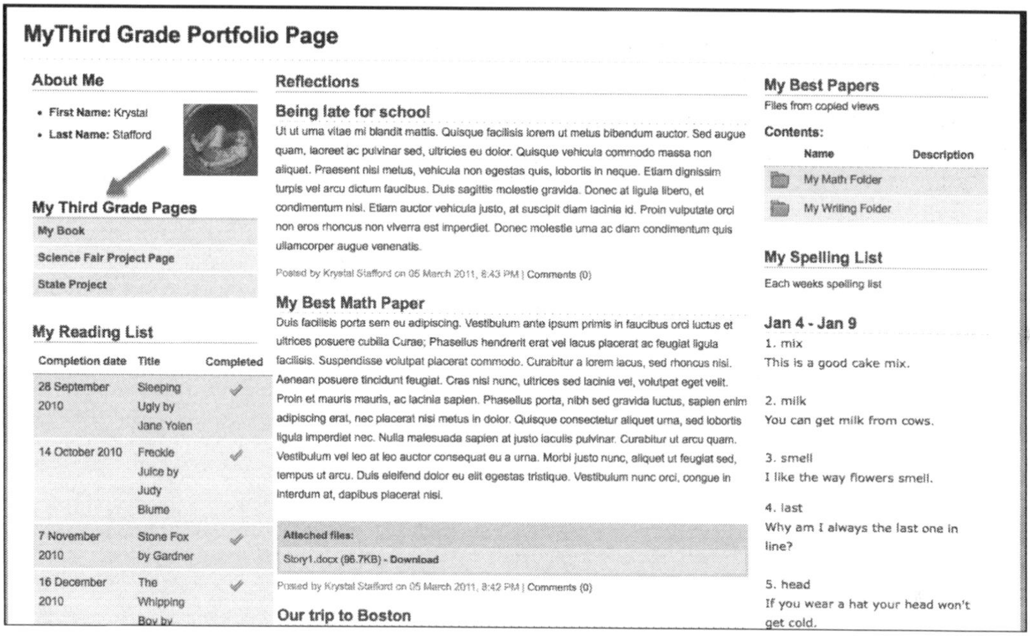

See also

- *Language acquisition journal* recipe in *Chapter 2, Literature and Writing*
- *A reading list (book reports)* recipe in *Chapter 5, The Primary Education Portfolio*
- *International project* recipe in *Chapter 5, The Primary Education Portfolio*

A student portfolio of the primary education years

Remember those folders filled with your work that you would bring home at the end of each school year? All those wonderful stories you wrote, projects you did, and pictures you drew? You can probably name a report (research paper) you wrote that you were really proud of, or that taught you some very important things, and maybe you still have it. Or maybe, like many of us, it was lost long ago. Having a digital portfolio of your best pieces is a true treasure and one that we can help our students give themselves.

The purpose of this recipe is to provide a vision of what a student's portfolio can look like after several years of building. The pages in this portfolio used the simple templates created in other parts of this chapter. In reality, a student's portfolio can become quite complex with collections inside collections, but even a simple portfolio can be a wonderful way of showing growth over time, and become a wonderful treasure for the student and his/her family. We will use tags to label artifacts, so that students can search for related artifacts more easily in the future.

In this recipe, we will build a collection that includes a homepage, the Kindergarten page, and the grades 1-5 template page. The home page and collection can be built in Kindergarten and changed over time. The home page should probably include a picture of the school, and a welcome by the student. pages can be added to the collection as the child progresses. This is the type of collection that can occur when an entire school supports the use of ePortfolios for teaching and learning.

The following screenshot shows an example of a complete portfolio:

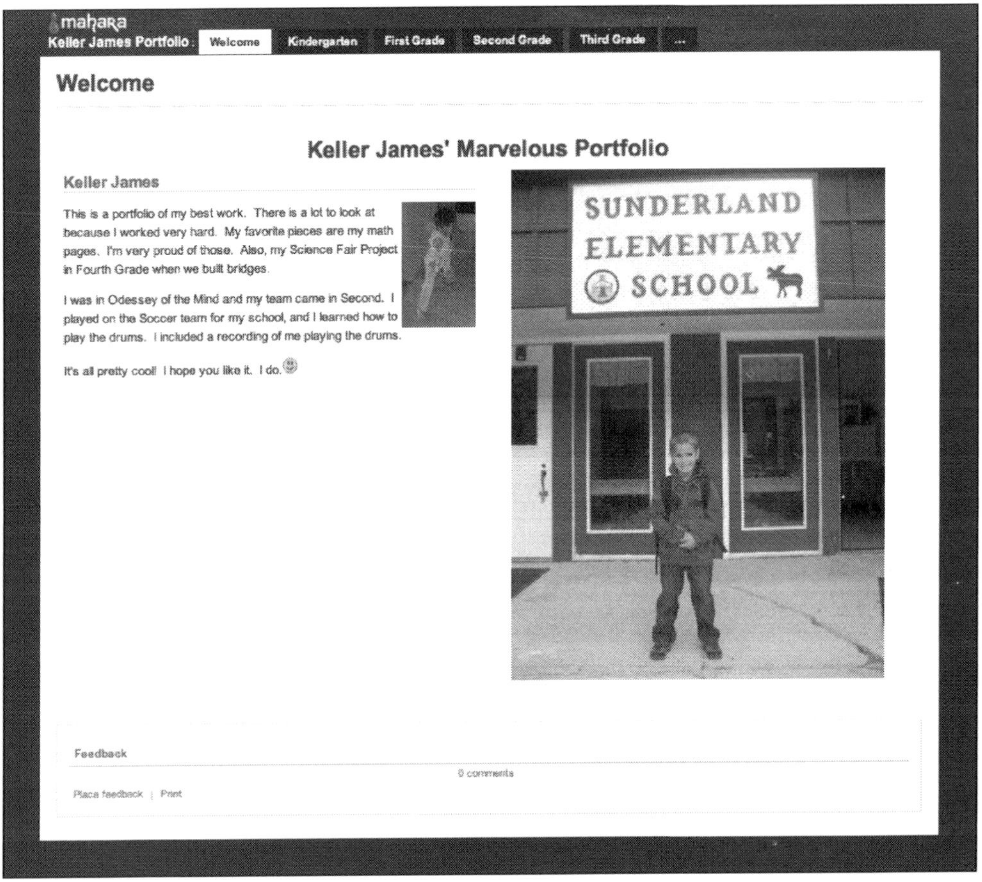

Getting ready

You will need to have a digital photo of the school or the school logo.

How to do it...

While we will be building this from the student's perspective, as mentioned in other recipes in this chapter, the home page can be built by the teacher and then copied by the students:

1. In the **Portfolio** section, go to **pages** and click **Create page**.
2. Click the **Edit Content and Layout** tab.
3. Select **2 columns, Equal widths**.
4. Click on **Save**.
5. From the drop-down menu labeled **Theme**, select a theme.
6. From the **Files, images and video** tab, click and drag **An Image** block into the right-hand side of the page you are creating.
7. Delete the text in the **Block Title**, leaving it blank.
8. Click in the small box next to **Upload file**.
9. Click the **Browse** button, find the image of your school, and upload it.
10. Set the **Width** to `400`.
11. Click on **Save**.
12. From the **Profile** tab, click and drag a **Profile Information** block into the left-hand side of your page.
13. In the **Block Title**, enter your name.
14. Do not select anything from the **Fields to show**.
15. Select a **Profile** icon.
16. In the section **Email Address**, choose **Don't show email address**.
17. In the **Introduction Text** box, type a welcome to your visitors. Tell them a little bit about yourself and some of the things they will discover in your portfolio.
18. Click on **Save**.
19. Click the tab to **Edit Title and Description**.
20. In the **page Title**, type `Welcome`.
21. In the **page Description**, type a banner for your homepage (for example, My Marvelous Portfolio).
22. Highlight the description and using the drop-down menu in the HTML editing toolbar, choose a **Font family**.

23. Make the text large by selecting **7(36pt)** from the **Font size** menu.
24. Click the tiny little arrow next to the upper-case **A**, in the top row of the HTML editing toolbar, to pick a color for your heading.
25. Center the heading by using the **center-alignment button** in the HTML editing toolbar.
26. Click on **Save**.
27. Click **Done**.

Now we will begin building the collection:

28. On the **Portfolio** tab, click the subtab **Collections**.
29. Click on **New Collection**.
30. In the **Collection name** field, type your name and `portfolio` (for example, Ellen Marie Murphy's Portfolio).
31. The **Collection description** will not display anywhere but is a place where you can add information about this collection that will be helpful to you. For example, this is a collection of all my work at my grammar school.
32. Make sure there is a checkmark in the box next to **page navigation bar**.
33. Click the button **Next: Edit Collection pages**.
34. You will see a list of the pages you can add to this collection in an area labeled **Add pages to collection**. Click in the small box next to **Welcome (the name of your page)**. Click **Add pages**.
35. If you have created a Kindergarten page, or other Grade Level pages, you can add them next. Click in the box next to each and click **Add pages**. If you don't have any other pages you can skip this step. If you want to reorder your pages, once you've added them, click the little arrows to left of each page.
36. Click **Done**.
37. To set the access for the collection, click the **Share** tab.
38. In the list of **pages & Collections**, you will see this collection. In the column labeled **Edit Access**, click the pencil tool next to the collection.
39. You will see this collection with a checkmark next to it. Use the **Add** button next to the access you would like to provide.
40. Click on **Save**. That access you set will be the same for all pages in the collection regardless of what they were before they were a collection.

How it works...

Mahara will automatically create navigation tabs at the top of each page in the collection.

There's more...

Everyone loves to look at pictures. A slideshow of photos can be a nice enhancement to a portfolio. You may also wish to add pages to the collection after its initial creation. We will discuss both of these now.

Adding a slideshow to the homepage

A nice option to consider is adding a slideshow from the student's years at the school. The images might be stored in the student's own portfolio, or in the files of a group, or perhaps even site files.

1. Open the Welcome page (homepage) in editing mode, by going to **pages** and clicking the small pencil tool next to it.
2. From the **Files, images and video** tab, click and drag an **Image Gallery** block into the page.
3. You can leave **Image Gallery** in the **Block Title**.
4. In the **Image Selection** area, select **I will choose individual images to display**.
5. In the **Images** section, you will see three tabs: **My Files**, **Group Files**, and **Site Files**. You can look for images in each of these areas. In **Group Files** and **Site Files**, you will only see files to which you have been given access, if any. To add an image to your gallery, click the **Select** button next to it.
6. You can also upload images to your files to use in your slideshow, by selecting the small box next to **Upload file** and clicking the **Browse** button.
7. In the **Style options**, choose **Slideshow**.
8. Change the **Width** to **300**.
9. Click on **Save**.

The following screenshot is an example of a homepage with a slideshow:

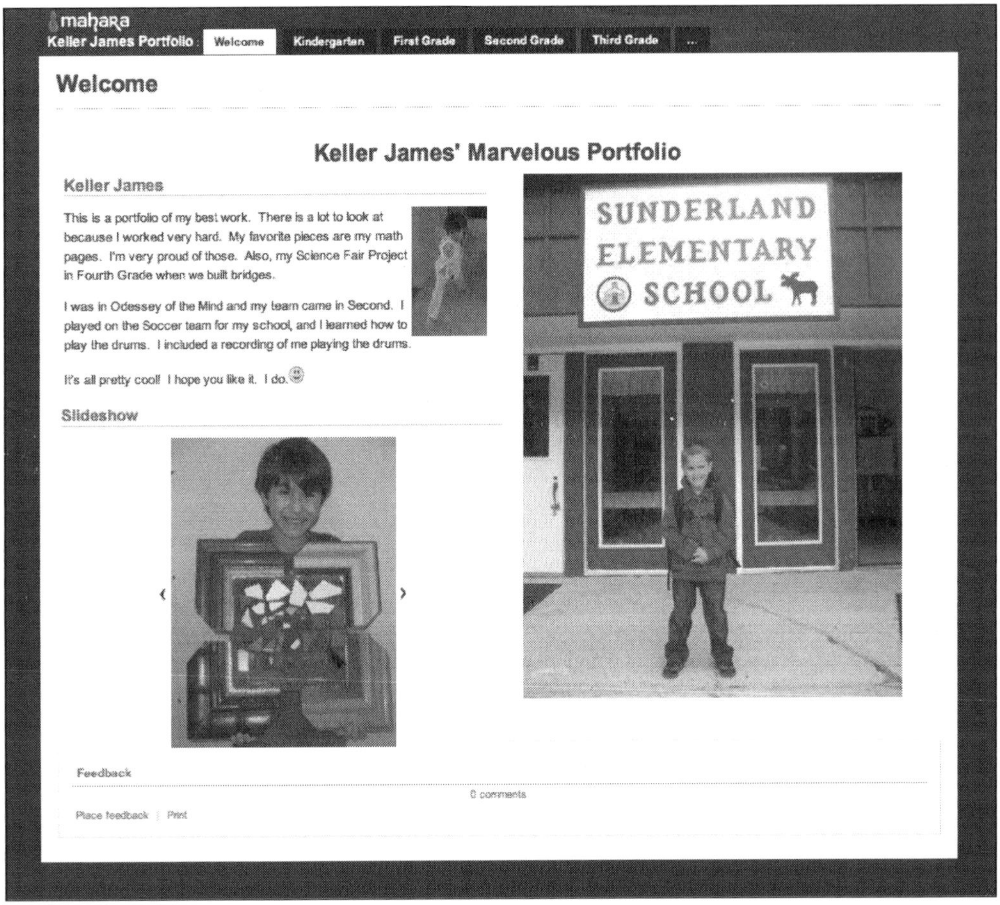

Adding pages to the collection

1. To add additional pages to the collection after it has been created, click the **Collections** tab in the **Portfolio** section.
2. You will see three icons to the right of each collection that allow for each of the following: **Manage pages, Edit title and description**, and **Delete**. Click the icon for **Manage pages**:

3. In the area labeled **Add pages to collection**, click in the small box next to each page you wish to add.
4. Click on **Add pages**.
5. Use the small arrows to the left of the pages to put them in the proper order.
6. Click **Done**.

See also

- A simple template for very young students recipe
- Creating & using a simple template recipe
- Using a Slideshow to create a book recipe

A reading list (book reports)

Book reports and reading lists are something every student is familiar with. They can provide good information regarding a particular student's reading interests and ability. Book reports written as reviews can help students develop an understanding of good writing as well. In this recipe, students will use plans to create a place where they can record and review the books that they read.

When added to a page, the list will appear in a collapsed format, as shown in the following screenshot:

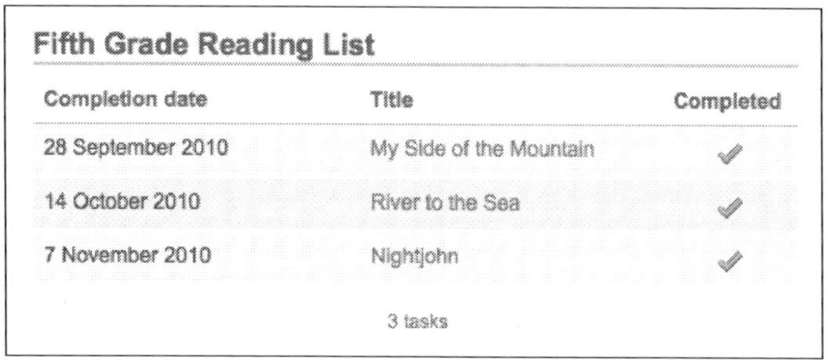

When a title is clicked, however, the block will expand revealing the student's review of the book, as shown in the following screenshot:

Fifth Grade Reading List

Completion date	Title	Completed
28 September 2010	My Side of the Mountain This was a really good book, but it probably wouldn't be too smart to do nowadays. I mean he has some strangers show up, and nowadays you are told not to speak to strangers. So, one of the things that I thought about is how different the world is now, but also how it is kind of the same. We care about sustainable living. That means living off the land. That's pretty much what Sam does. He finds a way to live without a grocery store, and without computers, and without electricity.	✓
14 October 2010	River to the Sea	✓
7 November 2010	Nightjohn	✓

How to do it...

Written for the student:

1. On the **Content** tab click **plans** and then the button labeled **New plan**.
2. In the **Title** field type something similar to `My 5th Grade Reading List`.
3. A **Description** is not necessary, but you can add one if you like.
4. Click the button **Save plan**.
5. Let's add our first book review by clicking the button **New task**.
6. In the **Title** field type the name of a book you are currently reading, or one that you just finished, and the name of the author.
7. The **Completion date** field is for the date you plan to finish reading the book. If you've already completed reading the book, put the approximate date you finished.
8. In the **Description** box type a review of the book—a book report.
9. If you've completed reading the book, put a checkmark in the small box next to **Completed** by clicking in the box.
10. Click on **Save task**.

At this point, only you can see this list. In order to share this with your teacher, or others, you will need to create a page and add a block that contains this reading list.

How it works...

Whenever you wish to add a new book to this list, add your review of the book, or the mark that you've completed the book, go to the plans section in the Content area of your portfolio. You will see this reading plan in your list of plans. Simply click the plan to open it.

You will see a list of the books you've added. Books that you've marked as completed will have a small green checkmark next to them. Books that have not been completed and that have passed the completion date, will be red—a little reminder that you need to finish the review.

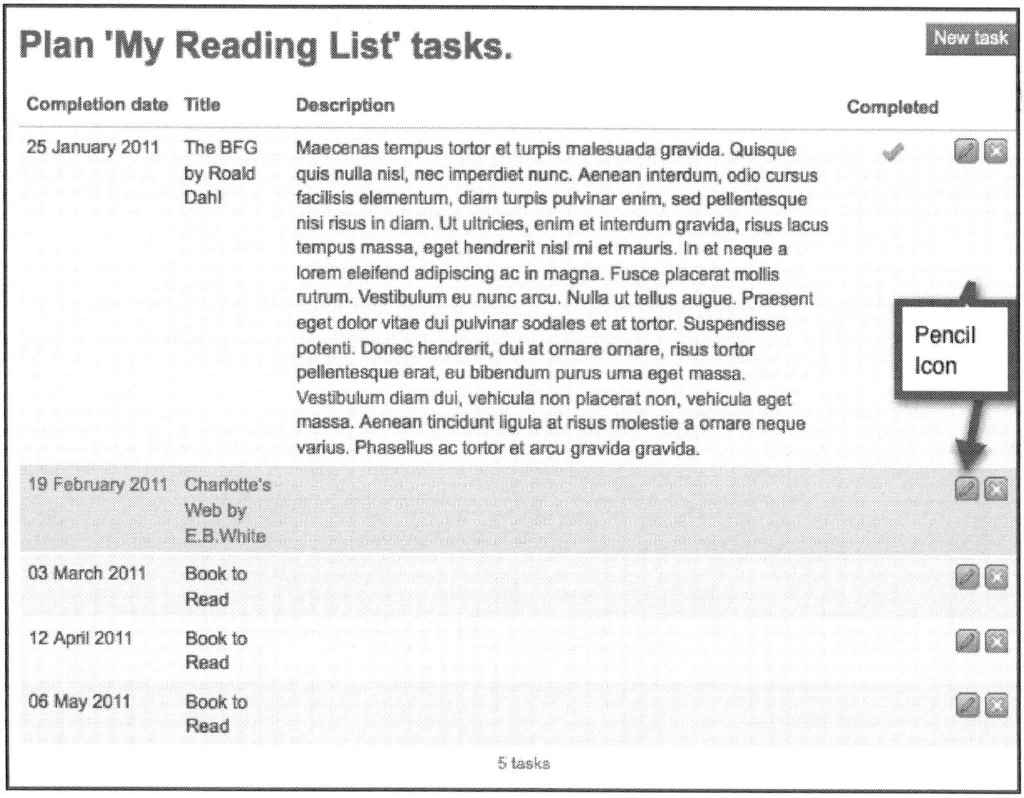

Plan 'My Reading List' tasks.
New task
Completion date
Title
Description
Completed
25 January 2011
The BFG by Roald Dahl
Maecenas tempus tortor et turpis malesuada gravida. Quisque quis nulla nisl, nec imperdiet nunc. Aenean interdum, odio cursus facilisis elementum, diam turpis pulvinar enim, sed pellentesque nisi risus in diam. Ut ultricies, enim et interdum gravida, risus lacus tempus massa, eget hendrerit nisl mi et mauris. In et neque a lorem eleifend adipiscing ac in magna. Fusce placerat mollis rutrum. Vestibulum eu nunc arcu. Nulla ut tellus augue. Praesent eget dolor vitae dui pulvinar sodales et at tortor. Suspendisse potenti. Donec hendrerit, dui at ornare ornare, risus tortor pellentesque erat, eu bibendum purus urna eget massa. Vestibulum diam dui, vehicula non placerat non, vehicula eget massa. Aenean tincidunt ligula at risus molestie a ornare neque varius. Phasellus ac tortor et arcu gravida gravida.
Pencil Icon
19 February 2011
Charlotte's Web by E.B.White
03 March 2011
Book to Read
12 April 2011
Book to Read
06 May 2011
Book to Read
5 tasks

To add a new book, click the **New task** button. To add a book review, or to mark that you've completed the book, click the little pencil icon next to the book you wish to edit. Add your review and/or click the **Completed** box and **Save task**. This will automatically update any pages in which you've put this plan, including your dashboard.

There's more...

There are other places to display your list. Let's examine a couple.

Adding the list to your dashboard

Adding the reading list to your dashboard will allow you to quickly see the status of your book reviews every time you log into Mahara. Here's how to add the list:

1. Click on the **Portfolio** tab and then **pages**.
2. The very first page in your list of **pages** will be your **Dashboard page**. To begin editing the page, click the little pencil tool to the right of the page. This will allow you to edit the content and layout.
3. From the **General** tab, click and drag a **Your plans** block into the left-hand column.
4. Leave the **Block Title** empty.
5. In the area labeled **plans to show**, you will see your Reading List plan. Click the small bubble next to it.
6. Click on **Save**.
7. Click **Done**.

Sharing the list with others

To share your reading list with your teacher, or parents, or friends, you will need to add it to a page and then provide access:

1. Go to the **pages** section of the **Portfolio** tab.
2. Click the button **Create page**.
3. You will now see two rows of tabs. On the top row of tabs, find the tab labeled **Edit Layout** and click on it.
4. Click the little bubble for **1 column, Equal widths**.
5. Click on **Save**.
6. If you would like to use a theme, click the drop-down menu **Theme** and select the one you would like.
7. From the **Genera**l tab, click and drag a **Your plans** block into white area beneath the **Theme** menu.
8. Leave the **Block Title** empty.
9. In the area labeled **plans to show**, you will see your Reading List plan. Click the small bubble next to it.
10. Click on **Save**.
11. Click **Done**.

12. To share your page, click the **Share** tab under **Portfolio**.
13. You will see a list of all your pages. To share this page with your teacher or friends, click the small pencil icon to the left of your page.
14. Click the **Add** button next to the individuals you would like to share this page with. And **Save**.
15. If you would like to share this page with your parents, click the pencil tool to the right of the page—in the column labeled **Secret URL**. Then click on **Add**.
16. You will see a long string of letters and numbers that begin with **http://**. That is the **Secret URL**, and you will need to give that to your parents in order for them to see your page.

Using slideshow to create a book

When I was in fourth grade, I wrote a marvelous little story about a fictional visit to "My Grandmother". I drew the pictures with colored pencils and wrote the text with a pen. I used crayons on purple construction paper to make a book cover, and stapled it all together. I still have a copy of the book. A great deal of our students' work is done with pencil and paper, but that does not mean it cannot become part of their permanent digital portfolio. This recipe will use the Slideshow block to create a digital booklet presenting various math problems that the student has worked on using pencil and paper.

This can be an ongoing project in that all of the images do not need to be taken and uploaded at the start. Instead, the book (slideshow) can be created with a minimal amount of images (even one will do). As new images are taken, they can easily be added to the slideshow.

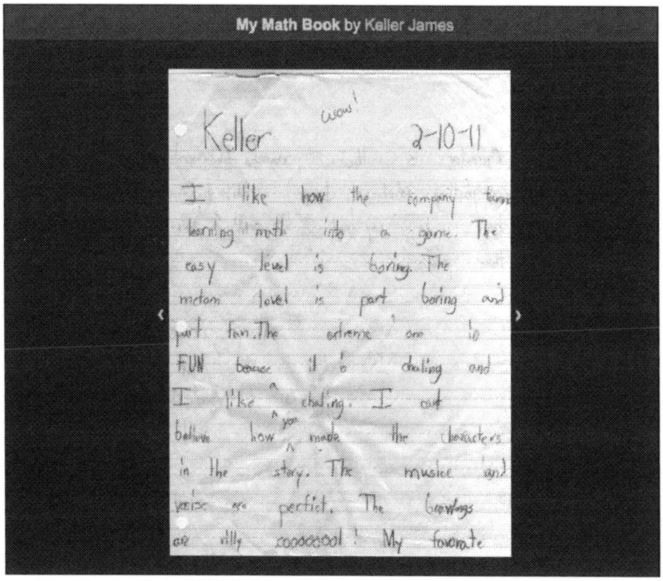

Getting ready

You will need to create digital copies of the student's documents. This can be done by either scanning in the documents, or by taking pictures of the documents using a digital camera. The images will need to be saved in a `.jpg`, `.gif`, or `.png` format in order for them to be displayed on the Web.

> The resolution of the images does not need to be more than 100 ppi, so if you are using a scanner you can set the ppi to anywhere between 72 and 100. Images with a higher resolution will not have any greater clarity on the computer screen, and will have unnecessarily large file sizes. If you are working with digital images already saved to your computer and/or coming from a digital camera, simply resize the images so that the largest dimension is no greater than 800 pxs. Larger sizes will take up unnecessary file space and will not improve the resolution of the image in the display.

How to do it...

Create a folder to contain the images:

1. Go to **Content** and then **Files**.
2. In the narrow textbox underneath **Home** type the name of the booklet, and then click the button **Create folder**.
3. You will see the new folder in your list of folders. Click on the name to open the folder.
4. Now, put a checkmark in the little box next to **Upload file**.
5. Click the **Browse** button to locate and upload the first image. You do not need to wait for the image to completely upload before clicking the **Browse** button again to find the next image.
6. After you have uploaded all of the images you wish to use initially, click the **Portfolio** tab.
7. In the **pages** section click the button **Create page**.
8. Click the tab **Edit layout**, and select **1 column, Equal widths**.
9. Click on **Save**.
10. From the drop-down menu **Theme**, choose a theme.
11. From the **Files, images and video** tab, click and drag the **Image Gallery** into the area beneath **Theme**.
12. Delete the text in the **Block Title**, leaving it empty.
13. In the **Image Selection** options choose **I will choose individual images to display**. This will allow you to control the order in which the images are displayed.

> While **Display all images from one of my folders** ensures that images added to the folder, after the initial creation of the slideshow, will be automatically added to the slideshow, the images will display in the reverse order; that is, the last image added will be displayed first. This can make creating a linear sequence difficult.

14. Click on the file you created in step 2 to open it.
15. Click the **Select** button next to each image you wish to be part of this booklet. Click them in the order you wish them to appear in the slideshow—that is the first image should be clicked first, the second next, and so on.
16. From the **Style options** choose **Slideshow**.
17. In the **Width** box you will find **400**. If your images are taller, rather than wider, you can leave it as 400. If your images tend to be wider rather than taller, change the **Width** to **600**.
18. Click on **Save**.
19. Click the **Edit Title and Description** tab.
20. In the field for **page Title**, type the title of the book.
21. Leave the **page Description** field empty.
22. In the field for **Tags**, add tags to identify the subject and grade level. Separate tags with a comma.
23. Click on **Save**.
24. Click the **Share page** tab.
25. By default, this page should have a checkmark next to it. If it doesn't, make sure you click the box next to it so that it is selected.
26. Choose the **Share with** option you would like by clicking the **Add** button next to your choice.
27. Click on **Save**.

How it works...

The page will display the first image in the list of images you added to the slideshow. To the right and left of the image there are small arrows that allow viewers to "turn the page".

There's more...

As mentioned in the introduction for this recipe, you can continue adding images even after creating the slideshow.

Adding images to the slideshow

1. Go to the **pages** tab in the **Portfolio** section of your portfolio.
2. Click the small pencil tool to the right of the page that contains your slideshow.
3. You will see your slideshow in the lower part of this page and directly above it and to the right will be two small icons. Click the one that will allow you to **Configure this block**:

4. You will see the list of images that are currently in the slideshow and a list of your files.
5. Put a checkmark in the small box next to **Upload file**.
6. Click the **Browse** button to find the new image you wish to upload.
7. Click the button labeled **Upload**.
8. You do not need to wait for the image to finish uploading before you add the next image; simply click the **Browse** button, find it, and **Upload**.
9. Click the **Select** button next to the images to add them.

> If you wish to add the new images to the folder you created, click and drag them into the folder before you click select. You cannot add them directly to the folder during the upload process for this item.

10. Click on **Save**.

See also...

- For more information on sizing digital images, see *A poetry page with a faux woodblock print created using GIMP* recipe in *Chapter 2, Literature and Writing*

International project

A common project in a grammar school is one that involves studying another country. Students pick the country they wish to study, and then complete a research project on what they've learned. The projects often conclude with an International Day, where students wear the folk costumes of their chosen country, offer some of the ethnic food, and so on.

This recipe presents one way that a student could complete their project using Mahara. With a little tweaking, this recipe can be used for any number of projects, from science projects, to history projects and more. In the end, the student will have actually created a website on their chosen topic—one that can be shared publically. What a wonderful way to display their hard work!

This recipe is for an upper level student. It is more difficult than many of the other recipes in this chapter. It also includes a banner which, while fun to do, can certainly be excluded from the recipe.

I've chosen to construct this recipe in a slightly different format than the previous recipes. I will first show you the various pages in a completed project and then talk about the elements that make up the page. Where there are elements that have not been discussed at length in other recipes, I will provide detailed instructions. Most of the elements in this project, however, can be found in more detail in recipes throughout this book.

The project is a collection of pages: the **Home page on France**, **Famous French People**, **French Cooking**, **French History**, and a page that contains a pretend travel blog to France called **My Trip to France**.

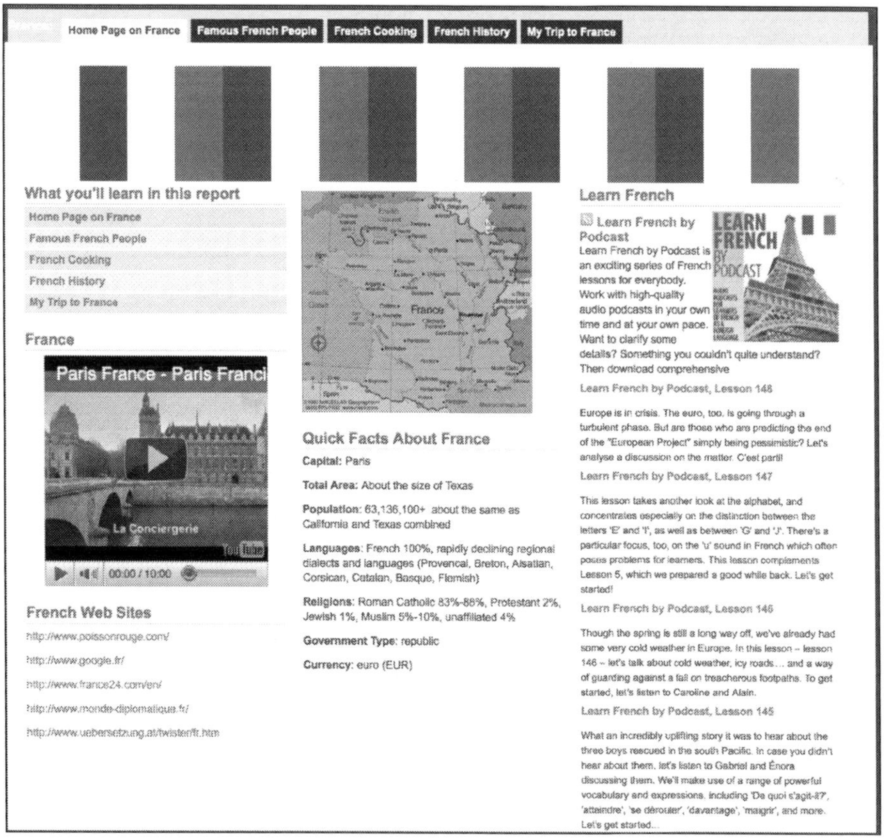

How to do it...

The home page consists of an RSS feed from another website, a YouTube video, a picture of a map hosted on another website, a textbox with quick facts about France, a textbox with links to French websites, and a Navigation block with links to each of the pages in this project. The banner was created using a table in the Description. Let's create our page and learn how to use tables to create the banner:

1. Go to **pages** and click **Create page**.
2. Click the tab **Edit Title and Description**.
3. In the **page Title**, type the name of the project and indicate that this is the homepage.
4. On the HTML toolbar for the **Description**, you will see several icons for adding and formatting tables. Click the icon for **Inserts a new table**:

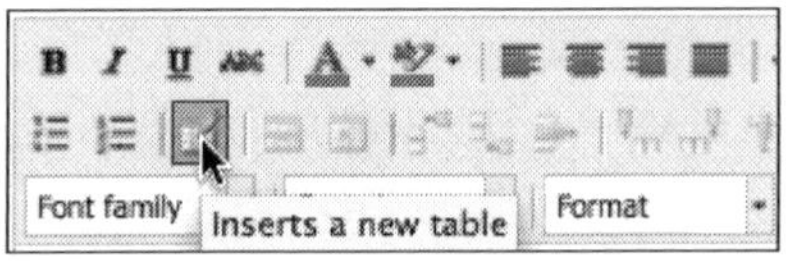

5. In the small field **cols** type `15`—this is the number of columns our table will have.
6. In the field for **rows**, type `1`.
7. From the drop-down for **Alignment**, choose **Center**.
8. For **Width** type `800`, for **Height** type `150`.
9. You can ignore all of the other fields and click **Insert**.
10. You will now see a row of boxes. Click inside the first box.
11. Click the icon for **Table cell properties**:

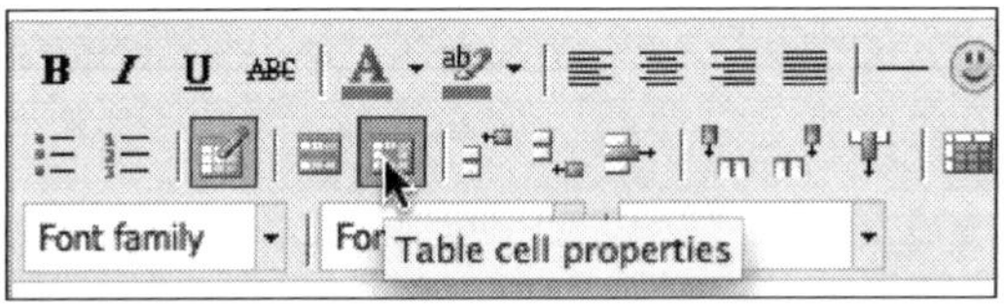

12. Click the **Advanced tab**.
13. At the very bottom of the option you will see an option for **Background color**. Click the small box with the down arrow.
14. Click the tab for **Palette** and then click the color you would like for the first cell.
15. Click on **Apply**.
16. Click on **Update**.

17. Click in the next cell you will add color to and repeat steps 11-16 until you have finished adding all of the colors you would like.
18. Click **Save**.

Now let's add an RSS feed. An RSS feed block embeds a block that is connected to another website. When that website is updated, the new information is displayed in your page. Many, many sites have RSS feeds. You will need to find a website on your topic that has an RSS feed.

19. You will see a small RSS icon, a page that has a feed. Click the icon and it will take you to the URL for the feed. Copy the URL.
20. Go back to the page you are editing and from the **External feeds** tab, click and drag an **External Feed** block into your page.
21. You can leave the **Block Title** blank.
22. In the **Feed Location** paste the URL you copied in step 19.
23. In the box for **Items to show**, type `5`.
24. Click the option to **Show feeds in full**.
25. Click on **Save**.

To add a textbox with links, click and drag a **Text Box** block, from the **General** tab, into your page. Copy the URLs from their various web addresses, and paste them in the textbox.

To add a YouTube video, drag an **External Video** block, from the **Files, images and video** tab, into your page. Paste the URL of the video in the field for **Video URL**.

To add an image from another website:

26. You will need the URL of the image (not the website). Find the image and put your cursor on the image. Right-click the mouse (PC) or *control* and click (Mac) and copy the **Image location**.
27. To add it to your page, drag a **Text Box** block into the page. Click in the body of the textbox and then click the icon to **Add an image** on the HTML toolbar (it looks like a small tree).
28. In the field for **Image URL**, paste the link you copied in step 26.
29. Click on **Save**.

The navigation menu in this homepage was added after the other pages were built and the collection was created.

The French Cooking page, the Famous French People page, and the French History page were all created using Image block and Text Box blocks.

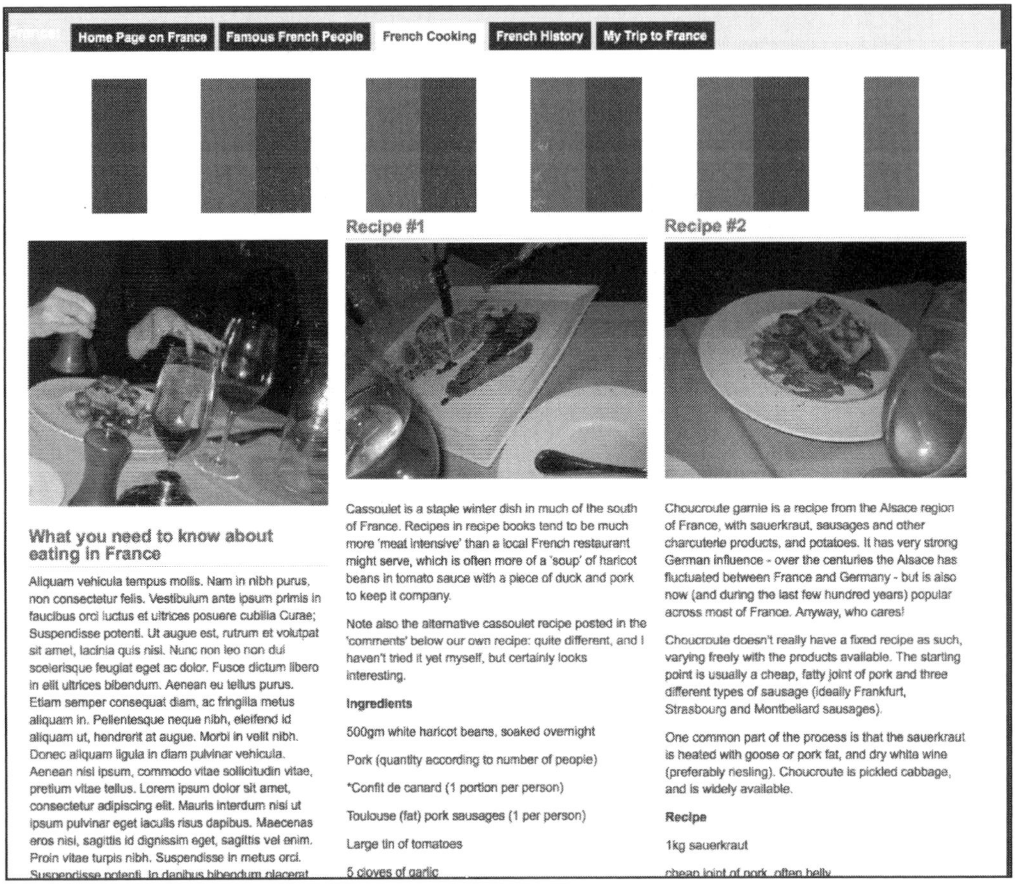

The banner was copied from the Description on the homepage, and pasted into the Description for each of the other pages. This provides a consistent look to the project.

30. To copy the banner, you will need to go to the home page for your project and click the button to **Edit page**.
31. Click the tab for **Edit Title and Description**.
32. Click in the **Description** box and then while holding down *Ctrl* (PC) or *Command* (Mac) on your keyboard, hit the letter *A* and then the letter *C* (this will highlight everything in the **Description** box, and then copy it).
33. Go to the **Edit Title and Description** tab for the page you want to add the banner to, and click inside the **Description** box.
34. While holding down the *Ctrl* or *Command* key, hit the letter *V*.

The final page in the project is a 1 column, equal widths page to which we add a journal. The journal will contain postings on a fictitious trip to the country of their choice (or a real trip if they've been there). In other projects, the journal could be used for any number of purposes.

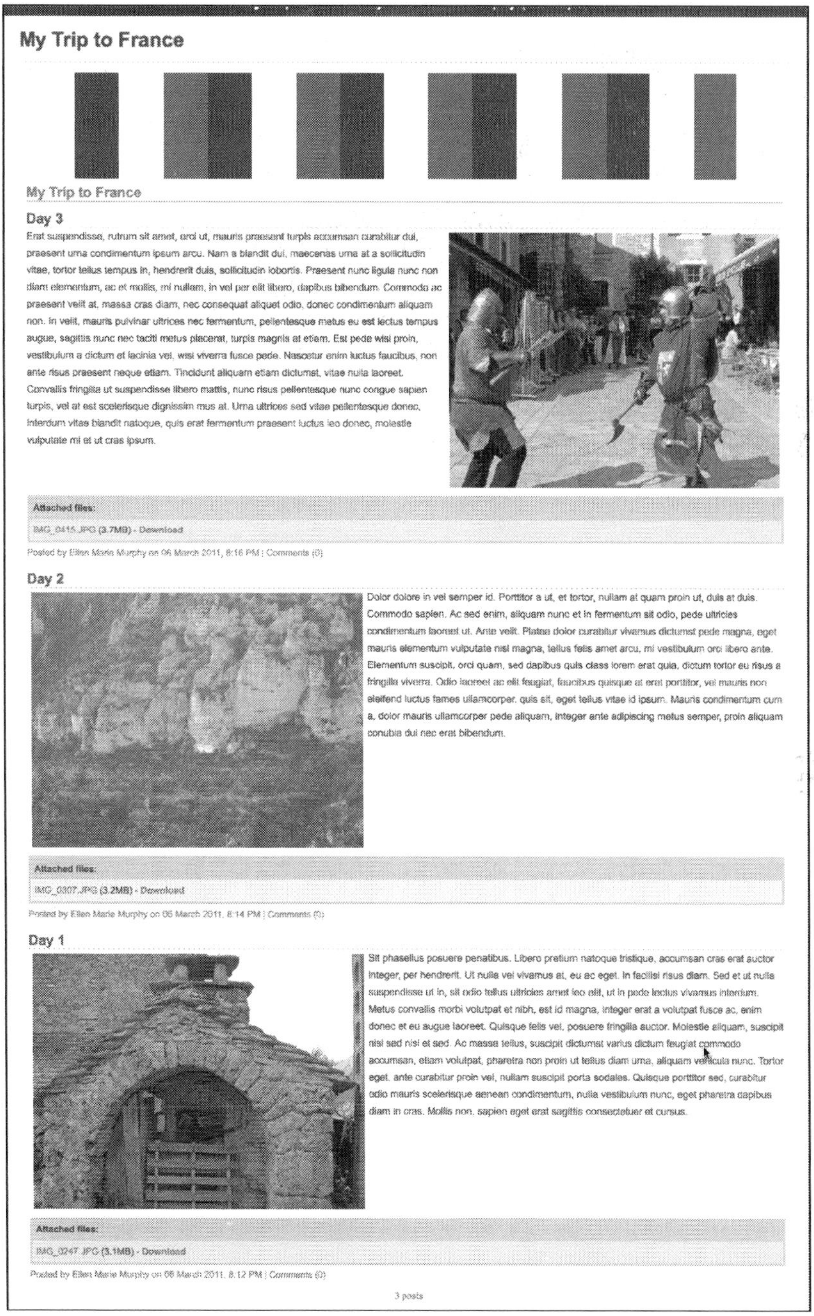

35. To package all of these pages in a collection, go to the **Collections** tab in the **Portfolio** section.
36. Click **New Collection**.
37. In the field for **Collection name**, you'll want to type the name of your project.
38. In the **Collection description**, type a brief description of the project.
39. Make sure that **page navigation** has a checkmark in the little box next to it.
40. Click **Next Edit Collection pages**.
41. The list of available pages will appear in an area labeled **Add pages to collection**.
42. Put a checkmark next to each of the pages that are part of this project.
43. Click the button to **Add pages**.
44. You will now see these pages in the section above the other pages. Use the small arrows to the left of each page to put them in the proper order (the homepage should be at the top of the list).
45. Click **Done**.
46. Now let's add the Navigation menu (or a Table of Contents) to the homepage. Go to **pages**, and in the list of your pages click and open the homepage for this project.
47. In the upper right-hand corner, click the button labeled **Edit this page**.
48. From the General tab, click and drag a Navigation block into your page.
49. In the **Block Title** type `What you'll learn in this report` or just simply `Table of Contents`.
50. From the drop-down menu for **Collection**, select your project.
51. Click on **Save**.
52. Since you've worked so hard on this, I would suggest you make it publicly accessible. Click the **Share page** tab.
53. This collection should be checked by default.
54. Click the **Add** button next to **Public**.
55. Click on **Save**.
5. That's it! Wow!

See also

- *Journaling a project from start to finish* recipe in *Chapter 1, Mahara for the Visual Art*
- *A daily gazette* recipe in *Chapter 2, Literature and Writing*

Creating a classroom page to share with families

It's always a nice idea to have a web page where families can find out the latest happenings in the classroom, download any documents they may need (like permission slips), and get ideas on how they can support what you are doing in the classroom.

In this recipe, we will create a page similar to this. The page includes a journal, a slideshow, documents to download, and contact information. It also provides places where parents can ask questions or post comments. It's extremely simple to build, but so effective. And, it can become part of your permanent portfolio (something that might be extremely useful when applying for recertification).

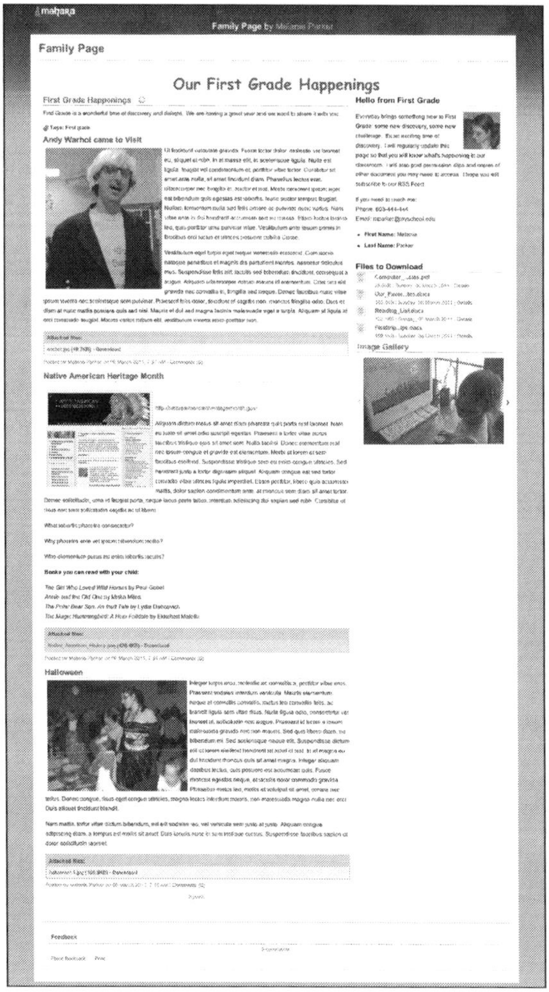

Getting ready

You will need to create a journal specifically for this recipe. You will also need to create a folder in the Files section of your portfolio, for class images. Finally you will want to create a folder for the various documents parents will be accessing throughout the year. Label the folder `Files to Download`.

How to do it...

1. Click on your **Portfolio** tab and then **pages | Create page**.
2. Click **Edit Layout**.
3. Select **2 columns, Larger left column**.
4. Click on **Save**.
5. From the **Journals** tab click and drag a **journal** block into the left-hand column.
6. You can leave the **Block Title** empty, as it will take the name of your journal.
7. Leave **Entries per page** at **5**.
8. Skip the **More options** area and click **Save**.
9. From the **File, images and video** tab click and drag an **Image Gallery** block into the right-hand column.
10. You can leave the text in the **Block Title: Image Gallery**.
11. From the **Image Selection** options, choose **Display all images from one of my folders (will include images uploaded later)**.
12. Click the **Select** button next to the folder you created for your class images.
13. For the **Style option** select **Slideshow**.
14. In the **Width** box replace the **400** with `300`.
15. Click on **Save**.
16. From the **Files, images and video** tab click and drag an **A Folder** block into the right-hand column above the slideshow.

> Using an **A Folder** block, instead of the **File(s) to Download** block, ensures that the page will automatically display any new documents you add to that folder.

17. Leave the **Block Title** empty.
18. Click the **Select** button next to the folder labeled **Files to Download**.
19. Click **Save**.

20. From the **Profile** tab click and drag **Profile Information** into the right-hand column above **Files to Download**.
21. In the **Block Title** type `Hello from First Grade` or something similar.
22. Select the information you wish to display by clicking in the small bubbles next to each item, including a **Profile icon**.
23. Use the **Introduction Text** box to type a personalized message. You can use this box to provide contact information if you did not do so in step 22. (The content of the Introduction Text box will appear only in this page.)
24. Click on **Save**.
25. Click the **Edit Title and Description** tab.
26. In the **Title** field type: Family page.
27. In the **Description** type a heading for the page, maybe something such as Ms. Or Mr. Teacher's First Grade Happening.
28. Highlight the text and choose the **center-alignment** icon on the HTML toolbar, **Comic Sans** from **Font family**, **7(36pt)** from **Font size**, and **Heading 1** from the drop-down that begins with **Paragraph**.
29. In the **Tags** field type "family page", so that you can easily locate this in the future.
30. Check the **Name display format** to make sure your professional name is what is displayed.
31. Click on **Save**.
32. Click the **Share page** tab.
33. In the **pages** section, you should see this page checked by default. If it's not, you should click the small box next to it.
34. Click the **Add** button next to **Public**. This will allow families to subscribe to an RSS feed from the journal on your page.
35. Click **Advance Options** to expand the menu.
36. There should be a checkmark next to **Allow comments**. Add a checkmark next to **Moderate comments**.
37. Click on **Save**.
38. You will be taken to the **Share** tab where you will see a list of your **pages & Collections** and information regarding the **Access** levels of each.
39. To provide families with a URL to the Family page, click its name in the list of **pages & Collections**. It will open in display mode. The URL for this page will be in the address bar at the top of the window. You will want to copy this and send it to the parents. To see the page as families will see it, you will need to log out of Mahara and go to the URL.

How it works...

You do not need to go to the page in order to keep it up-to-date. As you add posts to the journal, the page will automatically display them. When you have more than five posts, a navigation menu will appear in the page, underneath the journal, which will provide access to previous posts. As you add documents to the "Files to Download" folder, the page will automatically display the link to them. And, finally, as you add pictures to the class image file, they will be added to the slideshow on the page.

Families can subscribe to the journal by clicking the little RSS feed icon at the top of the journal:

At the bottom of your page, there will be a place where visitors can leave comments or ask question. It's actually a small link labeled **Comments**. When the link is clicked the comments section will expand. You will receive a notification that a comment has been added and that it awaits your approval, as shown in the following screenshot:

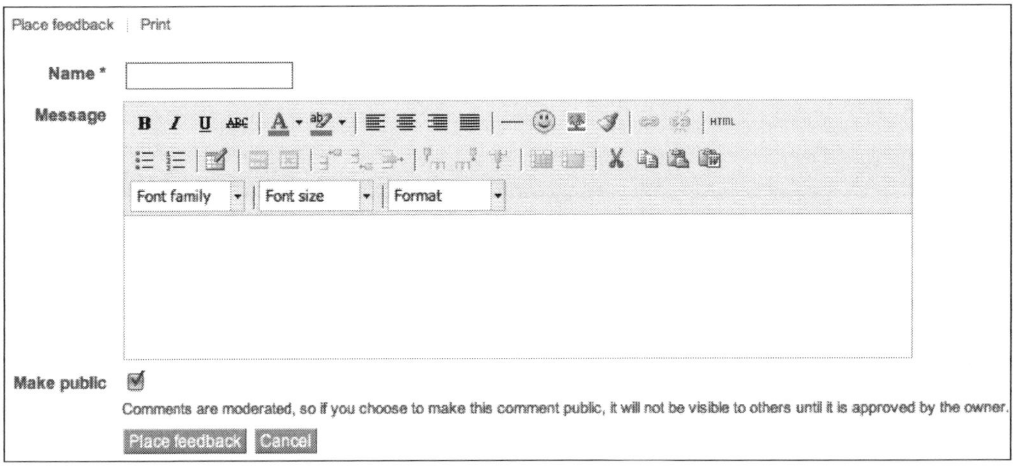

See also

- *Journaling a project from start to finish* recipe in *Chapter 1, Mahara for the Visual Arts*
- *A daily gazette* recipe in *Chapter 2, Literature and Writing*
- *Creating a group newspaper using news feeds from students' journals* recipe in *Chapter 4, Working with Groups*

6
The Social Portfolio

In this chapter, we will cover:

- Setting a theme and a layout for your profile page
- Posting comments to a wall
- Using the journal feature for your wall
- Adding a counter
- Adding a feed from Twitter
- Sending feeds to Twitter and/or Facebook
- Adding your external blog to your profile page

Introduction

Mahara includes a social networking component that allows you to communicate and share pieces of your portfolio with others. Your profile page is one of the best venues for this. Your Profile page can be personalized and can contain all sorts of items from images, to blogs, to Twitter feeds, and more. It has a Wall that visitors can write on. It has a Pages area that provides visitors easy access to other pages you've created. The Pages section will look somewhat like a table of contents. What appears in that box will be highly personalized—visitors will only see links to the pages they actually have access to.

In this chapter, we are going to look at some of the ways you can make your Profile page dynamic, a place that people will want to visit.

By default, everyone in your Mahara system has the ability to view your Profile page and you have the ability to view everyone else's. You can set up your Profile page for public access too.

Setting a theme and a layout for your profile page

In this recipe, we will begin the process of creating a dynamic Profile page. The recipes that follow this one will help you add elements to your page. The following screenshot is an example of mine:

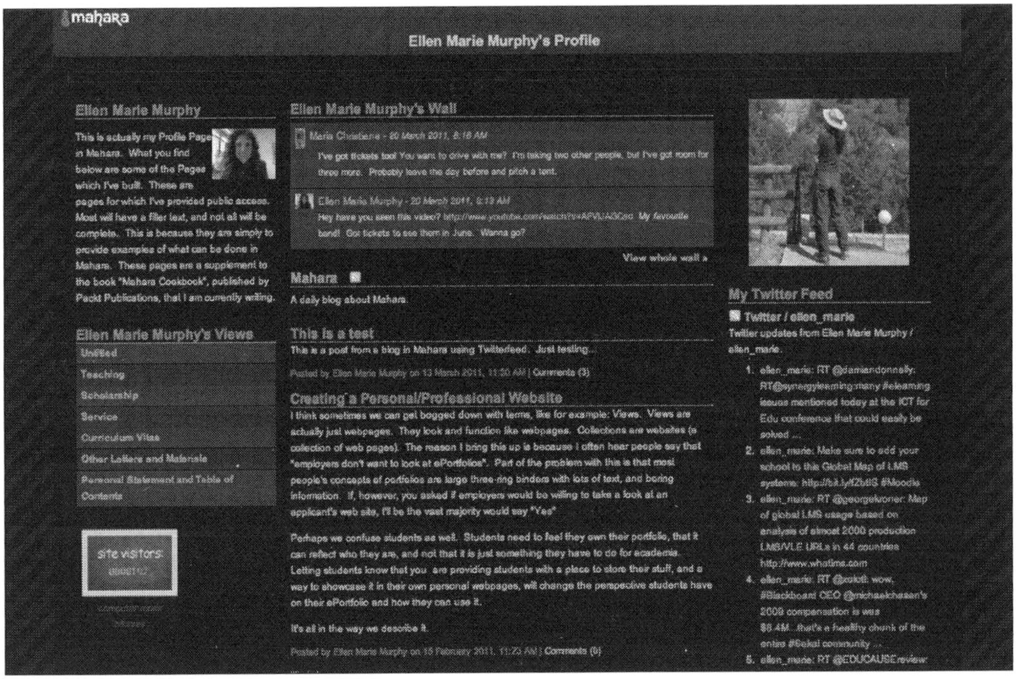

How to do it...

1. Click the **Portfolio** tab and then **Pages**.
2. In your list of pages, you will see a page called **Profile page**. Click the title to open it.

This is an image of a default Profile page:

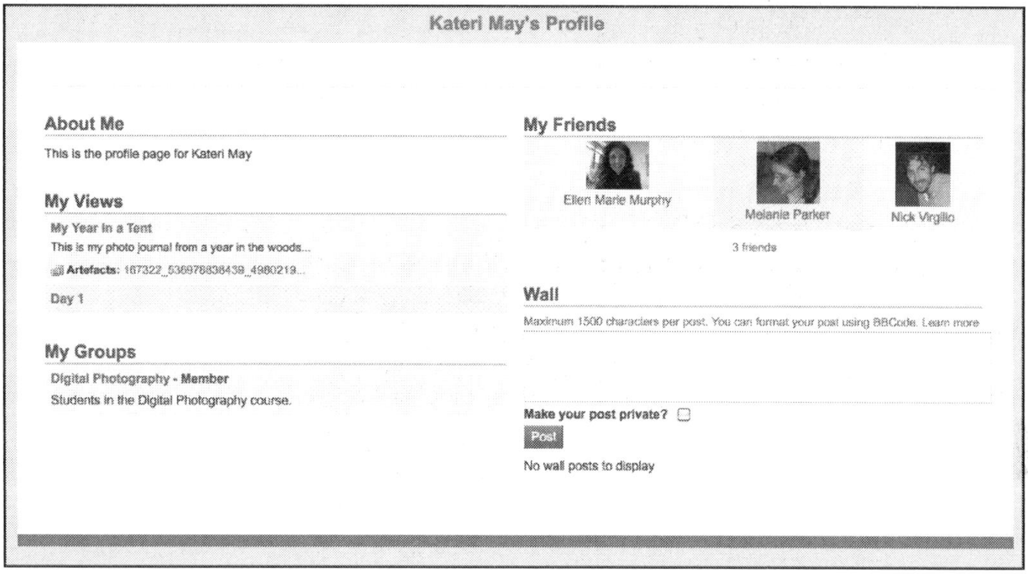

3. In the upper right-hand corner, you will see an option to edit the page.

> The exact wording of that *Edit* option depends on the theme that was applied to the page by default.

4. Click the tab labeled **Edit Layout**.
5. To make yours look similar to mine, click the option **3 columns, Larger centre column**.
6. Click **Save**.
7. From the drop-down menu for **Theme**, select **Fresh**.
8. The **About Me** block needs to be configured. Click the small icon to the right of **About Me**.
9. Select those items you wish to display on your Profile page, including a **Profile Icon**.
10. In the **Introduction Text** box, write a little bit about yourself.
11. Click **Save**.
12. You can delete any of the blocks you do not want to keep on your Profile page by clicking the small **x** in the corner of the block you wish to remove.

13. You can move blocks by hovering your cursor over the title of the block you wish to move. When you see a small hand appear, click and hold your mouse button down, and drag the block to wherever you wish.
14. Click **Done**.

Now, you're ready for the other recipes in this chapter.

Posting comments to a Wall

Your profile page comes with something called a **Wall**. The Wall is a place where visitors can post messages for you, and where you can post messages as well. It has limited formatting capabilities, but it does allow you to make text bold, or use italics, add an image, or add a URL (hyperlink). You can do this using something called BBCode. It's not quite HTML, but works a bit like it. In this recipe, we will learn how to use BBCode to post messages on a Wall.

How to do it...

1. First let's go to a friend's Profile page so we can leave a message. Click the **Groups** tab and then click on **My Friends**.
2. Click your friend's name to get to their profile page.
3. Unless they've deleted the **Wall** from their profile page, you will see a box labeled with their name and the word **Wall**. Click inside the box to begin typing.

The following is an example of a post that uses all of the BBCode available in Mahara:

[b]Cambridge Science Festival[/b] is in May. I've signed up as a volunteer. They are having some [i]really incredible[/i] events this year. Here's the link:[url]http://cambridgesciencefestival.org/Home.aspx[/url]. This is a pic of the laser show from last year's festival: [img]http://farm5.static.flickr.com/4066/4553165204_c8d921faab.jpg[/img]

It's a lot of fun!

4. If you want your post to be seen *only* by the individual who owns the Wall, click the box **Make your post private?**
5. Click the button labeled **Post**.

The following is a screenshot of what the previous text looks like after it's been posted:

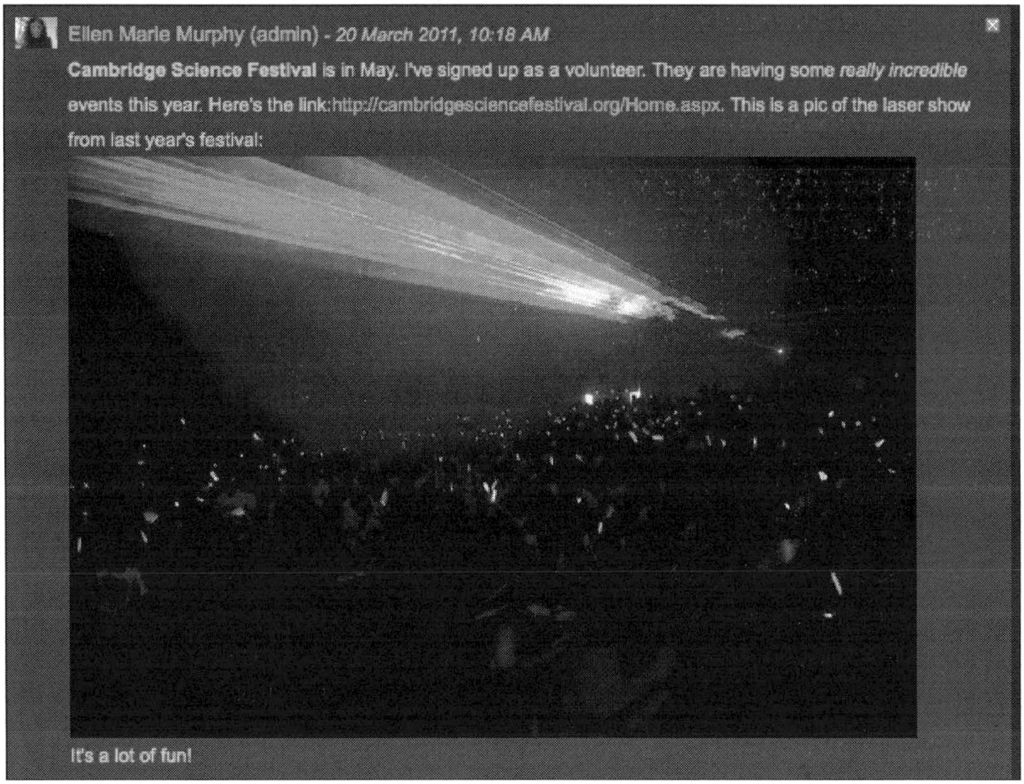

Ellen Marie Murphy (admin) - 20 March 2011, 10:18 AM
Cambridge Science Festival is in May. I've signed up as a volunteer. They are having some really incredible events this year. Here's the link:http://cambridgesciencefestival.org/Home.aspx. This is a pic of the laser show from last year's festival:
It's a lot of fun!

How it works...

In the previous example, Cambridge Science Festival is bold. To make text bold, put `[b]` in front of the text and `[/b]` at the end of the text. For italicized text, put `[i]` in front of the text you wish to italicize and `[/i]` at the end of it. To add an image, you will need the URL of the image. This is not necessarily the same thing as the URL of the page where you found the image. You have to actually isolate the image. The URL for an image ends with an image extension like `.jpg`, `.png`, or `.gif`. To get the link, you can usually just right-click the image and, in the menu of options that opens, select **Copy image location**. Then, use this code to add the image: `[img]` pasted URL of the image `[/img]`. This will not be a clickable image—that is, if someone clicks on it, it won't take them to the image location.

Images will not resize to fit the Wall, so, if you add a large image, it may overwhelm the page and bleed over into other columns. Use them carefully.

To add to your post a URL that will be a clickable link, put `[url]` in front of the URL and `[/url]` at the end of the URL.

> While BBCode has many optional codes, they do not currently work with Mahara.

Using the journal feature for your Wall

Your Wall is a great way to post messages and for others to leave messages for you. There is another method of doing that with some distinct advantages over using the Wall—the Journal. Bringing a journal into your profile page provides the means for you to share your thoughts and for others to post comments. There are several advantages that the journal provides: you can use the HTML editing tools to format your messages, individuals that post comments on your messages can also use HTML tools, and your posts (updates) can be automatically fed to Twitter and Facebook (see recipes in this chapter). The disadvantage is that friends can only post responses to your posts; they can't leave you messages apart from them. My recommendation is that you have both the journal and the Wall on your profile page.

In this recipe, we will add a journal to your Profile page for you to share your updates and thoughts. Later in this chapter, we'll provide a recipe that creates a feed from this journal to Facebook and Twitter.

Getting ready

By default, every Mahara account comes with a journal. In other words, even if you have not gone to the Journals sections of your portfolio and created a journal you already have one, and that's the journal we will use for this recipe. If you have already used this journal for something else, then you will want to create a new one before we begin. If you do not have that ability (the option **Create Journal** is not available) then you will need to go to your settings and select the option **Enable multiple journals**.

How to do it...

1. Click on the **Portfolio** tab and **Pages**.
2. Click the link for the **Profile page**.
3. In the upper right-hand corner of your **Profile** page, click the option **Edit this page**.

4. From the **Journals** tab, click and drag a **Journal** block into the area of your Profile page where you would like to add this blog (you can always move it later if you don't like where you dropped it).
5. The field for **Block Title** will be empty. You can specify a title such as `My Updates`, or `My Ruminations`, and so on. If you leave it blank, it will take on the name of your Journal.
6. Below the **Block Title**, you will see a list of your current journals. Click on the bubble next to the journal with your name (it is your default journal). For example, mine is called Ellen Marie Murphy's Blog. If you have created another journal for this recipe, then click the bubble next to that journal.
7. You can leave the **Entries per page** at **5**.
8. Skip the **More options** section.
9. Click **Save**.

How it works...

Although this blog/journal appears on your Profile page and others can subscribe to your blog, read your blog, and post comments to your blog from your Profile page, you will add your posts directly into the blog from the Journals section of your portfolio. You can read comments to your blog from here as well as from your Profile page. The advantage of this is that you can use this blog and its individual posts in a number of different pages, if you choose, and it allows you to keep this journal if you later decide to remove it from your profile page. The blog/journal becomes a permanent part of the content of your portfolio, whether it appears on a page or not. It works a little like Blogger, in that you can have multiple blogs.

We set the number of posts that will display on your Profile page to `5`. This means that the five latest posts will be displayed. However a small navigation menu will be created underneath your blog that will provide readers with access to your prior posts (to the archive).

So, let's add our first post:

1. Click on the **Content** tab and then on **Journals**.
2. Click on the **New Entry** button next to the title of the journal.
3. Give this first post a **Title**.
4. Add some text to the **Body**.
5. Leave **Allow comments** checked.
6. Click **Save**.

Your post will now appear on your Profile page and this is where visitors will be able to read and reply to it.

There's more...

As you may know, it is sometimes difficult to remember to go to your favorite web site or blog on a regular basis. That's why some individuals choose to "subscribe" to a blog or website. Subscribing allows them to automatically know when there is a new posting. It's possible to provide this option to fans of your Mahara journals. Let's see how.

Allowing others to subscribe to your journal

By default, individuals inside your Mahara system will have access to your blog, but unless you make the journal publically accessible, they won't be able to subscribe to it—that is, they won't be able to get an RSS feed from your journal.

When you have given public access to your Profile page, you will see a small orange icon next to the title of your journal, on your profile page. Readers who want to subscribe to your journal will click that icon. They will be taken to the feed page where they can select the program they use to receive RSS feeds (notification of updates to your journal), or where they can copy the URL for your feed and add it to a program not listed.

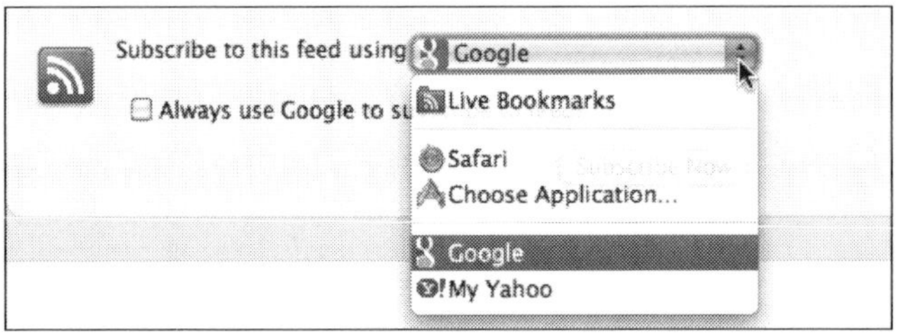

To make your profile page public, click the **Edit** link in the upper right-hand corner of the profile page. On the editing page, you will see a button labeled **Allow public access**. All you need to do is to click the button and click **Done**.

See also

- *Sending feeds to Twitter and/or Facebook* recipe

Adding a counter

The first site we will use for creating our counter, places a small text ad under your counter. If you chose an education counter from the list of options the site provides then the ad, which is just a very small link, will be related to education.

Getting ready

Open two windows or tabs. We will be going back and forth between the two.

How to do it...

1. In the first window/tab, log in to Mahara. You will notice that an area containing your profile information appears on the right-hand side of nearly every page. At the top of this area is your name. Click on your name.

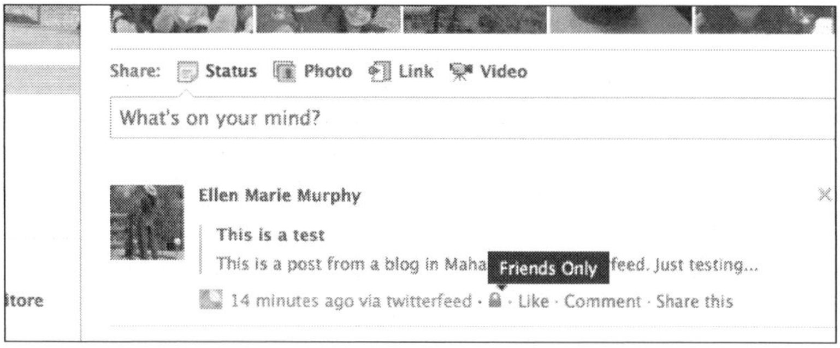

2. You will be taken to your profile page. Highlight and copy the URL that appears at the top of the window (in the address bar).

> While there are other ways to get to your profile page, clicking on your name in this manner is the best method for getting the proper URL.

3. Now we are going to switch to the other window/tab you have open. Go to `http://www.website-hit-counters.com/basic-hit-counters.html` and browse through the options to pick the counter you would like. When you've decided, click the little bubble next to your chosen option and a new window will open.
4. In the field for **Website URL**, paste the URL you copied in steps 1 and 2.
5. In the field for **Starting Count**, type the number you would like your counter to start at. You may opt for zero, but you could also enter 100 or even 1000.
6. For the option labeled **Increment on**, select the option **all hits**. This will increase the counter every time someone looks at your profile page. The other option, **unique visits only**, will only count the number of unique people that access your page—that is, only the first time an individual looks at your profile page, and not any of the times they may access it afterward.
7. Since this is most likely your first time using this tool, you will want to select **new** for the option labeled **Is this a new or existing account?**

8. Add your **email address**.
9. You do *not* need to select the option **I would like a Weekly Traffic Summary sent to this email**.
10. In the **Password** field, give yourself a password.
11. Click **Submit**.
12. Copy the code that appears next.
13. Now go back to the window/tab in which Mahara is open.
14. You should still be on your Profile page. If not, you will need to go there. On the Profile page, in the upper right-hand corner, you will see the option to **Edit this page**. Click on that option.
15. From the **General** tab, click-and-drag a **Text Box** block to the location you would like to add your counter.
16. Delete the text from the **Block Title** and replace it with `Site Visits` or simply leave it empty.
17. In the **Block Content** section, find **HTML** on the HTML editing toolbar, and select it:

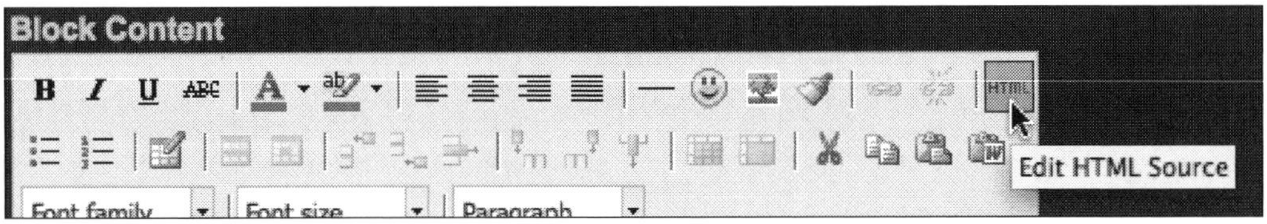

18. In the window that opens, paste the code you copied in step 12.
19. Click **Insert**.
20. Click **Save**.

How it works...

Every time someone, including you, visits your profile page, the counter will increase by one. The following image is a screenshot of mine:

There's more...

There are other sites that you can use to create your counter. Let's look at one now.

Another option (statcounter.com)

StatCounter is another option for creating a counter. It has more features than the previous one; you can log in and actually see graphs and charts that provide you with information about your various visitors. It does, however, display a large number of ads as you navigate the site. You have fewer options for counter display choices as well.

1. Follow steps 1 and 2 in the previous recipe.
2. Go to `http://statcounter.com`. Click the option **Register Now**.
3. You will need to create an account. Provide the required information including name and e-mail address.
4. Put a check mark in the box next to **I accept the terms and conditions**.
5. Click on **REGISTER MY ACCOUNT**.
6. Next, select your **Timezone**.
7. Click **PROCEED & ADD A PROJECT**.
8. In the field for **Website Title**, type the title of your page.
9. In the field for **Website URL**, paste the URL you copied in step 1.
10. Select a **Category**. I chose **Education**, but you might choose **Personal Homepage**.
11. Skip the next set of options and click **Next**.
12. Click **CONFIGURE AND INSTALL CODE**.
13. Select the option **Visible Counter**.
14. Click **Next**.
15. Select the option **Unique Visits Only** (this will still count visitors who return, just not if they return in 30 minutes or sooner).
16. You might want to start your counter at something other than zero. If so, put that number in the field for **Unique Visits**, and **Pageloads** (so that you can follow the stats a little better).
17. Click **Next**.
18. For the **Graphic or Text** option, select **Counter Image**.
19. Click **Next**.
20. For the **Number of digits**, choose **5**. You probably won't get 100,000 visitors to your page!
21. Select the other options as per your preferences. To see what your choices will look like, click the **Update** button. When you're satisfied with the results, click **Next**.

22. In this next window, leave the drop-down at **Default installation guide**. Skip the option for **HTML ONLY COUNTER**. Check the box for **XHTML COMPLIANT**.
23. Click **Next**.
24. Click in the box labeled **Your StatCounter Code** and copy the code.
25. In Mahara, open your Profile page and click the **Edit** option in the upper right-hand corner.
26. From the **General** tab, click and drag a **Text Box** block into your page. Put it in the location you would like your counter to appear.
27. In the **Block Title**, type `Site Visits`.
28. In the **Block Content** area, click the **HTML** option on the HTML toolbar. Paste the code you copied in step 24, into the **HTML Source Editor** box.

> If you paste the code directly into the **Block Content** area, it will not work. You will only see the code and not the counter.

29. Click **Update**. You will not see anything in the content area, but it's there.
30. Click **Save**.

To see more detailed information regarding your visitors, log in to the site using the username and password you created in step 3. Click **My Projects** and then the name of your page listed under **Project Name**.

Adding a feed from Twitter

Mahara out-of-the-box (that is without add-ons or plug-ins) does not have a *specific block* for adding a Twitter feed to a page but there is still a way to add a feed from Twitter. We will cover that method in this recipe.

> There is at least one plugin available for Mahara that can be used to add a Twitter gadget (`embed.ly`), but that would require installation by the System Administrator.

Getting ready

You can add a Twitter feed to your profile page even if you do not have a Twitter account, therefore there is no preparation needed for this recipe.

How to do it...

1. Go to `http://search.twitter.com`.
2. Type in your Twitter name, or any term that you would like to get the feed for. If you would like a particular individual's tweets (including your own), type in their Twitter name:

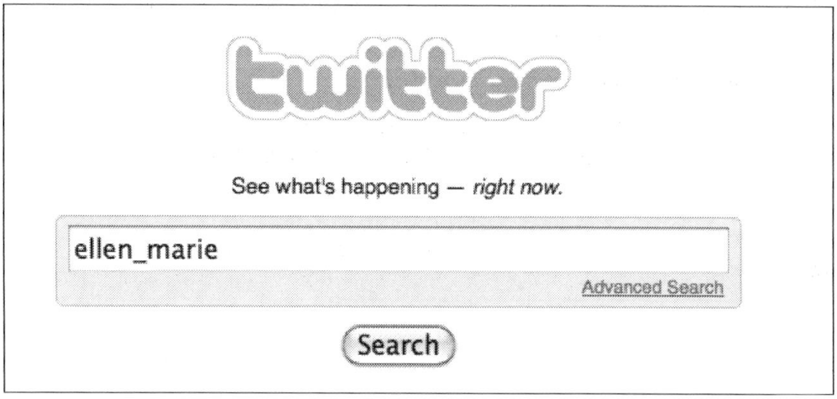

3. If you would like the tweets on a particular topic, type that in the search box:

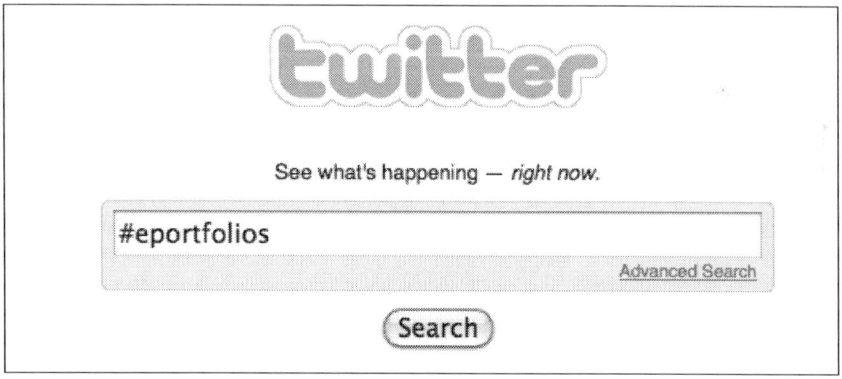

4. Click **Search**.
5. In the next window, you will see a list of the most recent tweets for the term that you searched for. Make sure these are the kind of tweets you wanted to get a feed for. In the case of using a Twitter name, you will get the user's tweets as well as tweets that mention the user.

6. In the upper right-hand corner, you will see a link labeled **Feed for this query**. Click that link:

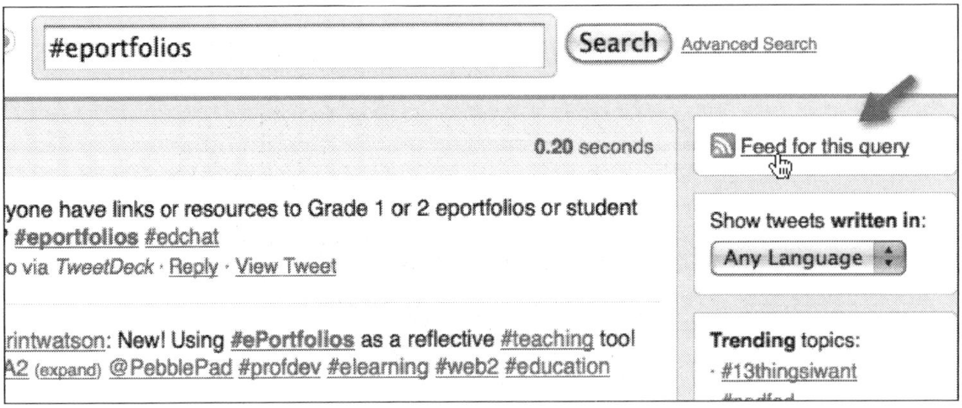

7. The next window that opens will be the actual feed page for those tweets. Copy the URL of the page (located in the address bar):

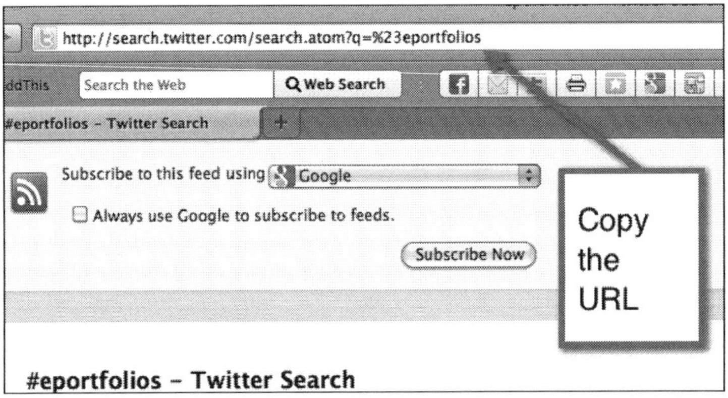

8. In your Mahara portfolio, go to your Profile page and in the upper right-hand corner click the link **Edit Content**.
9. From the **External feeds** tab, click-and-drag an **External feed** block into the column where you would like to add your Twitter feed.
10. You can leave the **Block Title** empty.
11. In the field for **Feed location**, paste the URL you copied in step 5.
12. You can leave the **Items to show** at the default, which is **10**. You can always change it later.

13. Do not check the box for **Show feed items in full**, as the tweets will be shown in full. If you check the box, each tweet will be displayed twice. The following image is what the feed, without the check mark, will look like:

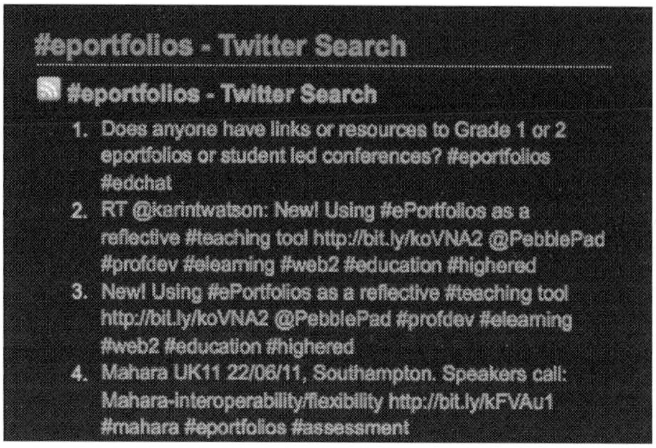

14. **Click Save**.

How it works...

As posts that contain your search term are added to Twitter, your Profile page will automatically be updated. It will show the most recent posts.

There's more...

Piers Dillon Scott has written about the previous idea and other ways to get an RSS feed from Twitter in the following Sociable blog post: `http://sociable.co/2011/04/30/twitter-hasnt-killed-rss-just-yet-heres-how-to-find-your-twitter-feed-rss-url`.

See Also...

- *Embedly and Google maps in Supplements* available on the Packt website *(Addons & Plugins)*
- *Twitter Tweet in Supplements* available on the Packt website *(Addons & Plugins)*

Sending feeds to Twitter and/or Facebook

In this recipe, we will create a journal that will feed to your profile page, as well as Twitter and Facebook. You can send a post from Mahara directly to Twitter and Facebook. I created a test post so I could show you how this works. You do not need to have both accounts for this and you do not need to send your tweets to both accounts if you do have them. You can select to send to one or the other or both.

> Please note that there are two add-ons that create this functionality: the Facebook Like add-on and the Twitter Tweet add-on. This recipe is for those who are using Mahara out-of-the-box.

Getting ready

By default, every member of Mahara has a journal/blog. It is located in the Journals section on the Content tab. The title of the journal is your name. For example, mine is called "Ellen Marie Murphy's Journal". We will add this journal to your Profile page so that your updates appear there as well as on Twitter and Facebook. In order for the feed to work, the journal/blog will need to allow public access. If you would prefer to use a different journal for this, you will need to create one. If you would like to have a journal that regularly updates to Twitter and Facebook, but you don't want to make your Profile publically viewable, you can add this journal to a different Page and set the access of that page to public (we'll cover that in the *There's more...* section below).

How to do it...

1. First, we'll need to copy the URL for the feed. To do this, go to your **Profile page**.
2. Next to the title of the journal, you will see a small RSS feed icon (it is orange and white in color). Click the icon.
3. You will be taken to the page that generates the feed. Copy the URL for this page (it is in the address bar at the top of the page).
4. Go to `http://twitterfeed.com`.
5. Click the button **Register Now**.
6. Provide an e-mail address and create a password, then click **Create Account**.
7. You'll now be at step 1 in the feed creation process. In the field for **Feed Name**, give this feed a name. This is primarily for your purpose.
8. In the field for **Blog URL or RSS Feed URL**, paste the URL you copied in step 3.
9. Leave **Active** checked.

10. In the **Advance Settings** section, **Update Frequency** indicates how frequently your blog posts will be fed. At **30 minutes**, it means that your posts will update 30 minutes after you post to your blog. The numbers of posts that will be sent out every 30 minutes are determined by the number you set. You can leave these options and all the other options at their default settings. You can change these at any time.

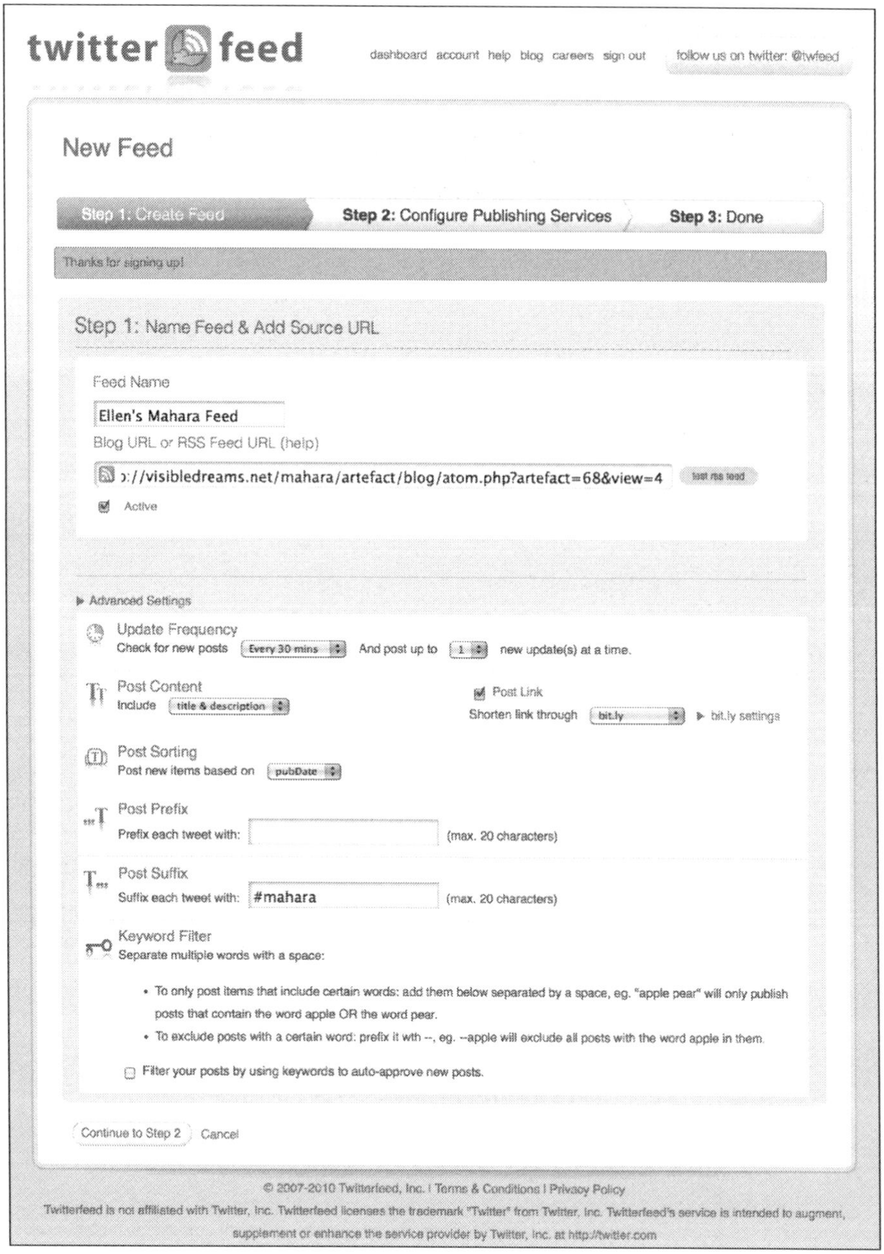

11. Click the button **Continue to Step 2**.
12. You will see that there are four available services. For this recipe, we will concentrate on Twitter and Facebook. Let's start with Twitter.
13. Click the **Twitter** link.
14. On the next page, click the big blue button labeled **Authenticate Twitter**.
15. Provide your Twitter name and password.
16. Click **Create Service**.
17. After you are brought back to **Available Services**, click the link for **Facebook**.
18. Click the button **Connect with Facebook**.
19. Again, you will need to provide access for Twitterfeed to access your Facebook account.
20. When Twitterfeed has successfully accessed your Facebook account, you will see something that looks like this:

21. Select **Create Service**.
22. Select **All Done!**
23. Now, click the button **Go to Dashboard**.

24. From the dashboard, you will be able to monitor your posts, edit your feeds, and create new feeds. You won't see any postings on the dashboard until you've added an entry to your blog. Any entries you had prior to creating the feed will not be sent out. Leave this page open and, in another window/tab, let's go back to Mahara so we can give this a test.

How it works...

To see how this works, we're actually going to run a test. Let's post a test post in our journal/blog and see what happens:

1. Go to Mahara and on the **Content** tab select **Journals**.
2. Click your journal to open it.
3. Click the button **New Post**.
4. In the **Title**, type `This is a test.`
5. In the **Body**, type `This is a post from my Page in Mahara. This is just a test.`
6. Click **Save Post**.
7. Go back to the window/tab that has been opened to your dashboard in Twitterfeed and click the link **check now!**

> Because the settings in Twitterfeed were set to **Check for new posts every 30 minutes**, you would normally have to wait 30 minutes to see the results of the feed. But, we can go to our dashboard in Twitterfeed and click the link **check now!**, which will post the feed immediately.

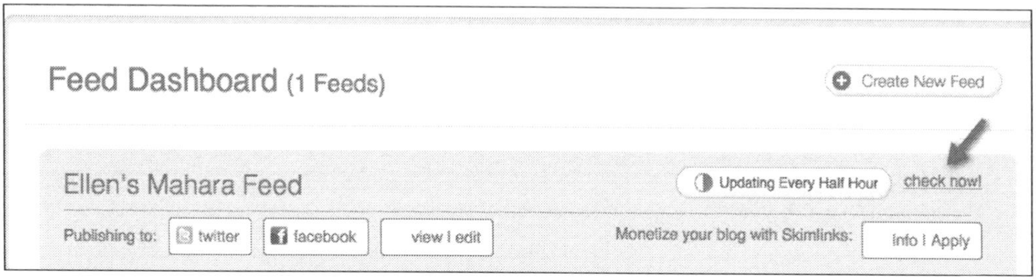

In Mahara, go to your Profile page and you will see the new blog post in the journal you added.

This is similar to the way it will look in Facebook. The Facebook post will adhere to your privacy settings.

The following screenshot is what the post looks like in Twitter. It contains the link to the post.

There's more...

There is additional functionality available, which we will explore next.

Adding hashtags and filtering

The **Advanced Settings** in your Twitterfeed account can be set to automatically include a Twitter hashtag in your published posts. Hashtags allow individuals to follow posts on certain topics. For example, if my post contains the hashtag **#mahara**, it allows individuals who are searching for posts on Mahara to easily find mine.

There are settings that can also regulate your feed so that Twitterfeed only sends out posts on a particular subject, or does not send posts on a particular subject:

1. To add these settings, log in to your Twitterfeed account. You will automatically be taken to your dashboard. Click **edit**, on the **view | edit** button, directly under the feed you want to edit.
2. Click **Advanced Settings** to expand that area:
    - To add hashtags, enter the hashtag in the field for **Post Suffix**.
    - To use the **Keyword Filter**, check the small box **Filter your posts by using keywords to auto-approve new posts** and follow the instructions provided:

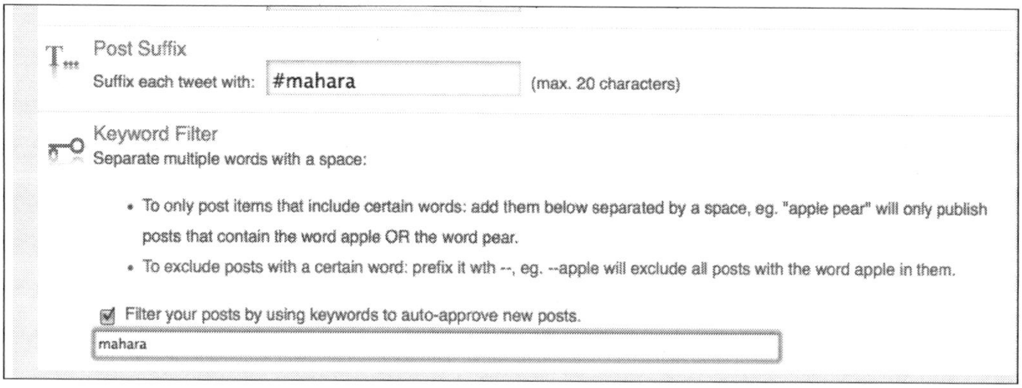

3. Click **Continue to Step 2**.
4. Click **All Done!**

See Also...

- *Facebook Like button in Supplements* available on the Packt website *(Addons & Plugins)*
- *Twitter Tweet in Supplements* available on the Packt website *(Addons & Plugins)*

Adding your external blog to your profile page

Often times, we either have blogs that we are following or our own blogs that are not hosted in Mahara. You can add these external blogs to your profile page. In this recipe that's just what we'll do.

How to do it...

On the home page for the blog, you will need to locate the button or link that will take you to a feed for the blog. The link may have an icon like the one shown in the following screenshot:

Or it might say **RSS Feed**, **Atom Feed**, or simply be labeled **Subscribe**.

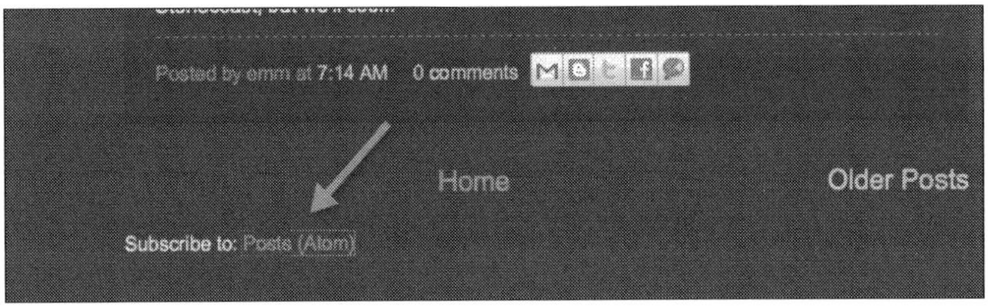

1. Click the link for the feed.
2. You will be taken to a page that looks something like the following screenshot (however, the title and URL that will be displayed, will be the title and url for your blog)

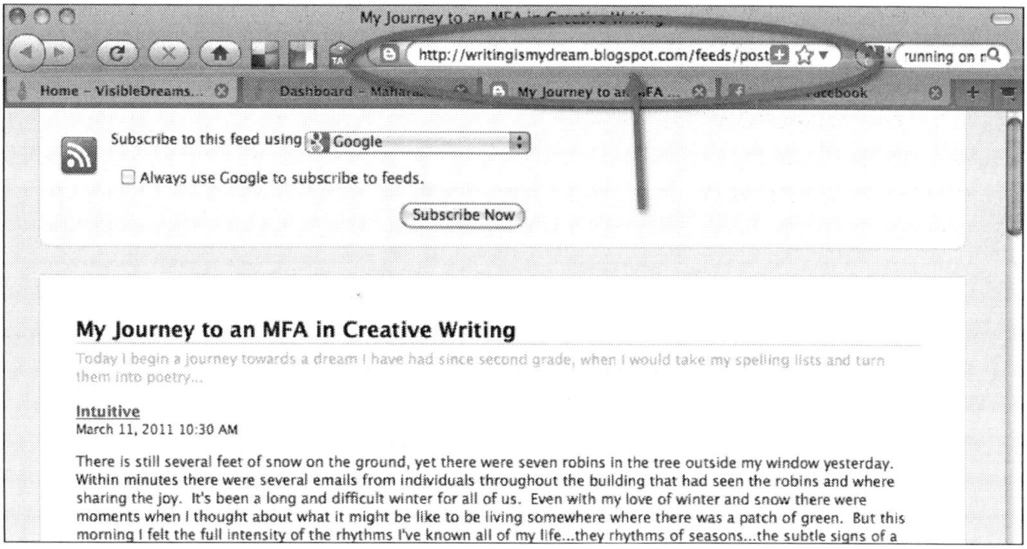

3. Copy the URL at the top of the page (in the address bar).
4. Go to your Profile page and click the **Edit** link in the upper-right corner.
5. From the **External feeds** tab, click and drag an **External feed** block into the section of your Profile page where you would like to add the blog.
6. Leave the **Block Title** empty as it will take its name from your feed.
7. In the field **Feed location**, paste the URL you copied in step 3.
8. In the field for **Items to show** type `5`.
9. Click the box **Show feed items in full?**
10. Click **Save**.

How it works...

Your Profile page will now display the five most recent posts to this blog. When the blog is updated, the new post will display in your Profile page as well. A navigation menu for previous posts will not appear on your page. The title of the blog will be a hyperlink to the original blog, and there will also be an RSS icon that will provide readers with the ability to subscribe to the RSS feed for this blog.

There's more...

You can add external feeds from sources that are not blogs.

Other RSS feeds

You don't have to limit your external feeds to blogs. Many websites have RSS feed capability including various news sites. You can use the steps in this recipe to add an RSS feed from any source. So, it's possible for you to share your favorite website(s) with your readers right from your Profile page.

See also

- *Adding a feed from Twitter* recipe

7

The College Application Portfolio

In this chapter, we will cover:

- The Art Portfolio and The Common Application: Art Supplement
- Using HTML to create your unofficial transcript
- Creating an academic achievements page
- The Common Application: Extracurricular Activities & Work Experience portion
- The Athletic Supplement

Introduction

There are a large number of recipes in this book that can be used for various activities in Secondary Education. These would include the various chapters on journals, the recipe on projects, and the recipes for building a resume. In this chapter, we are mostly concerned with preparing your portfolio for college applications and/or providing supplemental information for a traditional resume. This chapter includes the use of code that you can download from the Packt Publishing website for this book.

The Art Portfolio and The Common Application: Art Supplement

Nearly all programs for Schools of Art, whether they are Music, Theatre, Dance, Fine Arts, or Graphic Arts, require the submission of a portfolio. They almost always request the applicant to put the portfolio on a CD or DVD and mail it in. However, CDs and DVDs are rather old technologies and, when schools dispose of them, they contribute to the accumulation of waste. Creating a portfolio that can be viewed on the Web makes much more sense. Reviewers can zoom in on images and/or stream video. This is why using Mahara to create your portfolio is a very good idea. If the school still insists on a DVD, you can export your entire portfolio from Mahara. You can then burn it on to a CD or DVD, and it will be well-formatted.

This is a basic recipe for a Fine Arts portfolio. Though the portfolio we will be building is that of a student in the Studio Arts, this recipe can be used for some of the other arts as well. If this recipe is not applicable to your needs, hopefully you will find several of the recipes in this book helpful in designing your portfolio.

We will build the art performance piece of the portfolio first, but we will put everything together with a cover page that follows the Arts Supplement format for The Common Application.

Getting ready

Art schools generally require a certain number of images and examples of art in various genres and/or mediums. You will need to take photos of your artwork, and you will want to make certain to use high resolution and good lighting. The images from most digital cameras are in `.jpg` format, which is a web-ready format (can be viewed in a web browser). The easiest thing to do is to put all of the images into one folder and then "zip" or compress the folder. To compress a folder, you will simply have to right-click the folder and, from the menu of options, select to **compress** or **zip** the contents (on some computers, you may need to select **Sent to** and then select **compress**). We will unpack the compressed folder once we've uploaded it to Mahara. To begin, simply compress the folder.

You will also need a letter of recommendation from an instructor who is familiar with your work. They will need to send it to the school, or to The Common Application, directly. If they also give you a copy, you can attach it to this portfolio.

In the Profile section of your portfolio, add your contact information.

How to do it...

1. Click the **Content** tab in your portfolio, and then click **Files**.
2. Click the small box next to **Upload file**.

3. Click the **Browse** button and locate the compressed folder (not the original folder). It will have a **.zip** extension. Double-click it to begin uploading.
4. Once the compressed folder has finished uploading you will see it listed in your files. It will have a different icon than regular folders, however. You will see three icons to the its right. To unpack the contents, click the first icon to the right of the package. The icon will look somewhat like a vise holding a folder.

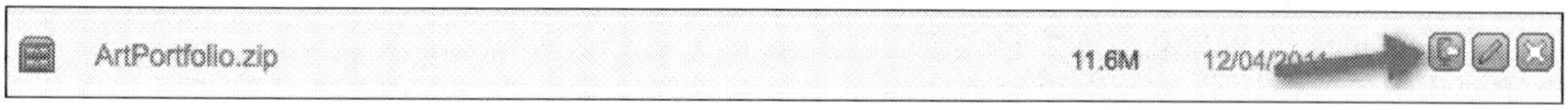

5. You will be taken to a new page that lists the contents of the folder. Click the button labeled **Unzip**.
6. You will see a band showing you the progress. When asked, click **Continue**.
7. You may now see your folder inside another folder of the same name. If you are on a Mac, you may see an additional folder labeled **_MACOSX**. You can delete the **_MACOSX** folder as it contains files you won't need, then hover your cursor over your art folder so that your cursor looks like a hand. Drag the folder into the **Parent folder**.

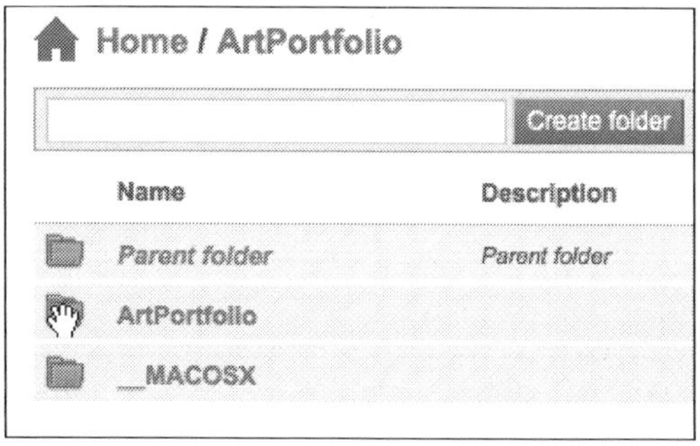

8. Now click on the link to the **Parent folder** to open it.
9. You will now see a list of all your folders and files. You will see that you have two **ArtPortfolio** folders with the exact same name. One will have a description that says **Files extracted from archive**. You can delete this folder because you removed the contents when you dragged the **ArtPortfolio** folder into the **Parent Folder**.
10. Delete the packaged folder as well (the one with the `.zip` extension).

Now let's add some information to the images:

1. Open your **ArtPortfolio** folder by clicking on it.
2. To the right of each image, you will see a small pencil icon. Use this icon to expand the **Edit file** options for one of your images.
3. Make sure the **Name** of the file is the name you will use in your list of images.

4. In the field for **Description**, provide information as to whether the art was **from life**, what medium was used to create the piece, and the approximate size of the original piece.
5. In the field for **Tags**, you can provide some keywords that will be helpful should you need to find this item in the future.

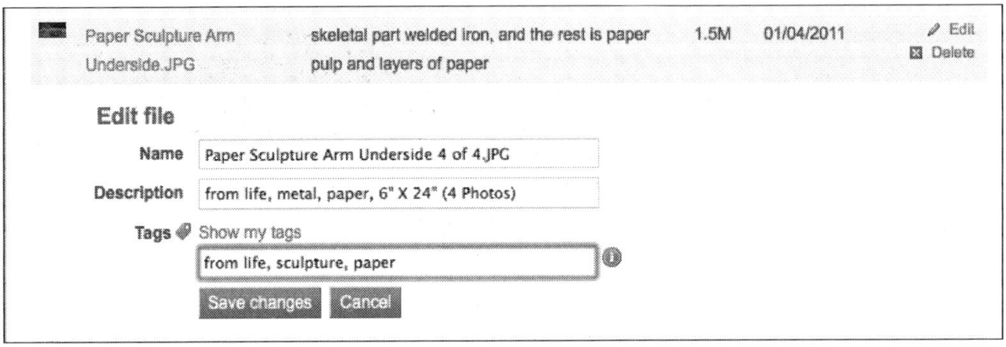

6. Click on the **Save changes** button.
7. Repeat steps 2-6 for each of your images.

   Now, let's build the pages that will become part of your official Art Portfolio. You may want to group your images into categories (for example, figure drawings, sculptures, landscapes, and so on) and then place each group of images on a separate page:

8. Click the **Portfolio** tab to go to the **Pages** section of your portfolio.
9. Click on the **Create Page**.
10. Click on the **Edit Layout** tab.
11. Select **4 columns, equal widths**.
12. Click the **Save** button.
13. Choose your theme from the drop-down menu labeled **Theme**.
14. On the **Files, images and video** tab, click and drag the **An Image** block into one of your columns.

> While you could use the **Image Gallery** block to quickly add your images, you will have much more control over how they display if you add them using the **An Image** block.

15. In the **Block Title**, type the name of the piece.
16. In the **Files** section, click on the **Art Portfolio** folder to open it.

17. Find your image and click the **Select** button next to it.
18. Click the small box beneath **Show Description**.
19. If your image is taller than it is wide, set the **Width** to **200**; if the image is wider than it is tall, set the **Width** to **250**.
20. Click the **Save** button.

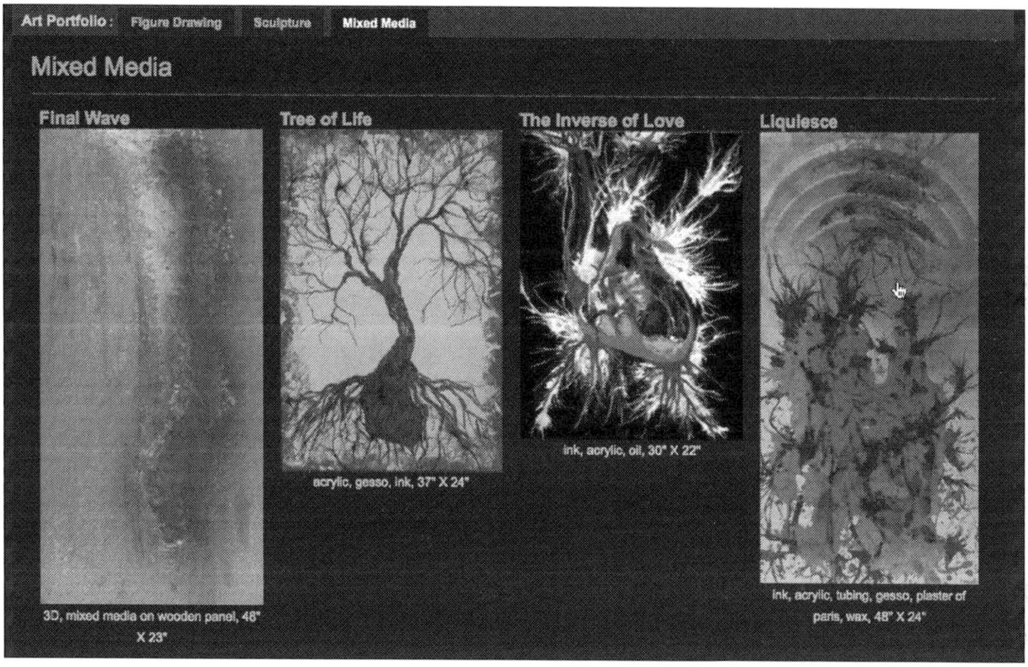

21. Repeat steps 7 - 13 for each of the images you want to add to this page.
22. Click the **Edit Title & Description** tab.
23. In the **Title** field, type the category of the images (for example, `Figure Drawing`).
24. Click the **Save** button.
25. Click **Done**.
26. Repeat the steps 1-18 for each page you want to create.

Now, we'll create the cover page:

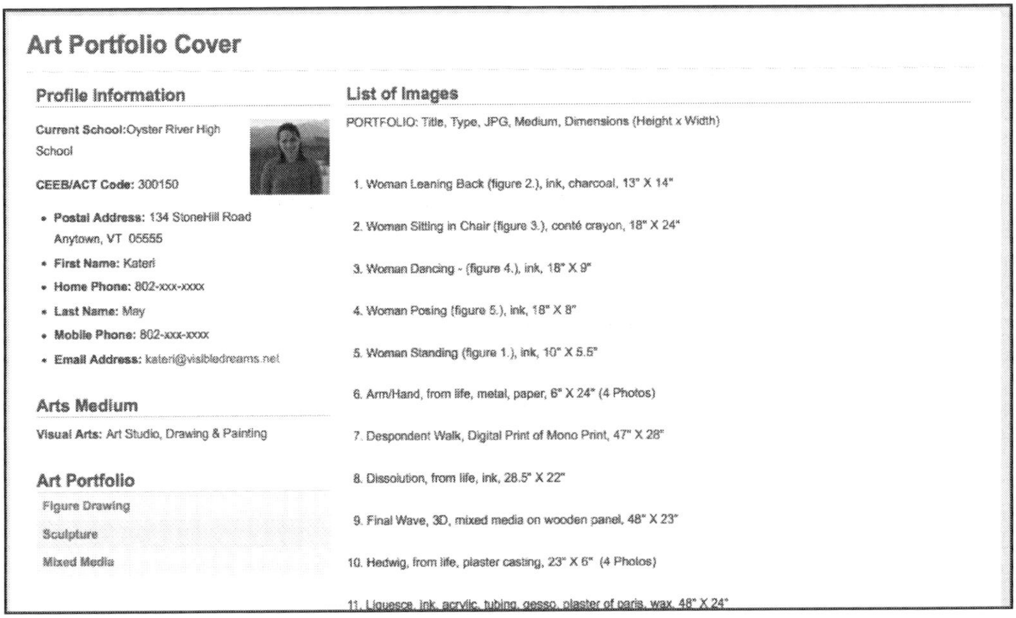

1. Go to the **Pages** tab and click **Create Page**.
2. Click on the **Edit Layout** tab.
3. Select **Larger right column** under **2 columns**.
4. Click on the **Save** button.
5. A list of the attached images (art portfolio contents) is almost always required, so let's add that first. From the **General** tab, click and drag a **Text Box** block into the right-hand column.
6. Delete the text in the **Block Title** and replace it with `List of Images`.
7. In the **Block Content area**, type your list. The institutions you are applying to and/or The Common Application will provide you with the information they would like in the list. Generally speaking, it should include the name of the image, the medium, and the approximate size of the actual piece.
8. Click the **Save** button.
9. From the **General** tab, click and drag a textbox into the left-hand column.
10. Change the **Block Title** to say `Arts Medium`.
11. In the **Block Content**, type your medium and area of interest. For this particular portfolio, the medium is **Visual Arts** and the areas of interest are **Drawing, Art Studio**, and **Painting**.
12. Click the **Save** button.

13. From the **Profile** tab, click and drag a **Profile Information** block into the left-hand column.
14. In the **Fields to Show**, select those items you need to display, such as, **First Name**, **Last Name**, **Postal Address**, and **Phone**.
15. You can select whether to display a profile icon or not.
16. Select your **Email Address**
17. In the **Introduction** text, type the name of your current school and the CEEB/ACT Code.
18. Click the **Save** button.
19. Click the **Edit Title and Description** tabs.
20. In the **Title field**, type `Art Portfolio Cover`.
21. You can leave the **Description** blank.
22. Click the **Save** button.
23. Click **Done**.

Now, let's package it all together:

1. Click the **Portfolio** tab and then **Collections**.
2. Click **New Collection**.
3. For the **Collection name** type: "`Art Portfolio and Supplement`".
4. You can leave the **Description** blank.
5. Make sure that there is a checkmark in the option for **Page navigation bar**.
6. Click **Next: Edit Collection Pages**.
7. In the **Add pages to collection** area, put a checkmark next to each of the pages that will be part of this collection.
8. Click **Add pages**.
9. Above the area labeled **Add pages to collection**, you will now see a list of the pages that will be part of the collection. Using the small up and down arrows, move the pages into the order in which you would like them to display. The cover page should be moved to the top.
10. Click **Done**.
11. Click the **Share** tab.
12. You will see this collection in the area labeled **Collections**. In the far-right column labeled **Secret URL**, click the pencil tool for your art portfolio.
13. In the next page, click the **Add** button next to **New Secret URL**.
14. A URL will be generated and will appear above the **Add** button. Copy and send it to the individuals you wish to provide access to.

How it works...

When an individual clicks on any of the images in your portfolio pages, they will be taken to a preview page. That page will display the image in a much larger size, and it will have a link that will provide access to details about the image. If they click on the image in this preview page, they will be given a magnifying glass cursor, which will allow them to zoom in on any portion of the image they would like to see in greater detail.

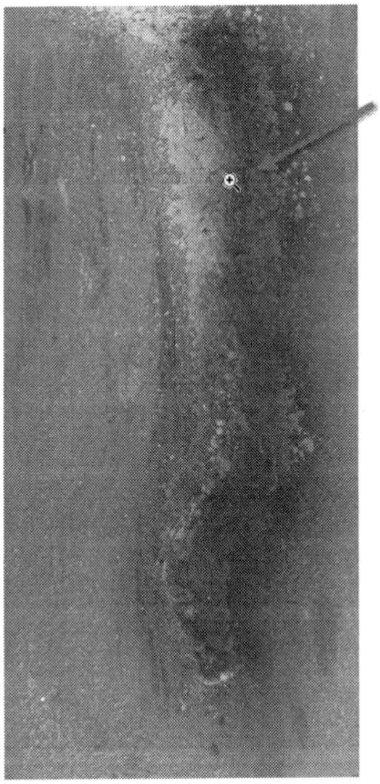

There's more...

Let's cover a few additional options for sending and creating this portfolio.

Exporting the portfolio

You can export your portfolio as a website, and burn it onto a CD or DVD. This allows the portfolio to be opened and viewed in a browser, without the need of the Internet or Mahara:

1. Click the **Portfolio** tab and then click **Export**.
2. Select **Standalone HTML Website** in the options for **Choose an export format**.
3. In the **What do you want to export?** list of options, select **Just some of my Collections**.

4. **Collections to export** will expand and display a list of your Collections. Put a checkmark next to **Art Portfolio**.
5. Click on **Generate export**.
6. When the program has finished it will ask you to save the file. Select the location where you wish to save the file. Click the **Save** button.

Using video and audio (for Music, Theatre, Film, and Dance)

If you are going to be using video or audio files, you will want to follow most of the steps outlined previously, however, it is best to upload video files one at a time. To add video and audio to a page, use the **Embedded Media** block and follow the same steps as you would for an image (as outlined previously). While you can add several audio files to a page, it is best to only add one video file per page. Unlike images, the name of the video and/or audio files will display on the page you create, but the description will not. Because of this, you will want to add a text box block with a brief description of the file.

Making each item in the list a link

On the cover page, we included a list of each image in the portfolio. You will need to include such a list for video and audio files as well. To make each item in the list a link to the actual file, follow these steps.

1. Open a simple text editing program (on a Mac open TextEdit; on a PC open Notepad).
2. Next, in Mahara, go to the **Files** section of your **Content** tab, and open the folder that contains your image, audio and/or video files (we named it **Art Portfolio**).
3. Place your cursor on the first file and click the right mouse button. From the menu that opens, select **Copy Link Location**:

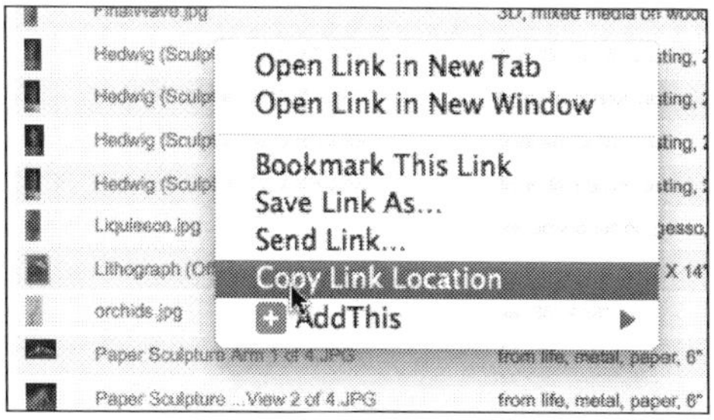

4. Click in the window of your text program and paste in the link location you just copied.
5. Repeat steps 2-4 for each file in the folder.
6. When you've copied the location of each file, click on the **Portfolio** tab in Mahara to go to the **Pages** area of your portfolio.
7. Click on the **Art Portfolio Cover page** to open it, and then select the **Edit** option in the upper right-hand corner.

8. Click the **Configure** icon in the upper right-hand corner of the text box block that contains your **List of Images** (or **List of Contents**).
9. Highlight the first item in the list, then click over to your text program and copy the link for that item.
10. Switch back to Mahara and, with the first item still highlighted, click the **Insert/edit link** icon on the HTML toolbar:

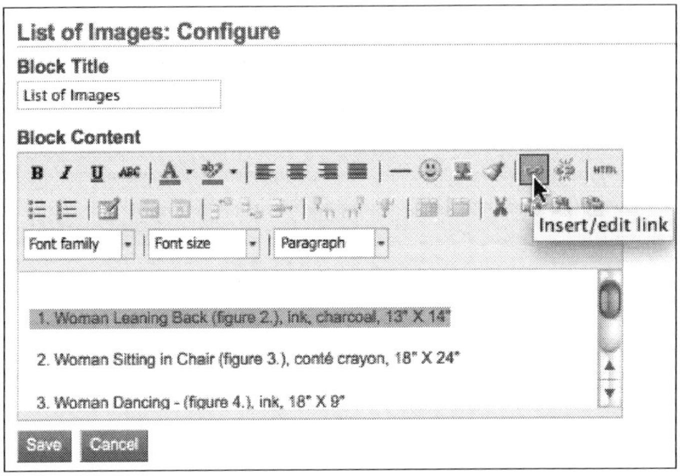

11. In the **Link URL** field, paste the link you copied in step 9.
12. Set the **Target** to **Open link in new window**.
13. You can leave the **Title** field empty, as you already have the filename in the list.
14. Click **Insert**.
15. Repeat steps 9-14 for each item in your list.
16. When you've finished editing the page, click **Done**.

See also

- *Mahara for the Visual Arts* recipe in *Chapter 1, Mahara for the Visual Arts*
- *Language acquisition journal* recipe in *Chapter 2, Literature and Writing*
- *Complex résumé* recipe in *Chapter 3, The Professional Portfolio*

Using HTML to create your unofficial transcript

While colleges and some employers will want copies of official transcripts, giving them access to your unofficial transcript can often help processes move along a bit quicker. While you could use a textbox in a page to create a table for your unofficial transcript, the textbox would not be saved as an artifact. This has a number of disadvantages. Instead, we are going to use a free web page composer, KompoZer, to create a document for our unofficial transcript. We will build a table to make a nice display for our transcript, and then save it as an HTML file. This will allow us to save this as an artifact, which we will be able to pull into multiple pages. This may be useful in the future.

Unofficial Transcript

Grade 12			
Course	Grade	Credit	GPA
AP English	A	1.0	4.0
AP Chemistry	A	1.0	4.0
AP History	B+	1.0	3.5
Drawing 1	A	.5	4.0
PE	B	.5	3.0
Linear Algebra	A	1.0	4.0
Statistics	B+	1.0	3.5
Grade 11			
English 12	A	1.0	4.0
Physics I & II	A	1.0	4.0
Mathematics IV	A	1.0	4.0
History 12	B	1.0	3.0
Latin II	B+	1.0	3.5
PE	B	.5	3.0
Music Composition	A	.5	4.0
Grade 10			
History 11	A	1.0	4.0
English 11	B+	1.0	3.5
Mathematics III	A	1.0	4.0
Chemistry	B+	1.0	3.5
Latin I	A	1.0	4.0
PE	B	1.0	3.0
Chorus	A	1.0	4.0
Grade 9			
English 10	A	1.0	4.0
Mathematics II	A	1.0	4.0
Biology	A	1.0	4.0
World History	A	1.0	4.0
English 9	A	1.0	4.0
PE	B	1.0	3.0
Chorus	A	1.0	4.0

Getting ready

As mentioned previously, we are going to be using an open source program called KompoZer to build our transcript. You do not need to be familiar with the program as I will walk you through the steps to build your HTML document. Before we begin, download and install KompoZer (available at `http://kompozer.net/`). On a piece of paper, sketch out the table you would like to create.

How to do it...

1. Open KompoZer.
2. At the bottom of the window you will see three tabs. The labels of the tabs will depend on the type of computer you are on. You might see **Design**, **Split**, and **Source**, or you might see **Normal**, **HTML Tags**, **Source**, and **Preview**. You will want to be on the **Design** or **Normal** tab.
3. Click **Table** on the top menu bar:

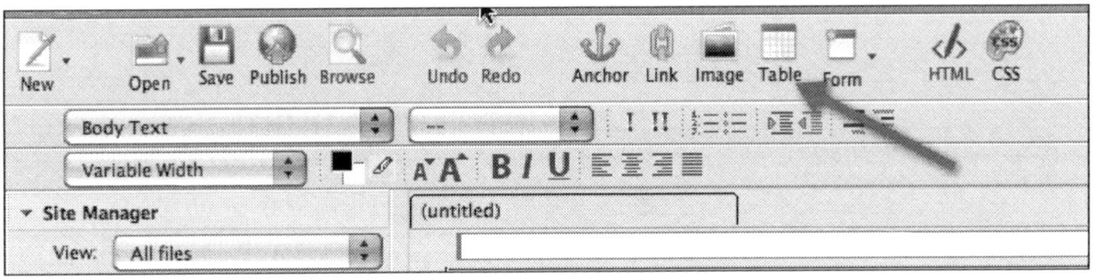

4. A small window with three tabs will open. Click the **Precisely** tab.
5. In the fields for **Rows** and **Columns**, type the number of rows and columns in the table you sketched out. Don't worry if you're not exactly sure, as you can always add or subtract rows or columns later.
6. In the field labeled **Width**, type `90` and ensure the drop-down menu is set to **%**.

> Using percentage, instead of a set width, will ensure that the table will fit in whatever size column you use when you add the table to your page.

7. Leave the **Border** at **1** for now.
8. Click **OK**.
9. You will now see the table in your page and it should have small boxes in the corners indicating that it is currently selected. If not, click on the table; in the menu at the top, click **Table** (the same **Table** you clicked in step 3). This will allow you to edit the table.

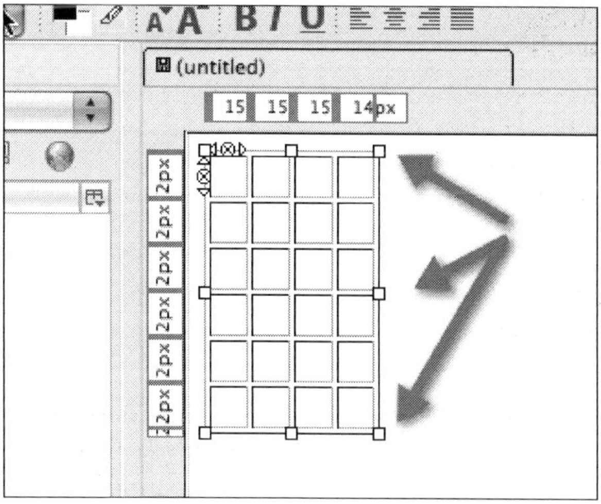

10. A window will open with two tabs. Click the tab labeled **Table**.
11. In the section labeled **Borders and Spacing**, you should see the default settings. For the moment, let's leave the settings at their defaults.
12. Change the **Table Alignment** to **Center**; leave the **Caption** at **None**.
13. If you would like to add a background color to your table, click the small rounded-rectangle.
14. Click **OK**.
15. To create headings in your table you can join several cells together. Simply put your cursor in the left-most cell of the row. Hold your mouse button down and drag it over the cells you'd like to join together, highlighting them. Then, click the right button on your mouse to open a menu, from which you should select **Join selected cells**.

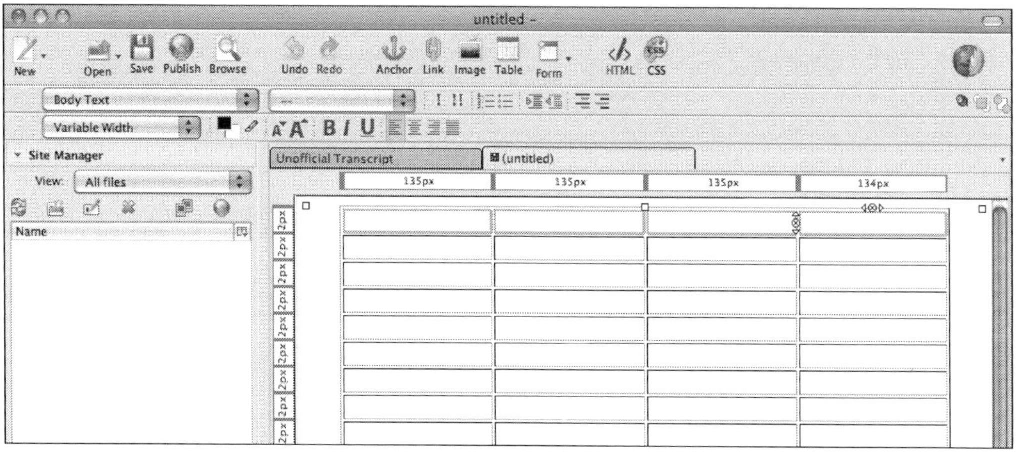

16. To give the heading a different color than the rest of the table, right-click in the cell and, from the menu that opens, select **Table** or **Cell Background Color**.
17. In the window that opens, make sure **Background for Cell(s)** is selected. Click on the color you want. Click **OK**.
18. Before adding text in the heading cell, click the center-align option in the toolbar at the top of the window and then add the text.
19. If you wish to change the color of the text, highlight it and use the little color boxes in the toolbar at the top of the page.

> If you hover your cursor above an icon on the toolbar, a small descriptor will appear providing information on the function of that particular icon.

20. Click inside each individual cell to add your content. You can use the formatting icons at the top of the window to centre the text, change the color of the text, the font, and more.
21. When you have finished the table, select **Save As** from the **File** menu; note that you will have to save this page with a `.html` extension. The **Format** will be an **HTML** file. Name the file "`Unofficial_Transcript`", then click the **Save** button.

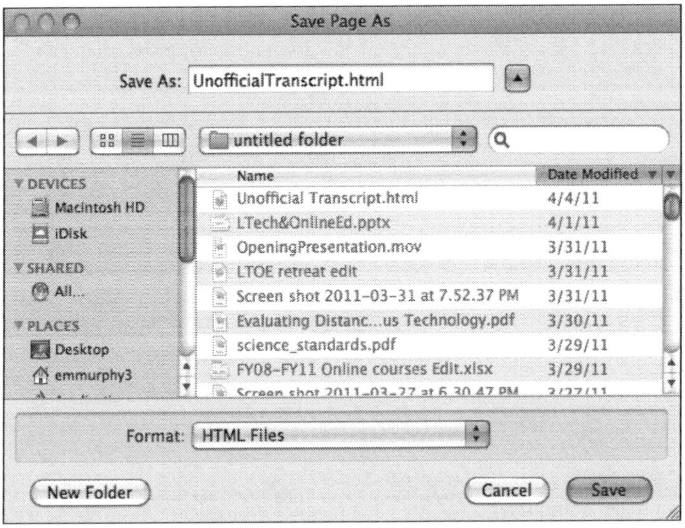

Now, let's upload this file to Mahara and add it to a page:

1. In Mahara, click on the **Content** tab and then click **Files**.
2. Click the small box next to **Upload file** and then click the **Browse** button to locate your unofficial transcript and upload it.

3. Go to the **Pages** area on the **Portfolio** tab.
4. Click **Create Page**.
5. Click the **Edit Layout** tab.
6. Select **1 column equal widths**.
7. Click the **Save** button.
8. From **Files, images and video** tab, drag and drop an HTML block into the page.
9. Delete the text in the **Block Title** field leaving it empty.
10. Click the **Select** button next to the file labeled **UnofficialTranscript**.
11. Click the **Save** button.
12. Click the **Edit Title and Description** tab.
13. In the field for **Page Title**, type: "`Unofficial Transcript`".
14. Make sure the name display format is your legal name.
15. Click the **Save** button.
16. Click **Done**. You can set the access level later.

There's more...

You may find that you need to add or remove some of the columns or rows. Here's how you can do that.

Adding additional rows and/or columns

It is best to edit your table before uploading it to Mahara, because an HTML document cannot be edited directly in Mahara (as can be done when using a textbox). If, however, you've already uploaded it, you will need to reopen the document in KompoZer—either download the file from Mahara and open it, or, if you have the original saved on your computer, you can open that. When you have finished editing it, you will need to re-upload it to Mahara. Delete the old file from Mahara before uploading this new file. Once it is uploaded, you will have to edit any pages that contained the older version of the document so that the HTML block points to this new version of the document.

1. To add an additional row or column, put your cursor inside a cell next to which you would like to add the row or column.
2. Click the right mouse button to pull up a menu of options.

3. Select the option **Table Insert**, and then select the addition that you would like:

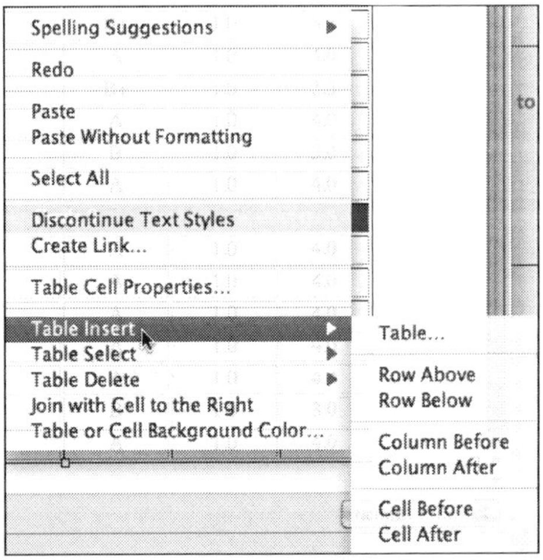

See also

- *Creating an academic achievements page* recipe in *Chapter 7, The College Application Portfolio*
- *Building the ECIS International Teacher portfolio* recipe in *Chapter 8, Certification and Accreditation Portfolio for Higher Education*

Creating an academic achievements page

You might want to include your unofficial transcript on a page that showcases your academic accomplishments. This page might include links to a collection of work, and writing samples. It should also include your academic awards (even if these are also listed in your résumé).

In this recipe, we will add your academic awards and achievements to your portfolio, we'll create a folder for writing samples, and we'll build a page that showcases your academic accomplishments.

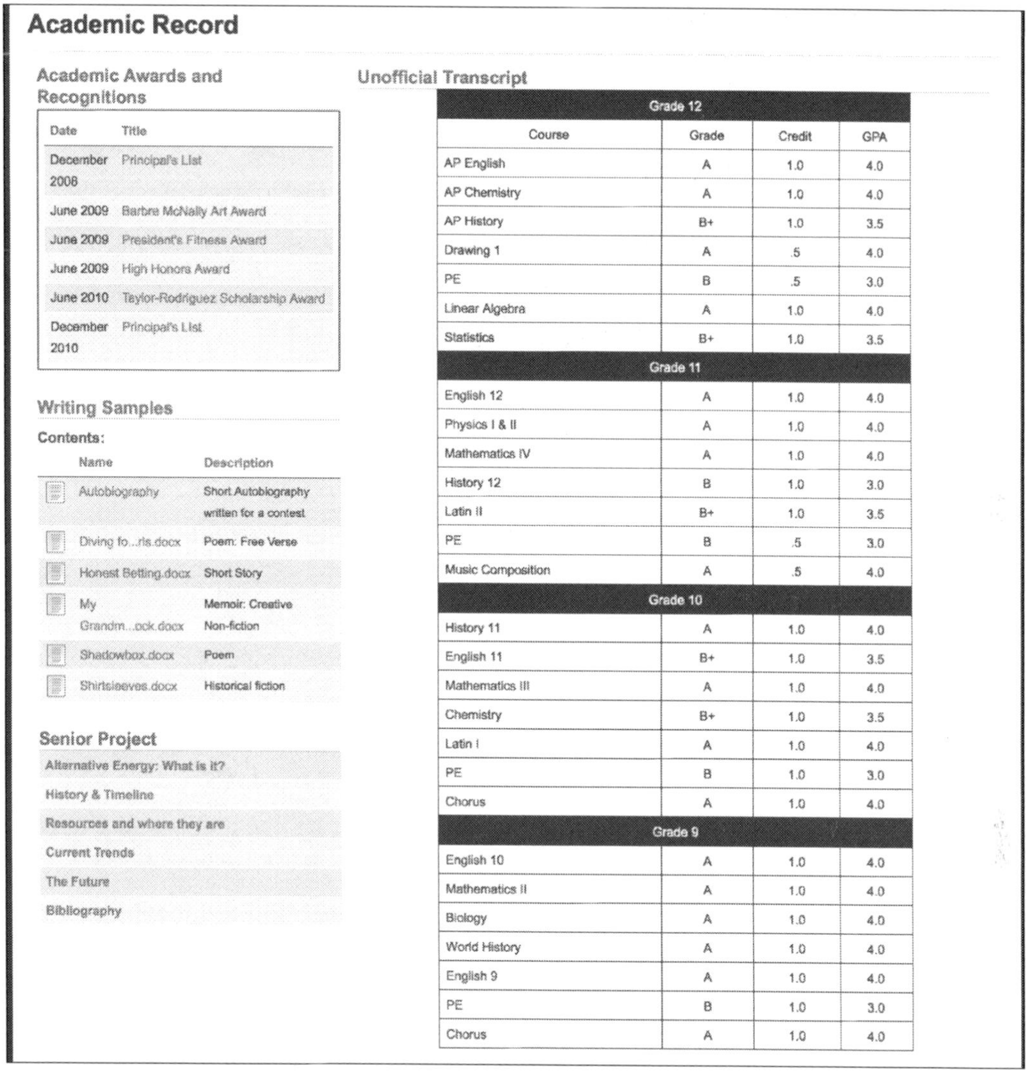

Academic Record

Academic Awards and Recognitions

Date	Title
December 2008	Principal's List
June 2009	Barbre McNally Art Award
June 2009	President's Fitness Award
June 2009	High Honors Award
June 2010	Taylor-Rodriguez Scholarship Award
December 2010	Principal's List

Writing Samples

Contents:

Name	Description
Autobiography	Short Autobiography written for a contest
Diving fo...rls.docx	Poem: Free Verse
Honest Betting.docx	Short Story
My Grandm...ock.docx	Memoir: Creative Non-fiction
Shadowbox.docx	Poem
Shirtsleeves.docx	Historical fiction

Senior Project

Alternative Energy: What is it?

History & Timeline

Resources and where they are

Current Trends

The Future

Bibliography

Unofficial Transcript

Course	Grade	Credit	GPA
Grade 12			
AP English	A	1.0	4.0
AP Chemistry	A	1.0	4.0
AP History	B+	1.0	3.5
Drawing 1	A	.5	4.0
PE	B	.5	3.0
Linear Algebra	A	1.0	4.0
Statistics	B+	1.0	3.5
Grade 11			
English 12	A	1.0	4.0
Physics I & II	A	1.0	4.0
Mathematics IV	A	1.0	4.0
History 12	B	1.0	3.0
Latin II	B+	1.0	3.5
PE	B	.5	3.0
Music Composition	A	.5	4.0
Grade 10			
History 11	A	1.0	4.0
English 11	B+	1.0	3.5
Mathematics III	A	1.0	4.0
Chemistry	B+	1.0	3.5
Latin I	A	1.0	4.0
PE	B	1.0	3.0
Chorus	A	1.0	4.0
Grade 9			
English 10	A	1.0	4.0
Mathematics II	A	1.0	4.0
Biology	A	1.0	4.0
World History	A	1.0	4.0
English 9	A	1.0	4.0
PE	B	1.0	3.0
Chorus	A	1.0	4.0

Getting ready

Follow the steps in the *Using HTML to create your unofficial transcript* recipe; do not, however, add it to a page (just skip that part).

In creating the following recipe, we will add a Collection called "**Senior Project**". Your collection might be some other project, just a group of pages that were created for various academic purposes, or you might not even have a collection. If you do not have a collection you can skip that part. If you want to include a collection of pages, but have not yet created the collection, you'll want to do that before beginning this recipe.

How to do it...

First, let's add your academic awards and achievements to your portfolio:

1. In Mahara, click the **Content** tab, then click **Résumé**, and then **Achievements**.
2. Click the **Add** button under the title **Certifications, Accreditations, and Awards**.
3. In the field labeled **Date**, provide the date of the recognition. It can be in any format that you'd like, for example, April 2009. Just make sure that whatever format you choose, you remain consistent and use that format for all of the awards and recognitions you list.
4. Next, in the field for **Title**, type the official name of the recognition.
5. In the **Description** area, type the criteria for the award. For example, `The award given to individuals recognized by students and faculty as having been a positive contributor to school and community, and one who has demonstrated leadership qualities.`
6. Click the **Save** button.
7. Repeat steps 2 – 6 for each recognition.

Next we'll create a folder for your writing samples as follows:

1. On the **Content** tab, click the sub-tab labeled **Files**.
2. In the box next to the button labeled **Create Folder**, type "`Writing Samples`".
3. Click **Create Folder**.
4. You will see the next folder in your list of folders. Click the title **Writing Samples** to open the folder.
5. To upload files, click the box next to **Upload** file, and then the **Browse** button.
6. When you find the file you'd like to upload, double-click it. You can continue uploading additional files while the files upload and you can always add more files to this folder in the future.
7. It is a good idea to add a description to each file. After the file has uploaded, click the little pencil icon to its right.
8. A list of options will expand with fields for a **Description** and **Tags**. Type a brief description in the designated field.
9. You might wish to add tags as well. Tags make it easy to search your portfolio and find specific items in the future. They are simply keywords you would associate with that particular item.
10. Click the **Save** button.
11. Repeat these steps for each sample you upload.

Now let's build our page:

1. Click the **Portfolio** tab and you should automatically be in the **Pages** section.
2. Click **Create Page**.
3. Click the **Edit Layout** tab.
4. Select **Larger right column** under **2 columns**:

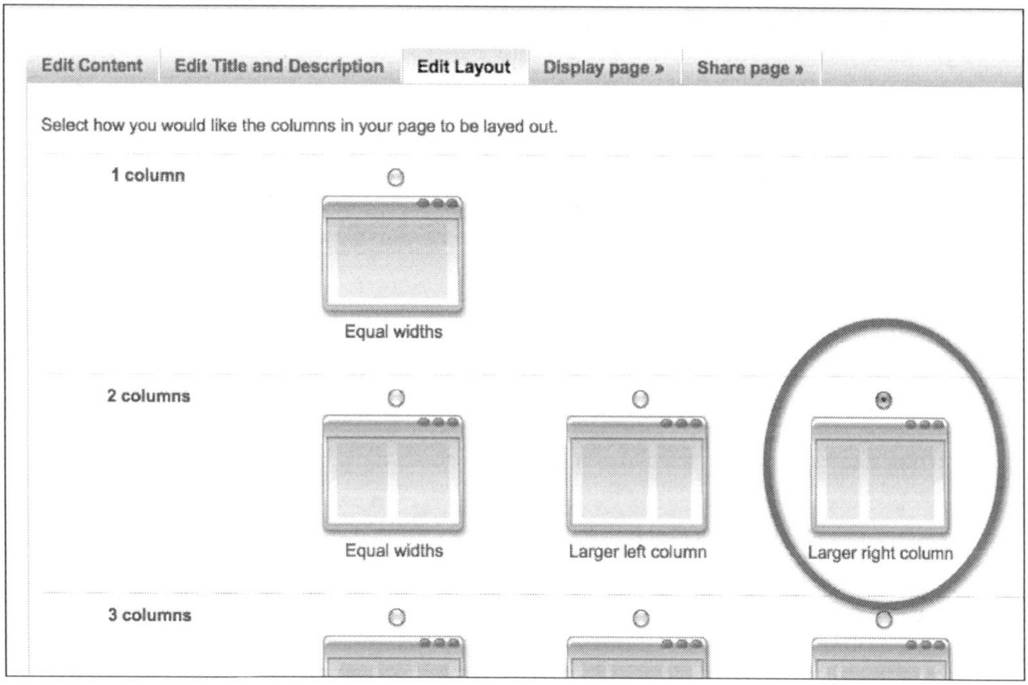

5. Click the **Save** button.
6. We're going to add a collection to this page first. If you do not have a collection, you can skip steps 6-9 and go directly to step 10.
7. From the **General** tab, click and drag a **Navigation** block into the left-hand column.
8. Leave the **Block Title** empty as it will take the name of the collection.
9. From the dropdown menu for **Collection**, select the collection you would like to add here.
10. Click the **Save** button.
11. From the **Files, images and video** tab, click and drag an **A Folder** block into the left-hand column.

> The **A Folder** block displays all documents in a particular folder. The block will automatically update if and when you add additional documents to the file folder in the future.

12. In the **Block Title**, type "`Writing Samples`".
13. Click the **Select** button next to your **Writing Samples** folder.
14. Click the **Save** button.
15. From the **Résumé** tab, click and drag a **One Résumé Field** block into the left-hand column.
16. In the field for **Block Title**, type "`Academic Awards & Recognitions`".
17. Click in the small bubble next to **Certifications, Accreditations, and Awards**.
18. Click the **Save** button.
19. From the **Files, images and video** tab, drag and drop an **HTML** block and drag it into the right-hand column.
20. Delete the text in the **Block Title**, leaving it empty.
21. Click the **Select** button next to the file labeled **UnofficialTranscript**.
22. Click the **Save** button.
23. Click the **Edit: Title and Description** tab.
24. In the field for **Page Title** type: "**Unofficial Transcript**".
25. Make sure the Name display format is your legal name.
26. Click the **Save** button.
27. Click **Done**. You can set the access level later.

How it works...

You can begin this page at the beginning of your secondary education, and continue working on it throughout the years. As you add content to the **Awards** section, this page will automatically reflect the additions. As you add content to your **Writing Samples** folder, the page will reflect that as well. Just remember that these additions are not made directly to the page but are done in the Content area of your portfolio.

To make additions to the transcripts, it would be easiest to create separate HTML files for each year of progress and add them by adding additional HTML blocks to the page. This is because you can't directly edit the documents in your file folder.

See also

- *A page of writing samples* recipe in *Chapter 2, Literature and Writing*.

The Common Application: Extracurricular Activities & Work Experience portion

Scholarship committees, colleges, and universities, and even potential employers take a great interest in the extra-curricular activities that individuals engage in. The activities can include volunteer work, paid employment, internships and job shadowing, club involvement, sports, and hobbies.

The work on building your portfolio should begin long before the end of your last year in school. You will want to collect a number of artifacts from the activities including news articles in which you are mentioned (either online or on the web), blog posts, images, video, audio files, letters of recommendation, links to web pages that are relevant, and more; building this page long before you need it is a good idea.

More and more institutions of higher education in the United States are asking applicants to use a set of documents called The Common Application. While this is specific for individuals interested in attending institutions of higher education in the U.S., this recipe can be altered and used for other types of similar applications.

In The Common Application, there is a section of the main application specifically titled **Extracurricular Activities & Work Experience**. It is followed by a short writing assignment, which asks for a brief elaboration on one of your extracurricular activities or work experiences (150 words or less). Some schools require additional supplements specifically for Athletics, the Arts, and Studies at International Schools.

In this recipe, we will create a table with the same structure as the **Extracurricular Activities & Work Experience** portion of The Common Application. We will also add the Short Answer Writing reflection piece. You will also learn how to save the finished document as a PDF file that can be attached to The Common Application.

In addition to this, we will add the information to a more detailed page. While the paper version of The Common Application does not provide you with the ability to attach images, newspaper clippings, links to websites, and so on, when you build your application using Mahara, you can add those things alongside the required information. Colleges are not yet prepared to accept electronic portfolios in lieu of The Common Application; however, conversations with admissions officers have revealed that they are considering this, particularly with the Extracurricular Activities, Employment, Athletics, and Arts sections. It could be that, by the time you graduate, you will be able to submit your Mahara portfolio in lieu of The Common Application.

Here's how the completed page will look like:

Extracurricular Activities & Work Experience

Extracurricular Activities & Work Experience

Grade level or post-graduate (PG)					Approximate time spent		When did you participate in the activity?			If applicable, do you plan to participate in college?
9	10	11	12	PG	Hours per week	Weeks per year	School Year	Summer/ School Break	Position held, honors won, letter earned, or employer	
x	x				2	26	x	x	Nursing Home Volunteer	np
Activity: This was part of a community action program at the High School. We would visit with the elderly at a local facility, approximately every other week and read to the residents. Each student was assigned to a particular individual, and would read materials chosen by that individual.										
x	x	x	x		1.5	18	x		Math Tutor	yes
Activity: Provided tutoring services in the tutorial center										
		x	x	x	40+	10		x	Youth Conservation Corp Leader	no
Activity: Worked as a part of a team repairing trails. We lived outdoors. I became a Certified Wilderness Guide										
		x	x		1	18	x		Member of Student Senate: Treasurer	yes
Activity: Participated as an elected officer on the Student Senate. In my Senior Year, I was the appointed Treasurer of my class.										
	x	x	x		8	47	x	x	Horse Groomer and Trail Guide	yes
Activity: Worked most weekends at an equestrian stable grooming horses and teaching visitors how to ride.										
	x	x	x		10	10	x		Performer at the Annual Pops Concert	
Activity: Performed with the Chorus, as well as with my band at the schools' Annual Pops Concert. Performers were chosen by audition.										

WRITING

Short Answer: A reflection on an extracurricular activity or work experience.

Curabitur eu nisl tortor. Proin vel nisl libero, id imperdiet leo. Aliquam id orci non tortor posuere lacinia eu ultrices nibh. Integer diam odio, aliquam quis mollis vitae, imperdiet ac sapien. Morbi eget tellus vel diam mattis pulvinar vel id velit. Nunc vel leo ante, ut interdum tellus. Phasellus porttitor tempus suscipit. Fusce scelerisque nibh viverra eros tincidunt varius. Cras euismod aliquet ante, sit amet vehicula sapien volutpat vel. Duis sed imperdiet risus. Sed eu velit leo. Mauris sapien diam, bibendum vel pharetra in, dapibus in elit. Vivamus scelerisque nisi nec justo consequat ut luctus eros lacinia. Lorem ipsum dolor sit amet, consectetur adipiscing elit.

Pellentesque lobortis hendrerit purus, eget mollis leo aliquam a. Donec odio est, tristique a lacinia eget, lobortis ut nulla. Praesent at urna ipsum, eu consectetur sapien. Fusce a metus nibh, vel imperdiet.

Feedback

0 comments

Place feedback | Print

Getting ready

All of the preparation should begin in your first year of secondary education. One thing that will be particularly helpful to you will be to keep a journal of your activities and to add pictures, news clippings, and hyperlinks to relevant web pages. If you are in the process of applying now, find a few relevant artifacts and add them to your portfolio. We will create a journal and write about a few of them. This will help you with the essay part of the application, as well as the Short Answer part of The Common Application.

While you could build the table yourself, using the HTML toolbar in Mahara or using a program like KompoZer, I've built the table for you and provided you with the code. The code can be downloaded from the Packt website.

How to do it...

1. Copy the code provided for the **Extracurricular Activities & Work Experience** table.
2. In Mahara, click on the **Content** tab, click **Résumé**, and then **Interests**.
3. Click **HTML** on the HTML toolbar.

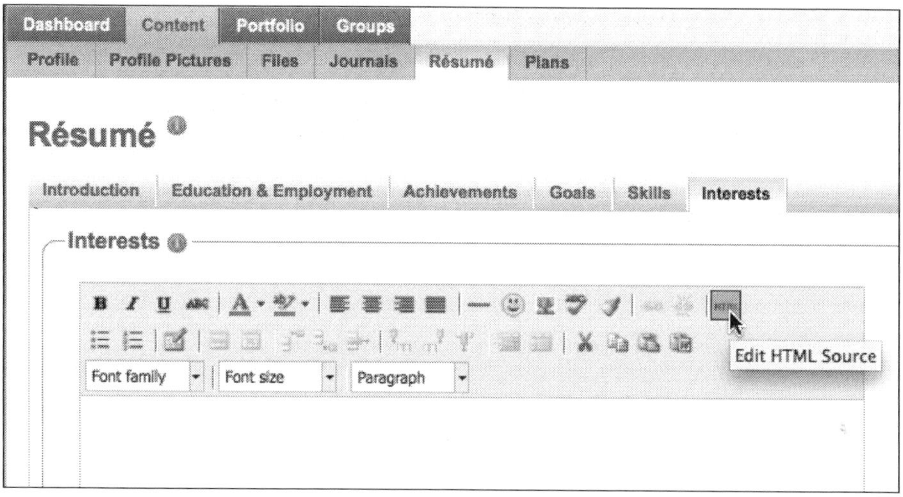

4. Using *command + V* on a Mac, or *Ctrl + V* on Windows, paste the code you copied in step 1 into the **HTML Source Editor**.
5. Click **Update**.
6. You will now have a table to work with. Add your information to this table by simply clicking in the individual cells and typing the appropriate information.
7. If you find you have too many rows, highlight the rows you wish to delete and click the **Delete row** icon in the HTML toolbar:

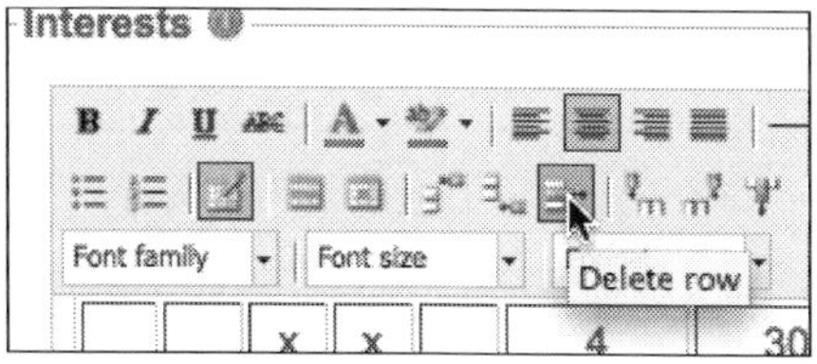

8. To begin adding the Short Answer Writing piece, place your cursor in the line below the table by clicking underneath it. Then using the *Enter* or *return* key on your keyboard, insert two lines.
9. Click the align-center option in the HTML toolbar.
10. From the drop-down menu for **Format**, select **Heading 2**:

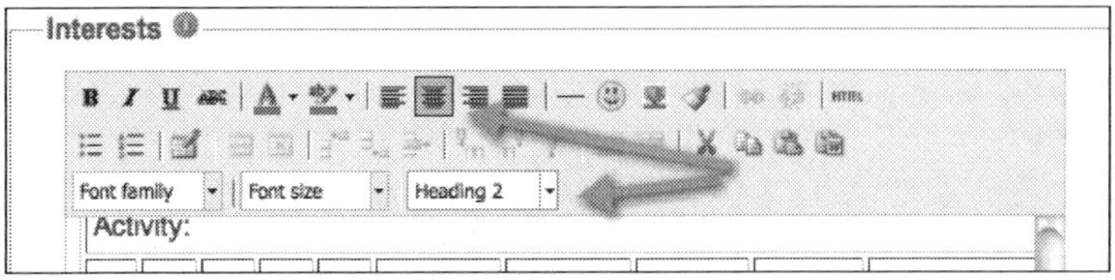

11. Using uppercase letters, type the word: `WRITING`.
12. Using the *Enter/return* key, insert one line. Your cursor should now be left-aligned.
13. Change the format to **Heading 3**.
14. Type this text:

    `Short Answer: A reflection on an extracurricular activity or work experience`
15. Using your *Return/Enter* key, insert one line and begin typing your reflection. Remember to keep it up to 150 words or less.

> You can monitor the number of words by typing in a word processing program like Microsoft Word first, and then copying and pasting the text. If you decide to do this, make sure to click the **Paste from Word** icon on the HTML toolbar before pasting the text.

16. Click the **Save** button.

Now let's create an actual page in which we will display this information:

1. Click on the **Portfolio** tab to get to the **Pages** section of your portfolio.
2. Click **Create Page**.
3. Click the **Edit Layout** tab.
4. Select **1 column, equal widths**.
5. Click the **Save** button.
6. From the **Résumé** tab, click and drag the **One Résumé Field** block into your page.
7. In the **Block Title**, type: "`Extracurricular Activities & Work Experience`".
8. In the area labeled **Fields to show**, select **Interests**.

9. Click the **Save** button.
10. Click the tab **Edit Title and Description**.
11. In the **Title** field, type: "`Extracurricular Activities & Work Experience`".
12. In the **Description**, simply put a space or two—it puts a little space at the top of your completed page.
13. Click **Save** and then click **Done**. (You can set the access levels later).

How it works...

Even though this table is meant to be included with The Common Application, completing it can be useful even for those who are not going to college or whose college does not accept The Common Application. You can actually begin building this table long before you are ready to apply for college, or a job.

When you participate in an activity, make sure to add it to the table. To do that, you will need to go to the **Résumé** section of the **Content** area in your portfolio, rather than the page itself. The page will automatically display any new content you add to **Interests** in the **Content** area of your portfolio.

To save the page as a PDF file, click the **Print** option at the bottom of the page. Select the option to save or print as a PDF.

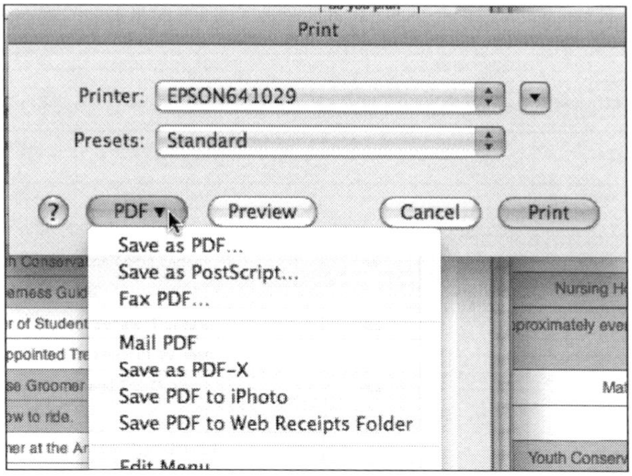

There's more...

Some individuals prefer to use their journals for developing and keeping artifacts of writing. Let's examine how that might work for this recipe.

Using a journal posting for the Short Answer section

If you have been keeping a journal on the activities you've performed, you may already have a marvelous post that would be perfect for the Short Answer part of the application. If not, you can write the post now. You don't even need to create a new journal to do this. You have your own personal journal, by default, in Mahara.

We're going to write a post and even add an image. Then we'll add it to a page:

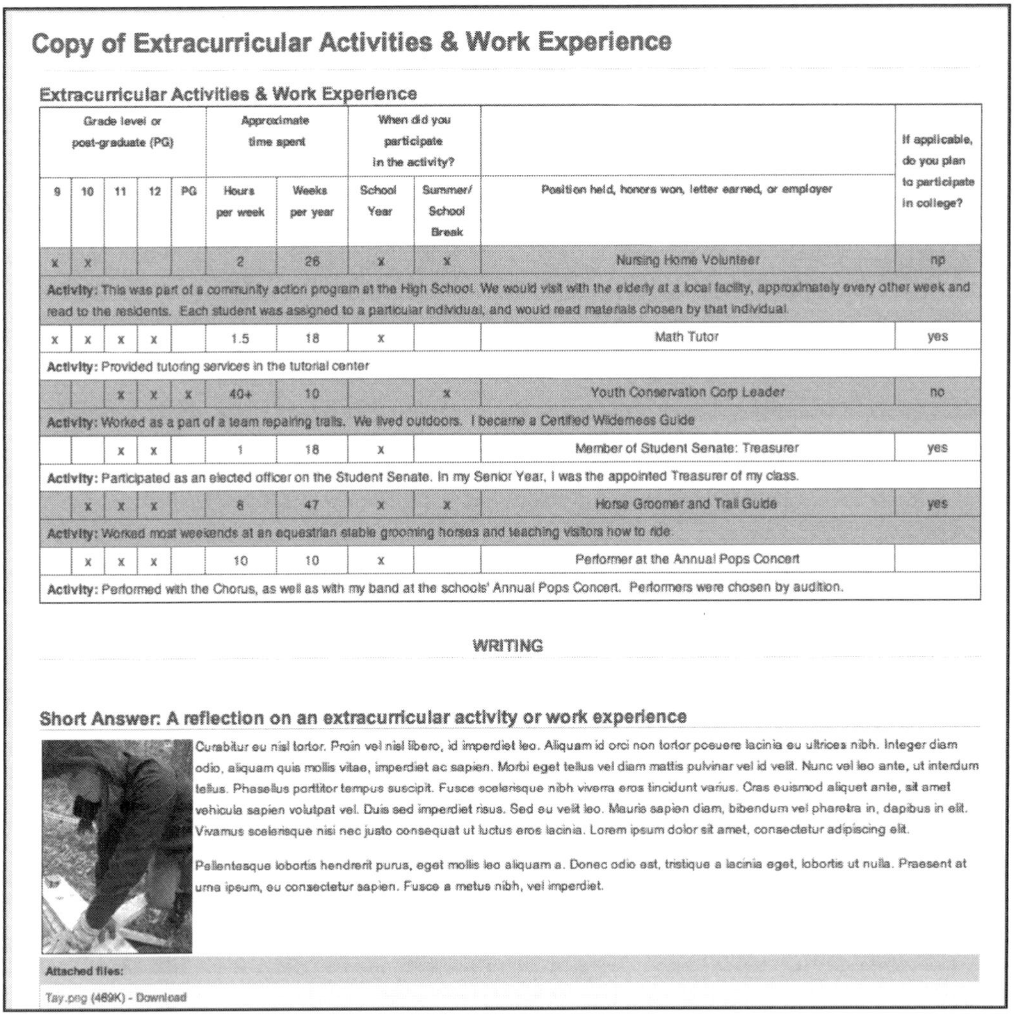

Copy of Extracurricular Activities & Work Experience

Extracurricular Activities & Work Experience

Grade level or post-graduate (PG)					Approximate time spent		When did you participate in the activity?			If applicable, do you plan to participate in college?
9	10	11	12	PG	Hours per week	Weeks per year	School Year	Summer/ School Break	Position held, honors won, letter earned, or employer	
x	x				2	26	x	x	Nursing Home Volunteer	np
Activity: This was part of a community action program at the High School. We would visit with the elderly at a local facility, approximately every other week and read to the residents. Each student was assigned to a particular individual, and would read materials chosen by that individual.										
x	x	x	x		1.5	18	x		Math Tutor	yes
Activity: Provided tutoring services in the tutorial center										
		x	x	x	40+	10		x	Youth Conservation Corp Leader	no
Activity: Worked as a part of a team repairing trails. We lived outdoors. I became a Certified Wilderness Guide										
		x	x		1	18	x		Member of Student Senate: Treasurer	yes
Activity: Participated as an elected officer on the Student Senate. In my Senior Year, I was the appointed Treasurer of my class.										
	x	x	x		6	47	x	x	Horse Groomer and Trail Guide	yes
Activity: Worked most weekends at an equestrian stable grooming horses and teaching visitors how to ride.										
	x	x	x		10	10	x		Performer at the Annual Pops Concert	
Activity: Performed with the Chorus, as well as with my band at the schools' Annual Pops Concert. Performers were chosen by audition.										

WRITING

Short Answer: A reflection on an extracurricular activity or work experience

Curabitur eu nisl tortor. Proin vel nisl libero, id imperdiet leo. Aliquam id orci non tortor posuere lacinia eu ultrices nibh. Integer diam odio, aliquam quis mollis vitae, imperdiet ac sapien. Morbi eget tellus vel diam mattis pulvinar vel id velit. Nunc vel leo ante, ut interdum tellus. Phasellus porttitor tempus suscipit. Fusce scelerisque nibh viverra eros tincidunt varius. Cras euismod aliquet ante, sit amet vehicula sapien volutpat vel. Duis sed imperdiet risus. Sed eu velit leo. Mauris sapien diam, bibendum vel pharetra in, dapibus in elit. Vivamus scelerisque nisi nec justo consequat ut luctus eros lacinia. Lorem ipsum dolor sit amet, consectetur adipiscing elit.

Pellentesque lobortis hendrerit purus, eget mollis leo aliquam a. Donec odio est, tristique a lacinia eget, lobortis ut nulla. Praesent at urna ipsum, eu consectetur sapien. Fusce a metus nibh, vel imperdiet.

Attached files:

Tay.png (469K) - Download

1. Begin with steps 1 – 11, and then follow steps 25 – 29, from the previous recipe, to begin the creation of your page. Next, we'll create the blog post.
2. Click the **Content** tab and then **Journals** tab.

3. Click the **New Entry** button next to the journal you want to add this post to.
4. In the **Title** field, type:

   `Short Answer: A reflection on an extracurricular activity or work experience.`
5. Enter your reflection in the **Body** area. Remember to keep it to 150 words or less.
6. If you wish to add an image, click the **Add a file** button under the **Body** area.
7. If you have previously saved the image to your files, click the **Select** button next to the image. If you have not previously uploaded it, click in the small box next to **Upload file**, click the **Browse** button to locate the image, and then click the **Upload** button.
8. When the image has finished uploading, click inside the body of your post, at the very beginning of the first sentence.
9. Click the edit image icon on the HTML toolbar.
10. Click the drop-down menu next to **Attached image** and select your image.
11. Type a brief description in the description field.
12. From the drop-down menu for **Alignment**, select **Left**.
13. For **Vertical space**, type `3`; for **Horizontal space**, type `3`.
14. Click **Insert**.
15. To resize the image, click on it then click on a corner and drag the corner either in or out to resize. Remember that the amount of text is relatively small, so you won't want a large image.
16. At the bottom of the window, deselect **Allow comments**.
17. Click the **Save entry** button

Now we'll add the blog post to your page, as follows:

1. Click the **Portfolio** tab to get to the **Pages** area of your portfolio.
2. In your list of pages, find the page for **Extracurricular Activities & Work Experience**. Click the small pencil tool to the right of the page title to open the page in the edit mode.
3. From the **Journals** tab, click and drag the **Journal Entry** block to the bottom of your page.
4. Leave the **Block Title** empty.
5. Click in the little bubble next to the post labeled **Short Answer: A reflection on an extracurricular activity or work experience**.
6. **Click the Save button.**
7. Click **Done**

See also

- *Journaling a project from start to finish* recipe in *Chapter 1, Mahara for the Visual Arts*
- *International project* recipe in *Chapter 5, The Primary Education Portfolio*

The Athletic Supplement

This recipe is very similar to the *Extracurricular Activities & Work Experience* recipe, but, this time, we will be creating a page similar to the Athletic Supplement to The Common Application. Again, you should begin using this at the start of your secondary education and regularly update it.

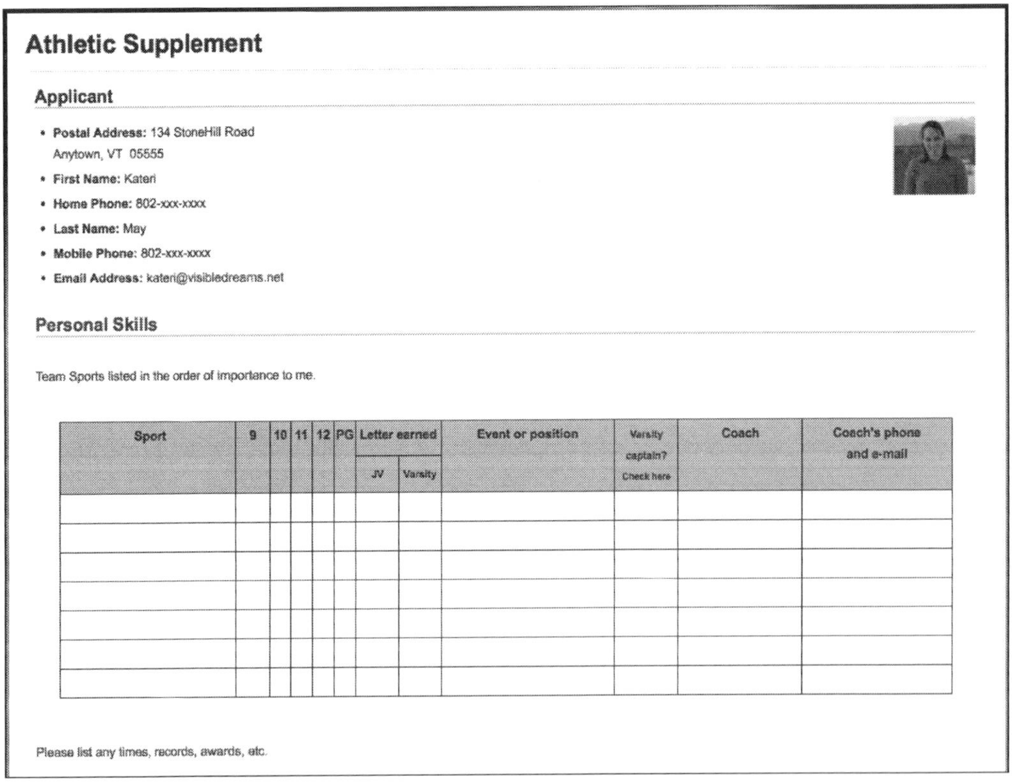

Athletic Supplement

Applicant

- **Postal Address:** 134 StoneHill Road
  Anytown, VT 05555
- **First Name:** Kateri
- **Home Phone:** 802-xxx-xxxx
- **Last Name:** May
- **Mobile Phone:** 802-xxx-xxxx
- **Email Address:** kateri@visibledreams.net

Personal Skills

Team Sports listed in the order of importance to me.

Sport	9	10	11	12	PG	Letter earned		Event or position	Varsity captain? Check here	Coach	Coach's phone and e-mail
						JV	Varsity				

Please list any times, records, awards, etc.

Getting ready

Download the Athletic Supplement code from the Packt website.

How to do it...

1. Copy the code provided for the Athletic Supplement table.
2. In Mahara, click on the **Content** tab, then click **Résumé**, and then **Skills**. We will use the Personal Skills portion of this section.

> This table can be added to the Goals section, instead of Skills, or the Interest section (if you did not use it for your Extracurricular Activities & Work Experience). We are not using a **Text Box** block in a page, because textboxes are not artifacts. They are associated only with the page in which they appear.

3. Click the **HTML** tab on the HTML toolbar.
4. Using *Command + V* on a Mac, or *Ctrl + v* on Windows, paste the code you copied in step 1, into the HTML Source Editor.
5. Click the **Update** button.
6. You will now have a table to work with. Add your information to this table, by simply clicking in the individual cells and typing the appropriate information.
7. Below the table is an area for you to list your times, records, and awards.
8. Click the **Save** button.

Now let's create an actual page in which we will display this information:

9. Click on the **Portfolio** tab to get to the **Pages** section of your portfolio.
10. Click the **Create Page** button.
11. Click on the **Edit Layout** tab.
12. Select **1 column, equal widths**.
13. Click the **Save** button.
14. From the **Résumé** tab, click and drag the **One Résumé Field** block into your page.
15. In the **Block Title**, type: "`Athletic Supplement`".
16. In the area labeled **Fields to show**, select **Personal Skills**.
17. Click the **Save** button.
18. From the **Profile** tab, click and drag a **Profile Information** block into the page above the table.
19. Change the **Block Title** to: "`Applicant`".
20. In the **Fields to show**, select the items you need to display, such as **First Name**, **Last Name**, **Postal Address**, and **Phone**.

21. You can select whether to display a **Profile Icon** or not.
22. Select your **Email Address**.
23. In the **Introduction text**, type the name of your current school and the CEEB/ACT Code.
24. Click the **Save** button.
25. Click on the **Edit Title and Description** tab.
26. In the **Title** field type: "`Athletic Supplement`".
27. You can leave the **Description** field blank.
28. Click the **Save** button.
29. Click **Done**. (You can set the access levels later.)

See also

- *The Common Application: Extracurricular Activities & Work Experience portion* recipe
- *The Art Portfolio and The Common Application: Art Supplement* recipe
- *Using HTML to create your unofficial transcript* recipe

8

Certification and Accreditation Portfolio for Higher Education

In this chapter, we will cover:

- Building the ECIS International Teacher portfolio
- Templates for meeting teacher certification standards
- Creating a portfolio access page for outside reviewers
- Archiving portfolios

Introduction

In this chapter, we will develop portfolios that can be used to demonstrate teaching abilities, to meet accreditation standards, and to fulfill teacher certification requirements.

Building the ECIS International Teacher portfolio

In this recipe, we will build a set of pages that could be used to meet Standard 1 of the ECIS International Teacher Certification Standards. We will follow the ITC Syllabus for 2010. Though we will focus on Standard 1, we can use similar formats for all of the standards and then put these together into a collection of standards.

The ITC requires three specific things for each standard: the Core Evidence, a Professional Log responding to each of the prompts, and a Reflective Report. In addition, you will need to keep a Reflective Journal. We'll look at a way of presenting all these artifacts together using Mahara. The method presented here is just one of the ways to do it.

Getting ready

For each standard, there is a practical activity, and so it is for Standard 1 as well. You will need to collect the required items for the Core Evidence, so let's take a look at what the Core Evidence requirements are for Standard 1. A visual record and outline plan of the activity (which should be photographs and a document), feedback from the students (which should be a video), critical moments that encourage intercultural awareness (pictures and a document), and local community involvement (audio mp3) are required. You will need to collect these items and upload them to the **Files** area in your portfolio.

You will also be working in two different journals, so you will need to ensure that your settings allow for multiple journals:

1. Log in to Mahara and click the **Settings** link in the upper right-hand corner.
2. Near the bottom of the **General account options**, you will see the option **Enable multiple journals**.
3. Make sure there is a check mark in the box next to that item.
4. Click on **Save**.

You will need a copy of the ITC Syllabus 2010, which is the document we are following in this recipe. It is available at `http://www.internationalteachercertificate.com/Documents/ITCSyllabus2010.pdf`.

And finally, you will need to have Microsoft Word or OpenOffice. OpenOffice is a free open source application similar to Microsoft Office. It is available for download at `http://www.openoffice.org/`.

How to do it...

Reflective Journal: The Reflective Journal is an informal journal used primarily for recording "critical events and outcomes, ideas, and reflections", which you can draw on as you respond to the prompts for the Professional Log. So, let's build this first:

1. Click on the **Content** tab and then **Journals**.
2. Click on **Create Journal**.
3. In the **Title** field, you'll want to type `Reflective Journal`.
4. In the **Description**, note that this is for International Teacher Certification.
5. Click on **Create Journal**.

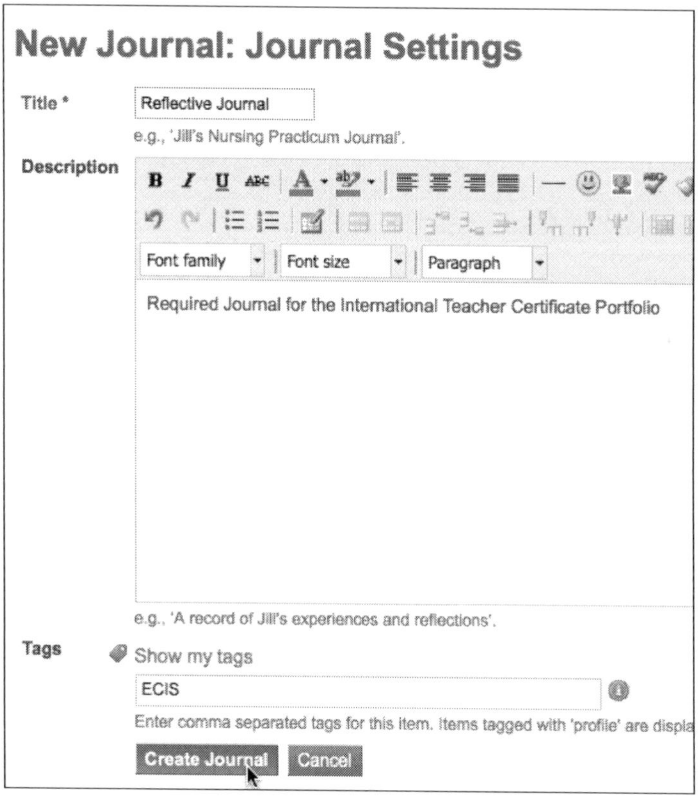

6. You will now be back to the page that contains your journals. To post an entry, click on **New Entry** next to the **Reflective Journal**.

Professional Log: Each standard requires a Professional Log with written responses to specific prompts. The Professional Log is composed of text entry boxes, each of which should contain responses of no more than 200 words. We will use a journal for our Professional Log.

7. Click on the **Content** tab and then on **Journals**.
8. Click on **Create Journal**.
9. In the **Title** field, you'll want to type `Professional Logs`.
10. In the **Description**, you might want to note that this is for International Teacher Certification.
11. Click on **Create Journal**.
12. You will now be taken back to your list of journals. Click the **New Entry** button next to **Professional Logs journal**. We will create a post for each of the prompts. You can then go into these posts and add your own responses, as you wish. Standard 1 has four prompts: 1.1, 1.2, 1.3, and 1.4. We will begin with 1.1.
13. In the **Title** field for this first entry, type `1.1 Designs activities that contribute to the cultural life of the school and involve the local community` (this is the text from the ECIS ITC syllabus for 2010).
14. In the **Body**, copy the prompt text in the ITC syllabus for this entry; see the following screenshot for the text:

1.1 Designs activities that contribute to the cultural life of the school and involve the local community

An internationally-minded teacher is expected to be involved in activities which introduce students to elements of the local culture and engage them with the local community.

In your professional log:

- state why you chose the extra-curricular activity and state the extent to which you were involved in its design
- explain how it contributed to the cultural life of your school and how it contributed to the local community
- explore how it changed the perceptions of those involved.

15. Click on **Save entry**.
16. Click **New Entry** and repeat steps 7-9 for each required post, using the appropriate text for each post.
17. When you are ready to begin responding to these prompts, you will go to the **Content** area of your portfolio and select **Journals**.

18. Open the journal by clicking on its title.
19. Next to each post, you will see a small pencil tool. Click the pencil tool to begin editing the post—that is, adding your response to it.
20. Click on **Save entry**.

Core Evidence: The Core Evidence portion of each standard requires very specific types of files, each of which must address specific criteria. Sometimes a video is required, sometimes a document, and sometimes an audio recording. The file sizes for each of these artifacts is limited as well.

21. Click on the **Content** tab and then on **Files**.
22. In the box next to **Create folder**, type `Core Evidence`, and the number of the standard (for example, `Core Evidence Standard 1`).
23. Click **Create folder**.
24. Click on the folder to open it.
25. Click in the small box next to **Upload file**.
26. Click the **Browse** button to locate one of your artifacts for the Core Evidence and begin uploading it.
27. You do not need to wait for the first artifact to upload before you begin uploading the next artifact. Click the **Browse** button to locate the next artifact and begin uploading it.
28. Repeat step 6 until you've uploaded all of the artifacts for Standard 1 Core Evidence.
29. Once you've uploaded all of the artifacts, you will need to edit the name and description for each. To do so, click the small pencil tool next to the artifact for **Core Evidence Item A**. This will expand a set of fields.

30. We will first work with the **Name** field. Keeping the file format extension as is (for example, `.pdf`), change the name to `A.Activity`.
31. In the field for the **Description**, type `A. Visual record and an outline plan of the activity`.
32. In the **Tags** field, type `ITC`.

33. Click on **Save Changes**.

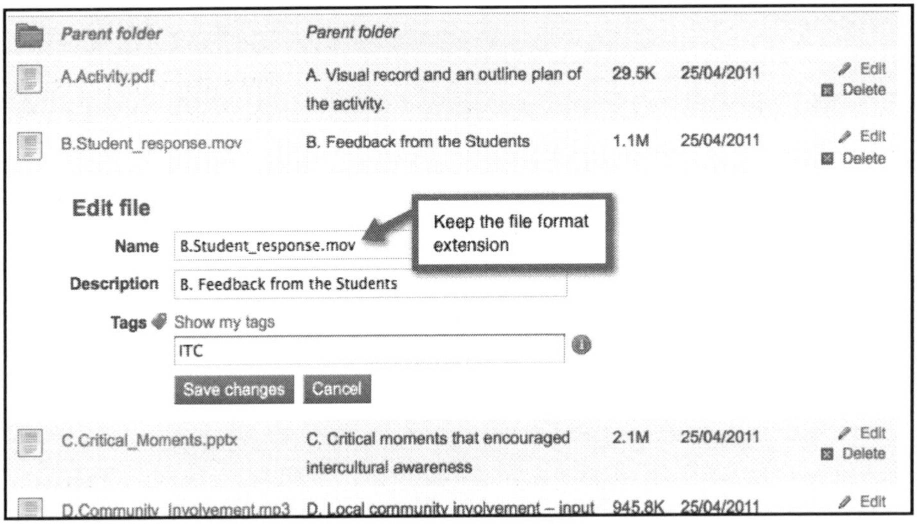

34. Click the pencil tool next to the artifact for **Core Evidence Item B**.
35. Keeping the file format extension, change the **Name** to `B.Student_response`.
36. In the **Description**, type `B. Feedback from the students`.
37. In the **Tags** field, type `ITC`.
38. Click on **Save Changes**.

We add the letters at the beginning of each name, so that they will appear in the proper order. The **Files** section lists files alphabetically.

39. Repeat steps 14-18 for each artifact, using the text from the ECIS ITC Syllabus.

Let's build the page for the Core Evidence and the Professional Log:

40. Go to **Portfolio** and then to **Pages**.
41. Click on **Create Page**.
42. Click the **Edit Layout** tab.
43. Select **1 column, equal widths**.
44. Click on **Save**.

45. From the drop-down menu labeled **Theme:**, select the theme you would like.
46. From the **Journals** tab, click and drag a **Journal Entry** block into the page.
47. Leave the **Block Title** empty.
48. From the list **Journal Entry**, select the one labeled **Professional Log: 1.4 Develops understanding between students from different backgrounds**.
49. Click on **Save**.
50. Repeat steps 7-10 for each of the Professional Log posts, dragging the blocks into the space above the previous post, and ending with **1.1** at the top.
51. From the **General** tab, click and drag a **Text Box** block into the top of the page.
52. Delete the text from the **Block Title**, leaving it blank.
53. Click the horizontal line icon in the HTML editing toolbar for the **Block Content** to add a horizontal bar.
54. Place your cursor under the ruler and type `Professional Log`.
55. Highlight the text and select **Heading 1** from the **Format** drop-down menu (it is the menu with **Paragraph** selected by default).
56. Click on **Save**.
57. From the **Files, images and video** tab, click and drag an **A Folder** block into the top of the page.
58. Leave the **Block Title** empty.
59. From the **Files** list, select the folder labeled **Core Evidence Standard 1**.
60. Click on **Save**.
61. In the tabs at the very top of the page, select the one labeled **Edit: Title and Description**.
62. In the **Title** field, type `Standard 1: Professional Log and Core Evidence`.
63. Click on **Save**.
64. Click on **Done**.

The following is an example of what the completed page will look like:

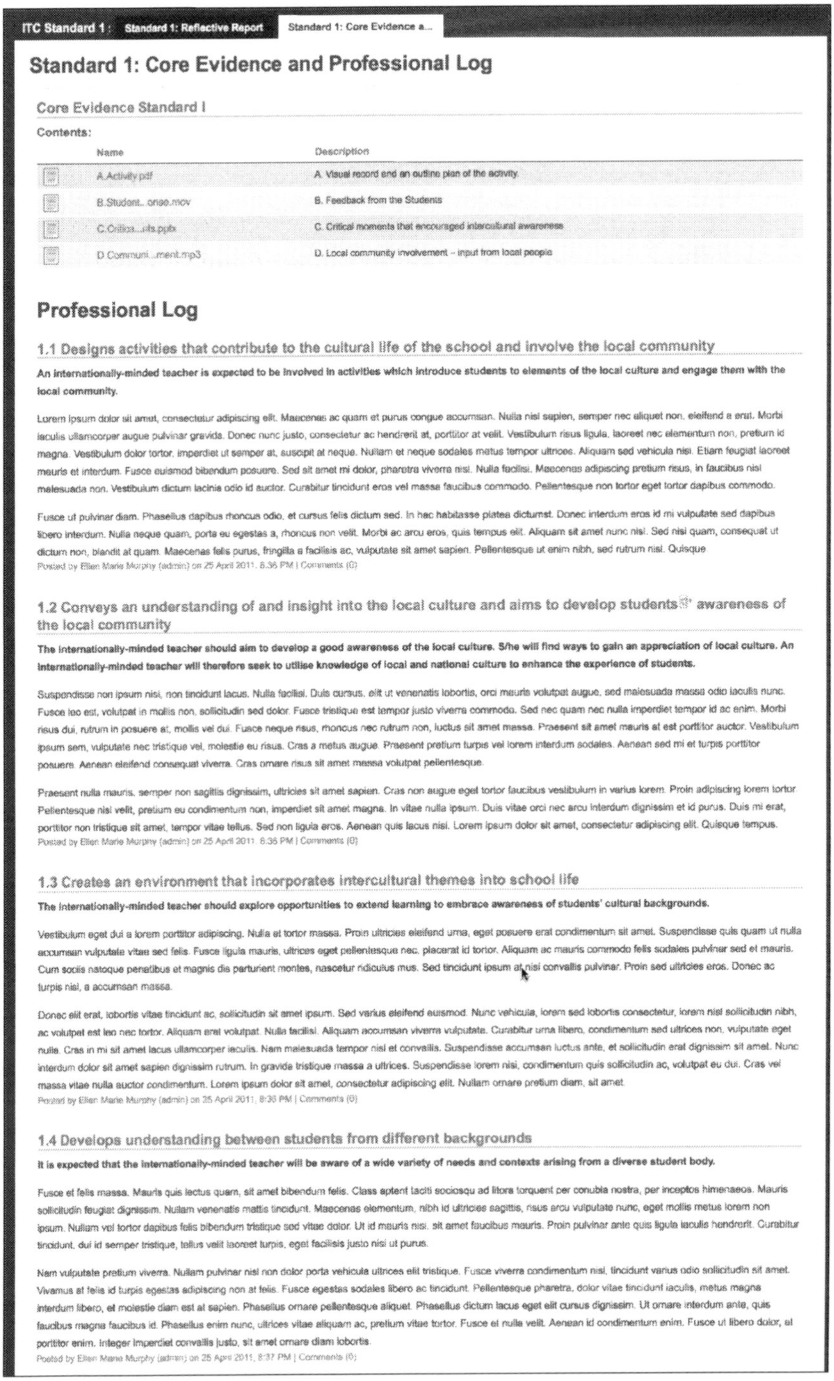

ITC Standard 1 : Standard 1: Reflective Report Standard 1: Core Evidence a...

Standard 1: Core Evidence and Professional Log

Core Evidence Standard I

Contents:

	Name	Description
	A.Activity.pdf	A. Visual record and an outline plan of the activity
	B.Student...onse.mov	B. Feedback from the Students
	C.Critica...nts.pptx	C. Critical moments that encouraged intercultural awareness
	D.Communi...ment.mp3	D. Local community involvement – input from local people

Professional Log

1.1 Designs activities that contribute to the cultural life of the school and involve the local community

An internationally-minded teacher is expected to be involved in activities which introduce students to elements of the local culture and engage them with the local community.

Lorem ipsum dolor sit amet, consectetur adipiscing elit. Maecenas ac quam et purus congue accumsan. Nulla nisi sapien, semper nec aliquet non, eleifend a erat. Morbi iaculis ullamcorper augue pulvinar gravida. Donec nunc justo, consectetur ac hendrerit at, porttitor at velit. Vestibulum risus ligula, laoreet nec elementum non, pretium id magna. Vestibulum dolor tortor, imperdiet ut semper at, suscipit at neque. Nullam et neque sodales metus tempor ultrices. Aliquam sed vehicula nisi. Etiam feugiat laoreet mauris et interdum. Fusce euismod bibendum posuere. Sed sit amet mi dolor, pharetra viverra nisi. Nulla facilisi. Maecenas adipiscing pretium risus, in faucibus nisl malesuada non. Vestibulum dictum lacinia odio id auctor. Curabitur tincidunt eros vel massa faucibus commodo. Pellentesque non tortor eget tortor dapibus commodo.

Fusce ut pulvinar diam. Phasellus dapibus rhoncus odio, et cursus felis dictum sed. In hac habitasse platea dictumst. Donec interdum eros id mi vulputate sed dapibus libero interdum. Nulla neque quam, porta eu egestas a, rhoncus non velit. Morbi ac arcu eros, quis tempus elit. Aliquam sit amet nunc nisl. Sed nisi quam, consequat ut dictum non, blandit at quam. Maecenas felis purus, fringilla a facilisis ac, vulputate sit amet sapien. Pellentesque ut enim nibh, sed rutrum nisl. Quisque

Posted by Ellen Marie Murphy (admin) on 25 April 2011, 8:36 PM | Comments (0)

1.2 Conveys an understanding of and insight into the local culture and aims to develop students' awareness of the local community

The internationally-minded teacher should aim to develop a good awareness of the local culture. S/he will find ways to gain an appreciation of local culture. An internationally-minded teacher will therefore seek to utilise knowledge of local and national culture to enhance the experience of students.

Suspendisse non ipsum nisi, non tincidunt lacus. Nulla facilisi. Duis cursus, elit ut venenatis lobortis, orci mauris volutpat augue, sed malesuada massa odio iaculis nunc. Fusce leo est, volutpat in mollis non, sollicitudin sed dolor. Fusce tristique est tempor justo viverra commodo. Sed nec quam nec nulla imperdiet tempor id ac enim. Morbi risus dui, rutrum in posuere at, mollis vel dui. Fusce neque risus, rhoncus nec rutrum non, luctus sit amet massa. Praesent sit amet mauris at est porttitor auctor. Vestibulum ipsum sem, vulputate nec tristique vel, molestie eu risus. Cras a metus augue. Praesent pretium turpis vel lorem interdum sodales. Aenean sed mi et turpis porttitor posuere. Aenean eleifend consequat viverra. Cras ornare risus sit amet massa volutpat pellentesque.

Praesent nulla mauris, semper non sagittis dignissim, ultricies sit amet sapien. Cras non augue eget tortor faucibus vestibulum in varius lorem. Proin adipiscing lorem tortor. Pellentesque nisl velit, pretium eu condimentum non, imperdiet sit amet magna. In vitae nulla ipsum. Duis vitae orci nec arcu interdum dignissim et id purus. Duis mi erat, porttitor non tristique sit amet, tempor vitae tellus. Sed non ligula eros. Aenean quis lacus nisi. Lorem ipsum dolor sit amet, consectetur adipiscing elit. Quisque tempus.

Posted by Ellen Marie Murphy (admin) on 25 April 2011, 8:36 PM | Comments (0)

1.3 Creates an environment that incorporates intercultural themes into school life

The internationally-minded teacher should explore opportunities to extend learning to embrace awareness of students' cultural backgrounds.

Vestibulum eget dui a lorem porttitor adipiscing. Nulla et tortor massa. Proin ultricies eleifend urna, eget posuere erat condimentum sit amet. Suspendisse quis quam ut nulla accumsan vulputate vitae sed felis. Fusce ligula mauris, ultrices eget pellentesque nec, placerat id tortor. Aliquam ac mauris commodo felis sodales pulvinar sed et mauris. Cum sociis natoque penatibus et magnis dis parturient montes, nascetur ridiculus mus. Sed tincidunt ipsum at nisi convallis pulvinar. Proin sed ultricies eros. Donec ac turpis nisi, a accumsan massa.

Donec elit erat, lobortis vitae tincidunt ac, sollicitudin sit amet ipsum. Sed varius eleifend euismod. Nunc vehicula, lorem sed lobortis consectetur, lorem nisl sollicitudin nibh, ac volutpat est leo nec tortor. Aliquam erat volutpat. Nulla facilisi. Aliquam accumsan viverra vulputate. Curabitur urna libero, condimentum sed ultrices non, vulputate eget nulla. Cras in mi sit amet lacus ullamcorper iaculis. Nam malesuada tempor nisl et convallis. Suspendisse accumsan luctus ante, et sollicitudin erat dignissim sit amet. Nunc interdum dolor sit amet sapien dignissim rutrum. In gravida tristique massa a ultrices. Suspendisse lorem nisi, condimentum quis sollicitudin ac, volutpat eu dui. Cras vel massa vitae nulla auctor condimentum. Lorem ipsum dolor sit amet, consectetur adipiscing elit. Nullam ornare pretium diam, sit amet

Posted by Ellen Marie Murphy (admin) on 25 April 2011, 8:36 PM | Comments (0)

1.4 Develops understanding between students from different backgrounds

It is expected that the internationally-minded teacher will be aware of a wide variety of needs and contexts arising from a diverse student body.

Fusce et felis massa. Mauris quis lectus quam, sit amet bibendum felis. Class aptent taciti sociosqu ad litora torquent per conubia nostra, per inceptos himenaeos. Mauris sollicitudin feugiat dignissim. Nullam venenatis mattis tincidunt. Maecenas elementum, nibh id ultricies sagittis, risus arcu vulputate nunc, eget mollis metus lorem non ipsum. Nullam vel tortor dapibus felis bibendum tristique sed vitae dolor. Ut id mauris nisi, sit amet faucibus mauris. Proin pulvinar ante quis ligula iaculis hendrerit. Curabitur tincidunt, dui id semper tristique, tellus velit laoreet turpis, eget facilisis justo nisi ut purus.

Nam vulputate pretium viverra. Nullam pulvinar nisl non dolor porta vehicula ultrices elit tristique. Fusce viverra condimentum nisi, tincidunt varius odio sollicitudin sit amet. Vivamus at felis id turpis egestas adipiscing non at felis. Fusce egestas sodales libero ac tincidunt. Pellentesque pharetra, dolor vitae tincidunt iaculis, metus magna interdum libero, et molestie diam est at sapien. Phasellus ornare pellentesque aliquet. Phasellus dictum lacus eget elit cursus dignissim. Ut ornare interdum ante, quis faucibus magna faucibus id. Phasellus enim nunc, ultrices vitae aliquam ac, pretium vitae tortor. Fusce et nulla velit. Aenean id condimentum enim. Fusce ut libero dolor, at porttitor enim. Integer imperdiet convallis justo, sit amet ornare diam lobortis.

Posted by Ellen Marie Murphy (admin) on 25 April 2011, 8:37 PM | Comments (0)

Reflective Report: Each standard requires a Reflective Report of approximately 600 words in response to a given prompt. For this part of the portfolio, we will use Microsoft Word (or OpenOffice) and save the file as an HTML document as well as `.doc` or `.docx`.

65. Open Word and type your Reflective Report making sure you have approximately 600 words.

> You can get the word count by clicking on the **Tools** option on the main menu bar and then selecting the option for **Word Count**.

66. When you've completed typing your Reflective Report, click on **File** at the top of the window and click **Save**.
67. Change the filename to `Standard 1 Reflective Report` and save as a `.docx` or `.doc`. Do not close the document.
68. Now we're going to save the file again, but this time as an HTML document:
    - If you are using Microsoft Word on a Mac, click on **File** again and select **Save as Web Page...**.

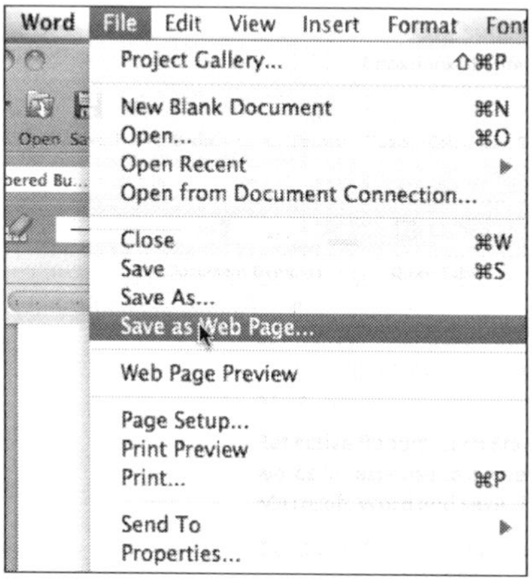

    - If you are using Microsoft Word on a Windows computer, click on **File** and then **Save As**. From the drop-down menu for **Save as type**, select **Web Page, Filtered**.

- If you are using Open Office, click on **File** and then **Save As**. From the drop-down menu for **File type**, select **HTML document**.

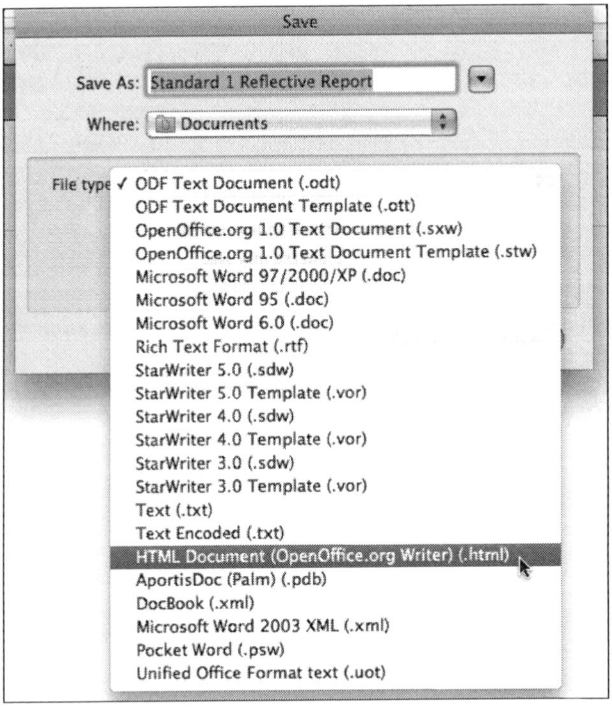

69. The name of your file should be the same as the one you gave it in step 3 (except that it will have a `.htm` or `.html` extension). Click on **Save**.
70. In Mahara, click on the **Contents** tab and then on **Files**.
71. Click the small box next to **Upload file**.
72. Click the **Browse** button, locate the `.doc` or `.docx` file, and upload it.
73. Click the **Browse** button again, locate the `.htm` or `.html` document, and upload it.
74. Click the **Portfolio** tab to get to the **Pages** area of your portfolio.
75. Click the button **Create Page**.
76. Click the tab labeled **Edit Layout**.
77. Select the option for **1 column, equal widths**.
78. Click on **Save**.
79. Set the same theme you picked earlier.
80. From the **Files, images and video** tab, click and drag a **Some HTML** block into the page.

81. Delete the text from the **Block Title**, leaving it empty.
82. Click the **Select** button next to the **Standard 1 Reflective Report**.
83. Click on **Save**.
84. From the **Files, images and video** tab, drag a **Files(s) to download** block into the page in the area below **Reflective Report**.
85. In the **Block Title** field, type `Download Reflective Report`.
86. Click the **Select** option next to the `.docx` file titled **Standard 1 Reflective Report**.
87. Click on **Save**.
88. Click the tab labeled **Edit: Title and Description**.
89. In the **Page Title** area type `Standard 1 Reflective Report`.
90. Leave the **Page Description** area empty.
91. If you wish to use any **Tags** to identify the page in the future, enter them now.
92. Click on **Save**.

The following is a screenshot of the completed page:

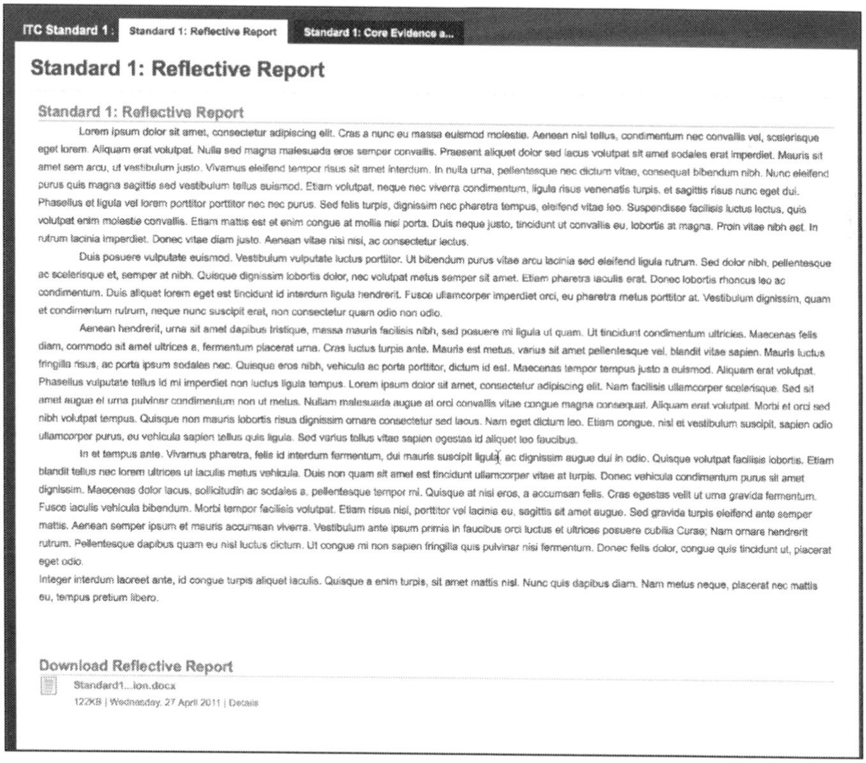

> There are several ways in which the Reflective Report could've been added to the portfolio. In this recipe, we use a typical word processing program, and save it as an HTML document. You could've also created the page in an HTML program such as KompoZer, which we discussed in a previous chapter, or you could've have copied the text into a Text Box block. If you decide to use the Text Box option, make sure you still upload a document with the text to your files so that you will have an artifact of the reflection. If you make a change to the text in the textbox, make sure to change your text in your original document as well, and re-upload it (so that they match). We keep a copy of the text in document format, because textboxes are not artifacts. They are only associated with the page in which they appear.

To make the collection for Standard 1:

93. Click the **Portfolio** tab and then **Collections**.
94. Click **New Collection**.
95. In the field for **Collection name**, type `ITC Standard 1`.
96. You can leave the **Description** empty.
97. Make sure the option for **Page navigation bar** is selected.
98. Click **Next: Edit Collection pages**.
99. In the area labeled **Add pages to collection**, click in the small boxes next to the pages for Standard 1.
100. Click **Add pages**.
101. Your pages will appear at the top of the page. Using the small arrows, arrange the pages so that the Reflective Report is first.
102. Click **Done**.
103. Click the **Share** tab to set the Access level.

How it works...

In this recipe, we created a collection for each standard. These individual collections will later be accessed through a page in the completed all-encompassing portfolio that may, itself, be a collection containing all the required documentation and all of the standards. There is also the option of not making these smaller collections and, instead, making one collection that includes tabs for each individual page. There are advantages and disadvantages for each method, which are discussed with each method.

In addition to the standards, the final portfolio will need to include several elements. Before continuing with the following *There's more...* section (to bind this all together), you will want to make sure you've created a page or pages for those elements. They are:

- An Introduction to your portfolio (which includes the Short Statement and Description of Personal Context)
- A Personal Statement
- A Written Report of a senior colleague

There's more...

There are two ways of putting this all together.

The final portfolio, a collection that contains collections for each standard

This *There's more...* activity assumes that you have created a collection for each standard. In this section, we will create the introductory page for the standards, and we will create the collection for all of the pages in the ITC Portfolio. The advantage of putting your portfolio together in this manner is that it is more highly organized; the disadvantage is that each of the collections (and therefore pages) for the various standards, can only be accessed from the ITC Standards page, where we will build a table of contents. See the following screenshot:

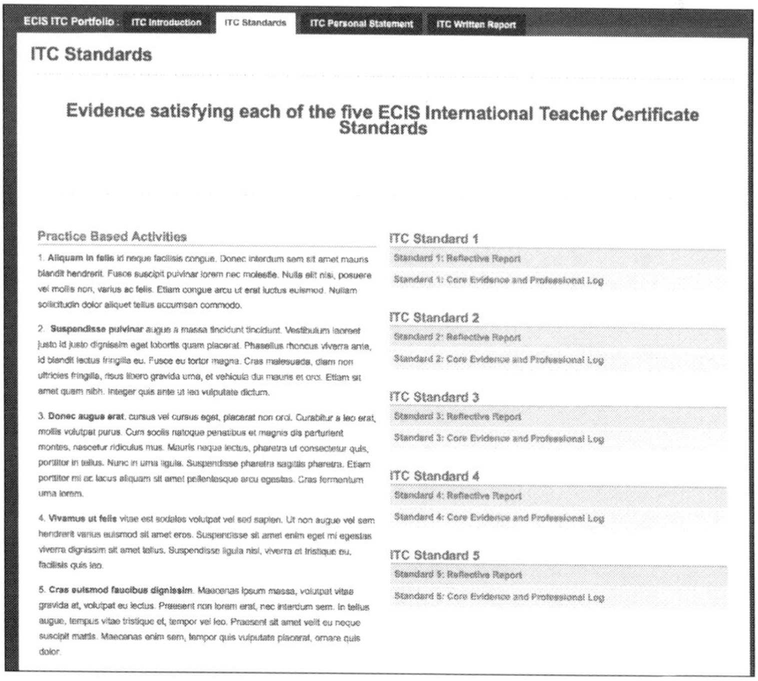

1. Click on **Portfolio** and then on **Pages**.
2. Click **Create Page**.
3. Click the **Edit Layout** tab.
4. Select **2 columns, Equal widths**.
5. Click on **Save**.
6. From the **General** tab, click and drag a **Text Box** block into the left-hand column.
7. Change the **Block Title** to **Practice Based Activities.**
8. In the **Block Content**, list the five activities you conducted to meet the standards and provide brief descriptions for each.
9. Click on **Save**.
10. From the **General** tab, click and drag a **Navigation** block into the right-hand column.
11. Leave the **Block Title** empty.
12. From the **Collection** drop-down menu, select **ITC Standard 5**.
13. Click on **Save**.
14. Repeat steps 10–13 for each standard, concluding with **ITC Standard 1** at the top of the column.
15. Select the **Edit: Title and Description** tab.
16. In the **Title** field, type `ITC Standards`.
17. In the **Description** field, choose to align to center and type `Evidence satisfying each of the five ECIS International Teacher Certificate Standards`.
18. Highlight the text in the description and, using the formatting drop-down menu, apply **Heading 1**.
19. Click on **Save**.
20. Click on **Done**.

To build the collection:

21. Click the **Portfolio** tab and then **Collections**.
22. Click the **Create Collection** button.
23. In the **Collection Name** field, type `ECIS ITC Portfolio`.
24. You can leave the **Collection Description** empty.
25. Make sure the **Page navigation bar** option is checked.
26. Click **Next: Edit Collection Pages**.
27. In the area labeled **Add pages to collection**, click in the small boxes next to **ITC Introduction**, **ITC Standards**, **ITC Personal Statement**, and **ITC Written Report**.
28. Click **Add pages**.

29. The ITC pages will now appear above the area labeled **Add pages**. They should be in the order listed in step 27. If they aren't, use the small arrows to move them into place.
30. Click on **Save**.

To export your portfolio, follow the steps in the *Archiving portfolios* recipe.

The final portfolio: one collection containing individual pages

As mentioned previously, you can choose not to make a collection for each standard and instead make one collection for the entire portfolio. The benefit of this option is that each page in the portfolio will be accessible from every other page through the use of the tabs at the top of each page. If you wish to set up your portfolio in this manner, skip the steps in the main recipe that create a collection for each standard.

We will create an ITC Standards Introduction page, and the final collection.

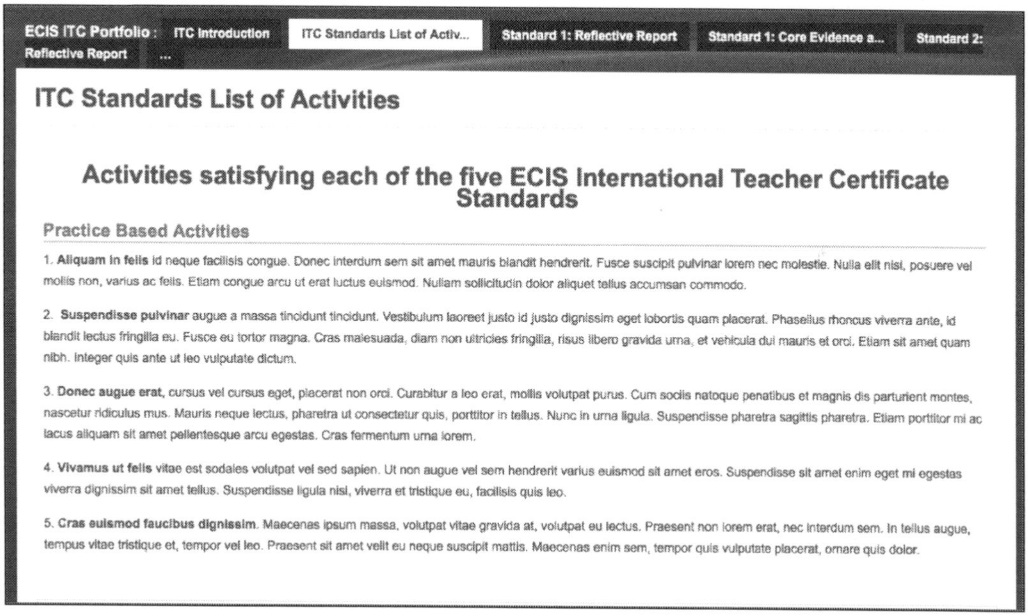

31. Go to the **Pages** section of the **Portfolio** tab.
32. Click **Create Page**.
33. Click the **Edit Layout** tab.
34. Select **1 column, Equal widths**.
35. Click on **Save**.
36. From the **General** tab, click and drag a **Text Box** block into the page.

37. Change the **Block Title** to **Practice Based Activities**.
38. In the **Block Content**, list the five activities you conducted to meet the standards and provide brief descriptions of each.
39. Click on **Save**.
40. Click the **Edit: Title and Description** tab.
41. In the **Title Field**, type `ITC Standards List of Activities`.
42. In the **Description** field, type `Activities satisfying each of the five ECIS International Teacher Certificate Standards`.
43. Highlight the text in the description and, using the formatting drop-down menu, apply **Heading 1**.
44. Click on **Save**.
45. Click on **Done**.

To build the collection:

46. Click the **Portfolio** tab and then **Collections**.
47. Click the **Create Collection** button.
48. In the **Collection Name** field, type `ECIS ITC Portfolio`.
49. You can leave the **Collection Description** empty.
50. Make sure the **Page navigation bar** option is checked.
51. Click **Next: Edit Collection Pages**.
52. In the area labeled **Add pages to collection**, click in the small boxes next to the appropriate pages such as ITC Introduction, ITC Standards List of Activities, Standard 1 Reflective Report, Standard 1 Core Evidence and Professional Log, Standard 1 Reflective Report, Standard 1 Core Evidence and Professional Log, Standard 2 Reflective Report, Standard 2 Core Evidence and Professional Log, Standard 3 Reflective Report, Standard 3 Core Evidence and Professional Log, Standard 4 Reflective Report, Standard 4 Core Evidence and Professional Log, Standard 5 Reflective Report, Standard 5 Core Evidence and Professional Log, ITC Personal Statement, and ITC Written Report.
53. Click **Add pages**. Each of these pages will have a tab accessible from every other page in the collection.
54. The ITC pages will now appear above the area labeled **Add pages**. Use the **small arrows icons** next to each of them, to arrange them in the order listed in step 22.
55. Click on **Save**.

To export your portfolio (in order to burn it to a CD or transfer to some other storage device), follow the steps in the *Archiving portfolios* recipe.

See also

- *Archiving portfolios* recipe
- *Using HTML to create your unofficial transcript* recipe in *Chapter 7, The College Application Portfolio*

Templates for meeting teacher certification standards

It is best if students become familiar with the standards for their particular certification and begin building their teaching portfolio at the beginning of their studies. This would allow them, among other things, to chronicle the building, implementation, and assessment of lesson plans. This would also make the final portfolio much richer. However, many students do not do this and many programs do not require and/or assess the portfolio until a final capstone course, or similar. This means that students have to write the reflections, which nearly all certification portfolios require, while they are building the final portfolio. With that in mind, the template we will be building in this recipe will provide instructors and students with a method for creating a final portfolio, with the idea that the students do not already have a journal in which they have been chronicling their process.

This recipe is for instructor use.

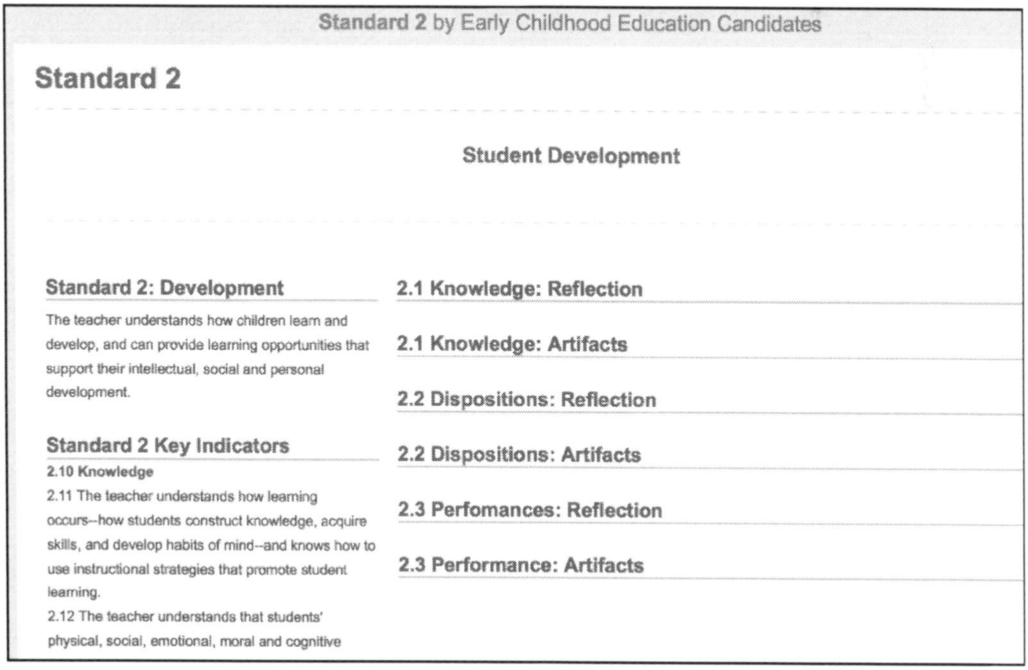

Standard 2 by Early Childhood Education Candidates
Standard 2
Student Development
Standard 2: Development
The teacher understands how children learn and develop, and can provide learning opportunities that support their intellectual, social and personal development.
Standard 2 Key Indicators
2.10 Knowledge
2.11 The teacher understands how learning occurs--how students construct knowledge, acquire skills, and develop habits of mind--and knows how to use instructional strategies that promote student learning.
2.12 The teacher understands that students' physical, social, emotional, moral and cognitive
2.1 Knowledge: Reflection
2.1 Knowledge: Artifacts
2.2 Dispositions: Reflection
2.2 Dispositions: Artifacts
2.3 Perfomances: Reflection
2.3 Performance: Artifacts

Getting ready

The template is a page that students can copy. While it is possible for an instructor to build the template from within their own personal account, it is best if templates are created within a group. This is so that access to the template will not be dependent on the account of a particular instructor.

While the type of group is not of particular importance in the development of a template, only Course Groups provide instructors with the ability to lock student Pages after submission so that students cannot edit the Page. For this recipe, we are going to use a Standard—Request Membership group. To create your group:

1. Click the **Groups** tab in **Mahara**.
2. You should find yourself in the **My Groups** area; if not; select the tab for **My Groups**. Click the **Create Group** option.
3. In field for **Group Name**, give the group a name that will allow students who will be using the template, to find it easily. For example, **Early Childhood Education Candidates**.
4. In the **Group Description** field, provide information that will further clarify the group's purpose.
5. In the drop-down menu for **Group type**, select **Request Membership**. This will create a Standard group (as opposed to a Course group). Students become members by selecting to do so. Their request will need to be approved by an administrator for the group (the instructor that creates the group is automatically an administrator).
6. If your institution has established group categories, select the category for this type of a group from the drop-down menu for **Group category**. Otherwise, skip this option.
7. The **Publically Viewable Group?** option should not be selected.
8. The **Shared page notifications** option should have a check mark next to it.
9. Click on **Save Group**. After saving the group, you should find yourself at the group's home page, where you can begin building the template.

How to do it...

For this example, we are going to use Standard 2 of the Interstate New Teacher Assessment and Support Consortium (INTASC) Standards. Please substitute the following text examples with those from the standards you are using:

1. On the group's home page, click the tab labeled **Pages**.
2. Click **Create Page**.
3. Click the **Edit Layout** tab.
4. Select **2 columns, Larger right column**.

5. Click on **Save**.
6. From the **General** tab, click and drag a **Text Box** block into the left-hand column of the page.
7. Change the **Block Title** to `Standard 2: Student Development.`
8. In the **Block Content** area, enter the general description of the standard. For example:

The teacher understands how children learn and develop, and can provide learning opportunities that support their intellectual, social, and personal development.

9. Click on **Save**.
10. From the **General** tab, click and drag another **Text Box** block into the left-hand column, beneath the textbox you added in step 6.
11. Change the text in the **Block Title** to `Standard 2 Key Indicators.`
12. In the **Block Content** area, add the descriptions of the key indicators. For example:

2.10 Knowledge.

2.11 The teacher understands how learning occurs—how students construct knowledge, acquire skills, and develop habits of mind—and knows how to use instructional strategies that promote student learning.

2.12 The teacher understands that students' physical, social, emotional, moral, and cognitive development influence learning and knows how to address these factors when making instructional decisions.

2.13 The teacher is aware of expected developmental progressions and ranges of individual variation within each domain (physical, social, emotional, moral, and cognitive), can identify levels of readiness in learning, and understands how development in any one domain may affect performance in others.

2.20 Dispositions.

2.21 The teacher appreciates individual variation within each area of development, shows respect for the diverse talents of all learners, and is committed to helping them develop self-confidence and competence.

2.22 The teacher is disposed to use students' strengths as a basis for growth, and their errors as an opportunity for learning.

2.30 Performances.

2.31 The teacher assesses individual and group performance in order to design instruction that meets learners' current needs in each domain (cognitive, social, emotional, moral, and physical) and that leads to the next level of development.

2.32 The teacher stimulates student reflection on prior knowledge and links new ideas to already familiar ideas, making connections to students' experiences, providing opportunities for active engagement, manipulation, and testing of ideas and materials, and encouraging students to assume responsibility for shaping their learning tasks.

2.33 The teacher accesses students' thinking and experiences as a basis for instructional activities by, for example, encouraging discussion, listening and responding to group interaction, and eliciting samples of student thinking orally and in writing.

13. Use the tools in the HTML editing toolbar to format the text. For example, apply **Heading 4** to each of the central key indicators, 2.10, 2.20, 2.30, and so on.
14. Click on **Save**.
15. From the **Files, images and video** tab, click and drag a **File(s) to download** block into the right-hand column.
16. Change the **Block Title** to the last key indicator category, for example, `2.3 Performance`, and add the word `Artifacts`.
17. Click on **Save**.
18. From the **Files, images and video** tab, click and drag a **Some HTML** block into the top of the right-hand column.
19. Change the **Block Title** to the last key indicator category, for example, `2.3 Performance`, and add `Reflection`.
20. Repeat steps 15-19 for each of the key indicator categories for this standard.
21. When finished, click the **Edit: Title and Description** tab.
22. In the field for **Page Title**, enter the text indicating the standard (for example, `Standard 2`).
23. You can leave the **Page Description** empty or you can add a description of the Standard (for example, `Student Development`).
24. In the field for **Tags**, enter they type of standard (for example, `INTASC`).
25. Click on **Save**.
26. Click the tab **Share page**.

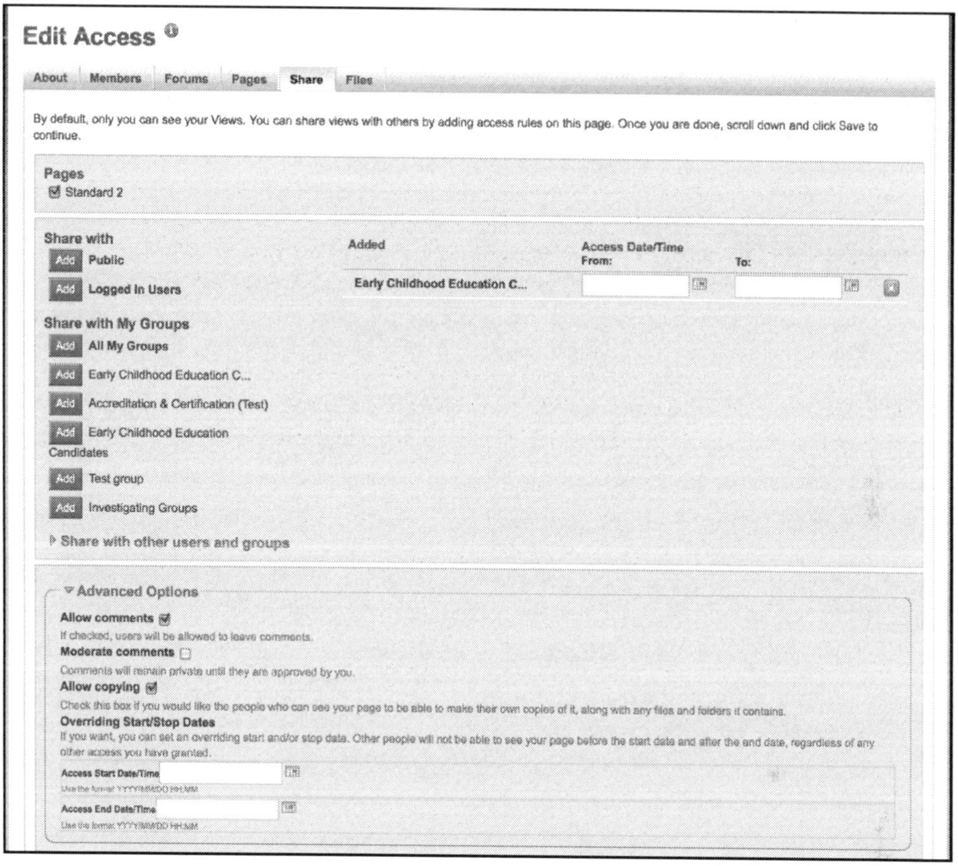

27. You will see a page called **Standard 2** listed in the **Pages** section with a check mark next to it. In the **Share with** section, you will see that your group has already been provided access.
28. Click the link labeled **Advanced Options** to expand that section.
29. Put a check mark next to **Allow copying** by clicking in the small box next to that option.

> The **Allow copying** option is what actually makes a page a template. It allows the individuals with access to the page to copy it and use it as their own page.

30. Click on **Save**. Your template is now ready for the students that are members of your group to copy and use.

> While you may have several Pages that students will need to copy (each of which will eventually become part of a Collection), only individual Pages can be copied in the current version of Mahara. In other words, it is not possible to copy a Collection. Rather, each individual Page must be copied one at a time. The copying of Collections is purposed for Mahara 1.5.

How it works...

When writing their reflections, students should either use a web page authoring program (such as KompoZer) or a word processing program that provides the option of saving the document as a web page (Microsoft Word and OpenOffice both offer this option). They will need to upload their artifacts and reflections to the **Files** section of their portfolio. They will also need to join your group, so that they will have access to template(s). Because we set the access level for this group as Request Membership, you will have to approve the students' requests in order for them to become members of the group. The following are the instructions for students:

To join a group:

1. Click the **Groups** tab, and then click **Find Groups**.
2. Find your group in the list (use the search tool if necessary). Click the button labeled **Request to join this group**.
3. You will receive a notification once the instructor has approved your membership. Until the instructor has done so, you will not be able to copy the templates.

To copy and use the templates:

4. Click the **Portfolio** tab.
5. In the **Pages** section, click the button labeled **Copy a page**.
6. You will see a list of all the pages you are able to copy. To find the templates for this group, type its name in the box for **Search owners**, and click the icon that looks like a magnifying glass.
7. All of the templates for this group should now appear in the list. Click the **Copy Page** button next to the first template you wish to copy, and the template will open, ready for editing.
8. The text in the left-hand column is a description of the standard; the items on the right are blocks to which you will add your reflections and artifacts. You will see two icons to the right of each of those items. The **x** icon will delete the item while the other icon will allow you to edit (or configure) the item.
9. Click the **configure** icon next to one of the items with a label that indicates it is for artifacts.

10. The **Files** section of your portfolio will open. Click the **Select** option next to each artifact for this specific standard and key indicator.
11. Click on **Save**.
12. Next click the **configure** icon next to an item with a label that indicates it is for a reflection.
13. The **Files** section of your portfolio will open again. This time click the **Select** option next to the `.html` page that you created and uploaded for this standard and key indicator.
14. Click on **Save**.
15. Repeat steps 9-14 for each of the key indicators.
16. When finished, click the **Edit: Title and Description** tab.
17. The **Page Title** field will contain the name of the standard as well as the words **Copy of**; delete the **Copy of** portion of the title, leaving the rest intact.
18. Click on **Save**.
19. Click the **Share page** tab.
20. You should see this new page in the list of your pages, and it should have a check mark next to it. If not, click the small box next to this page to add a check mark.
21. For this exercise, we are only going to share your new page with the administrators/instructors of your group. Click the **Share with other users and groups** link to expand the options.

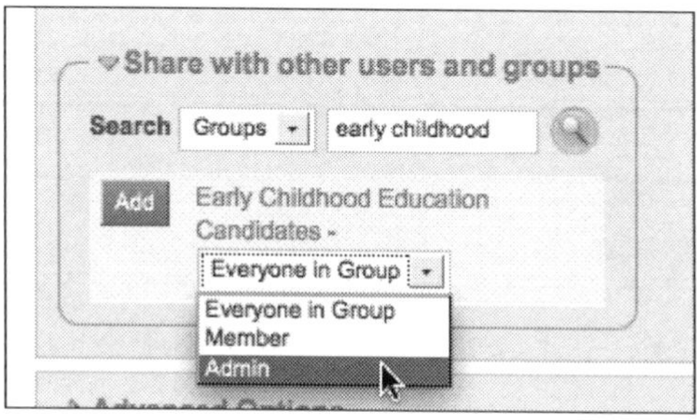

22. From the drop-down menu next to **Search**, select **Groups**.
23. Type in the name of the group and select the magnifying tool.
24. The group should appear below the search window, along with an **Add** button and a drop-down menu. In the drop-down menu, select **Admin**.
25. Click **Add**.
26. Click **Save**.

There's more...

Let's look at another option for creating artifacts.

Using journal posts to share artifacts and reflections

The Journal feature of Mahara can provide another method for the collection of reflections and artifacts. If this is the method you choose, have each student create a journal called Standards. Instruct them to create a post for each key indicator and attach the related artifact(s) to the post. To build your template, follow steps 1-9 in the *Getting Ready* section of this recipe, and steps 1-14 in the *How to do it...* section.

Let us begin with step 15 in the *How to do it...* section:

1. From the **General** tab, click and drag a **Text Box** block into the right-hand column.
2. In the **Block Title**, type `2.4 Reflection & Artifacts`.
3. In the **Block Content**, area type the following instructions for your students:

```
[From the Journal tab, click and drag a Journal Entry block
below this entry. Select the posting you had created for this
key indicator from the list of journal entries and click
Save. When that journal entry has been added to this page,
delete this text box by clicking the x in its upper right-
hand corner]
```

4. Click on **Save**.
5. Repeat these steps for each key indicator.
6. Continue building the template using steps 21-30 of the *How to do it...* section.

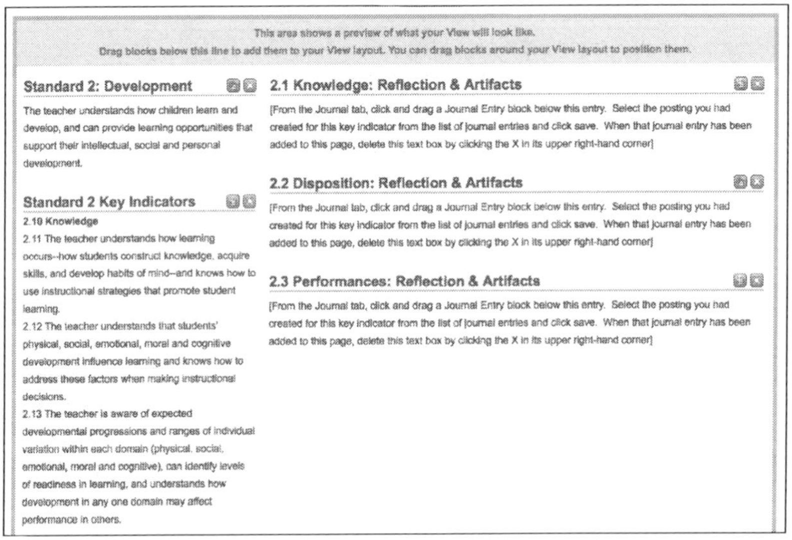

You will also need to change the instructions you provide to students. The instructions for students are in the *How it works...* part of this recipe. The part that you will need to change is covered in steps 9-14. Students will not need to complete those steps. Instead, they merely need to follow the text in the textboxes you added to the template, and then continue with step 15 in their instructions.

See also

- *Chapter 4, Working with Groups*
- *Language acquisition journal* recipe in *Chapter 2, Literature and Writing*
- *Building the ECIS International Teacher portfolio* recipe
- *A simple template for very young students* recipe in *Chapter 5, The Primary Education Portfolio*
- *Creating and using a simple template* recipe in *Chapter 5, The Primary Education Portfolio*

Creating a portfolio access page for outside reviewers

Some accreditation reviews require that reviewers have access to student portfolios. In this recipe, we will examine one method for providing reviewers access, without requiring them to have an account in your Mahara instance. The access we will be providing will not be to permanent archives of student portfolios, but to locked student portfolio pages.

When we use the term *archived portfolio*, we refer to a portfolio that the student has exported. It is an exact copy of a portfolio as it appeared at the moment it was exported. On the other hand, a locked page is one that still exists in the student's portfolio, but which the student cannot edit. The page(s) can, however, be updated. For example, if a locked page contains a journal, and the student adds a new entry to the journal, the page will display the new post.

Getting ready

Create a Course Group and add, as members, the students whose portfolios you need to display. These students will now have a drop-down menu next to each page in their list of pages on the Portfolio tab. The drop-down menu will allow them to submit a particular page for assessment. When they select that option, the page will be sent to the administrators of the Course Group and will be visible to the administrators on the group home page. The page will be locked. Ask the students to submit the Portfolio page or collection in this manner. In addition, ask them to create a Secret URL as well, and to send you the URL. You will need to keep a list of these URLs and the name of the student associated with it. It is best to keep that list in a text-editing program like Text Edit (Mac) or Notepad (PC). We will be using that list in this recipe.

The following screenshot is an example of what this page may look like:

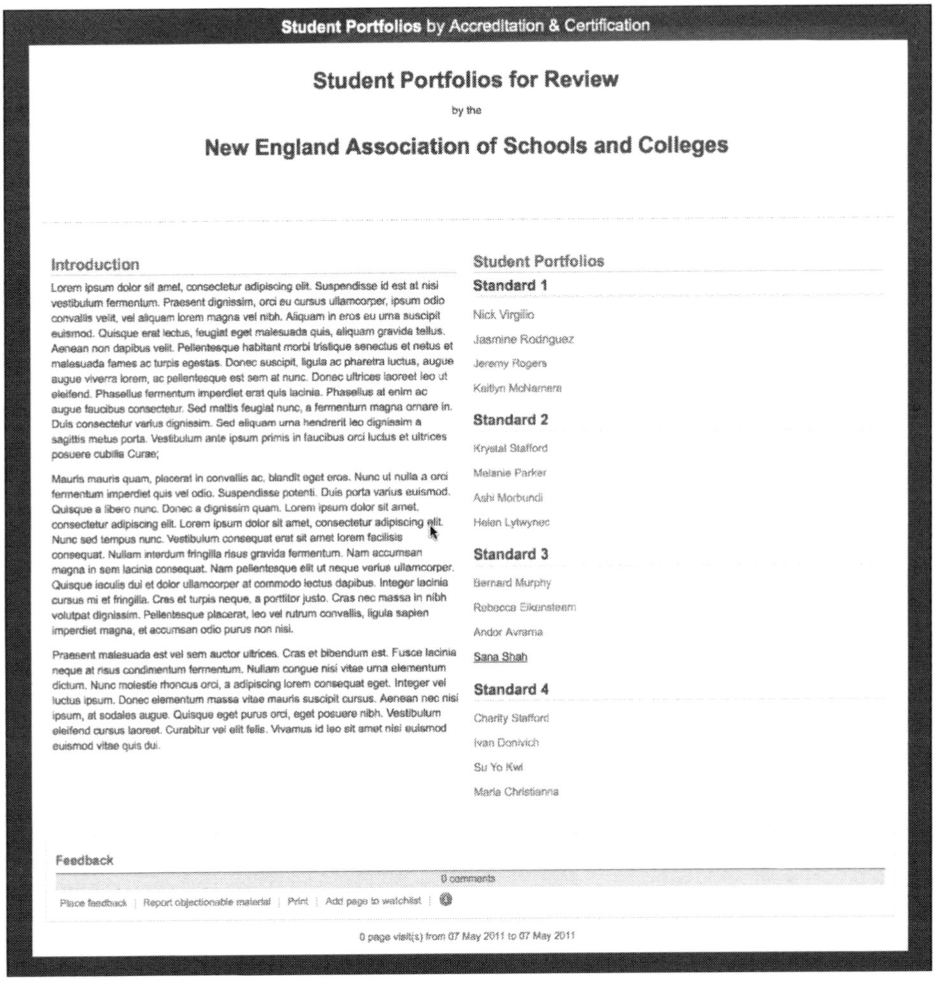

How to do it...

1. You will need to open two windows—one will be your browser window opened to Mahara; the other will be the document that contains your list of Secret URLs (see the preceding *Getting ready* section).
2. Go to the home page for your group, click on the tab labeled **Groups**, then on **My Groups**. Find this new group in the list of groups and click on the name to open the home page.

3. On the home page, you will see several tabs; click the tab labeled **Pages**.
4. Click the button labeled **Create Page**.
5. Click the **Edit Layout** tab.
6. Select **2 columns, Equal width**.
7. Click on **Save**.
8. From the **General** tab, click and drag a **Text Box** block into the left-hand column.
9. In the **Block Title**, change the text to say `Introduction`.
10. In the **Block Content** area, add your introductory text for the reviewers.
11. Click on **Save**.
12. From the **General** tab, click and drag a **Text Box** block into the right-hand column.
13. Change the text in the **Block Title** to say `Student Portfolios`.
14. Put your cursor in the **Block Content** field.
15. If you are going to organize the portfolios by standards, type `Standard 1`, highlight the text, and, using the formatting option on the HTML toolbar, apply **Heading 2**.

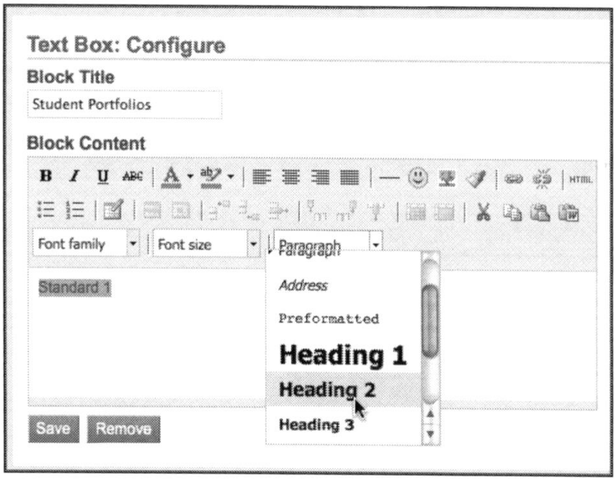

16. Type the name of the student whose portfolio you are going to list first.
17. Without closing Mahara, go to window that contains your list of Secret URLs.
18. Highlight and copy the URL associated with this particular portfolio.
19. Go back to Mahara and highlight the student's name that you typed in, in step 16.

20. Click the **Insert/edit link** icon on the HTML toolbar:

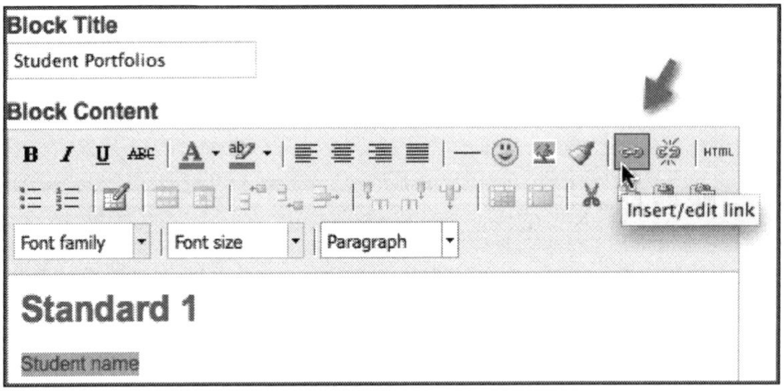

21. A small window will open. In the field for **Link URL**, paste the URL you copied in step 18.
22. From the drop-down menu for **Target**, select **Open in new window**.
23. In the field for **Title**, type `Portfolio`.
24. Click **Insert**.
25. Repeat steps 17-24 for each portfolio.
26. For each standard heading, repeat step 16.
27. When completed, click the **Edit: Title and Description** tab.
28. In the field for **Page Title** type `Student Portfolios`.
29. In the **Description** field, click the **align center** icon.
30. Type `Student Portfolios for Review` and the name of the accrediting agency reviewing the portfolios. Highlight the text and, using the drop-down menu for formatting, select **Heading 1**.
31. Insert two lines using the *Enter* or *return* key on your keyboard.
32. Add a horizontal line by clicking the **Insert horizontal ruler** icon on the HTML toolbar:

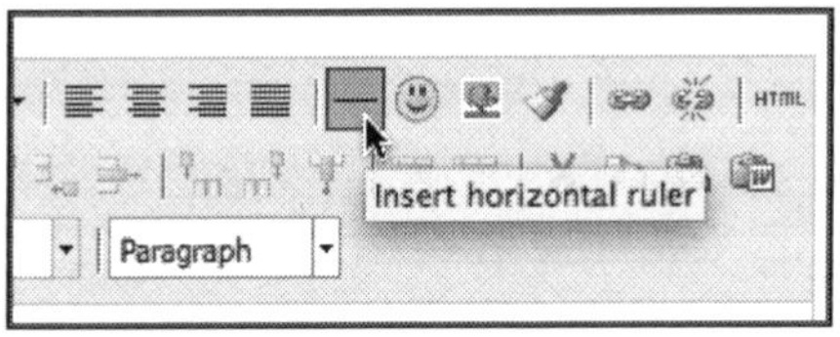

33. Click on **Save**.
34. Click **Done**.

35. You should now find yourself back at the **Pages** section for the group. There will be several tabs near the top of the page. Select the tab labeled **Share**.

36. You will see a table that looks similar to the one shown in the next screenshot. Find the page called **Student Portfolios** in the column labeled **Pages & Collections**. To the right, you will see a pencil tool in the column labeled **Secret URL**. Click on that pencil tool:

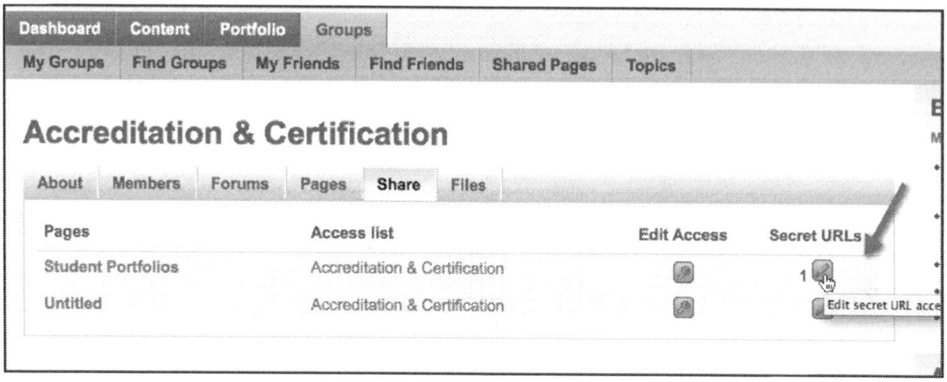

37. In the page that opens, click the **Add** button. This will generate a Secret URL, which will appear above the **Add** button. Copy this URL and give it to the reviewers. This is the URL they will need to use to access the page with student portfolios.

38. You can close Mahara.

How it works...

The student portfolios will be locked and will be viewable only by those who are either administrators of the group or access the portfolio using the Secret URL. Administrators of the group will see links to the student portfolios on the group home page. Only administrators of the group will see these links. These links were created when the student submitted the portfolio using the drop-down menu for Course Groups (see the *Getting Ready* section). This step also locked the portfolio, which means they cannot edit the page(s) unless, and until, the group administrator releases it.

This recipe added one other method to access the student portfolio, the Secret URL. Secret URLs create a condition that provides access to individuals who enter the page(s) directly by means of the Secret URL. Reviewers will be using the Secret URL to access the group page, as well as the various student portfolios.

See also

- *Chapter 4, Working with Groups*

Archiving portfolios

Some institutional programs are required to save copies (permanent records) of students' final portfolios, especially those used for certification. Archives can be created and downloaded for permanent storage; however, the archives of individual portfolios can only be created by the users themselves. In this case, that would be the students. Once created, the archives can be given to the institution for permanent storage or for submission to an agency. This recipe provides instructions for users on how to create a permanent archive of their portfolio (or of a portion of a portfolio). Students will need to perform these steps themselves and, once completed, send the archive to their instructor.

How to do it...

1. Click the **Portfolio** tab, and then the **Export** tab.
2. From the options for **Choose an export format**, select **Standalone HTML Website**.
3. From the list of options under **What do you want to export?**, select either **Just some of my collections** (if you need to archive an entire collection) or **Just some of my pages**.

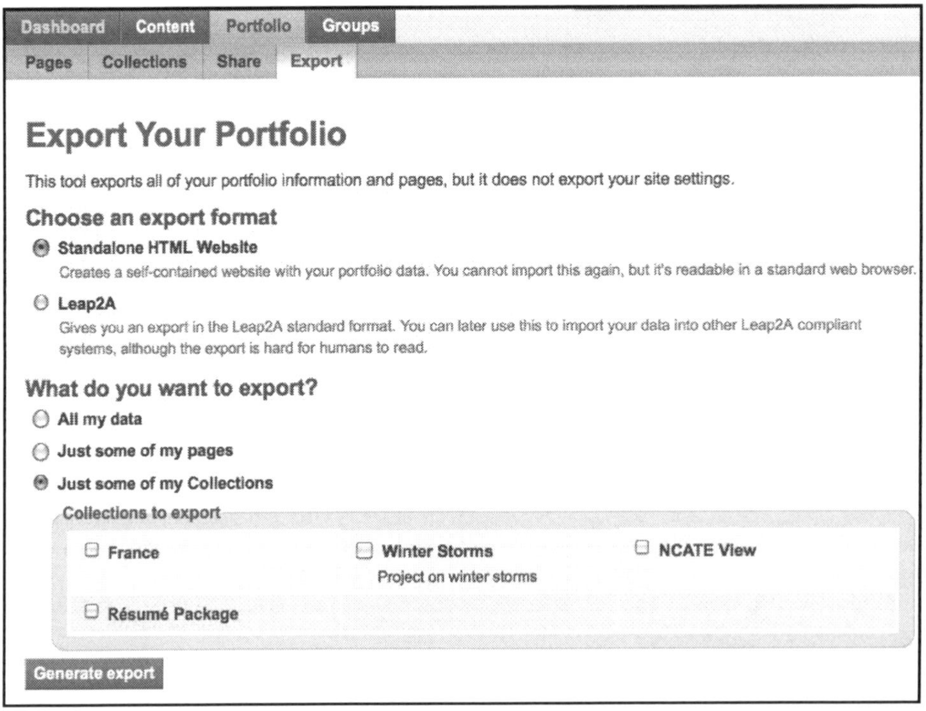

4. The page will expand to reveal your options for selection. Your options will depend on what you selected in step 3; you will be able to choose from either a list of your collections or from a list of your pages. Click in the small box next to the item you wish to archive.

> You can export several Collections or Pages at one time but they will all be part of a single archive. As such, the items cannot easily be separated to send to different individuals.

5. When you've finished making your selections, click the **Generate export** button.
6. When your file is done exporting, you will see a message that says **Export generated successfully** and a window will open with the options: **Open** or **Save file**. If the window does not automatically open, click the **Continue** link and it will open.
7. Select the **Save File** option and click **OK**.

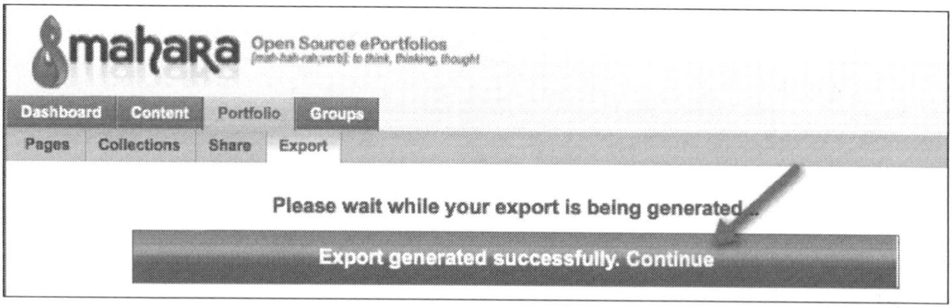

8. In the next window, select the location where you wish to store the file and click **Save**.
9. Your archive will be saved as a `.zip` file (a compressed folder). This is the file you will need to give your institution.

How it works...

To view the archive contents, unzip the archive (this can usually be done by simply double-clicking the file). Once unpackaged, you should see a folder with a title indicating it contains a portfolio and including the name of the individual who created the portfolio. Inside the folder will be a number of files, including a file called `index.html`. To view the portfolio, click on the `index.html` file.

There's more...

You may wish to upload the archived portfolio to a website, where it will be more easily accessible. Now we will look at how this can be done.

Access to an archived portfolio from a website

If you would like to make an archived portfolio viewable on the web, you will need to have access to a web server. Upload the zipped portfolios to the web server. Unzip them on the web server. This will create a set of folders, each with the name of the individual whose portfolio is contained within. Leave the contents of the folders exactly as they are. Each folder will contain an index page. This is the page that needs to be selected in order to view the portfolio. If you create a web page to contain links to archived portfolios, make sure the links point to the index pages. You can delete the zipped packages.

See also

- *The Art Portfolio and the Common Application: Art Supplement* recipe in *Chapter 7, The College Application Portfolio*

Index

D

E

F

G

R

S

[PACKT] open source
community experience distilled
PUBLISHING

Thank you for buying
Mahara 1.4 Cookbook

About Packt Publishing

Packt, pronounced 'packed', published its first book "*Mastering phpMyAdmin for Effective MySQL Management*" in April 2004 and subsequently continued to specialize in publishing highly focused books on specific technologies and solutions.

Our books and publications share the experiences of your fellow IT professionals in adapting and customizing today's systems, applications, and frameworks. Our solution based books give you the knowledge and power to customize the software and technologies you're using to get the job done. Packt books are more specific and less general than the IT books you have seen in the past. Our unique business model allows us to bring you more focused information, giving you more of what you need to know, and less of what you don't.

Packt is a modern, yet unique publishing company, which focuses on producing quality, cutting-edge books for communities of developers, administrators, and newbies alike. For more information, please visit our website: `www.packtpub.com`.

About Packt Open Source

In 2010, Packt launched two new brands, Packt Open Source and Packt Enterprise, in order to continue its focus on specialization. This book is part of the Packt Open Source brand, home to books published on software built around Open Source licences, and offering information to anybody from advanced developers to budding web designers. The Open Source brand also runs Packt's Open Source Royalty Scheme, by which Packt gives a royalty to each Open Source project about whose software a book is sold.

Writing for Packt

We welcome all inquiries from people who are interested in authoring. Book proposals should be sent to author@packtpub.com. If your book idea is still at an early stage and you would like to discuss it first before writing a formal book proposal, contact us; one of our commissioning editors will get in touch with you.

We're not just looking for published authors; if you have strong technical skills but no writing experience, our experienced editors can help you develop a writing career, or simply get some additional reward for your expertise.

[PACKT] open source
community experience distilled
PUBLISHING

Mahara 1.2 E-Portfolios: Beginner's Guide

ISBN: 978-1-847199-06-5 Paperback: 264 pages

Create and host educational and professional e-portfolios and personalized learning communities

1. Create, customize, and maintain an impressive personal digital portfolio with a simple point-and-click interface
2. Set customized access to share your text files, images, and videos with your family, friends, and others
3. Create online learning communities and social networks through groups, blogs, and forums
4. A step-by-step approach that takes you through examples with ample screenshots and clear explanations

---

Moodle 1.9 for Teaching 7-14 Year Olds: Beginner's Guide

ISBN: 978-1-847197-14-6 Paperback: 236 pages

Effective e-learning for younger students using Moodle as your Classroom Assistant

1. Focus on the unique needs of young learners to create a fun, interesting, interactive, and informative learning environment your students will want to go on day after day
2. Engage and motivate your students with games, quizzes, movies, and podcasts the whole class can participate in
3. Go paperless! Put your lessons online and grade them anywhere, anytime

Please check **www.PacktPub.com** for information on our titles

15284068R00164

Made in the USA
Lexington, KY
18 May 2012